# Corporate Finance

Foundations of Value Optimization and Survival

FIRST EDITION

# Corporate Finance

## Foundations of Value Optimization and Survival

EDITED BY Jay Brandi

*University of Louisville*

SAN DIEGO

Bassim Hamadeh, CEO and Publisher
Jennifer Codner, Senior Field Acquisitions Editor
Michelle Piehl, Senior Project Editor
Emely Villavicencio, Senior Graphic Designer
Stephanie Kohl, Licensing Coordinator
Natalie Piccotti, Director of Marketing
Kassie Graves, Vice President of Editorial
Jamie Giganti, Director of Academic Publishing

cognella® | ACADEMIC PUBLISHING
3970 Sorrento Valley Blvd., Ste. 500, San Diego, CA 92121

# CONTENTS

# MODULE 1

# Financial Management and the Business Environment

*Until input thought is linked to a goal purpose there can be no intelligent accomplishment.*

**Paul G. Thomas**

*The only responsibility of business is to make profits.*

**Milton Friedman**

The ultimate financial goal of a for-profit firm should be to increase the value of that firm over time. Achieving that goal is not easy, and it requires careful analysis, planning, and decision-making.

In his paper "Value Maximization, Stakeholder Theory, and the Corporate Objective Function," Michael Jensen clarifies the difference between stakeholder theory and value maximization. Stakeholder theory, he notes, has its foundations in the disciplines of "sociology, organizational behavior, the politics of special interests, and managerial self-interest." It is a theory in which "managers should make decisions that take account of the interests of all the stakeholders in a firm," to include not only owners but customers and all others who can "substantially affect, or be affected by, the welfare of the firm."

Value maximization, Professor Jensen points out, has its roots "in 200 years of research" and "means not just the value of the equity, but the sum of the values of all financial claims on the firm—debt, warrants, and preferred stock, as well as equity."

The managers responsible for making the decisions that affect the value of a firm are not isolated from the rest of the world. They must constantly be aware of the environment in which they operate. To be effective and efficient, the best managers receive, review, and accept or reject information obtained from a variety of sources, both internal (within the business firm) and external (outside the business firm). To correctly understand and utilize this information, the manager must have an understanding of the ever-changing environment in which the firm operates.

Given that managers operate in a dynamic environment, they must be flexible and capable of adjusting to rapid changes in the financial marketplace in which they operate. Within this framework, financial managers perform several functions. These functions can be categorized into the three separate decision areas of financing (a.k.a. capital acquisition or capital procurement), investment (a.k.a. capital distribution or capital allocation), and operations (a.k.a. capital management or capital operations).

The financing decision is concerned with raising funds for the firm. It includes not only identifying the types and sources of funds to be raised but also identifying the most favorable terms and constraints on those funds.

The investment decision deals with identifying those resources, both short- and long-term, that should be purchased or leased by the firm. In other words, the investment decision concerns the determination of the manner in which the funds obtained as financing can be most efficiently allocated to the firm.

Operating decisions deal with the disbursement of funds received by the firm from everything that it does. This decision is complex, since it deals with the disbursement or retention of funds from both operating and nonoperating sources and because it also involves allocation of funds for future operations. Operating decisions include activities such as financial analysis, the decision to pay or not to pay cash or stock dividends, the issuance or repurchase of stock and debt, and financial forecasting and planning.

It is also important to managers in all areas of the business environment to have some understanding of financial management. Simply making a profit is not enough to ensure the long-term success of a business firm. Whether a manager has control of an entire conglomerate corporation or just one small department in that corporation, it is necessary to make decisions rationally and objectively. Since all decisions have some direct or indirect financial implications, all managers, not just financial managers, should have an understanding of the financial ramifications of each decision made.

There is always a risk that the actual results of a decision will differ from those desired. This suggests that managers should always consider not just the expected outcome but also the best, the worst, and the various shades-of-grey outcomes associated with a decision.

No managerial decision should be made without considering the timeframe in which the decision will be implemented. Financial management decisions must also be made in consideration of both their long- and short-term effects. Further, no decision should be made without consideration of both the direct and the indirect costs and benefits associated with that decision.

Another area of managerial concern is compliance with government regulation and constraints. All business firms must operate within the confines of the regulatory constraints imposed on them by government. These regulations may be domestic or foreign.

There are three basic types of regulation that currently exist. These are regulations controlling industry concentration, such as monopolies; regulations providing a right to monopoly for those firms operating in industries that are severely regulated; and third, regulations that attempt to protect the health or financial stability or quality of the environment.

Regulations that attempt to control the concentration of an industry are aimed at encouraging competition. Competition is encouraged in certain industries because of the belief that where monopoly situations exist, it is possible for firms to restrict the amount and/or quality of the product that is delivered to the consumer. As a result, prices will be higher than would normally be the situation in a competitive environment. Consequently, competition is encouraged by regulation in the hopes that the result will be less costly and more efficient products and services.

In certain cases, it is believed that monopolistic power would be beneficial to the public good. Such cases occur in industries, such as public utilities, where costs to enter a business are extremely high and it is believed that monopolistic industry concentration will provide a more efficient and cost-saving product to the public.

The last type of regulation is enacted with the goal of providing an increase in public welfare in terms of health or financial stability or quality. These types of regulations are generally created to control the financial services industry or manufacturing industries. For the financial services industry, such regulations typically restrict the way in which institutions such as commercial banks or savings and loans operate. Financial regulations may also provide requirements for the issuance of financial securities—such as common and preferred stock and bonds and debentures—in order to provide protection of public investors. For manufacturing entities, these regulations generally prescribe acceptable methods of control in areas such as air pollution and reclamation of land by mining concerns

In "On Financial Regulation, the Financial Crisis and the End of GE Capital," Jeffrey Jarrett (2015) discusses the financial crisis of 2007–2008, the effects of that crisis, the implications for regulation, and the Glass-Steagall Act, created to protect banking customers. Jarrett concludes that while the United States suffered through the crisis, the country's neighbor to the north, Canada, which has provincial regulations that work harmoniously, did not. The author posits that the financial regulations in the United States are more discordant across the country, creating a greater negative impact in the United States.

The successful management of a firm requires the pursuit of a stated goal or objective. The major alternative goals most often cited by managers are stakeholder-theory management, profit maximization, size maximization, and value maximization. The most theoretically or academically acceptable financial objective for a firm is to pursue the maximization of the firm's value, alternatively defined as shareholder wealth. It is also an extremely difficult objective to pursue.

In any business, the objectives and goals of the owners should always supersede those of the nonowner managers of the firm. In a corporation, managers are employed as the agents of the shareholders and are thus appointed to act on their behalf. When managerial decisions do not benefit both management and shareholder groups in the same way, it is possible for management to act in its own best interests at the expense of the shareholders.

This problem, referred to as the principal-agent or agency problem, is an important consideration in assessing managerial performance. The agency problem exists when there is a dissimilarity between the interests of managers and shareholders. This means that management appointed by the stockholders to run the firm may pursue objectives not geared toward the best interests of the firm's owners but rather toward the best interests of the managers.

Agency problems often occur when management compensation is tied to profit improvement. Decisions geared toward the improvement of profits are often short-term in nature, as opposed to value-maximization decisions, which are generally more long-term in nature. A similar problem may exist with the determination of salaries and fringe benefits for management. Agency issues may occur in this area as well unless those salaries and fringes are set with the objective of keeping or obtaining the best-qualified managers.

Eugene Fama, in his paper "Agency Problems and the Theory of the Firm," provides some insight as to the issues related to both organizational ownership and managerial control. To make his point, Professor Fama clarifies that the defining issue of importance is not necessarily ownership or entrepreneurship but rather survival in a competing economy. It is, he concludes, this competitive environment that requires managers to "face both the discipline and opportunities provided by the markets for their services, both within and outside the firm."

# Recommended Readings

Fama, Eugene F. "Agency Problems and the Theory of the Firm." *Journal of Political Economy* 88, no. 2 (April 1980): 288–307.

Jensen, Michael C. "Value Maximization, Stakeholder Theory, and the Corporate Objective Function." *Journal of Applied Corporate Finance* 14, no. 3, (Fall 2001): 8–21.

Friedman, M. "The Social Responsibility of Business is to Increase its Profits." *New York Times Magazine* (September 13, 1970).

Fu, X., T. Tang, and Y. Yan. "Why Do Institutions Like Corporate Social Responsibility Investments? Evidence from Horizon Heterogeneity." *Journal of Empirical Finance* (forthcoming, 2018).

# Selected Readings

Jarrett, Jeffrey E. "On Financial Regulation, the Financial Crisis and the End of GE Capital." *Journal of Business & Financial Affairs* 4, no. 1 (2015): 146.

# On Financial Regulation, the Financial Crisis and the End of GE Capital

By Jeffrey E. Jarrett

## Introduction

During the financial crisis of 2007–2008, the public observed the great economic crisis with the heavy losses in employment, great decrease the prices of new and existing homes, increases in foreclosures on home and business properties and reduction of businesses to increase their size of business activities through the ability to borrow and later to raise funds through the selling of equity instruments and bonds. As part of the solution, the federal banking system induce lending of major United States Bank by the injection of huge amounts into these banks in the form of creating additional large sums of cash and cash equivalents to increase the size of the major banks resulting in more liquidity in markets for borrowing by firms to raise capital. General Electric, in difficulties and did lobby for huge manufacturing corporation with a significant amount of assets in financial markets found itself Lobbying for Federal Reserve action to liquefy financial markets to borrow funds to keep its extensive manufacturing divisions in operation. Regulations designed to produce better liquidity in financial markets did increase the size of the major banking institutions in the United States.

The public cried out against the policy of "to big to fail" and financial regulation was enacted to prevent another economic failure by attempting to regulate action taken by the major banks. Large parts of this regulatory activity come from the well-known "Dodd-Frank" legislation. Being an extremely long and detailed legislation enacted into law, the purpose here is not to debate the details but to examine its results.

Recently, General Electric (GE), a major manufacturer in a number of industries also containing a significant amount of its capital in financial assets including real estate, insurance, mutual funds and the like announced a reorganization of its assets. The program began with sales of $26.5 million in real estate assets and a return to its roots in manufacturing of oil drilling equipment, jet engines,

Jeffrey E. Jarrett, "On Financial Regulation, the Financial Crisis and the End of GE Capital," *Journal of Business & Financial Affairs*, vol. 4, no. 1, pp. 146. Copyright © Jeffrey E. Jarrett (CC by 4.0) at https://www.omicsonline.org/open-access/on-financial-regulation-the-financial-crisis-and-the-end-of-ge-capital-2167-0234-1000e146.php?aid=52871.

and medical devices produced in operational facilities throughout the world. GE Capital is to be reduced greatly in size if not eliminated entirely. All this is a result emanating from financial regulation which makes financial operations more risky for GE to remain heavily invested in operation outside of its main mission in manufacturing. GE is only one, albeit a big one, of financial companies that are changing with the landscape of finance.

How does this changing landscape preview what has happened in financial markets and how do we wish it to look like? By contrast none of this financial failure in markets occurred in Canada. The United States and Canada both have regulations in financial markets. How they operate to provide the same services differs greatly between the two nations even when both are operating well. Both provide the same basic services service to financial institutions. What are the striking differences?

First, The USA contains more than 7000 chartered banks and a great number of regulators. Banks may be regulated by the Federal Reserve, The Federal Deposit Insurance Corporation, FDIC, the Office of the Comptroller of the Currency and in addition possible fifty state regulating bodies. There are also a number of regulators for non-Bank Financial Institutions. Canada has only about 80 banks and the big six hold 93 percent of the assets. There are only thirteen provinces with only one federal regulator, i.e. the Office of the Superintendent of Financial Institutions (OIFI).

The result is that banks have not been free to establish branches in other states in the USA whereas, in Canada, branch banking is far more common than in the USA. Provincial regulations in Canada are largely in harmony with each other. This is not true for the USA. Small farmers in the USA are against branch banking because the banks may take their capital to another area if the economy in one sector is below the median due to a drought, incidence of Earthquakes, fracking by the local extraction industry, and the effects of climate change. We know that regional shocks to the farming sectors produces bank runs and other destabilizing features. The US had had experience with bank runs but Canada has not.

In addition in the USA, branching restrictions which protect small banks from were coupled with new laws designed to protect small banking institutions were enacted after the "Great Depression" of the 1930's. The Federal Deposit Insurance Corporation and the Glass-Steagall Act designed to protect depositors also protect the smaller institutions form competition. Steagall support was necessary to gain enough votes from agrarian representatives in the House of Representative for passage. Additional regulations were eventually passed to put limits on what institution could pay depositors, served to keep banks small. These laws also prevented banks from growing resulting in a fragmented regulatory system in the USA with respect to Canada.

In sum, the Canadian system did not have a 2007–2008 financial crisis. Their regulatory control operated much more efficiently and produced a financial healthier result than in the USA. Although GE is not a bank but has a large stake in financial operations, we should observe their recent decisions concerning their withdrawal from financial activities. Banking can be a more stable industry if somehow the USA could reduce the number of regulators and harmonize their regulations across the nation. Using Canada as simply a small nation about one-tenth the economic size of the US is not an excuse for improving the regulatory systems.

# MODULE 2

# Annual Reports and Financial Statements

*Don't ever let your business get ahead of the financial side of your business. Accounting, accounting, accounting. Know your numbers.*

**Tilman J. Fertitta**

A ny analysis of a firm, whether to assess performance for investment or to make managerial decisions, should include a review of the organization's financial statements. These include the balance sheet, income statement, statement of retained earnings, and statement of cash flow. A review of the firm's annual report or its filings with the Securities Exchange Commission (SEC) to include the footnotes to the annual financial statements is also generally undertaken.

Annual reports all contain several sections of importance that disclose significant material information to the reader. One section provides the financial statements for one or more years, another the footnotes that help to explain or clarify the information provided in the statements. Another section of significant importance is the report of the audit committee.

Audit committees are comprised of members of the company's board of directors. The members of the committee are responsible for reviewing the accounting policies, financial reporting, and information disclosure activities of the firm to ensure accuracy and the appropriate degree of disclosure. To be listed on the New York Stock Exchange, at least one of the committee's members should be a financial expert, and all members should be independent.

The findings of a 2009 study provide some insight that is not entirely comforting with regard to the value of the information disclosed by publicly held firms. Don E. Giacomino, Michael D. Akers, and Joseph Wall, in their August 2009 *CPA Journal* article "Testing the Financial Literacy and Expertise of Audit Committee Members," provide insight as to audit committee requirements to include those of the Sarbanes-Oxley Act of 2002 and both New York Stock Exchange (NYSE) and National Association of Securities Dealers Automated Quotations (NASDAQ). The article discusses surveys defined as the Deloitte Quiz and the FEI quiz. The authors introduce the importance of their review, given their belief that it was important to consider the financial literacy of audit committees in three areas of critical importance for their companies, to include whether audit committee members understood

> the transactions that require the judgements described; the accounting and measurement issues for the policies and estimates; management's choices among policies and methods for making estimates and the reasons for them; the implications of management choices for the potential manipulation of financial reporting.

In their concluding remarks, the authors note, based on the results of the FEI study surveying FEI (Financial Executives Institute) members, that

> directors and audit committee members are financially illiterate, and given the financial literacy requirements for audit committee members, the authors propose that companies consider measuring and improving the financial literacy of their audit committee members.

To remedy the problem, they provide several recommendations for improving financial literacy.

Along the same lines, it is important to be able to recognize whether financial statements are, or are not, fraudulent. Arthur Pinkasovitch, in a 2018 article for Investopedia Academy entitled "Detecting Financial Statement Fraud," cites firms previously found to commit such fraud, to include both Enron and WorldCom as examples of the reality of financial statement fraud and the problems it can cause. Pinkasovitch notes that financial statement fraud comes in several flavors, to include

- "fictitious sales
- improper expense recognition
- incorrect asset valuation
- hidden liabilities
- and unsuitable disclosures."

The author goes on to note several "red flags" for detecting such fraud, to include looking for "a rapid and unexplainable rise in the number of day's sales in receivables, growing inventories, a large buildup of fixed assets, and a significant surge in the company's performance" within the final fiscal year. He also suggests the use of quantitative models such as the Beneish model, which combines eight different financial ratio values into one value known as the M-score and which can be useful in identifying possible fraud problems.

As to the financial statements themselves, items such as accounts receivable and inventories are reported on the firm's balance sheet. The balance sheet identifies the financial position of a firm as of a specific date. The statement is therefore also often called the statement of financial position. Utilizing the balance sheet, the analyst may examine a firm as a portfolio of resources or assets, which are equal to the sources or claims against those assets in the form of either liabilities or equity. Those sources or claims against the assets are the sources of funding utilized to acquire the assets and may be in the form of debt or borrowed funds or equity in the form of either common or preferred ownership shares.

The income statement identifies the amount of profit or loss earned by a firm over a specified period of time. It provides a measure of the ability of the firm to attain one basic objective of earning an acceptable level of profit for the owners of the firm. As presented, the statement reduces the sales or revenues earned by the firm by the amount of expense required to earn that revenue.

Income statements can be presented as either single-step or multistep statements. The difference is simply that single-step statements show fewer layers of profit than are presented with multistep statements. Single-step statements, for example, might show only one operating profit value by lumping all operating expenses between the net sales or revenue value and net operating profit. Multistep statements will instead show multiple layers of profit, to include items such as gross profit and then net operating profit.

One important item to note with income statements is the presence of noncash items, such as depletion and depreciation expenses. These items are noncash expense write-offs and thus do not affect the actual cash flow of the firm. Depreciation, for example, is a cost charged against revenue representing an estimate of the periodic loss of value of the depreciating asset over time from the usage of that asset. The true rate of economic depreciation for the asset is dependent on a number of things, to include the rate of usage of the asset, the type of asset involved, the quality of the maintenance utilized for the asset, and a number of other factors.

The statement of retained earnings identifies the amount of dividends paid to stockholders for a specified period of time and also provides a method of identifying the amount of income that has alternatively been retained and reinvested in the firm. Retained earnings, also referred to as earned surplus, provides the total cumulative value of the profits and losses of the firm over time minus any dividends that have been paid to the owners of the firm as cash dividends.

The statement of cash flow is directly related to the other financial statements. It provides, therefore, a picture of the changes in the firm's cash position from one period to the next. As a cash flow statement, it converts the firm's accounting profit-oriented income statement to a cash flow–based statement. As a result, the statement provides an indication of the sources of cash as well as the uses of those cash funds.

The statement will provide the sources and uses of cash by segmenting those flows as operating, financing, or investment cash flows. The flows include net income or losses for the specified period, an adjustment for noncash expenses, changes in balance sheet items from one period to another, and sources or uses of cash provided by financing activities, such as the sale or repurchase of common stock, and investment activities, such as the purchase or sale of existing assets.

One of the primary considerations of both organization formation and most management decisions is the effect of taxation. The effects of tax laws and the ability of a firm to manage taxes are critical. The annual reports, financial statements, financial footnotes, and the performance of the firm all reflect the effects of taxation.

It is important to recognize, then, that most significant managerial decisions require consideration of the tax ramifications of those decisions. Financing decisions, for example, require the consideration of the pretax expense of debt interest payments relative to the post-tax payment of stock dividends.

Some decisions, such as the decision to pay dividends or to repurchase stock, are also affected by tax regulations. When dividends are paid, the same revenue providing those dividends may have been subject to double or even triple taxation.

Double taxation occurs when an individual owns corporate stock. The firm issuing that stock is a legal entity and pays tax on its earnings and then pays dividends from the after-tax income. The stockholder then pays a tax on these dividends. Thus, the same earnings have been taxed twice.

Triple taxation occurs when a corporation owns the stock of another corporation. The first corporation pays a dividend to its stockholders. As a stockholder, the second corporation is entitled to these dividends. It receives the dividends as income and subsequently passes those dividends on as its own dividends to its stockholders. This means that the stockholders' dividend has been previously taxed at two levels: it has been taxed as taxable income from the first corporation prior to the paying of the dividend to the corporation in which the stockholder owns shares, and then it has been taxed again as income to the second corporation.

This means that by the time this dividend has gotten to the stockholder, who must also pay taxes, the income has already been taxed twice. Thus, the same dividend income has been taxed three times.

## Recommended Readings

Amiram, D., Z. Bozanic, and E. Rouen. "Financial Statement Errors: Evidence from the Distributional Properties of Financial Statement Numbers." *Review of Accounting Studies* 20, no. 4 (2015): 1540–1593.

## Selected Readings

Giacomino, Don E., Michael D. Akers, and Joseph Wall. "Testing the Financial Literacy and Expertise of Audit Committee Members." *The CPA Journal* 79, no. 8 (August 2009): 66–71.

Pinkasovitch, Arthur. *Investopedia Academy.* January 3, 2018. https://www.investopedia.com/articles/ financial-theory/11/detecting-financial-fraud.asp.

READING 2

# Testing the Financial Literacy and Expertise of Audit Committee Members

By Don E. Giacomino, Michael D. Akers, and Joseph Wall

I n recent years, several laws and regulations have set new requirements for the financial literacy and expertise of members of audit committees. In 1999, the New York Stock Exchange (NYSE) added a rule requiring that each company have an audit committee comprising independent directors who are financially literate and including at least one financial expert. In that same year, the NYSE and the National Association of Securities Dealers (NASD) formed a Blue Ribbon Committee to make recommendations on improving the effectiveness of audit committees. Recommendation 3 of that report advocated the following:

> [T]he NYSE and NASD [should] require listed companies with a market capitalization above $200 million ... to have an audit committee comprised of a minimum of three directors, each of whom is financially literate (as described in the section of this Report entitled "Financial Literacy") or becomes financially literate within a reasonable period of time after his or her appointment to the audit committee, and further that at least one member of the audit committee have accounting or related financial management expertise.

Current NYSE (section 303A.06) and Nasdaq rules rely heavily on SEC Rule 10A-3(b), which sets required standards of independence, prohibiting an audit committee member from accepting directly or indirectly any consulting, advisory, or other compensatory fee from the issuer or any subsidiary under most eases. The NYSE Listed Company Manual section 3O3A.O7 and Nasdaq Rule 4350(d) both include the three-member minimum and financial literacy requirements.

The Sarbanes-Oxley Act of 2002 (SOX) requires that each issuer of periodic reports to the SEC disclose "whether or not, and if not, the reasons therefor, the audit committee is comprised of at least 1 member who is a financial expert, as such term is defined by the Commission." Under SOX, expertise is measured by specific knowledge, experience, or a combination thereof. It has been suggested that non-accounting experts who fit the definition may be less competent to perform this role than those with accounting-specific expertise (Gopal V. Krishnan and Gnanakumar Visvanathan, "Does the *SOX* Definition of an Accounting Expert Matter?" July 29, 2009, papers.ssm.com/sol3/papcrs.cfm?abstractid=X66K&4).

Some recent attempts at measuring the financial (accounting) knowledge of current and prospective board members have been made in the studies of financial literacy cited below. With this background, the authors explored whether companies have formal processes in place for measuring or improving the financial literacy of audit committee members. The result is proposed content for testing financial literacy and financial expertise.

## Financial Literacy

Current regulations and laws vary as to the meaning of financial literacy and financial expertise. Audit committee members are required to be able to read and understand fundamental financial statements under the rules of both the NYSE (Listed Company Manual section 303A.07) and Nasdaq (Rule 4350-4). Both regulations refer to SEC Regulation S-K [section 407(d)(5)] for the acceptance of a financial expert's qualifications.

The Blue Ribbon Committee did not define financial literacy but indicated that literacy includes the ability to read and understand fundamental financial statements, including a company's balance sheet, income statement, and cash flow statements. As Roman Weil, a professor at the University of Chicago observes. "It is clear they mean accounting literacy and not financial literacy." In their presentations to board members, Weil and his colleagues defined financial literacy by developing four criteria based on the "critical accounting policies and estimates" section of a company's Management's Discussion and Analysis (MD&A):

- Understand the transactions that require the judgments described.
- Understand the accounting and measurement issues for the policies and estimates.
- Understand management's choices among policies and methods for making estimates and the reasons for them.
- Understand the implications of management choices for the potential manipulation of financial reporting.

1. Retained earnings on the balance sheet is an account usually referring to:

   a. Cash and other liquid assets generated by income with which the firm can pay dividends

   b. Net assets (assets minus liabilities) generated by income that the firm can distribute its dividends

   c. Part of the firm's owners' claims to net assets of the *firm*

   d. None of the above

   e. More than one of the above

2. If a firm uses the indirect method for the statement of cash flows (SCF), which of the following is true? (indicate all that apply)

   a. The SCF lists cash receipts from customers.

   b. The SCF shows cash spent for acquiring other firms in the financing section of the statement.

   c. The SCF shows stock issued to acquire other firms.

   d. The SCF shows the change in accounts receivable.

3. Which of the following is true of the accounting for derivatives? (indicate all that apply)

   a. Derivatives always appear at fair value (market value) on the balance sheet.

   b. The accounting for derivatives under U.S. GAAP can induce volatility into earnings.

   c. By definition in U.S. GAAP, accounting derivatives are instruments that require large cash investments at inception.

   d. Derivatives can never be assets for accounting purposes.

4. The accounting for inventories in the United States can be based on either LIFO or FIFO. Which of the following statements describes LIFO and FIFO accounting under U.S. GAAP? (indicate all that apply)

   a. LIFO inventory accounting always results in lower financial statement income.

   b. LIFO inventory accounting always reduces income taxes paid for a given period.

   c. A given firm must use either LIFO or FIFO for all its inventories; it is not legal under tax law to use LIFO for some inventories and FIFO for other inventories.

   d. A firm that uses LIFO must display the difference between costs of beginning and ending inventories as reported and the costs of inventories that would have been reported had the firm been using FIFO (or current cost).

**Financial Statements and Accounting Literature**

1. The balance sheet
   a. Is a financial snapshot, taken at a point in time, of the assets the company owns and the claims against those assets.
   b. Records the flow of financial resources over time.
   c. Reports the operating results of a company for a period of time.
   d. Is prepared by the auditors.
   e. Both a and d are correct

2. Financial statements to be filed with the SEC should be prepared
   a. Following the IRS code
   b. As the company's financing agreements dictate or prescribe
   c. Following generally accepted accounting principles (GAAP)
   d. Using the practices followed by others in the industry
   e. All of the above

**Disclosure Rules**

1. Which of the following financial information is not covered by the independent auditor's report?
   a. Earnings announcements
   b. Pro forma earnings releases
   c. The footnotes to the financial statements
   d. MD&A
   e. All of the above

**Form and Content of SEC Filings**

1. Which of the following is true about the Form 10-K?
   a. Contains the annual financial statements of the company
   b. Contains an audit report on the included financial statements
   c. Is subject to SEC review
   d. All of the above are true

**Exhibit 2.2**     Sample Questions from the Deloitte Basic Financial
Literacy Assessment Tool (*Continued*)

**Internal Controls**

1.   Who is responsible for the design and effectiveness of the company's internal controls?

   a.   Management

   b.   Internal audit

   c.   External audit

   d.   The audit committee

   e.   All of the above

For the purposes of discussion, Weil's definition of financial literacy is used below.

# Financial Expertise

SOX and the SEC require only that at least one member of the audit committee meets the SEC definition of a "financial expert." SEC Regulation S-K section 229.407(d)(5)(ii) defines an audit committee financial expert as a person who has all of the following attributes:

- An understanding of U.S. GAAP and financial statements;
- The ability to assess the general application of U.S. GAAP in connection with accounting for estimates, accruals, and reserves;
- Experience preparing, auditing, analyzing, or evaluating financial statements that present a breadth and level of complexity of accounting issues that can reasonably be expected to be raised by the company's financial statements, or experience actively supervising persons engaged in such activities;
- An understanding of internal controls and procedures for financial reporting; and
- An understanding of audit committee functions.

These attributes must be acquired through education and experience as described in Regulation S-K.
    The Chartered Financial Analyst (CFA) Centre and the CFA Institute provide specific qualifications for audit committee membership:

- All board members should be financially literate, though not necessarily a financial or accounting professional. (See www.cfainstitute.org/centre/topics/govemance/official/

committee_qualifications.html and April 10, 2002 Letter to NYSE on Issues of Corporate Accountability at www.cfainstitute.org/centreAopics/comment/2002/02aimrcom_corpgov. html.)

- Regarding financial expertise, members of the committee overseeing auditors and auditor activities should possess a considerable, if not thorough and in-depth, understanding of financial reports and the auditing process. Regulators should recognize individuals holding the CFA designation as meeting the standard of financial expert for audit committees. (See September 3, 2002, Letter to SEC on Improvement of Oversight of the Auditing Process at www.cfainstitute.org/centre/topics/comment/2002/02 financial_info.html, and November 6, 2003, Letter to Ontario Securities Commission on Multilateral Instrument 52–110 Audit Committees at www.cfainstitute.org/centre/topics/comment/2003/03audit_comm.html.)

## Testing for Financial (Accounting) Literacy

Recently, several parties have constructed and administered tests or quizzes that gauge financial literacy. Professors at the University of Chicago devised their own instrument for MBA students, corporate officers, directors, and legal counsel. Financial Executives International (FEI) has constructed a quiz for its members. Deloitte has created a self-assessment tool for audit committees of its audit clients.

## The Weil and Schipper Quiz

Professors Katherine Schipper and Roman Weil of the University of Chicago have conducted programs and made presentations on financial accounting knowledge to corporate executives and board members. Using their criteria described above, they developed and administered their own quiz for testing participants' knowledge of financial accounting. Their quiz consists of 13 questions whose answers can be found in a basic accounting text for first-year MBA students and 12 questions on advanced topics (special purpose entities, use of reserves, restructuring, issuance of shares for I.O.U., stock options, derivatives, and income manipulation.) Alter testing 1,466 directors and officers who attended the programs from 2002 to 2005, Weil concluded the following:

> The individual quiz taker, self-selected from larger audiences, are likely more confident of their financial literacy than those who did not take the quiz. The people who took this quiz, likely the better half of our board member attendees, are not yet financially literate.

*Exhibit 2.1* provides sample questions from the Weil and Schipper quiz.

| **Exhibit 2.3** | Sample Questions from the FEI Quiz |

1. Who is responsible for the proper preparation and presentation of the financial statements?

   a. Board of Directors

   b. Management

   c. External auditor

   d. Audit Committee

2. Which of the following is NOT typically included among "current assets" on the balance sheet?

   a. Accounts receivable

   b. Fixed assets

   c. Inventory

   d. Prepaid expenses

   e. All of the above are typically included.

3. Cash flow per share is defined by GAAP as:

   a. Net income plus depreciation divided by shares outstanding

   b. Cash flow from operations on the cash flow statement divided by shares outstanding

   c. The change in cash in the balance sheet divided by the shares outstanding

   d. There is no GAAP definition. Analysts/companies devise one to suit their own purposes.

4. The audit committee of a public company should be composed of:

   a. The CFO, CEO, and at least three outside directors

   b. At least three independent directors, all financially literate, and at least one financial expert

   c. The CFO, the CEO, and the Chairman of the Board

Over a four-year period, Weil and Schipper administered the quiz to attendees at executive education sessions for board members. The sessions were held at the University of Chicago Graduate School of Business, Stanford Law School, and the Wharton School. Weil also gave the quiz to MBA students at the University of Chicago. The median score for directors and officers, self-selected from larger audiences, has remained consistent at 32% (eight correct out of 25 questions). The MBA

# Exhibit 2.4 Topical Content

| Topic | Weil and Schipper Quiz | FEI Quiz | D&T Quiz | Proposed Financially Literate | Proposed Financial Expert |
|---|---|---|---|---|---|
| Responsibilities (Management, Board of Directors, Audit Committee) | 1 | 1 | | 2 | 2 |
| MD&A (Purpose and Content) | | | 1 | 2 | 2 |
| U.S. GAAP Sources | | | 1 | 1 | 2 |
| Basic Concepts (Revenue, Cost, etc.) | 1 | 1 | 1 | 2 | 2 |
| Statement of Cash Rows | 1 | 1 | | 1 | 2 |
| Cash vs. Accrual | | | | 1 | 2 |
| Current Assets | 1 | 1 | | 2 | 2 |
| Fixed Assets | 1 | | | 1 | 2 |
| Pensions | | | | 1 | 2 |
| Intangible Assets | 1 | 1 | | 1 | 2 |
| Inventory Cost | 1 | 1 | | 2 | 2 |
| Current Liabilities | | | 1 | 2 | 2 |
| Restructuring | 2 | 1 | | 1 | 2 |
| Derivatives | 2 | 1 | | 1 | 2 |
| Long-term Liabilities | | | 1 | 1 | 2 |
| Leases | 1 | | | 1 | 2 |
| Purchase Commitments | 1 | | | 1 | 2 |
| Reserves | 2 | | 1 | 1 | 2 |
| Stock Options | 2 | | | 1 | 2 |
| Deferred Taxes | 1 | 1 | | 1 | 2 |
| Shareholder Equity | | 1 | 1 | 1 | 2 |
| Income Manipulation | 1 | 1 | | 1 | 2 |
| Revenue Recognition | | | 1 | 1 | 2 |
| Earnings per Share | 1 | 1 | 1 | 1 | 2 |
| Gross Margin | | | 1 | 2 | 2 |
| Income from Continuing Operations | | | | 1 | 2 |
| Bad Debt Expense | | | | 1 | 2 |
| Impairment of Assets | 1 | 1 | 1 | 1 | 2 |
| Off-balance-sheet Financing | | | | 1 | 2 |
| Consolidations | | | 1 | 1 | 2 |
| Footnote Disclosures | | | 1 | 1 | 2 |
| Extraordinary Gains/Losses | | | | 1 | 2 |
| Accounting Changes | | | | 1 | 2 |
| Related Party Transactions | | | 1 | 1 | 2 |
| Discontinued Operations | | | | 1 | 2 |
| Internal Controls | | | 1 | 1 | 2 |
| SEC Reporting Requirements | 1 | | 1 | 1 | 2 |
| Special Purpose Entities | 2 | | | 1 | 2 |
| Segment Reporting | | 1 | | 1 | 2 |
| Audit Reports | | | 1 | 2 | 2 |
| Non-U.S. GAAP Earnings per Share | | | | 1 | 2 |
| Principles vs. Rules | | | | 1 | 2 |
| Contingencies | | | | 1 | 2 |

**Note:** The number "1" indicates basic knowledge and the number "2" indicates advanced knowledge.

students answered only the 13 basic accounting questions. Weil and Schipper reported only the top 30 of 155 University of Chicago students who completed the quiz.

The authors administered the Weil and Schipper quiz to undergraduate finance and accounting majors at a private Midwestern university. As opposed to the FEI and Weil and Schipper respondents, these undergraduate students were not self-selected and results were not self-reported. To make meaningful comparisons between these undergraduates and the University of Chicago MBAs, the results for the top 19% of the undergraduates are reported. The results show that the top 19% of MBA students who answered the 13 basic questions scored higher than the top 19% of undergraduate students and directors. These results are not surprising: MBAs are expected to perform at a higher level than undergraduate students. Also, it is expected that as the time a person has been out of school increases, the likelihood of that person performing well on examinations decreases. The difference between the undergraduate students and the directors was expected, though not to the extent actually seen.

The undergraduate students do not appear to have an appropriate level of knowledge of the accounting topics addressed in the Weil and Schipper quiz. While the Weil and Schipper quiz specifically tests accounting knowledge, the Deloitte Basic Financial Literacy Self-Assessment Tool and the FEI Financial Literacy quiz measure financial literacy and also incorporate questions relating to auditing skills and knowledge.

## The Deloitte Quiz

Deloitte has developed two assessment tools that are available to its audit clients: the Basic Financial Literacy Self-Assessment Tool and the Advanced Self-Assessment Tool. Deloitte encourages audit committees to consider and tailor each tool as part of a broad assessment of financial literacy. The basic tool is a 30-question quiz that covers basic knowledge in four areas: financial statements and accounting literature, disclosure rules, form and content of SEC filings, and internal controls. Deloitte advises: "Audit committee members should not inter that answering most, or even all, of these questions correctly represents a 'passing' grade in basic financial literacy." The tool was designed to identify audit committee members who may require more focused financial literacy education than others. Those who take the quiz do not report their scores; therefore, performance results are not available.

*Exhibit 2.2* provides sample questions from the Deloitte Basic Financial Literacy Assessment Tool.

Thirty-seven undergraduate students in finance and accounting completed the Deloitte quiz. Undergraduate students were strongest on questions related to basic financial statements (section 1) and the form and content of SEC filings. They were weakest on internal control and disclosure rules. Because there are only five questions on internal control and only two of the 37 students answered one specific internal control question correctly, further testing on internal controls may yield very different results.

# The FEI Quiz

Philip B. Livingston, president and CEO of FEI, with contributions from University of Chicago professors Roman Weil and V. Duane Rath, as well as John Stewart, a former partner at Arthur Andersen, developed the FEI Financial Literacy quiz. Available to members online, the 24-question quiz covers basic financial statements and responsibilities of directors, managers, and audit committee members. *Exhibit 2.3* provides sample questions from the FEI quiz.

The authors have only self-reported results from FEI members who took the quiz and chose to inform FEI of their scores. In 2007, FEI indicated that the self-reported members scored an average of 67% on the quiz. The authors administered the FEI quiz to 98 undergraduate finance (juniors) and accounting (seniors) students at a private, Midwestern university. The average undergraduate student scored 68%—very close to the self-reported scores from FEI members. The students scored highest on questions related to balance-sheet accounts and lowest on board of directors' responsibility, cash flow per share, restatement causes, segment reporting, purpose of the MD&A, valuation of stock warrants, audit committee responsibility, and NYSE and Nasdaq models.

# Company Efforts to Improve or Test Financial Literacy

An examination of the existing research finds that only Weil and Schipper have attempted to measure the extent to which companies are measuring or improving financial literacy of their audit committees. Weil and Schipper surveyed audit committee chairs to find out if—

- The company assesses the financial literacy of audit committee members, or
- The company or its board has taken steps since 1999 to increase the financial literacy of the members of the audit committee.

None of the 27 respondents reported any formal process to assess financial literacy of audit committee members. In addition, none of the respondents indicated that their board had any formal process for increasing the financial literacy of the audit committee members.

# A Proposal

In addition to examining and administering each of the three quizzes to the students, the authors sought the opinions of members of their Accounting Advisory Board regarding topical content and level of knowledge expected. *Exhibit 2.4* shows the topical content of each of the three financial literacy quizzes. The exhibit's two right-hand columns present the authors' proposal for topical content for testing financial literacy and financial expertise. Forty topics are listed as either basic knowledge or advanced knowledge. Only three of the topics—basic concepts (revenue, cost, materiality, matching), earnings per share, and impairment of assets—appear on all three quizzes. Based on feedback from accounting firm partners and advisory board members who looked at the topical content of the three quizzes, the authors added the following 11 topics to the proposed content:

- Cash vs. accrual,
- Pensions,
- Income from continuing operations,
- Bad debt expense,
- Off-balance-sheet financing,
- Extraordinary gains and losses,
- Accounting changes,
- Non-U.S. GAAP earnings per share,
- Principles vs. rules,
- Contingencies, and
- Discontinued operations.

Given the findings by Weil and Schipper that directors and audit committee members are financially illiterate, and given the financial literacy requirements for audit committee members, the authors propose that companies consider measuring and improving the financial literacy of their audit committee members. Companies can construct their own assessment tools or use one of the tools identified [...]. Many audit committee members are likely to have access to the FEI or Deloitte tools. Audit committee members can also participate in the programs conducted by Weil on financial (accounting) literacy.

A national financial literacy testing procedure or certification may be advisable. Professional organizations such as FEI or the AICPA could write and administer the exams. As suggested in Exhibit 2.4, the topics for testing financial literacy would be the same as those for financial expertise. The difference is the level of knowledge expected. Two levels of examination are suggested to address this.

Many current business students will eventually serve on corporate boards. Colleges and universities can play a role by setting financial accounting standards and testing business majors on financial literacy during the students' senior year, regardless of the quiz used. The authors' findings for undergraduate finance and accounting majors at just one university suggest that students need to improve their financial accounting knowledge. In addition, students' knowledge of the basics of auditing and taxation could also be tested. Additional testing for financial literacy at other universities can provide greater insight as to the extent to which business majors have the requisite knowledge for serving on audit committees and how they compare to directors and audit committee members.

*Don E. Giacomino, CPA,* is a professor and Flynn Chair Holder, and ***Michael D. Akers, CPA, CMA, CFE, CIA,*** is the Horngren Professor and department chair, both in the department of accounting at Marquette University, Milwaukee, Wis. ***Joseph Wall, MBA,*** is the managing director of Ideas in Motion, LLC, as well as an assistant professor of business administration at Carthage College, Kenosha, Wis.

READING 3

# Detecting Financial Statement Fraud

By Arthur Pinkasovitch

..........................................................................................................................................................

Looking back at Enron, perhaps the company best known for committing accounting fraud, you can see the many methods that were utilized in order to improve the appearance of its financial statements. Through the use of off balance sheet special purpose vehicles, the firm hid its liabilities and inflated its earnings. In 1999, limited partnerships were created for the purpose of purchasing Enron shares as a mean of improving performance of its stock. It all worked for a while. But Enron's aggressive accounting practices and financial statement manipulation began to spiral out of control, and its doings were eventually uncovered by *The Wall Street Journal*. Shortly after, on December 2, 2001, Enron filed for Chapter 11 in what was the largest U.S. bankruptcy in history ... only to be surpassed by WorldCom less than a year later.

The U.S. government responded with preventative measures. Despite passage of the Sarbanes-Oxley Act–a direct result of the Enron, WorldCom and Tyco scandals–financial statement improprieties remain too common an occurrence. And complex accounting fraud such as that practiced at Enron is usually extremely difficult for the average retail investor to discover. However, there are some basic red flags that help. After all, the Enron fraud was not exposed by high-paid Ivy League MBA-holding Wall Street analysts, but by news reporters who used journal articles and public filings in their due diligence process. Being first on the scene to uncover a fraudulent company can be very lucrative from a short seller's perspective and can be rather beneficial to a skeptical investor who is weighing in the overall market sentiment.

## What Is Financial Statement Fraud?

According to a study conducted by the Association of Certified Fraud Examiners (ACFE), fraudulent financial statement accounts for approximately 10% of incidents concerning white collar crime. Asset misappropriation and corruption tend to occur at a much greater frequency, yet the financial impact of these latter crimes is much less severe. ACFE defines fraud as "deception or misrepresentation that an individual or entity makes knowing that the misrepresentation could result in some unauthorized benefit to the individual or to the entity or some other party." Greed and work pressure are the most common factors pushing management to deceive investors and creditors.

Financial statement fraud can surface in many different forms, although once deceptive accounting practices are initiated, various systems of manipulation will be utilized to maintain the appearance of sustainability. Common approaches to artificially improving the appearance of the financials include: overstating revenues by recording future expected sales, understating expenses through such means as capitalizing operating expenses, inflating assets' net worth by knowingly failing to apply an appropriate depreciation schedule, hiding obligations off of the company's balance sheet and incorrect disclosure of related-party transactions and structured finance deals.

Five basic types of financial statement fraud exist:

- fictitious sales
- improper expense recognition
- incorrect asset valuation
- hidden liabilities
- unsuitable disclosures

Another type of financial statement fraud involves cookie-jar accounting practices, a procedure by which a firm will understate revenues in one accounting period and maintain them as a reserve for future periods with worse performance. Such procedures remove the appearance of volatility from the operations.

And then, of course, there is the total fabrication of statements. In the spring of 2000, financial fraud investigator Harry Markopolos approached the SEC, claiming that the $65 billion wealth management business of Bernard Madoff was fraudulent. After modeling Madoff's portfolio, Markopolos realized that the consistent returns achieved were impossible. For example, according to an interview with the Certified Fraud Investigator, he "concluded that for Madoff to execute the trading strategy he said he was using he would have had to buy more options on the Chicago Board Options Exchange than actually existed." Fortunately, this sort of fraud is pretty rare.

## Financial Statement Fraud Red Flags

Financial statement red flags provide a general overview of the warning signs investors should take note of. They do not necessarily indicate an occurrence of financial statement fraud, but merely signal that further in-depth research must be conducted to assess the validity of the corporate documents. Creditors would find such information useful to ensure that loans are not provided to firms operating with an elevated amount of risk. Investors, on the other hand, may want to take note of the following factors to discover new shorting opportunities.

The most common financial statement fraud red flags:

- Accounting anomalies, such as growing revenues without a corresponding growth in cash flows. Sales are much easier to manipulate than cash flow but the two should move more or less in tandem over time.

- Consistent sales growth while established competitors are experiencing periods of weak performance. Of course, this may be due to efficient business operations rather than fraudulent activity.

- A rapid and unexplainable rise in the number of day's sales in receivables in addition to growing inventories. This suggests obsolete goods for which the firm records fictitious future sales.

- A significant surge in the company's performance within the final reporting period of fiscal year. The company may be under immense pressure to meet analysts' expectations.

- The company maintains consistent gross profit margins while its industry is facing pricing pressure. This can potentially indicate failure to recognize expenses or aggressive revenue recognition.

- A large buildup of fixed assets. An unexpected accumulation of fixed assets can flag the usage of operating expense capitalization, rather than expense recognition.

- Depreciation methods and estimates of assets' useful life that do not correspond to those of the overall industry. An overstated life of an asset will decrease the annual depreciation expense.

- A weak system of internal control. Strong corporate governance and internal controls processes minimize the likelihood that financial statement fraud will go unnoticed.

- Outsized frequency of complex related-party or third-party transactions, many of which do not add tangible value (can be used to conceal debt off the balance sheet).

- The firm is on the brink of breaching their debt covenants. To avoid technical default, management may be forced to fraudulently adjust its leverage ratios.

- The auditor was replaced, resulting in a missed accounting period. Auditor replacement can signal a dysfunctional relationship while missed accounting period provides extra time to "fix" financials.

- A disproportionate amount of management compensation is derived from bonuses based on short term targets. This provides incentive to commit fraud.

- Something just feels off about the corporation's business model, financial statements or operations

# Financial Statement Fraud Detection Methods

Spotting red flags can be extremely challenging as firms that are engaged in fraudulent activities will attempt to portray the image of financial stability and normal business operations. Vertical and horizontal financial statement analysis introduces a straightforward approach to fraud detection. Vertical analysis involves taking every item in the income statement as a percentage of revenue and comparing the year-over-year trends that could be a potential flag cause of concern. A similar approach can also be applied to the balance sheet, using total assets as the comparison benchmark, to monitor significant deviations from normal activity. Horizontal analysis implements a similar approach whereby rather than having an account serve as the point of reference, financial information is represented as a percentage of the base years' figures. Likewise, unexplainable variations in percentages can serve as a red flag requiring further analysis.

Comparative ratio analysis also allows analysts and auditors to spot discrepancies within the firm's financial statements. By analyzing ratios, information regarding day's sales in receivables, leverage multiples and other vital metrics can be determined and analyzed for inconsistencies. A mathematical approach, known as the Beneish Model, evaluates eight ratios to determine the likelihood of earnings manipulation. Asset quality, depreciation, gross margin, leverage and other variables are factored into the analysis. Combining the variables into the model, an M-score is calculated; a value greater than -2.22 warrants further investigation as the firm may be manipulating its earnings while an M-score less than -2.22 suggests that the company is not a manipulator Similar to most other ratio-related strategies, the full picture can only be accurately portrayed once the multiples are compared to the industry and to the specific firm's historical average. [...]

# The Bottom Line

Having proper knowledge of the red flags to avoid companies indulging in unscrupulous accounting practices is a useful tool to ensure the safety of your investments. [...]

# MODULE 3

# Financial Analysis

*Causal analysis provides absolutely no value judgment, and a value judgment is absolutely not a causal explanation.*

**Max Weber**

In order to place a proper value on a firm in the marketplace, investors, whether they are institutional or individual, often attempt to perform the exercise of fundamental analysis. Similarly, the management of a firm must undertake an analysis of the organization to increase the probabilities that managerial decisions are profit and/or value oriented—in short, that the organization's resources are utilized in the best interests of the firm and its owners.

Fundamental analysis deals with the analysis of material information about a firm. Material or fundamental information is information based on items such as historical and forecasted financial statements, the management of the firm, and the products of the firm. To be more specific, material information is information that makes a difference. If the information will affect a decision to take or not take action, it is material.

Analysis of a firm provides insight regarding past performance, strengths, weaknesses, and the potential for profit, cash flow, and growth. The basic financial statements included in an analysis include the balance sheet, the income statement, the statement of retained earnings, and the statement of cash flow.

Perhaps the most common approach to financial analysis is ratio analysis. Ratio analysis is primarily concerned with evaluating the ability of management to obtain a level of profitability and increased investment value for the firm. Ratio analysis generally considers such items as asset investment, the efficiency of the usage of those assets, the type of financing utilized to purchase those assets, the amount of shareholder return earned, and the ability of the firm to provide safety to creditors.

Analysis of appropriately constructed ratios provides an analyst with insight as to issues such as a firm's financial strengths and weaknesses, efficiency, profitability, sources of risk, and market perception. Ratio analysis can be utilized not only to evaluate a firm at a single point in time but also for comparison to both the internal trends of the firm itself and to other firms or an industry standard.

One of the important characteristics of ratios is that they do not provide answers or solutions. They are simply indicators suggesting something is good, bad, unchanged, or changed with regard to the operations of the firm. The question then is why the ratio provided that indication, whether it was something that was intended, whether it was or was not preventable if not desired, and finally, whether it can be continued if desirable or prevented if not.

In examining ratio results, the interrelationship of ratios must be considered. Often, one ratio may provide an indication of something that appears to be good or bad. The analysis of separate ratios can provide additional insight as to whether the initial indication has merit or perhaps appears negated.

As a result of the findings of ratio analysis, appropriate management action may be taken to ensure the value of the firm is strengthened in the future. Care must always be taken to ensure the size of the firm being examined and the economic conditions under which the firm was or will be operating are considered in the analysis. For those analyses conducted within a year—quarter-to-quarter, for example—the differences in the business cycle of the firm must be considered to ensure that no erroneous conclusions are reached.

Perhaps one of the most common problems encountered in the discussion or presentation of ratio analysis is the plethora of ratio titles encountered in the financial world. The simple fact is that there are various ways ratios can be constructed, and various names have been attached to ratios over time.

Jeffrey A. Mankin and Jeffrey J. Jewell address these issues in their paper entitled "A Sorry State of Affairs: The Problems with Financial Ratio Education." The 2014 paper discusses their study of accounting and finance textbooks, and they note that for the "Top 20" ratios cited in business textbooks, "only four of the Top 20 ratios have 100% consensus on the formula" to calculate the ratio. Further, many of the ratios "have several commonly used 'aliases' or alternate names." While this can cause confusion in the professional world as the results of ratio analysis are discussed and reported, the authors note the confusion around calculations and naming "is currently a barrier to learning financial ratios." Since students may take several classes using different texts, any "subtle changes in names or formulas may be a source of frustration and an impediment to learning."

Financial analysts typically segregate ratios into several groups. One of the more popular approaches is to classify them as liquidity, activity or operating, leverage, profitability, and market or valuation ratios. As with the names of the ratios themselves, ratios can also be classified a number of different ways.

Liquidity ratios provide the analyst with insight as to the ability of a firm to meet its short-term obligations as they mature. The current ratio and the quick ratio (also known as the acid-test ratio) are the two most often considered liquidity ratios. The difference between the current ratio and the quick ratio is the removal of the most illiquid current assets from the current ratio to obtain the quick ratio. The concern of course is that, when necessary, current assets might be liquidated as a means of paying off short-term debt obligations. More marketable and more easily liquidated assets improve liquidity and reduce the risk of not being able to pay bills as they come due.

Activity or operating ratios are geared towards explaining or attempting to explain exactly how efficiently and effectively a firm's management controls its investment in assets. Any investment in assets or resources should be with the intent of providing revenue or sales, to reduce expenses, or both in an effort to improve the value of the firm. Some of the most commonly utilized operating or activity ratios include the inventory turnover, average collection period, fixed asset turnover, and total asset turnover ratios.

Leverage ratios are created as a means of providing some insight as to the effectiveness with which management is handling its financing. The issues of most concern to an analyst in the leverage area is the level of debt financing—since debt financing incurs fixed-cost interest charges that must be covered and therefore increases a firm's level of risk—and the extent to which those charges are covered by the funds available to pay them. Fixed charges also provide leverage or magnification of profits. Thus, in profitable periods of operation, fixed financing costs can magnify those profits. The downside is that in periods of losses, fixed financing costs can magnify those losses as well. The most commonly utilized leverage ratios include the debt, debt-equity, times interest earned or interest charges coverage, and the fixed charges coverage ratios.

Profitability ratios, as their name implies, are utilized to identify the effectiveness of the firm at earning a profit, thus providing cash flow and, ultimately, value to the firm's owners. Profitability ratios are often classified as returns relative to sales, assets, or equity investment.

Common profitability ratios include the net margin, earning power, return on investment, return on common equity, and return on total equity ratios.

Some analysts may include ratios such as the price-earnings multiple, dividend payout, and market-to-book ratios in the profitability grouping. Others may separate these types of ratios into another group commonly referred to as market ratios.

In a 2011 article entitled "What Is Your ROA? An Investigation of the Many Formulas for Calculating Return on Assets," authors Jeffrey Jewell and Jeffrey Mankin cited a 2010 study and noted that "eleven different versions of ROA" were found in "business textbooks."

The authors note that differences in the definition of the numerator or the denominator of the ratio can significantly affect the results of the computation but also that the use of the different formats can be of use if the differences are understood. For example, the version with operating profit in the numerator and total assets in the denominator is "particularly useful when comparing different firms that have varying levels of non-operating items." They also discuss the effects of certain variables such as interest expense, noting, for example, that "higher interest expense leads to higher values of ROA in one version" (version 8) of the ratio. They point out, however, that "this seemingly perverse result actually makes sense if we interpret version 8 as being an 'all investors' ROA. In other words, version 8 is measuring the total return on assets available to pay both debt and equity holders of the firm." The ratio in question is determined as follows:

## (Net Income − Interest Expense)/Total Assets

Keeping in mind the interrelationships of ratios and the many facets of business management, one method of presenting these interrelationships is DuPont analysis, which is sometimes expanded to a more expansive modified DuPont analysis. DuPont analysis is so called because the E.I. du Pont de Nemours or DuPont Company has traditionally been credited with being the first firm to include the analysis in its annual reports.

Simple DuPont analysis involves determining the product resulting from multiplying the net margin ratio times the total asset turnover ratio. The resulting ratio is the return on investment ratio. The approach provides a method of explaining how that return was obtained, why it increased, or why it fell. A key question here is whether the firm is obtaining most of its returns from the turnover of products or from pricing and expense controls as evidenced in the net margin value.

An extension of the DuPont model is to add in a measure of leverage called the equity multiplier. Fixed-cost debt financing can provide a magnification of profits and losses, and thus, the addition of the equity multiplier provides insight as to how much debt the firm has relative to equity and thus how much magnification is provided from fixed-cost financing or financial leverage.

A second commonly utilized analytical approach is the creation and analysis of normalized or comparative statements. Normalized statements are statements that are presented in a relative form. These statements provide for ease of comparison between firms that have different size or volume characteristics and quick insight as to the importance of various factors to a firm as well as to how those factors have changed over time. The two common approaches are vertical statement analysis and horizontal statement analysis.

## Selected Readings

Jewell, Jeffrey J., and Jeffrey A. Mankin. "What Is Your ROA? An Investigation of the Many Formulas for Calculating Return on Assets." *Academy of Educational Leadership Journal* 15, Special Issue (2011): 79–91.

Mankin, Jeffrey A., and Jeffrey J. Jewell. "A Sorry State of Affairs: The Problems with Financial Ratio Education." *Academy of Educational Leadership Journal* 18, no. 4 (2014): 195–219.

# What is Your Roa?

An Investigation of the Many Formulas for
Calculating Return on Assets

By Jeffrey J. Jewell and Jeffrey A. Mankin

## Abstract

[This reading] compares the eleven different versions of computing return on assets that can be found in current business textbooks. To illustrate the practical differences between the different versions, each version of ROA is calculated for eight slightly different example firms. The results are then compared and analyzed. Pros and cons are then discussed for each version of ROA. A practical ROA taxonomy is proposed to organize the several different versions and to improve comparability.

## Introduction

A recent study by Mankin and Jewell (2010) of ratios in 77 current business textbooks made several interesting discoveries. The study included accounting, finance, management, marketing, and financial statement analysis textbooks. Two of the most interesting points are as follows. First, textbook authors are in unanimous agreement on how to calculate very few ratios. The current ratio, gross profit margin, and dividend yield are the most notable of these ratios. Second, most ratios, even the most commonly used ones, have several alternate formula versions. Common ratios with substantial disagreement in the formulas are return on assets, quick ratio and inventory turnover.

This research focuses on return on assets (ROA) because it is a popular ratio with many different formula variations. [This reading] the eleven different ratio formulas found in current business textbooks and propose three additional ROA formulas that would be possible based on the sample data.

# Literature Review

## Financial Ratios

Financial ratios are used for several important purposes. Whittington (1980) summarized two basic uses of financial ratios: normative and positive. Normative uses include measuring a firm's ratios to a standard such as another company or to an industry average. Positive uses include estimation of financial variables such as profit margins, returns, leverage, and stock prices. Positive uses can also include researchers using predictive models for corporate failure, bankruptcy, and credit risk.

Normative uses of financial ratios involve two primary functions: financial analysis and business education. Financial analysis involves evaluating a firm's profitability and riskiness and then comparing them to industry averages. Ratios generally involve a mathematical proportion of X/Y that allows analysts control in two ways (Barnes, 1987). First, ratios control for the size of the financial information. Because of this characteristic, different firms' current ratios can be compared even if the firms' current assets and/or current liabilities are not comparable. Second, ratios control for industry factors. Industries often have unique characteristics that are seen if a firm's financial ratios are compared to the industry average. It is axiomatic that a firm's financial ratios should be compared to industry averages. Both financial researchers (Lev, 1969) and textbook authors (White, Sondhi, & Fried, 2003) recommend that financial analysis should include industry averages. This type of recommendation is a normative use of ratios.

A second normative use of financial ratios includes their use in business education. Financial ratios are an important tool in business education. Students learn to use financial ratios in accounting, finance, marketing, and management classes. Huefner (2002) argued that financial ratio preparation and analysis is an important part of the very first accounting course. Recently, the New York State Society of Certified Public Accountants (NYSSCPA) has issued a white paper of educational goals for CPA candidates (Fierstein, 2008). The preparation and interpretation of financial ratios were included in the NYSSCPA goals for students preparing for careers as CPAs.

Besides normative uses, financial ratios also have positive uses. Positive uses of financial ratios include estimating certain financial variables or predicting future outcomes such as bankruptcy or business failure. Financial ratios are used in many financial research studies to predict certain outcomes. Several studies have tested whether financial ratios are normally distributed. For example, Deakin (1976) concluded that a normal distribution could not be assumed for financial ratios with the possible exception of the debt/assets ratio.

One of the more well-studied positive uses of financial ratios is in the area of business failures. Beaver (1966) used financial ratios of failed firms and non-failed firms to predict business failure. Since each ratio was analyzed separately, this was essentially a univariate technique. He identified financial ratios that were predictive in identifying failed firms. Altman (1968) expanded this into multivariate research by using multiple discriminant analysis (MDA). This research led to the Z-score model that is widely used in business failure analysis (Krantz, 2010). Altman (2000) later expanded the Z-score model into a second-generation predictive model called Zeta® analysis.

## Return on Assets

Return on Assets (ROA) is one of the most popular and useful of the financial ratios. ROA has been used in industry since at least 1919 when the DuPont Company used it as the top of its ratio triangle system. The ratio was called return on investment and was calculated as Profit / Total Assets. The base of the DuPont triangle was the expanded ROA formula: Profit Margin (Profit / Sales) and Capital Turnover Ratio (Sales / Total Assets) (Horrigan, 1968).

The importance that educators and practitioners place on ROA can be seen in three ways. First, at least one ROA formula is presented in most business textbooks. ROA was the third most frequently presented ratio in a study of business textbooks, appearing in 70 of the 77 textbooks (Mankin & Jewell, 2010). Only the current ratio and inventory turnover ratio occurred more often than ROA.

Second, at least one version of ROA is used often in failure prediction studies. The original Altman (1968) Z-Score included ROA as one of its five factors used to predict business failure using a version defined as Earnings Before Interest and Taxes / Total Assets (EBIT / TA). Beaver (1966) also used ROA as one of the six ratios used to predict business failure. The ROA version in the Beaver study was Net Income / Total Assets (NI / TA). Hossari and Rahman (2005) ranked the popularity of all financial ratios used in studies predicting business failures. Their study included 53 previous studies from 1966 to 2002 and ranked 48 separate ratios. The ROA version Net Income / Total Assets (NI / TA) was the single most common ratio in all the failure prediction studies.

Third, analysts often use ROA in their investigation of a firm's financial position, performance, and future prospects. Gibson (1987) surveyed Chartered Financial Analysts about the importance of many financial ratios. The study included four different versions of ROA, and each version was selected by at least 90% of the CFA respondents as a primary measure of profitability.

## Return on Assets in Textbooks

Of all of the ratios presented in business textbooks, authors disagree the most about return on assets. In the Mankin and Jewell (2010) study, 70 of the 77 textbooks included ROA. The study found eleven different versions of ROA in business textbooks. The different versions of ROA are shown in Table 4.1, along with the frequency with which they appear in the sample.

In the Table 4.1 data, 28 textbooks, or 40% of the textbooks in the sample, define ROA as Net Income / Total Assets. To simplify the discussion, a version number has been assigned to each ROA formula. So, the most popular formula for ROA has been assigned version 1, the second most popular is version 2, etc.

It is important to understand that Table 4.1 does not include "semantic" differences in how the ratio is defined or how the formula is displayed. Table 4.1 has standardized all insignificant differences

**Table 4.1** ROA Formulas and Frequencies (Mankin & Jewell, 2010)

| Version | Formula | Number in Sample | Percent in Sample |
|---|---|---|---|
| 1 | Net Income / Total Assets | 28 | 40.00% |
| 2 | Net Income / Average Total Assets | 11 | 15.71% |
| 3 | (Net Income + Interest Expense) / Average Total Assets | 8 | 11.43% |
| 4 | [Net Income + Interest Expense × (1-Tax Rate)] / Average Total Assets | 7 | 10.00% |
| 5 | Earnings Available to Common Shareholders / Total Assets | 5 | 7.14% |
| 6 | Earnings Before Interest and Taxes / Average Total Assets | 3 | 4.29% |
| 7 | Operating Profit / Total Assets | 2 | 2.86% |
| 8 | (Net Income + Interest Expense) / Total Assets | 2 | 2.86% |
| 9 | [Net Income + Interest Expense × (1-Tax Rate)] / Total Assets | 2 | 2.86% |
| 10 | Earnings Before Tax / Total Assets | 1 | 1.43% |
| 11 | Earnings Before Interest and Taxes / Total Assets | 1 | 1.43% |
| **Totals** | | **70** | **100.00%** |

in terminology, of which there were many. All eleven versions of ROA can be economically and mathematically different in different situations, sometimes by large amounts. Each version should also be defined and interpreted in slightly different ways in an economic or accounting sense. This idea will be expanded on later. It is also important to realize that each of the eleven versions was simply called "Return on Assets" or "Return on Total Assets" or some other synonymous term in the textbook. These naming issues have the potential to cause considerable confusion among students and practitioners who may assume that the version of ROA in a given textbook is the only version of ROA, or the definitive version of ROA.

This is not to say that the ratios above are only known as "Return on Assets." For example, five other textbooks in the sample include the ratio Earnings Before Interest and Taxes / Total Assets (EBIT / TA). However, in those five texts that ratio is known as "Basic Earnings Power." Therefore those five observations are not included in Table 4.1.

A few basic observations about the various versions of ROA can be made simply by noting the details of Table 4.1. First, the most widely used version of ROA is also the simplest version, Net Income / Total Assets (NI / TA). Second, the top two versions comprise about 56% of the sample, while the bottom nine versions comprise the other 44%. Third, several versions of ROA have identical numerators but differ in that one version averages total assets in the denominator while the other does not. Version 1 and 2 of ROA fit this pattern, as do versions 3 and 8, 4 and 9, and 6 and 11. So, out of the eleven versions of ROA there are only seven unique numerators. Fourth, the ratios can be categorized not only based on their denominators, but also based on the "size" of their numerators. The versions with Operating Profit, EBIT, or EBT in the numerator will obviously give answers of larger magnitude in most situations than those with after-tax numbers in the numerator.

Table 4.2 attempts to organize the various versions of ROA in a more logical manner. The ratios are separated based on whether or not the denominator averages total assets; they are also arranged in descending order of typical magnitude. Although the study found only eleven versions of ROA

**Table 4.2** ROA Versions by Size and Denominator

| Version | Formula | Abbreviated Formula |
|---------|---------|---------------------|
| **Panel A: Denominator = Total Assets** | | |
| 7 | Operating Profits / Total Assets | OP / TA |
| 11 | Earnings Before Interest and Taxes / Total Assets | EBIT / TA |
| 10 | Earnings Before Tax / Total Assets | EBT / TA |
| 8 | (Net Income + Interest Expense) / Total Assets | (NI + IntExp) / TA |
| 9 | [Net Income + Interest Expense × (1-Tax Rate)] / Total Assets | [NI + IntExp(1-T)] / TA |
| 1 | Net Income / Total Assets | NI / TA |
| 5 | Earnings Available to Common Shareholders / Total Assets | EACS / TA |
| **Panel B: Denominator = Average Total Assets** | | |
| 12* | Operating Profits / Average Total Assets | OP / ATA |
| 6 | Earnings Before Interest and Taxes / Average Total Assets | EBIT / ATA |
| 13* | Earnings Before Tax / Average Total Assets | EBT / ATA |
| 3 | (Net Income + Interest Expense) / Average Total Assets | (NI + IntExp) / ATA |
| 4 | [Net Income + Interest Expense × (1-Tax Rate)] / Average Total Assets | [NI + IntExp(1-T)] / ATA |
| 2 | Net Income / Average Total Assets | NI / ATA |
| 14* | Earnings Available to Common Shareholders / Average Total Assets | EACS / ATA |

in textbooks, there are three additional valid versions that can be constructed by combining three of the existing numerators with average total assets as the denominator. These new versions are all denoted with a * on the version number. For example, there is no version of ROA in the sample defined as Earnings Available to Common Shareholders / Average Total Assets (EACS / ATA). This version is introduced in Table 4.2 and given the version number 14*. This new version 14* has the same numerator as ROA version 5. Table 4.2 also introduces an abbreviated formula for each version.

Since the versions are now organized in a logical way, the differences can be analyzed. The two denominators, total assets and average total assets, can be compared.

Why do some authors average total assets while others do not? It is interesting to note that of the 70 textbooks in the sample that include a formula for ROA, 29 (41.4%) of the texts average the total assets in the denominator while 41 (58.6%) of the textbooks do not. It is even more interesting to note that 24 of 29 (82.8%) of all the texts that use average total assets are accounting textbooks. The accounting texts used average total assets in 24 of the 28 (85.7%) textbooks. Only 4 of the 42 (9.5%) non-accounting texts used average total assets. The reason for this is very simple. ROA compares an income number (a flow measure) to total assets (a stock measure). Whenever comparing flow measures to stock measures accountants like to average the stock measure in order to preserve the matching principle. Apparently, however, the authors of the finance, management and marketing texts in the sample feel no compulsion to preserve the matching principle in their versions of ROA.

## Comparing the Denominator

So what is the practical impact of averaging the denominator versus not averaging? A very simple example can answer this question. In this example, consider the two most basic and popular versions of ROA, versions 1 and 2. These two versions have the same numerator, net income, but version 2 averages the denominator while version 1 does not. Holding net income constant, each ratio is calculated for several years and several different levels of total assets. This will isolate the effect of averaging the denominator. Calculations are shown in Table 4.3.

**Table 4.3** The Impact of Averaging the Denominator

|         |              | 2006      | 2007     | 2008      | 2009      | 2010      |
|---------|--------------|-----------|----------|-----------|-----------|-----------|
|         | Net Income   | $12,000   | $12,000  | $12,000   | $12,000   | $12,000   |
|         | Total Assets | $100,000  | $90,000  | $100,000  | $110,000  | $120,000  |
| **Version** |          |           |          |           |           |           |
| 1       | NI / TA      | 12.00%    | 13.33%   | 12.00%    | 10.91%    | 10.00%    |
| 2       | NI / ATA     | —         | 12.63%   | 12.63%    | 11.43%    | 10.43%    |

There are several interesting observations can be made from this example. First, and most obviously, one extra year of ROA can be calculated with version 1. Since averaging the denominator requires two years worth of total assets, analysts must have at least two years of data before they can calculate an ROA with version 2. Second, based on the results for 2007, when total assets are falling, averaging the denominator yields a lower ROA (version 2 < version 1). Third, the reverse is true for 2008. When total assets are rising, averaging the denominator yields a higher ROA (version 2 > version 1). Fourth, focusing on 2007—2010, averaging the denominator may make ROA slower to recognize trends. In this case the firm appears to be adding non-productive assets (assets that do not contribute to income). This makes both ROA's fall, but version 1 begins to fall more quickly than version 2. The reverse would be true as well. If the firm were to shed inefficient assets the positive trend should be detected more quickly by version 1. Of course if variation in total assets were not informative for some reason, analysts would prefer an ROA that was less affected by the "noisy" changes. Assume for the moment that the variation of total assets from 2006—2008 was not meaningful. Version 2 has the advantage of being unaffected by these noisy changes in total assets. A summary of the advantages of each denominator can be found in Table 4.4.

**Table 4.4** Advantages of Each Denominator

| Denominator | Advantages |
|---|---|
| Average Total Assets | 1. Preserves the matching principle |
| | 2. Less affected by "random" changes in total assets |
| | 3. Higher ROA when assets are rising |
| Total Assets | 1. Simplicity |
| | 2. Requires less data to calculate ROA |
| | 3. Quicker to react to trends |
| | 4. Higher ROA when assets are falling |

## Comparing the Numerator

Table 4.5 begins the process of comparing the seven different numerators. Once again simple examples will illustrate the practical differences between the ratios. In order to fully explore the differences between the seven numerators, ROA is calculated for eight different example firms. These example firms have identical operating income and total assets; however, they each differ in one important variable, such as interest expense. In order to simplify the analysis even further only a few firms will be compared at a time. The first comparison, highlighting the effects of non-operating items, appears in Table 4.5.

**Table 4.5** The Effects of Non-Operating Items on ROA

| | Firm Description | Firm A Base | Firm B Non-Operating Income | Firm C Non-Operating Loss |
|---|---|---|---|---|
| | Total Assets | $500,000 | $500,000 | $500,000 |
| | Tax Rate | 40% | 40% | 40% |
| | Income from Operations | $100,000 | $100,000 | $100,000 |
| | **Plus: Non-Operating Income** | **0** | **10,000** | **(10,000)** |
| | EBIT | 100,000 | 110,000 | 90,000 |
| | Less: Interest Expense | 0 | 0 | 0 |
| | EBT | 100,000 | 110,000 | 90,000 |
| | Less: Tax | 40,000 | 44,000 | 36,000 |
| | Net Income | 60,000 | 66,000 | 54,000 |
| | Less: Preferred Dividends | 0 | 0 | 0 |
| | EACS | 60,000 | 66,000 | 54,000 |
| **Version** | | | | |
| 7 | OP / TA | **20.00%** | **20.00%** | **20.00%** |
| 11 | EBIT / TA | 20.00% | 22.00% | 18.00% |
| 10 | EBT / TA | 20.00% | 22.00% | 18.00% |
| 8 | (NI + IntExp)/ TA | 12.00% | 13.20% | 10.80% |
| 9 | [NI + IntExp(1-T)] / TA | 12.00% | 13.20% | 10.80% |
| 1 | NI / TA | 12.00% | 13.20% | 10.80% |
| 5 | EACS / TA | 12.00% | 13.20% | 10.80% |

Table 4.5 compares Firm A, the base firm, to Firm B, which has non-operating income, and Firm C, which has non-operating losses. Note that version 7 of ROA is exactly the same for all three firms. Every other version is higher for firm B, due to the presence of non-operating income. Likewise, every other version is lower for firm C, due to the presence of non-operating losses. So, version 7 of ROA has the distinct benefit of being completely unaffected by non-operating items. This makes version 7 particularly useful when comparing different firms that have varying levels of non-operating items.

The second comparison, highlighting the impacts of interest expense, appears in Table 4.6. Here important differences among the various versions really start to emerge. In this example we are comparing Firm A, the base firm, to Firms D and E. Firm D is a low debt firm with low interest expense, while Firm E is a high debt firm with high interest expense. We can make four interesting observations from Table 4.6. The first two observations will certainly not be surprising, while the latter two may be.

**Table 4.6** The Effects of Interest Expense on ROA

|  |  | Firm A | Firm D | Firm E |
|---|---|---|---|---|
|  | **Firm Description** | **Base** | **Low Debt** | **High Debt** |
|  | Total Assets | $500,000 | $500,000 | $500,000 |
|  | Tax Rate | 40% | 40% | 40% |
|  | Income from Operations | $100,000 | $100,000 | $100,000 |
|  | Plus: Non-Operating Income | 0 | 0 | 0 |
|  | EBIT | 100,000 | 100,000 | 100,000 |
|  | **Less: Interest Expense** | **0** | **10,000** | **30,000** |
|  | EBT | 100,000 | 90,000 | 70,000 |
|  | Less: Tax | 40,000 | 36,000 | 28,000 |
|  | Net Income | 60,000 | 54,000 | 42,000 |
|  | Less: Preferred Dividends | 0 | 0 | 0 |
|  | EACS | 60,000 | 54,000 | 42,000 |
| **Version** |  |  |  |  |
| 7 | OP / TA | **20.00%** | **20.00%** | **20.00%** |
| 11 | EBIT / TA | **20.00%** | **20.00%** | **20.00%** |
| 10 | EBT / TA | 20.00% | 18.00% | 14.00% |
| 8 | (NI + IntX)/ TA | 12.00% | 12.80% | 14.40% |
| 9 | [NI + IntX(1-T)] / TA | 12.00% | 12.00% | 12.00% |
| 1 | NI / TA | 12.00% | 10.80% | 8.40% |
| 5 | EACS / TA | 12.00% | 10.80% | 8.40% |

First, both version 7 and 11 of ROA are completely unaffected by interest expense. Second, higher interest expense leads to lower values of ROA for versions 10, 1, 5. Comparing the results for Firm D and Firm E shows this. Third, higher interest expense leads to higher values of ROA for version 8. This seemingly perverse result actually makes sense if we interpret version 8 as being an "all investors" ROA. In other words, version 8 is measuring the total return on assets generated for both debt and equity holders. To restate, version 8 is measuring the total return on assets available to pay both debt and equity holders of the firm. Fourth, version 9, like versions 7 and 11, is also completely unaffected by debt levels and interest expense. However, since version 9 is based on Net Income it yields a smaller value than versions 7 or 11, which are both based on pretax numbers.

So, if an analyst wanted to compare the ROA's of various firms while eliminating any differences caused by debt policy he could use version 7 or 11 for a pre-tax ROA or version 9 for an after-tax ROA. If the analyst wanted to compare ROA's while considering the differences caused by debt policy, he would use version 10 for a pre-tax ROA or version 1 or 5 for an after-tax ROA. Finally, if an analyst wanted to know an "all investors" ROA she would use version 8.

Table 4.7 shows the effects of taxes and dividends on ROA. In this example, the base firm is compared to firms with different levels of taxes and dividends. Firm F has tax loss carry-forwards that cut its tax expense for the current year in half. Firm G pays a preferred dividend, while firm H pays a common dividend. There are several observations we can draw from Table 4.7.

First, Firm F's tax situation highlights the fact that we have three pre-tax versions of ROA, versions 7, 11, and 10, and four after-tax versions of ROA, versions 8, 9, 1, and 5. The pre-tax versions of ROA are unaffected by Firm F's tax loss carry-forward. However, the after-tax versions of ROA all benefit from higher values caused by the reduced taxes. Second, Firm G's preferred dividend only affects version 5 of ROA, causing it to be lower than version 5 for the base firm. Since version 5 is the only version to subtract preferred dividends, it can be thought of as a "common shareholders ROA." Finally, it is interesting to note that all of the versions of ROA are identical for Firm A and Firm H. This highlights the fact that none of the versions of ROA are affected by common dividends.

The examples above illustrate that each version of ROA can be useful in the proper context. The various numerators are all measuring something slightly different. Table 4.8 summarizes the advantages of each numerator.

Earlier in the paper, the issue of "naming confusion" was mentioned. This "naming confusion" potentially arises from calling so many different formulas that all measure slightly different things "return on assets." To help alleviate this problem we propose new names for many of the versions of ROA. The proposed taxonomy serves two different purposes: the proposed names are descriptive of the mathematics involved with the ratio and the proposed names will help differentiate each version of ROA from every other version. The proposed taxonomy is shown in Table 4.9.

**Table 4.7** The Effects of Taxes and Dividends on ROA

| | | Firm A | Firm F | Firm G | Firm H |
|---|---|---|---|---|---|
| | **Firm Description** | **Base** | **Tax Loss Carryforwards** | **Preferred Dividends** | **Common Dividends** |
| | Total Assets | $500,000 | $500,000 | $500,000 | $500,000 |
| | Tax Rate | 40% | 40% | 40% | 40% |
| | Income from Operations | $100,000 | $100,000 | $100,000 | $100,000 |
| | Plus: Non-Operating Income | 0 | 0 | 0 | 0 |
| | EBIT | 100,000 | 100,000 | 100,000 | 100,000 |
| | Less: Interest Expense | 0 | 0 | 0 | 0 |
| | EBT | 100,000 | 100,000 | 100,000 | 100,000 |
| | Less: Tax | 40,000 | 20,000 | 40,000 | 40,000 |
| | Net Income | 60,000 | 80,000 | 60,000 | 60,000 |
| | Less: Preferred Dividends | 0 | 0 | 10,000 | 0 |
| | EACS | 60,000 | 80,000 | 50,000 | 60,000 |
| | Less: Common Dividends | 0 | 0 | 0 | 10,000 |
| | Additions to RE | 60,000 | 80,000 | 50,000 | 50,000 |
| **Version** | | | | | |
| 7 | OP / TA | 20.00% | 20.00% | 20.00% | 20.00% |
| 11 | EBIT / TA | 20.00% | 20.00% | 20.00% | 20.00% |
| 10 | EBT / TA | 20.00% | 20.00% | 20.00% | 20.00% |
| 8 | (NI + IntExp)/ TA | 12.00% | 16.00% | 12.00% | 12.00% |
| 9 | [NI + IntExp(1-T)] / TA | 12.00% | 16.00% | 12.00% | 12.00% |
| 1 | NI / TA | 12.00% | 16.00% | 12.00% | 12.00% |
| 5 | EACS / TA | 12.00% | 16.00% | 10.00% | 12.00% |

**Table 4.8** The Advantages of Each Numerator

| Numerator | Advantages |
|---|---|
| Operating Profit | 1. Unaffected by non-operating items, debt levels, taxes, or dividends |
| | 2. Useful for comparing firms with different exposure to non-operating items |
| EBIT | 1. Unaffected by debt levels, taxes, and dividends |
| | 2. Useful for comparing pre-tax returns of firms with different capital structures |
| EBT | 1. Unaffected by taxes and dividends |
| | 2. Useful for comparing firms with different tax situations |
| (NI + IntExp) | 1. Measures "all investors" ROA |
| | 2. Shows the total ROA available to "pay" investors a return |
| [NI + IntExp(1-T)] | 1. Eliminates the effects of different debt levels and interest expense |
| | 2. Useful for comparing after-tax returns of firms with different debt levels |
| Net Income | 1. Simplicity |
| | 2. The "bottom line" ROA for all equity holders |
| EACS | 1. The only version that considers preferred dividends |
| | 2. The "bottom line" ROA for common shareholders |

**Table 4.9** Proposed Taxonomy for the Different Versions of ROA

| Version | Formula | Proposed Name |
|---|---|---|
| 7 | OP / TA | Operating Return on Assets |
| 11 | EBIT / TA | Basic Earning Power (This name is already widely used for this version) |
| 10 | EBT / TA | Pre-tax Return on Assets |
| 8 | (NI + IntExp) / TA | All Investors Return on Assets |
| 9 | [NI + IntExp(1-T)] / TA | Debt Neutral Return on Assets |
| 1 | NI / TA | Net Return on Assets |
| 5 | EACS / TA | Common Shareholders Return on Assets |
| 12* | OP / ATA | Operating Return on Average Assets |
| 6 | EBIT / ATA | Basic Earning Power of Average Assets |
| 13* | EBT / ATA | Pre-tax Return on Average Assets |
| 3 | (NI + IntExp) / ATA | All Investors Return on Average Assets |
| 4 | [NI + IntExp(1-T)] / ATA | Debt Neutral Return on Average Assets |
| 2 | NI / ATA | Net Return on Average Assets |
| 14* | EACS / ATA | Common Shareholders Return on Average Assets |

# Conclusion

Return on assets (ROA) is a popular and well-known ratio. It is used by analysts to measure the profitability of a firm and by researchers to make predictions on financial variables and events. However, the current study shows that there are eleven different versions of ROA in current business textbooks. One of the problems with the existence of so many disparate versions is that it makes comparability between versions more difficult. Imagine analysts, sitting around a boardroom, or students in a study group attempting to discuss the ROA of a firm. Unless they have previously agreed upon the ROA version to be used, there could be considerable confusion. It is possible, even likely, that different participants will have different "correct" answers and draw different conclusions about the profitability of the firm depending on the version of ROA used.

Now imagine a student or a professional researching a firm using Yahoo!Finance, Morningstar, or any other financial data service. Unless she understands the version of ROA used by that site, she is very likely to misuse and misinterpret the data. This problem is compounded when comparing different ROA's from different data sources.

Therefore, based on the analysis above, it is appropriate not to think of ROA as a single ratio but as a "category of ratios." This category includes almost any ratio that compares an earnings related number from the income statement to Total Assets or Average Total Assets. This study shows each of the eleven versions of ROA can have a valid use in the proper context, but that none should be presented as the only or the definitive version of ROA. In the future, it would be beneficial for both students and practitioners if textbook authors would use names that would more accurately reflect the uses and highlight the differences among the various versions of ROA. Perhaps a decade from now, instead of multiple versions of ROA all sharing the same name, there will be a less confusing and more descriptive nomenclature in use.

# References

Altman, E. I. (1968). Financial Ratios Discriminant Analysis and the Prediction of Corporate Bankruptcy. *Journal of Finance*, 23(4), 589–609.

Altman, E. I. (2000). *Predicting Financial Distress of Companies: Revisiting the Z-Score and Zeta® Models.* Unpublished manuscript, New York University.

Barnes, P. (1987). The Analysis and Use of Financial Ratios: A Review Article. *Journal of Business Finance & Accounting*, 14(4), 449–461.

Beaver, W. H. (1966). Financial Ratios as Predictors of Failure. *Journal of Accounting Research*, 4(3), 71–111.

Deakin, E. B. (1972). A Discriminant Analysis of Predictors of Business Failure. *Journal of Accounting Research*, 10(1), 167–179.

Fierstein, S. S. (2008). Examination of Pre-Certification Education. *The CPA Journal*, 78(8), 26–33.

Gibson, C. (1987). How Chartered Financial Analysts View Financial Ratios. *Financial Analysts Journal*. May-June.

Horrigan, J. (1968). A Short History of Financial Ratio Analysis. *Accounting Review*, 43(2), 284–294.

Hossari, G., & Rahman, S. (2005). A Comprehensive Formal Ranking of the Popularity of Financial Ratios in Multivariate Modeling of Corporate Collapse. *Journal of American Academy of Business, Cambridge*, 6(1), 321–327.

Huefner, R. J. (2002). Redesigning the First Accounting Course. *The CPA Journal*, 72(10), 58–60.

Krantz, M. (2010). The Altman Z-Score: A Tool to Predict Financial Trouble. *USA Today*, July 13.

Lev, B. (1969). Industry Averages as Targets for Financial Ratios. *Journal of Accounting Research*, 7(2), 290–299.

Mankin, J. A. & J. J. Jewell (2010). A Sorry State of Affairs: The Problems With Financial Ratio Education. Unpublished working paper.

White, G. I., A. C. Sondhi & D. Fried. (2003). *The Analysis and Use of Financial Statements* (3rd ed.). Hoboken, NJ: John Wiley & Sons.

Whittington, G. (1980). Some Basic Properties of Accounting Ratios. Journal of Business Finance and Accounting, 7(2), 219.

# A Sorry State of Affairs

## The Problems with Financial Ratio Education

By Jeffrey J. Jewell and Jeffrey A. Mankin

......................................................................................................................................

## Abstract

[This reading] examines a large sample of accounting, finance, management, marketing, and financial statement analysis texts. The "Top 20" ratios in business textbooks are identified and discussed. [The reading] finds two major problems with ratio presentation in business textbooks: formula confusion and naming confusion. Many ratios bearing the same name are presented with different mathematical formulas. Only four of the Top 20 ratios have 100% consensus on the formula. Many ratios also have several commonly used "aliases" or alternate names. These two issues may cause considerable difficulty for both students and practitioners.

## Introduction

A basic understanding of financial ratios and financial analysis is considered by most professors to be a fundamental component of business literacy. This is demonstrated, in part, by the inclusion of financial ratios in a wide variety of business textbooks, including those for financial and managerial accounting, corporate finance, investments, business strategy, marketing research, and financial statement analysis. Business students typically encounter ratios for the first time in an introductory accounting class. They are then periodically re-exposed to them throughout their academic careers, culminating in what is probably a heavy dose of ratios and financial analysis in a capstone business policy or strategy class. Accounting and finance majors probably receive more instruction on ratios than other business students, but all business majors are probably exposed to ratios in at least three classes: accounting, finance, and business policy.

One of the great strengths of ratio analysis is its flexibility. Since there is no governing body in charge of ratios, users of ratios are free to customize or create their own ratios to address their

Jeffrey A. Mankin and Jeffrey J. Jewell, "A Sorry State of Affairs: The Problems with Financial Ratio Education," *Academy of Educational Leadership Journal*, vol. 18, no. 4, pp. 195–219. Copyright © 2014 by Elsevier B.V. Reprinted with permission. Provided by ProQuest LLC. All rights reserved.

particular analytical needs. This, of course, leads to the existence of many different ratios that each addresses a different issue.

Though flexibility is a strength of ratio analysis, unlimited flexibility has the potential danger of resulting in chaos. Users of financial ratios should have some expectation of consistency in ratio names and calculations. It is reasonable to assume that once a student learns a particular ratio that knowledge can be applied in a variety of situations with little potential for error or confusion. The data, however, show that that is probably not the case. There is little consistency in ratio names or formulas among the business textbooks in the sample. It appears that the textbook authors' choices to exercise their flexibility have resulted in a bewildering array of minor variations in ratio formulas and names.

We have long been aware of anecdotal evidence, primarily in the form of student complaints, that ratios are presented quite differently in different textbooks and classes. Many students have complained about different classes emphasizing completely different sets of ratios. To some extent this is to be expected, as different business disciplines will find different ratios more useful. So this complaint may have little merit. More importantly, many students have complained about two specific problems they have experienced. First, ratio formulas are inconsistent. Many ratios with the same name have different formulas in other textbooks. Second, ratio names are inconsistent. Many ratios with the same formulas have different names in other textbooks.

Financial ratio calculations need to be precise so they have precise meanings to users, consistency between years and comparability among firms. Students, professors, and professionals naturally expect the ratios to have a high level of precision. However, the ratio formulas in the sample suffer from a lack of standardization and precision. Two of the primary student complaints about ratio instruction appear to have some merit. There are many "competing" mathematical formulas for ratios with the same name. Likewise many ratios with identical mathematical formulas have different names. This "formula confusion" and "naming confusion" creates a lack of consistency in financial ratio formulas and in financial ratio terminology that likely creates a lack of precision in financial analysis.

Checking several textbooks from different classes is enough to confirm the basic truth of the student complaints. However, a casual review is insufficient to assess the magnitude of the ratio problem. A certain amount of inconsistency in ratio names and formulas must be expected, due to the flexibility discussed above. However, it is difficult, without a thorough understanding of the issue, to know when we have crossed the line from a reasonable amount of inconsistency into the area of "chaos." Because of the same complaints year after year, we decided that a more thorough study of these issues was appropriate.

One way to illustrate the problem of formula confusion is to compare ratios from a variety of popular investment websites. Many of these websites provide financial ratios of publicly traded companies. However, these websites frequently "disagree" on the values of various ratios. To illustrate this problem, an online search was performed to compare Return on Assets (ROA) numbers for the Coca-Cola Company. We chose ROA because it is a very common ratio that has many different formulas. These ROA numbers for Coca-Cola are shown on Exhibit 5.1.

| Exhibit 5.1 | Return on Assets Coca-Cola Company |
| --- | --- |

| 2/23/2011 | |
| --- | --- |
| **Website** | **Return on Assets** |
| Daily Finance | 19.86% |
| Google Finance | 19.51% |
| MSN Money | 19.50% |
| Morningstar | 14.98% |
| Yahoo Finance | 9.60% |

These ROA numbers were taken from these popular sites on the same day. The results ranged from 9.60% to 19.86%. The most common formula for ROA is Net Income / Assets [see Table 5.8]. However, there are several ways to calculate ROA that can give dramatically different results. The websites do not have to provide the formulas used in calculating the ratios, but Yahoo does provide a glossary for its key ratios. Yahoo calculates ROA as Earnings from Continuing Operations / Average Total Assets, which is a "non-standard" version of ROA. This simple example using a common ratio for a widely followed company shows the real problem of formula confusion.

Because of these problems with inconsistent ratio names and formulas, this paper will attempt to answer the following questions:

1. What ratios are most commonly being taught to business students?

2. How consistently are these ratios being taught, in terms of both formulas and names?

3. To what extent is inconsistency in ratio presentation explained by the business discipline? (Do accounting professors teach ratios differently from finance professors?)

## Literature Review

> It is inconceivable that accounting data can be analyzed without transferring it
> into ratios, in one way or another ... (Horrigan, 1965, 568)

Financial ratios were developed to be useful for investors, creditors, and managers. A historical review of the development and the use of financial ratios is helpful to show how these ratios are important to decision makers. This review of the financial ratio literature is provided in three sections. The first section gives a history of the early development of financial ratios. The second section discusses the many uses of financial ratios. The third section attempts to show which ratios are important to professionals.

## Early Development of Financial Ratios

The Industrial Revolution in the late 19th century changed business from small firms with owner-managers to large firms with professional managers and stockholders. This drove the need for financial statements and financial analysis. Commercial bank requests for company financial statements that began in the 1870's became widespread by the 1890's. The current ratio was the first financial ratio developed, in the 1890's, and remained the only ratio for several years. The passage of the Federal Income Tax in 1913 and the establishment of the Federal Reserve Board in 1914 were two important events in the United States that increased the demand for and the quality of financial statements. There were two innovations in 1919 that were very influential in expanding the use of financial ratios. The first was the Alexander Wall publication of *Study of Credit Barometrics*, and the second was the DuPont Company's development of its famous ratio triangle (Horrigan, 1968).

Alexander Wall (1919b) was a banker and credit manager who developed a system of seven ratios that he applied to 981 firms that he divided into nine geographic regions and nine industries. Wall's analysis was published as *Study of Credit Barometrics* in the *Federal Reserve Bulletin* in 1919. Because the Federal Reserve Board published the study, it was widely read and highly influential (Horrigan, 1968). Wall used the term 'barometrics' to show the dynamic nature of the ratios' changing during business cycles the ratios' variation by industry and region.

Wall championed the idea of using more than one single ratio based on a single absolute standard when he questioned the axiom that the current ratio should be at least 2.0. Wall asserted:

> Experience has fixed upon a ratio of two dollars of quick assets for every dollar of quick liabilities. There has, however, been no scientific method used in establishing this ratio or requirement, and in many cases it is neither sound nor economic, and least of all safe as a credit guide. It is, however, a law of comparative analysis and serves a purpose, as it tends to create a margin of safety (Wall 1919a, 132).

Wall's analysis showed wide variability of the current ratio by industry and by geographic region. He argued for the use of relative standards to compare a firm's ratios by industry. Wall termed this industry analysis the "law of averages" to encourage evaluations based on industry criteria rather than absolute standards.

Wall presented his findings by summarizing his seven ratios by industry and by region. He explained how to calculate these ratios, what information they provided and why they were necessary for credit decisions. This study gave credit managers a way to calculate these seven ratios for a firm and compare them to the average for that industry in the proper region (Wall 1919b). Wall was one of the founders and the first secretary-treasurer of the professional trade organization Robert Morris

**Exhibit 5.2**  Original *Credit Barometrics* Ratios (Wall 1919b)

| |
|---|
| Current Ratio |
| Receivables to Merchandise |
| Net Worth to Non-Current Assets |
| Total Debt to Net Worth |
| Sales to Receivables |
| Sales to Merchandise |
| Sales to Net Worth |
| **Additional Ratio Included in *Analytical Credits* Book (Wall 1921)** |
| Sales to Non-Current Assets |

Associates, now known as the Risk Management Association (Kansas Chapter, 2008). His work was continued by RMA as its *Annual Statement Studies* that has remained in continuous publication. The list of seven ratios for 981 financial statements has grown to nineteen ratios for more than 200,000 financial statements (RMA, 2010). The original seven ratios calculated by Wall with his additional eighth ratio added two years later are shown in Exhibit 5.2.

In addition to the Wall study, the second important financial ratio development in 1919 began with the DuPont Company. The company created a triangle model to evaluate its operating results. Specifically, the model decomposes Return on Assets (ROA) into Net Profit Margin and Total Asset Turnover (Barnes, 1987). This model was not initially accepted as widely as the Wall study, but the DuPont model has since become a classic financial analysis technique (Horrigan, 1968). A depiction of the DuPont triangle is shown in Figure 5.1. The Wall study and the DuPont triangle were early financial ratio developments that helped make financial ratios popular for many uses. The following section discusses some of these uses of financial ratios.

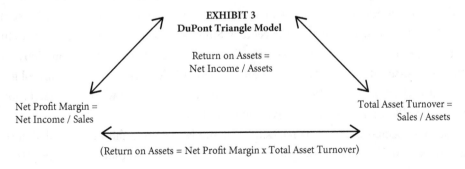

**EXHIBIT 3**
**DuPont Triangle Model**

Return on Assets =
Net Income / Assets

Net Profit Margin =
Net Income / Sales

Total Asset Turnover =
Sales / Assets

(Return on Assets = Net Profit Margin x Total Asset Turnover)

**Figure 5.1**

## Uses of Financial Ratios

Financial ratios are used for several important purposes. Whittington (1980) summarized two basic uses of financial ratios as normative and positive. Normative uses include comparing a firm's ratios to another company or to an industry average. Positive uses include estimation of future variables such as profit margins, returns, debt, and market prices. Positive uses can also include using predictive models for corporate failure, bond ratings, and credit risk.

Normative uses of financial ratios involve two primary functions: financial analysis and business education. Financial analysis involves evaluating a firm's profitability and riskiness and then comparing them to benchmarks such as industry averages. Ratios generally involve a mathematical proportion that allows analysts control for two factors: size and industry (Barnes, 1987). First, ratios control for the size of the firm. Different firms' ratios can be compared even if the firms' sizes are not comparable. For example, a small company with thousands of dollars in debt may have a higher debt ratio than a large company with debt in the millions of dollars. Second, ratios control for industry factors. Industries often have unique characteristics that are seen if a firm's financial ratios are compared to the industry average. It is a maxim that a firm's financial ratios should be compared to its industry averages. Both financial researchers (Lev, 1969) and textbook authors (White, Sondhi, & Fried, 2003) recommend that proper financial analysis should include industry averages. This recommendation is a normative use of ratios.

A second normative use of financial ratios includes their use in business education. Financial ratios are an important tool in business education. Students learn to use financial ratios over several business courses in their college careers. Huefner (2002) argued that financial ratio preparation and analysis is an important part of the very first accounting course. The New York State Society of Certified Public Accountants (NYSSCPA) issued a recommendation of educational goals for CPA candidates (NYSSCPA, 2008). Included in that recommendation was the preparation and interpretation of financial ratios for students preparing for careers as CPAs.

Financial ratios also have positive uses. Positive uses of ratios include estimating certain financial variables or predicting future outcomes such as business failure or bankruptcy. Financial ratios are used in many financial research studies to predict certain outcomes.

One of the well-studied areas of financial ratios is business failure. These studies attempt to identify which companies may experience financial hardship, default, or bankruptcy. These studies began in rudimentary form early in the 20th century. Smith and Winakor (1930) were one of the first researchers to use ratios as predictors of failure. Their study used 21 ratios in the predictive model. One of the weaknesses of their study is that it only included failed firms and not a control group of successful firms. Merwin (1942) also used ratios as failure predictors in what Horrigan (1968, 289) called the "first really sophisticated analysis of ratio predictive power."

The 1960's were a classic era in financial studies to predict business failure. Several of the studies of this era are seminal studies in using financial ratios as failure predictors. Beaver (1966) used financial ratios of failed firms and non-failed firms to predict business failure using a univariate technique. He found certain financial ratios that had predictive power in identifying failed firms. Altman (1968) expanded this into multivariate research by using multiple discriminant analysis (MDA). This research led to the well-known Altman's Z-score model that is widely used in business failure analysis (Krantz, 2010).

Another positive use of ratios is in determining which financial ratios are most useful. Obviously, the utility of these ratios is governed by how they are used. For example, in studying business failure Tamari (1966) found the Current Ratio to be useful because failed firms had lower current ratios than successful firms. Beaver (1966) found that a Cash Flow to Debt ratio was the most useful in his business failure study. Hossari and Rahman (2005) analyzed 53 business failure studies from 1966–2002 and ranked 48 separate ratios. They found that Return on Assets (ROA) was the single most common ratio in all the studies. Pinches, Mingo, and Carruthers (1973) used factor analysis to determine which ratios had long-term stability. They identified not a single ratio but a set of seven ratios that were stable over time.

Many financial ratios have been used in normative uses such as financial analysis. Also many ratios have been used in positive uses such as failure prediction studies. The following section attempts to determine which financial ratios are important to financial analysts.

## Using Financial Ratios

To attempt to identify which ratios financial analysts find valuable, Gibson (1987) asked financial analysts which ratios they thought were the most significant in a set of 60 ratios. The participants were asked to provide the level of significance on a scale from 0–9, with 9 being the most significant. The twenty ratios that financial analysts rated the highest are shown in Exhibit 5.3. This exhibit shows what ratios financial analysts value the most. Of the twenty ratios, eight are related to returns and profitability, including four of the top five ratios. Another eight of the top twenty give information about a firm's liquidity and debt. The other ratios relate to market valuations and operating leverage.

# The Sample

This study used a sample of business textbooks to evaluate the state of financial ratio education. The following process was used to accept textbooks and ratios into the sample:

1. The text had to be a current edition available for sale by the publisher.
2. Authors were permitted to have more than one textbook in the sample as long as the texts were for different courses or different audiences. For example, Needles & Powers (2009) *Financial Accounting, 10th ed.* and Needles, Powers, & Crosson (2011) *Principles of Accounting, 11th ed.* are both included in the sample because these books are different versions and not simply different editions of the same text.

**Exhibit 5.3** Top 20 Highest Rated Financial Ratios By Analysts (Gibson, 1987)

| Rank | Ratio Name | Significance (0–9) |
|------|------------|--------------------|
| 1 | Return on Equity After Tax | 8.21 |
| 2 | Price / Earnings Ratio | 7.65 |
| 3 | Earnings Per Share | 7.58 |
| 4 | Net Profit Margin After Tax | 7.52 |
| 5 | Return on Equity Before Tax | 7.41 |
| 6 | Net Profit Margin Before Tax | 7.32 |
| 7 | Fixed Charge Coverage | 7.22 |
| 8 | Quick Ratio | 7.10 |
| 9 | Return on Assets After Tax | 7.06 |
| | Times Interest Earned | 7.06 |
| 11 | Debt to Equity Ratio | 7.00 |
| 12 | Return on Total Invested Capital After Tax | 6.88 |
| 13 | Stock Price / Book Value | 6.75 |
| 14 | Degree of Financial Leverage | 6.61 |
| 15 | Long-Term Debt / Total Invested Capital | 6.52 |
| 16 | Debt / Assets | 6.50 |
| 17 | Total Debt / Total Assets | 6.42 |
| 18 | Return on Total Invested Capital Before Tax | 6.40 |
| 19 | Degree of Operating Leverage | 6.36 |
| 20 | Current Ratio | 6.34 |

3. Generally speaking, electronic copies of the texts had to be available at CourseSmart.Com. A few texts were obtained in hardcopy form from the publisher.

4. The text had to have a clearly defined chapter, section, or appendix on financial ratios. The sections were typically called "Financial Analysis," "Performance Measurement" or some similar name.

5. Many texts have a chapter or section on financial ratios but then also have various other ratios scattered through other chapters. Only ratios appearing in the main chapter, section, or appendix were included in the sample.

6. Ratios or calculations containing any math more sophisticated than simple arithmetic were omitted. Therefore, measures like alpha, beta, and correlation were not defined as ratios for the purposes of this study.

7. Differences in ratio formula format or terminology that did not result in mathematical differences in the ratio were standardized away.

8. Different formulas with the same ratio name were recorded as different "versions" of a ratio. For example, there are four mathematically different versions of the Quick Ratio in the sample.

9. Identical formulas with different names were logged as the same ratio, but the "aliases" were recorded.

The sample included 77 textbooks containing a total of 1427 ratios, an average of 18.53 ratios per textbook. There are 129 unique ratios in the sample. For these purposes, a unique ratio has a unique name and a formula that is mathematically different from all other ratios in the sample. Different versions of the same ratio are not counted as unique. For example, the four different versions of the Quick Ratio only count as one unique ratio since they are all called "Quick Ratio."

Accounting textbooks are the most common in the sample, representing 31 books. There are 27 finance textbooks in the sample. For the sake of comparisons the 13 management and marketing books were combined into one group. Since financial statement analysis courses are frequently taught as a hybrid of finance and accounting, the 6 textbooks for these courses were also placed in a separate category. A complete breakdown of the sample by business discipline can be found below in Table 5.1.

**Table 5.1** Data Set By Discipline

|  | Accounting | Finance | MGT/MKT | FSA | Total |
|---|---|---|---|---|---|
| Textbooks | 31 | 27 | 13 | 6 | 77 |
| Textbook % | 40.3% | 35.1% | 16.9% | 7.8% | 100.00% |
| Total Ratios | 573 | 485 | 196 | 173 | 1427 |
| Mean | 18.48 | 17.96 | 15.08 | 28.83 | 18.53 |
| Minimum | 13 | 11 | 4 | 15 | 4 |
| Maximum | 26 | 28 | 27 | 37 | 37 |

A complete description of the sample can be found in the appendix [...]. Table 5A shows a summary of the sample tabulated by publisher and business discipline. Table 5B shows a summary of the sample tabulated by copyright date and business disciple. Tables 5C–5F show the complete sample of textbook titles and authors for each business discipline.

# Results

We hoped to find exactly what ratios were being covered most frequently in the classroom. As previously mentioned, we found a total of 129 unique ratios in the sample. However, these ratios were not all present with the same frequency. In fact some ratios were present in almost all of the textbooks, while many show up in only a very small handful of books. Table 5.2 shows the Top 20 ratios ranked by the frequency with which they appear in the sample.

There are several interesting points in Table 5.2. First, the current ratio is the most popular ratio in business textbooks, appearing in 74 of the 77 texts in the sample. It is interesting to note that none of the ratios appear in every textbook. Second, very few of the ratios are present in the vast majority of the texts. Only three ratios appear in over 90% of the sample, while only seven of the ratios appear in over 80% of the sample. The bottom few ratios in the top 20 appear in only about 40% of the sample. Third, while this table only shows 20 of the 129 unique ratios in the sample, it actually accounts for over 73% of the total ratios in the sample. The Top 20 ratios account for 1,051 of the 1,427 (73.65%) observations in the sample.

**Table 5.2** Top 20 Ratios By Frequency

| Rank | Ratio Name | Frequency | Percent Of Books |
|------|-----------|-----------|------------------|
| 1 | Current Ratio | 74 | 96.10% |
| 2 | Inventory Turnover | 72 | 93.51% |
| 3 | Return on Assets (ROA) | 70 | 90.91% |
| 4 | Quick Ratio | 69 | 89.61% |
| 5 | Times Interest Earned | 68 | 88.31% |
| 6 | Net Profit Margin (Return on Sales) | 66 | 85.71% |
| 7 | Days Sales Outstanding (DSO) | 62 | 80.52% |
| 8 | PE Ratio | 61 | 79.22% |
| 9 | Total Asset Turnover | 60 | 77.92% |
| | Return on Equity (ROE) | 60 | 77.92% |
| 11 | Receivables Turnover | 51 | 66.23% |
| | Debt Ratio | 51 | 66.23% |
| 13 | Debt to Equity | 49 | 63.64% |
| 14 | EPS | 42 | 54.55% |
| 15 | Days Sales in Inventory (DSI) | 37 | 48.05% |
| | Gross Profit Margin | 37 | 48.05% |
| 17 | Dividend Payout | 32 | 41.56% |
| 18 | Dividend Yield | 31 | 40.26% |
| | Fixed Asset Turnover | 31 | 40.26% |
| 20 | Market to Book | 28 | 36.36% |
| | **Total Ratios** | **1,051** | |

The second fact we hoped to explore is the consistency with which ratios are being presented, both in terms of ratio formulas and names. When exploring the issue of formula consistency we decided to focus only on differences that would create mathematical differences in the computed values for the ratios. In other words, we choose to ignore, or more accurately standardize away, any semantic differences in how the formulas were presented. This proved to be a bigger challenge than originally anticipated. Sadly, there is an appalling lack of standardized vocabulary when it comes to financial analysis. To pick a simple example, all of the following phrases have exactly the same meaning to an experienced analyst: Net Income, Net Profit, Net Earnings, After-Tax Profit, Earnings After Tax (EAT), Income After Tax. However, to a novice student each of those phrases may appear to represent a different number or value. In examples like this we simply choose a preferred term, Net Income in this case, and standardized all of the ratios to use that term.

A second issue revolved around terms that were near synonyms, but not perfect synonyms. One example of this would be Sales and Net Sales. For a small subset of firms there is a significant difference between those two accounts, but for most firms they can be used interchangeably. There did not seem to be any great logic behind a text choosing to use Sales vs. Net Sales. Furthermore there was not a single ratio in the sample where both terms were used. This led us to conclude that we could standardize away the possible difference between them. So for our purposes, the two ratios Net Income / Sales and Net Income / Net Sales were treated as two observations of the same ratio.

A counter-example of near synonyms that we choose to treat as separate items is Earnings Before Interest and Taxes (EBIT) and Operating Profits. Many texts appear to use these terms interchangeably. However the mathematical difference between the two terms, non-operating items, can be large and economically significant for many firms. Therefore we treated those terms as separate entities. For example Operating Profit / Total Assets and EBIT / Total Assets both show up in the sample as Return on Assets (ROA). We treated those two formulas as two separate versions of ROA rather than two observations of the same version of ROA.

A third issue arose involving how to classify ratios when different books used the same name for different formulas or used different names for the same formula. For example, the ratio Net Income / Total Assets is known by several names in the sample, two of which are Return on Assets and Return on Total Capital. This would imply that Total Assets and Total Capital have the same value. In fact, some textbooks seemed to use these terms interchangeably while others went to great lengths to explain the difference between the two. (The most common explanation is that Total Capital does not include Current Liabilities. So, Total Capital = Long-Term Debt + Equity). Some texts even had one formula for Return on Assets and another for Return on Total Capital. So, if a text gave the name Return on Total Capital to the formula Net Income / Total Assets and did not have another ratio called Return on Assets, we classified this as an observation of Return of Assets and noted the "alias" Return on Total Capital. If a text gave the name Return on Total Capital to a formula other than Net Income / Total Assets it was recorded as Return on Total Capital, not Return on Assets. However, if a book gave the name Return on Assets to a completely different formula, like EBIT / Average Total Assets, this was recorded as a separate version of Return on Assets.

Beyond the differences in terminology described above, there were also significant challenges due to the different methods of mathematical presentation of the ratios. The differences in terminology and presentation were significant enough that we sometimes had to put pencil to paper and work out examples to determine if two formulas were mathematically equivalent or not. In short, this process of trying to compare the textbooks in detail turned out to be more complex and to involve much more judgment we had originally anticipated. The end result of this process has been summarized in Tables 5.3 and 5.4 below.

For the sake of simplicity Table 5.3 limits itself to considering the same 20 ratios from Table 5.2. The ratios have been re-sorted so they are no longer in order of frequency. They are now in order of the "consensus" about how to define them. The table shows the most common formula for the ratios, the degree of consensus among the textbooks about how to define the ratios, and the number of different versions for each ratio. For these purposes the "consensus" is defined as the percentage of the textbooks containing the ratio that use the most popular version of the ratio formula. For example, we know from Table 5.2 that 73 textbooks contain the Current Ratio. Of these 73 books, all define the Current Ratio exactly the same way, as Current Assets / Current Liabilities. We know from Table 5.2 that 69 textbooks contain the ratio Return on Assets. Table 5.3 tells us that of those 69 textbooks, only about 40% of them define ROA with the most popular formula, Net Income / Total Assets, and that there are eleven mathematically different versions of ROA in the sample.

There are several interesting observations about Table 5.3. First, only four ratios enjoy 100% consensus on their mathematical formulas from the textbooks. This certainly gives a bit of credence to student complaints about different formulas in different books. Second, the twelve different versions of Return on Assets are fairly compelling evidence of chaos in defining this ratio. Third, the average, median, and mode for the number of different versions of each ratio are all very near 4.0. The fact that even the most commonly used ratios have about four mathematically different versions on average is somewhat alarming. This also gives credence to student complaints about ratio inconsistency.

Table 5.4 is not a simple re-sort of Tables 5.2 and 5.3. Rather, it shows all of the ratios in the sample that have at least three different names. This cutoff of three names was simply for the sake of brevity. Many more ratios had two different names. A total of 16 ratios have at least three names, with four ratios having five names, four ratios having four names, and eight ratios having three names. The process used to analyze the sample only classified a ratio name as an alias if it had the same formula, after standardizing terminology, as a ratio with a different name. In other words, there are ratios in the sample called Debt to Equity, Book Debt to Equity, and Liabilities to Stockholders' Equity that all give mathematically identical answers. This "naming confusion" problem illustrated in Table 5.4 helps explain some of the difficulties students have in learning and using ratios.

**Table 5.3** Top 20 Ratios by Degree of Consensus

| Rank | Ratio Name | Ratio Formula | Percent | Total Versions |
|------|------------|---------------|---------|----------------|
| 1 | Current Ratio | Current Assets / Current Liabilities | 100.00% | 1 |
| | Gross Profit Margin | Gross Profit / Sales | 100.00% | 1 |
| | Dividend Yield | Dividends Per Share / Market Price | 100.00% | 1 |
| | Market to Book | Market Price / Book Value | 100.00% | 1 |
| 5 | Debt Ratio | Debt / Assets | 96.00% | 3 |
| 6 | PE Ratio | Market Price / EPS | 95.08% | 4 |
| 7 | Net Profit Margin (Return on Sales) | NI / Sales | 90.91% | 3 |
| 8 | Debt to Equity | Debt / Equity | 87.76% | 3 |
| 9 | Times Interest Earned | EBIT / Interest Expense | 82.35% | 4 |
| 10 | Fixed Asset Turnover | Sales / Fixed Assets | 73.33% | 2 |
| 11 | Earnings Per Share (EPS) | (NI–Preferred Dividends) / WAvg Common Shares | 64.29% | 2 |
| 12 | Total Asset Turnover | Sales / Assets | 59.32% | 4 |
| 13 | Return on Equity (ROE) | NI / Equity | 57.63% | 5 |
| 14 | Dividend Payout | Dividends Per Share / EPS | 56.25% | 3 |
| 15 | Quick Ratio | (Cash + AR + Mkt Sec) / Current Liabilities | 49.28% | 4 |
| 16 | Receivables Turnover | Sales / Average AR | 46.00% | 6 |
| 17 | Days Sales in Inventory (DSI) | 365 / Inventory Turnover | 45.95% | 5 |
| 18 | Days Sales Outstanding (DSO) | 365 / Receivables Turnover | 45.90% | 5 |
| 19 | Inventory Turnover | COGS / Average Inventory | 44.44% | 4 |
| 20 | Return on Assets (ROA) | NI / Assets | 40.00% | 11 |

AR = Accounts Receivable
COGS = Cost of Goods Sold
EBIT = Earnings Before Interest and Taxes
EPS = Earnings Per Share
Mkt Sec = Marketable Securities
NI = Net Income
WAvg = Weighted Average

| | |
|--|--|
| Minimum | 1 |
| Maximum | 11 |
| Mean | 3.60 |
| Median | 3.50 |
| Mode | 4.00 |

**Table 5.4** Top 16 Ratios For Naming Confusion

| Name | Total Names | Aliases |
|---|---|---|
| Days Sales Outstanding (DSO) | 5 | Days Sales in Receivables, Average Collection Period (ACP), Days Sales Uncollected, Collection Period |
| Cash Conversion Cycle | 5 | Operating Cycle, Net Trade Cycle, Cash to Cash Operating Cycle, Cash to Cash Period |
| Equity Multiplier | 5 | Leverage Ratio, Financial Leverage Ratio, Financial Structure Ratio, Assets to Equity |
| Days Payables Outstanding (DPO) | 4 | Average Payment Period, Payables Period, Days Purchases in Payables |
| Debt Ratio | 4 | Total Debt to Total Assets, Debt to Total Capital, Total Debt Ratio |
| Net Profit Margin | 4 | Profit Margin, Return on Sales (ROS), Profit Margin on Sales |
| Return on Assets (ROA) | 4 | Return on Total Assets, Rate Earned on Total Assets, Return on Total Capital |
| Operating Cash Flow to Income | 4 | Cash Flow Yield, Quality of Income, Cash Flow from Operations to Income |
| Operating Cash Flow to Total Assets | 3 | Cash Flow to Assets, Cash Return on Assets |
| Return on Equity (ROE) | 3 | Return on Stockholders' Equity, Rate Earned on Stockholders' Equity |
| Long-Term Debt Ratio | 3 | Long-Term Debt to Total Capital, Debt to Total Capital |
| Days Sales in Inventory (DSI) | 3 | Average Age of Inventory, Days Inventory Held |
| Total Asset Turnover | 3 | Turnover Ratio, Net Sales to Assets |
| Fixed Asset Turnover | 3 | Sales to Fixed Assets, PP&E Turnover |
| Times Interest Earned | 3 | Interest Coverage Ratio, Number of Times Interest Charges are Earned |
| Debt to Equity | 3 | Book Debt to Equity, Liabilities to Stockholders' Equity |

The third issue we wanted to explore is whether or not there are consistent differences in presentation of ratios among textbooks from the different business disciplines. In other words, to what extent is the variability we see in ratio formulas simply because accounting textbooks are consistently different from finance textbooks and finance textbooks are consistently different from management textbooks, etc. Our original hypothesis, based on anecdotal evidence, was that there was probably a good bit of difference between finance and accounting textbooks. We did not have any real opinion on how management, marketing, or financial statement analysis books would compare to the finance and accounting texts. In order to examine this issue, we constructed detailed tables for each of the Top 20 ratios. These tables each show every version of the ratio and the frequency with which that version appears in each category of textbook. We will discuss the detail tables for three specific ratios below, and attempt to draw some general conclusions from them. The remaining detail tables may be found in the appendix. (We did not include the detail tables for the ratios with 100% consensus, as they are completely uninteresting.)

The most frequent cause of inconsistency in ratio formulas in the sample has to do with the philosophy of the authors in comparing income statement accounts to balance sheet accounts. The matching principle of accounting tries to match revenues with the expenses that generate them. A matching problem occurs when comparing income statement and balance sheet numbers. This is because the income statement shows results from a period of time (flow numbers), while the balance sheet shows numbers from a specific point in time (stock numbers). When comparing income statement numbers to balance sheet numbers, averaging the balance sheet numbers preserves the matching principle. It is very clear in the sample that the accounting texts are far more likely to use this averaging approach than texts from the other disciplines. Eight of the top 20 ratios involve comparing income statement accounts to balance sheet accounts. The issue of whether or not to average the balance sheet account is a major source of inconsistency for all eight of those ratios.

Days Sales in Inventory (DSI) is a good example of the impact the "averaging issue" can have on a ratio's consistency. Table 5.5 shows the detail information for DSI. Notice that the first three versions of DSI in the list, comprising about 95% of the observations, are identical except in their treatment of the averaging issue. The majority of the accounting texts (14/20) average the inventory in the denominator. The clear majority of the finance, management and marketing texts (9/12) do

**Table 5.5** Days Sales In Inventory (DSI)

| | | Accounting | Finance | Mgt/Mkt | FSA | Total | Percent |
|---|---|---|---|---|---|---|---|
| 1 | 365 / (COGS / Inventory) | 6 | 5 | 4 | 2 | 17 | 45.95% |
| 2 | 365 / (COGS / Average Inventory) | 14 | 1 | | 2 | 17 | 45.95% |
| 3 | 365 / (COGS / Beginning Inventory) | | 1 | | | 1 | 2.70% |
| 4 | 365 / (Sales / Inventory) | | 1 | | | 1 | 2.70% |
| 5 | 360 / (COGS / Inventory) | | | | 1 | 1 | 2.70% |
| | | **20** | **8** | **4** | **5** | **37** | **100.00%** |

COGS = Cost of Goods Sold

**Table 5.6** Times Interest Earned

| | | Accounting | Finance | Mgt/Mkt | FSA | Total | Percent |
|---|---|---|---|---|---|---|---|
| 1 | EBIT / Interest Exp | 23 | 23 | 6 | 4 | 56 | 82.35% |
| 2 | Operating Profit / Interest Exp | 5 | 2 | 2 | 1 | 10 | 14.71% |
| 3 | (Pretax Operating Profit + Interest Exp) /Interest Exp | 1 | | | | 1 | 1.47% |
| 4 | Recurring Earnings / Interest Exp | | | | 1 | 1 | 1.47% |
| | | **29** | **25** | **8** | **6** | **68** | **100.00%** |

EBIT = Earnings Before Interest and Taxes, Interest Exp = Interest Expense

not average the denominator, using ending inventory instead. One author chooses not to average, but uses beginning inventory instead of ending inventory in the denominator. This is a pattern that shows up over and over again in the sample: accounting texts have a clear preference for averaging while finance, management, and marketing texts do not. Interestingly, the Financial Statement Analysis texts are virtually split down the middle on the issue, showing no clear preference for averaging or not averaging. The other two versions of DSI are caused by minor changes that are unrelated to the averaging issue. Notice that each of these versions only appears one time in the sample. This is another pattern in the sample. Many of the ratio versions in the sample have only one or two observations. In fact every single ratio in the sample with more than three versions has at least one version with only one or two observations.

A second cause of inconsistency in ratio formulas in the sample has to do with the use of near, but not quite, synonyms in the ratio formulas. Examples of this include using Operating Profit in lieu of EBIT or Common Equity in lieu of Stockholders' Equity. This creates ratios that will have similar values most of the time, but could potentially be very different some of the time. The Times Interest Earned Ratio is a good example of this.

The difference between EBIT and Operating Profit is non-operating items, which is usually assumed to be zero in classroom examples but can be very significant for real companies. It is difficult to say in this case whether the authors were assuming non-operating items away, in which case the first two versions would give identical answers, or whether they intended to differentiate between EBIT and Operating Profit. Our basic methodology in situations like this was to take the formula at face value. In other words, we assumed that Operating Profit meant Operating Profit, not EBIT. Notice again that the third and fourth versions of TIE only show up one time in the sample.

A third cause of inconsistency in ratio formulas in the sample has to do with the authors trying to measure slightly different things, but using the same name for the measurement. Net Profit Margin is a good example of this. Table 5.7 shows the detail information for Net Profit Margin. Note that over 90% of authors prefer version 1, Net Income / Sales, which is by far the best known and most widely

**Table 5.7** Net Profit Margin (Return On Sales)

| | | Accounting | Finance | Mgt/Mkt | FSA | Total | Percent |
|---|---|---|---|---|---|---|---|
| 1 | NI / Sales | 25 | 19 | 10 | 6 | 60 | 90.91% |
| 2 | EACS / Sales | | 5 | | | 5 | 7.58% |
| 3 | (NI + Interest Exp (1-Tax Rate)) / Sales | 1 | | | | 1 | 1.52% |
| | | **26** | **24** | **10** | **6** | **66** | **100.00%** |

EACS = Earnings Available to Common Shareholders = (Net Income–Preferred Dividends), Interest Exp = Interest Expense, NI = Net Income

used version of the ratio. However, a significant minority of the finance texts (5/23) prefer version 2, Earnings Available to Common Shareholders (or EACS) / Sales. The difference between Net Income and EACS is preferred dividends. (EACS = Net Income–Preferred Dividends). Net Income is a broader measure since it includes money that can be claimed by all shareholders, both common and preferred. EACS is claimable only by common shareholders. Clearly Net Income and EACS are two measures that are closely related, yet significantly different, at least for firms with preferred shareholders. EACS / Sales is certainly a useful measure for firms with preferred shareholders, but it is measuring something different from Net Income / Sales. EACS / Sales might more accurately be called Common Shareholders Net Profit Margin or something similar, yet none of the authors in the sample were that descriptive, choosing instead to use Profit Margin or Net Profit or Return on Sales, all common aliases for Net Income / Sales. This pattern of making a very useful, but perhaps situational, variation of the "standard" version of a ratio, but giving it the same name is quite common in the sample.

Table 5.8 shows the detail information for Return on Assets (ROA). ROA exhibits all three of the problems with ratio consistency discussed above. Notice that several versions of the ratio are identical except for the averaging issue. Also note that we see both the "synonym" issue (EBIT and Operating Profit) and the "slightly different" issue (Net Income and EACS) represented. Further, note that we have a "quite a bit different" issue with some of these versions. The numerators feature pre-tax values as large as Operating Profit and after-tax numbers as small as EACS. This will result in potentially vast differences between the calculated values of the various versions. Finally, note that two of the versions only appear once in the sample while another three only appear twice in the sample. For whatever reason, ROA is certainly the ratio where authors have most chosen to exercise their flexibility. For a more complete discussion of the many different ROA formulas, see Jewell and Mankin (2011).

**Table 5.8** Return On Assets

| | | Accounting | Finance | Mgt/Mkt | FSA | Total | Percent |
|---|---|---|---|---|---|---|---|
| 1 | NI / Assets | 3 | 16 | 7 | 2 | 28 | 40.00% |
| 2 | NI / Average Assets | 9 | 1 | | 1 | 11 | 15.71% |
| 3 | (NI + Int Exp) / Average Assets | 8 | | | | 8 | 11.43% |
| 4 | (NI + Int Exp (1-Tax Rate)) / Average Assets | 6 | | | 1 | 7 | 10.00% |
| 5 | EACS / Assets | | 5 | | | 5 | 7.14% |
| 6 | EBIT / Average Assets | 1 | 1 | | 1 | 3 | 4.29% |
| 7 | Operating Profit / Assets | | 1 | 1 | | 2 | 2.86% |
| 8 | NI + Int Exp / Assets | | | 2 | | 2 | 2.86% |
| 9 | (NI + Int Exp (1-Tax Rate)) / Assets | 1 | 1 | | | 2 | 2.86% |
| 10 | EBIT / Assets | | | 1 | | 1 | 1.43% |
| 11 | EBT / Assets | | | 1 | | 1 | 1.43% |
| | | **28** | **25** | **12** | **5** | **70** | **100.00%** |

EACS = Net Income–Preferred Dividends, EBIT = Earnings Before Interest and Taxes, EBT = Earnings Before Taxes, Int Exp = Interest Expense, NI = Net Income

# Conclusion and Recommendation

Professionals and business students use financial ratios extensively. Professors and employers expect students to learn to use and interpret financial ratios in their business courses and throughout their careers. However, there is currently a barrier to learning financial ratios caused by the use of different names and different formulas for the same ratio. An experienced professional may already have a preferred set of standardized ratios or may easily adjust to differences in names or formulas. However, this may not be the case with business students moving through a typical business curriculum. For these students subtle changes in names or formulas may be a source of frustration and an impediment to learning.

There is a certain amount of tension in the world of ratios between the flexibility analysts and authors have in creating their own ratios and the potential for confusion that a myriad of different ratio names and formulas can cause. It is difficult to fully assess the true costs and benefits of flexibility in ratio construction. This study attempts to illustrate some of the costs of unconstrained flexibility, or the lack of ratio standardization, by highlighting the two issues of naming confusion and formula confusion in financial ratio education. These issues are a problem because financial ratios need to be precise and consistent in order to avoid confusion and improve understanding of financial results.

The solution to the problems of naming confusion and formula confusion is quite simple in theory, but quite complex in practice. Both problems could be largely eliminated by simply having analysts and authors agree on more descriptive names for the various ratios. No actual flexibility would be lost; authors would simply have to use unique names for mathematically different ratios, rather than recycling existing ratio names. For example the ratio Net Income / Total Assets would retain the name Return on Assets, but the ratio Net Income / Average Total Assets could be named Return on Average Assets and the ratio EACS / Total Assets could be named Common Shareholders' Return on Assets. Similar "common sense" naming systems could in theory be devised for all of the ratios with competing formulas and names. Of course the practical impediment to this solution is that there is no simple way to achieve consensus on the best name for each ratio formula. Even if a set of descriptive and less confusing ratio names could be devised there is no easy way to insure compliance with the naming system.

The solution described above is not likely to happen anytime soon. In the mean time professors should take whatever steps they can in the classroom to make ratio education less confusing for students.

# References

Altman, E. I. (1968). Financial Ratios Discriminant Analysis and the Prediction of Corporate Bankruptcy. *Journal of Finance*, 23(4), 589–609.

Barnes, P. (1987). The Analysis and Use of Financial Ratios: A Review Article. *Journal of Business Finance & Accounting*, 14(4), 449–461.

Beaver, W. H. (1966). Financial Ratios as Predictors of Failure. *Journal of Accounting Research*, 4(3), 71–111. New York State Society of Certified Public Accountants. (2008). Examination of Pre-Certification Education. *The CPA Journal*, 78(8), 26–33.

Gibson, C. (1987). How Chartered Financial Analysts View Financial Ratios. *Financial Analysts Journal*. May-June.

Horrigan, J. O. (1965). Some Empirical Bases of Financial Ratio Analysis. *Accounting Review*, 40(3), 558.

Horrigan, J. O. (1968). A Short History of Financial Ratio Analysis. *Accounting Review*, 43(2), 284–294.

Hossari, G., & Rahman, S. (2005). A Comprehensive Formal Ranking of the Popularity of Financial Ratios in Multivariate Modeling of Corporate Collapse. *Journal of American Academy of Business, Cambridge*, 6(1), 321–327.

Huefner, R. J. (2002). Redesigning the First Accounting Course. *The CPA Journal*, 72(10), 58–60.

Jewell, J. J. and Mankin, J. A. (2011). What Is Your ROA? An Investigation of the Many Formulas for Calculating Return on Assets. *Academy of Educational Leadership Journal*, Forthcoming.

Kansas Chapter, Risk Management Association. (2008, Fall). *Borrowed Times*. Newsletter.

Krantz, M. (2010). The Altman Z-Score: A Tool to Predict Financial Trouble. *USA Today*, July 13.

Lev, B. (1969). Industry Averages as Targets for Financial Ratios. *Journal of Accounting Research*, 7(2), 290–299.

Merwin, C. L. (1942). Financing Small Corporations: In Five Manufacturing Industries, 1926–36. National Bureau of Economic Research.

Pinches, G. E., Mingo, K. A., & Caruthers, J. K. (1973). The Stability of Financial Patterns in Industrial Organizations. *Journal of Finance*, 28(2), 389–396.

Risk Management Association. (2010). Annual Statement Studies: Financial Ratio Benchmarks 2010–2011.

Smith, R. F. & Winakor, A. H. (1930). *A Test Analysis of Unsuccessful Industrial Companies.* Bulletin No. 31. University of Illinois Bureau of Business Research.

Tamari, M. (1966). Financial Ratios as a Means of Forecasting Bankruptcy. *Management International Review (MIR)*, 6(4), 15–34.

Wall, A. (1919a). *The Banker's Credit Manual.* Indianapolis: Bobbs-Merrill Company.

Wall, A. (1919b, March). Study of Credit Barometrics. *Federal Reserve Bulletin.* Federal Reserve Board.

Wall, A. (1921). *Analytical Credits.* Indianapolis: Bobbs-Merrill Company.

White, G. I., Sondhi, A. C., & Fried, D. (2003). *The Analysis and Use of Financial Statements* (3rd ed.). Hoboken, NJ: John Wiley & Sons.

Whittington, G. (1980). Some Basic Properties of Accounting Ratios. Journal of Business Finance and Accounting, 7(2), 219.

# Appendix

**Table 5A**  Textbooks by Publisher

| Publisher | Accounting | Finance | MGT/MKT | FSA | Total | Percent |
|---|---|---|---|---|---|---|
| Cengage | 13 | 9 | 2 | 2 | 26 | 33.8% |
| McGraw-Hill | 8 | 9 | 4 | 1 | 22 | 28.6% |
| Prentice Hall | 4 | 5 | 6 | 1 | 16 | 20.8% |
| Wiley | 5 | 2 | 1 | 1 | 9 | 11.7% |
| Cambridge Business | 1 | | | 1 | 2 | 2.6% |
| Textbook Media | | 2 | | | 2 | 2.6% |
| **TOTAL** | **31** | **27** | **13** | **6** | **77** | **100%** |

**Table 5B**  Textbooks By Copyright Date

| Date | Accounting | Finance | MGT/MKT | FSA | Total | Percent |
|---|---|---|---|---|---|---|
| 2011 | 4 | 4 | 2 | 1 | 11 | 14.3% |
| 2010 | 8 | 7 | 7 | 1 | 23 | 29.9% |
| 2009 | 7 | 8 | 1 | | 16 | 20.8% |
| 2008 | 4 | 7 | 1 | 1 | 13 | 16.9% |
| 2007 | 6 | 1 | 2 | 2 | 11 | 14.3% |
| 2006 or earlier | 2 | | | 1 | 3 | 3.9% |
| **TOTAL** | **31** | **27** | **13** | **6** | **77** | **100%** |

**Table 5C** Accounting Textbooks

| Authors | Title | Date | Publisher |
|---|---|---|---|
| Ainsworth | Introduction to Accounting: An Integrated Approach, 6ed | 2011 | McGraw-Hill |
| Albrecht, Stice, Stice | Financial Accounting, 10ed | 2008 | Cengage |
| Anthony, Hawkins, Merchant | Accounting: Text and Cases, 12ed | 2007 | McGraw-Hill |
| Breitner, Anthony | Core Concepts of Accounting, 10ed | 2006 | Prentice Hall |
| Brewer, Garrison, Noreen | Introduction to Managerial Accounting, 4ed | 2008 | McGraw-Hill |
| Edmonds, Edmonds, Olds, McNair, Ysay, Schneider, Milam | Fundamental Financial and Managerial Accounting, 1ed | 2007 | McGraw-Hill |
| Harrison, Horngren, Thomas | Financial Accounting, 8ed | 2010 | Prentice Hall |
| Hartgraves, Morse, Davis | Managerial Accounting, 5th ed | 2009 | Cambridge Business |
| Horngren, Harrison, Oliver | Accounting, 8ed | 2009 | Prentice Hall |
| Horngren, Harrison, Oliver | Financial and Managerial Accounting, 2ed | 2009 | Prentice Hall |
| Ingram, Albright | Financial Accounting, 6ed | 2007 | Cengage |
| Kieso, Weygandt, Warfield | Intermediate Accounting, 12ed | 2008 | Wiley |
| Kimmel | Financial Accounting: Tools for Business Decision Making, 5ed | 2009 | Wiley |
| King, Lembke, Smith | Financial Accounting: A Decision-Making Approach | 2001 | Wiley |
| Libby, Libby, Short | Financial Accounting, 5ed | 2007 | McGraw-Hill |
| Marshall, McManus, Viele | Accounting: What the Numbers Mean, 7ed | 2007 | McGraw-Hill |
| Needles, Powers | Financial Accounting, 10ed | 2009 | Cengage |
| Needles, Powers, Crosson | Principles of Accounting, 11ed | 2011 | Cengage |
| Nikolai, Bazley, Jones | Intermediate Accounting, 11ed | 2010 | Cengage |
| Porter, Norton | Financial Accounting: Impact on Decision Makers, 6ed | 2010 | Cengage |
| Porter, Norton | Using Financial Accounting Information: The Alternatives to Debits & Credits, 6ed | 2010 | Cengage |
| Reeve, Warren, Duchac | Accounting: Using Excel for Success | 2011 | Cengage |
| Rich, Jones, Hietger, Mowen, Hansen | Cornerstones of Financial & Managerial Accounting, 1ed | 2009 | Cengage |
| Stice, Stice, Skousen | Intermediate Accounting, 17ed | 2010 | Cengage |
| Stickney, Weil, Schipper, Francis | Financial Accounting, An Introduction to Concepts, Methods, and Uses, 13ed | 2010 | Cengage |
| Warren | Survey of Accounting | 2011 | Cengage |
| Warren, Reeve, Duchac | Financial and Managerial Accounting, 10ed | 2009 | Cengage |
| Weygandt, Kieso, Kimmel | Accounting Principles, 8ed | 2008 | Wiley |
| Weygandt, Kieso, Kimmel | Financial Accounting, 7ed | 2010 | Wiley |
| Wild, Larson, Chiappetta | Fundamental Accounting Principles, 18ed | 2007 | McGraw-Hill |
| Williams, Haka, Bettner, Carcello | Financial and Managerial Accounting, 15ed | 2010 | McGraw-Hill |

**Table 5D** Finance Textbooks

| Authors | Title | Date | Publisher |
|---|---|---|---|
| Berk, DeMarzo | Corporate Finance: The Core | 2009 | Prentice Hall |
| Berk, DeMarzo, Harford | Fundamentals of Corporate Finance | 2009 | Prentice Hall |
| Besley, Brigham | Essentials of Managerial Finance, 14ed | 2008 | Cengage |
| Block, Hirt | Fundamentals of Investment Management, 9ed | 2008 | McGraw-Hill |
| Block, Hirt, Danielson | Foundations of Financial Management, 13ed | 2009 | McGraw-Hill |
| Bodie | Essentials of Investments, 8ed | 2010 | McGraw-Hill |
| Booth, Cleary | Introduction to Corporate Finance, Canadian ed | 2008 | Wiley |
| Brealey, Myers, Allen | Principles of Corporate Finance, 10ed | 2011 | McGraw-Hill |
| Brigham, Daves | Intermediate Financial Management, 10ed | 2010 | Cengage |
| Brigham, Ehrhardt | Financial Management: Theory and Practice, 12ed | 2008 | Cengage |
| Brigham, Houston | Fundamentals of Financial Management, 12ed | 2009 | Cengage |
| Brooks | Financial Management: Core Concepts | 2010 | Prentice Hall |
| Cornett, Adair, Nofsinger | Finance: Application and Theory, 1ed | 2009 | McGraw-Hill |
| Gallagher | Financial Management, 5ed | 2009 | Textbook Media |
| Gitman, Joehnk | Fundamentals of Investing, 10ed | 2008 | Prentice Hall |
| Graham, Smart, Megginson | Corporate Finance, 3ed | 2010 | Cengage |
| Hawawini, Viallet | Finance for Executives: Managing for Value Creation, 3ed | 2007 | Cengage |
| Hirschey, Nofsinger | Investments, 2ed | 2010 | McGraw-Hill |
| Jordan, Miller | Fundamentals of Investments, 5ed | 2009 | McGraw-Hill |
| Keown, Martin, Petty | Foundations of Finance, 7ed | 2011 | Prentice Hall |
| Lasher | Practical Financial Management, 6ed | 2011 | Cengage |
| Mayo | Investments: An Introduction, 10ed | 2008 | Cengage |
| Megginson, Smart | Introduction to Corporate Finance, 2ed | 2009 | Cengage |
| Melicher, Norton | Introduction to Finance: Markets, Investments, and Financial Management, 13ed | 2008 | Wiley |
| Ross, Westerfield, Jaffe | Corporate Finance, 9ed | 2010 | McGraw-Hill |
| Ross, Westerfield, Jordan | Essentials of Corporate Finance, 7ed | 2011 | McGraw-Hill |
| Werner, Stoner | Modern Financial Managing: Continuity and Change, 3ed | 2010 | Textbook Media |

**Table 5E** Management and Marketing

| Authors | Title | Date | Publisher |
|---|---|---|---|
| Bamford, West | Strategic Management: Value Creation, Sustainability, and Performance, 1ed | 2010 | Cengage |
| Barney, Hesterly | Strategic Management and Competitive Advantage, 3ed | 2010 | Prentice Hall |
| Coulter | Strategic Management in Action, 5ed | 2010 | Prentice Hall |
| David | Strategic Management: Concepts and Cases, 13ed | 2011 | Prentice Hall |
| de Kluyver | Strategy: A View from the Top | 2009 | Prentice Hall |
| Dess, Lumpkin, Eisner | Strategic Management: Creating Competitive Advantages, 5ed | 2010 | McGraw-Hill |
| Gamble, Thompson | Essentials of Strategic Management, 2ed | 2011 | McGraw-Hill |
| Grant | Contemporary Strategy Analysis, 7ed | 2010 | Wiley |
| Harrison, St. John | Foundations in Strategic Management | 2010 | Cengage |
| Kerin, Peterson | Strategic Marketing Problems: Cases and Comments, 11ed | 2007 | Pearson |
| Peter, Donnelly | Marketing Management: Knowledge and Skills, 8ed | 2007 | McGraw-Hill |
| Thompson, Strickland, Gamble | Crafting and Executing Strategy: The Quest for Competitive Advantage, 16ed | 2008 | McGraw-Hill |
| Wheelen, Hunger | Strategic Management and Business Policy: Achieving Sustainability, 12ed | 2010 | Prentice Hall |

**Table 5F** Financial Statement Analysis Textbooks

| Authors | Title | Date | Publisher |
|---|---|---|---|
| Easton, McAnally, Fairfield, Zhang, Halsey | Financial Statement Analysis & Valuation, 2ed | 2010 | Cambridge Business |
| Fraser, Ormiston | Understanding Financial Statements, 9ed | 2007 | Prentice Hall |
| Gibson | Financial Reporting & Analysis, 12ed | 2011 | Cengage |
| Palepu, Healy | Business Analysis & Valuation, 4ed | 2008 | Cengage |
| White, Sondhi, Fried | The Analysis and Use of Financial Statements | 2003 | Wiley |
| Wild, Subramanyam, Halsey | Financial Statement Analysis, 9ed | 2007 | McGraw-Hill |

**Table 5G** Inventory Turnover

| | Accounting | Finance | MGT/MKT | FSA | Total | |
|---|---|---|---|---|---|---|
| COGS / Average Inventory | 26 | 2 | 1 | 3 | 32 | 44.44% |
| COGS / Inventory | 5 | 14 | 4 | 2 | 25 | 34.72% |
| Sales / Inventory | | 8 | 5 | 1 | 14 | 19.44% |
| COGS / Beg Inventory | | 1 | | | 1 | 1.39% |
| | **31** | **25** | **10** | **6** | **72** | **100.00%** |

COGS = Cost of Goods Sold

**Table 5H** Quick Ratio

| | | Accounting | Finance | Mgt/Mkt | FSA | Total | |
|---|---|---|---|---|---|---|---|
| 1 | (Cash + AR + Mkt Sec) / Current Liabilities | 24 | 5 | | 5 | 34 | 49.28% |
| 2 | (Current Assets – Inventory) / Current Liabilities | 1 | 17 | 11 | 1 | 30 | 43.48% |
| 3 | (Cash + AR) / Current Liabilities | 1 | 3 | | | 4 | 5.80% |
| 4 | (Current Assets – Inventory – Ppd) / Current Liabilities | 1 | | | | 1 | 1.45% |
| | | **27** | **25** | **11** | **6** | **69** | **100.00%** |

AR = Accounts Receivable, Ppd = Prepaid Expenses

**Table 5I** Days Sales Outstanding

| | | Accounting | Finance | Mgt/Mkt | FSA | Total | |
|---|---|---|---|---|---|---|---|
| 1 | 365 / (Sales / AR) | 5 | 15 | 6 | 2 | 28 | 45.16% |
| 2 | 365 / (Sales / Average AR) | 18 | 1 | 1 | 2 | 22 | 35.48% |
| 3 | 365 / (Credit Sales / AR) | 2 | 5 | 2 | | 9 | 14.52% |
| 4 | 360 / (Sales / AR) | | 1 | | 1 | 2 | 3.23% |
| 5 | 365 / (COGS / Beg Inventory) | | 1 | | | 1 | 1.61% |
| | | **25** | **23** | **9** | **5** | **62** | **100.00%** |

AR = Accounts Receivable, COGS = Cost of Goods Sold

**Table 5J** Price / Earnings Ratio

|   |   | Accounting | Finance | Mgt/Mkt | FSA | Total |   |
|---|---|---|---|---|---|---|---|
| 1 | Market Price / EPS | 25 | 24 | 7 | 2 | 58 | 95.08% |
| 2 | Market Cap / Net Income | 1 |   |   |   | 1 | 1.64% |
| 3 | Average Market Price / EPS | 1 |   |   |   | 1 | 1.64% |
| 4 | Market Price / Diluted EPS |   |   |   | 1 | 1 | 1.64% |
|   |   | **27** | **24** | **7** | **3** | **61** | **100.00%** |

EPS = Earnings Per Share

**Table 5K** Total Asset Turnover

|   |   | Accounting | Finance | Mgt/Mkt | FSA | Total |   |
|---|---|---|---|---|---|---|---|
| 1 | Sales / Assets | 6 | 21 | 7 | 2 | 36 | 60.00% |
| 2 | Sales / Average Assets | 17 | 2 |   | 3 | 22 | 36.67% |
| 3 | Sales / Beginning Assets |   | 1 |   |   | 1 | 1.67% |
| 4 | Sales / (Average Assets – LT Inv) | 1 |   |   |   | 1 | 1.67% |
|   |   | **24** | **24** | **7** | **5** | **60** | **100.00%** |

LT Inv = Long-Term Investments

**Table 5L** Return On Equity

|   |   | Accounting | Finance | Mgt/Mkt | FSA | Total |   |
|---|---|---|---|---|---|---|---|
| 1 | NI / Equity | 6 | 16 | 11 | 2 | 35 | 58.33% |
| 2 | NI / Average Equity | 13 | 2 |   | 3 | 18 | 30.00% |
| 3 | EACS / Common Equity |   | 3 |   |   | 3 | 5.00% |
| 4 | EACS / Average Equity | 2 |   |   |   | 2 | 3.33% |
| 5 | NI / Common Equity |   | 2 |   |   | 2 | 3.33% |
|   |   | **21** | **23** | **11** | **5** | **60** | **100.00%** |

EACS = Net Income – Preferred Dividends, NI = Net Income

**Table 5M** Receivables Turnover

| | | Accounting | Finance | Mgt/Mkt | FSA | Total | |
|---|---|---|---|---|---|---|---|
| 1 | Sales / Average AR | 21 | | | 2 | 23 | 45.10% |
| 2 | Sales / AR | 2 | 8 | 1 | 2 | 13 | 25.49% |
| 3 | Credit Sales / AR | | 3 | 5 | | 8 | 15.69% |
| 4 | Credit Sales / Average AR | 4 | 1 | | | 5 | 9.80% |
| 5 | Sales / Beginning AR | | 1 | | | 1 | 1.96% |
| 6 | Sales / Average Gross AR | | | | 1 | 1 | 1.96% |
| | | **27** | **13** | **6** | **5** | **51** | **100.00%** |

AR = Accounts Receivable

**Table 5N** Debt Ratio

| | | Accounting | Finance | Mgt/Mkt | FSA | Total | |
|---|---|---|---|---|---|---|---|
| 1 | Debt / Assets | 17 | 19 | 10 | 3 | 49 | 96.08% |
| 2 | LT Debt / (LT Debt + Equity) | 1 | | | | 1 | 1.96% |
| 3 | Debt / (LT Debt + Equity) | | | | 1 | 1 | 1.96% |
| | | **18** | **19** | **10** | **4** | **51** | **100.00%** |

LT Debt = Long-Term Debt

**Table 5O** Debt To Equity

| | | Accounting | Finance | Mgt/Mkt | FSA | Total | |
|---|---|---|---|---|---|---|---|
| 1 | Debt / Equity | 19 | 8 | 10 | 6 | 43 | 87.76% |
| 2 | LT Debt / Equity | 1 | 4 | | | 5 | 10.20% |
| 3 | (LT Debt – Deferred Taxes) / Equity | 1 | | | | 1 | 2.04% |
| | | **21** | **12** | **10** | **6** | **49** | **100.00%** |

LT Debt = Long-Term Debt

**Table 5P** Earnings Per Share

|   |   | Accounting | Finance | Mgt/Mkt | FSA | Total |   |
|---|---|---|---|---|---|---|---|
| 1 | EACS / WAvg Common Shares | 20 | 2 | 2 | 3 | 27 | 64.29% |
| 2 | NI / WAvg Common Shares | 6 | 5 | 3 | 1 | 15 | 35.71% |
|   |   | **26** | **7** | **5** | **4** | **42** | **100.00%** |

EACS = Net Income − Preferred Dividends, WAvg = Weighted Average

**Table 5Q** Dividend Payout

|   |   | Accounting | Finance | Mgt/Mkt | FSA | Total |   |
|---|---|---|---|---|---|---|---|
| 1 | Dividend Per Share / EPS | 8 | 5 | 4 | 1 | 18 | 56.25% |
| 2 | Common Dividends / NI | 8 | 2 |   | 3 | 13 | 40.63% |
| 3 | Dividend Per Share / Diluted EPS |   |   |   | 1 | 1 | 3.13% |
|   |   | **16** | **7** | **4** | **5** | **32** | **100.00%** |

EPS = Earnings Per Share, NI = Net Income

# MODULE 4

# Financial Statement Forecasting and Planning

*Everything that is beautiful and noble is the product of reason and calculation.*

**Charles Baudelaire**

F inancial forecasting and planning involves an exercise in, as the name implies, trying to predict what an organization's financial statements will look like in the future. The statements are prepared based on certain assumptions related to economic and industry conditions: the firm, its assets, its financing, policies, revenues, expenses, and any legal, regulatory, tax, or self-imposed constraints. Forecasted statements can be used to plan, to provide insight for purposes of obtaining financing, and to estimate firm value.

Two types of forecasted statements are generally prepared. These are: first, the pro forma or forward-looking financial statements, to include the balance sheet, the income statement, the statement of retained earnings, and the statement of cash flow; and second, the cash budget.

There are four basic approaches to forecasting financial statements. The first and most obvious is to obtain actual dollar values for estimated sales, expenses, and other financial statement items. This can be defined as a budgeted-expense approach. The second method utilized is the ratio approach. The ratio method utilizes expected or desired ratio results together with forecasts of financial statement values to predict other values.

A third approach, referred to as the percentage-of-sales approach, requires first the determination of each value on the income statement and the balance sheet, which will vary with sales. Then, using a base historical time period, the percentage of each of those items on the income statement and the balance sheet is determined as a percentage of the historical sales value. Those percentage values, together with any policy, constraint, and restriction requirements, are then utilized to prepare a forecast of the income statement, statement of retained earnings, balance sheet, and, if desired, statement of cash flow for the future time frame.

The fourth possibility for pro forma income statement construction is some combination or hybrid of the percentage of sales, ratio, and budgeted-expense methods. This is generally the most appropriate approach, since minor deviations in expense values are not worth the effort or the cost involved in making budgeted-expense calculations.

It might be best, therefore, to express these values as a percentage of sales, while other more important or large expense values may best be expressed as true budgeted numbers simply because of their importance. Unless budgeted properly, errors in those values deemed important to the end result might lead to particularly erroneous expectations with regard to income or other measures of performance in the forecast period. Further, the use of ratios can often provide the best estimates when a firm is trying to achieve specified levels of performance, such as hitting target current, turnover, rate of return, or debt ratios.

From the basic accounting equation, we know that assets must equal liabilities plus equity, and therefore, if the total of liabilities plus equity balances on a forecasted balance sheet does not equal the asset total, this difference suggests that a firm has forecasted too little or too much in financing. When a difference exists, it is always appropriate to consider the forecasted asset total to be correct. The rationale is that the balance sheet values were estimated based on a forecast of sales. The assets estimated are then the appropriate level of assets necessary to produce those sales, given all other constraints.

Thus, if the asset total exceeds the financing total, more financing will be needed to attain that level of assets and thus the forecasted sales level. Conversely, if the asset level is below the forecast financing balance, an excess of funding is estimated, and this excess can be used over the forecast period to pay off debt, pay higher dividends, purchase other assets, or perhaps to invest in marketable securities.

Accountants are able to create financial statements in a format that is understandable by users of those statements by utilizing standard reporting formats familiar to the reader. There are two distinctly different approaches to standard creation. Generally accepted accounting principles (GAAP) and International Financial Reporting Standards (IFRS) are two approaches, as pointed out by Lori Solsma and W. Mark Wilder in their paper "Pro Forma Disclosure Practices of Firms Applying IFRS" (2015), which provides a review of the two distinctly different theoretical approaches.

As the authors note, GAAP is a "rules-based standard," while IFRS is a "more principles-based" approach to setting reporting standards. The biggest issue here is the use of judgement by the reporting entity when applying the IFRS standards. IFRS reporting thus requires more information disclosure, as the use of judgement implies providing some rationale for the reported information.

The Solsma and Wilder study compares the "pro forma disclosures of US-listed IFRS firms" with "US-listed foreign firms that report results using the USA's generally accepted accounting principles," finding the "reporting standard is associated with pro forma disclosure behavior." US-listed foreign firms use IFRS disclosure standards more than they do GAAP standards, suggesting investors of all types should become more familiar with those standards.

The users of financial statements typically utilize both the historical statements and the pro forma statements provided when possible. In their paper "The Effect of Managerial Forecasted Financial Statements on Security Analysts' Judgement" (1998), Robert L. Webster and T. Selwyn Ellis note that "management-forecasted financial statements used in conjunction with historical statements, *vice* historical statements, produced consistently higher levels of reported confidence in assessing the financial condition of the firm." The authors further present the arguments both for and against disclosure of financial forecasts, as stated in another article by Kieso and Weygandt (1995).

It is extremely important to realize that the construction of pro forma statements does not just provide the financial manager an ability to look at a predicted position of the firm in financial statement form. All of the financial analysis—to include ratios, vertical statements, and horizontal statements that can be applied to historical statements—can also be applied to forecasted pro forma statements. Such analysis provides insight with regard to the effects of the assumptions and constraints used to create the statements and to possible changes in policies for the future.

Ratios can, for example, be helpful in identifying areas in which operating performance is or is not considered acceptable. Management can utilize this information to make changes in policies as well as plans for proposed financing or investment. This allows managers to take action to correct potential problems before they are realized as real ones.

It is important for managers to remember that the theoretically appropriate objective of the firm should be to maximize the firm's value, not to maximize sales, size, or the satisfaction of a single group. It is also important to recognize that growth can be as deadly to a firm as the lack of sales opportunities.

Growth can present problems when that growth takes place too rapidly for the firm to handle effectively. This implies that growth is also not an acceptable target for maximization. Thus, identifying a level of growth that is reasonable and acceptable should be pursued, and this objective, which does not overutilize existing resources, is in line with the pursuit of maximizing value and is therefore a desirable outcome of financial forecasting and planning.

## Recommended Readings

Kieso, D. E., and J. J. Weygandt. *Intermediate Accounting*, 8th ed. New York, John Wiley, 1995, 1368–70.

## Selected Readings

Solsma, Lori, and W. Mark Wilder. "Pro Forma Disclosure Practices of Firms Applying IFRS," *International Journal of Accounting & Information Management* 23, no. 4 (2015): 383–403.

Webster, Robert L., and T. Selwyn Ellis. "The Effect of Managerial Forecasted Financial Statements on Security Analysts' Judgment." *Journal of Management Psychology* 13, no. 1/2 (1998): 102–112.

# Pro forma Disclosure Practices of Firms Applying IFRS

By Lori Solsma and W. Mark Wilder

....................................................................................................

## Abstract

**Purpose**—The purpose of this paper is empirically investigate the pro forma disclosure behavior of US-listed foreign firms applying International Financial Reporting Standards (IFRS).

**Design/methodology/approach**—The annual earnings press releases of US-listed foreign firms on the New York Stock Exchange are analyzed to compare the effect that reporting standard (specifically IFRS) has on pro forma disclosure frequency, disclosure characteristics and benchmarking.

**Findings**—US-listed foreign firms applying IFRS report pro forma disclosures more frequently than firms using the USA's generally accepted accounting principles (GAAP), but less opportunistically.

**Originality/value**—This paper extends Epping and Wilder's (2011) study and contributes to the pro forma disclosure literature by providing a cross-country analysis of non-GAAP disclosure based on reporting standard (IFRS or US GAAP). Understanding the non-GAAP disclosure of firms applying IFRS is useful to investors and regulators, as more countries adopt IFRS.

**Keywords** International, Standards, Disclosure, Non-GAAP, Opportunistic, Pro forma

**Paper type** Research paper

## Introduction

The purpose of this paper is to observe the pro forma disclosure behavior of US-listed foreign firms applying International Financial Reporting Standards (IFRS). The pro forma disclosures of US-listed IFRS firms are compared with those of US-listed foreign firms that report results using the USA's generally accepted accounting principles (GAAP), as well as US firms (US firms are required to use US GAAP). A non-GAAP (pro forma) financial amount is a numerical

Lori Solsma and W. Mark Wilder, "Pro Forma Disclosure Practices of Firms Applying IFRS," *International Journal of Accounting & Information Management*, vol. 23, no. 4, pp. 383–403. Copyright © 2015 by Emerald Group Publishing Limited. Reprinted with permission.

representation of an amount that if presented in accordance with GAAP would appear in a historical, current, or projected balance sheet, income statement, or statement of cash flows. The pro forma number excludes amounts that are included (and/or includes amounts that are excluded) from the most comparable GAAP amount (SEC, 2003). The Securities and Exchange Commission's (SEC) Regulation G clarifies that for foreign firms whose financial statements are prepared using IFRS or domestic GAAP, GAAP refers to the principles under which the financial statements are prepared.

Regulation G requires that public disclosure of such financial measures be accompanied by the most directly comparable GAAP financial measure and be reconciled to this measure. Regulation G applies to both foreign and domestic companies, with limited exceptions for foreign registrants. Regulation G does not apply to foreign private issuers that are listed on a securities exchange outside the USA, report a pro forma financial measure that is not derived from a US GAAP measure and report the disclosure outside the USA (SEC, 2003). Because the exceptions are limited, the SEC believes that US investors will be protected.

In a 2011 meeting, the IFRS Advisory Council acknowledged the important role of non-GAAP disclosures, providing management's perception of entity performance and financial health (IFRS Advisory Council, 2011). The Council also discussed problems associated with the use of non-GAAP disclosures, such as the lack of rigor, and evolved literature supporting these disclosures. Differences in reporting standards and exchange requirements result in non-GAAP disclosures that lack common definitions and regulations. Therefore, the Council is concerned that non-GAAP disclosures lack consistency and comparability across regions. At the February 2014 meeting, the Advisory Council included non-GAAP/non-IFRS reporting as a possible future research project (IFRS, 2014).

Extant literature has examined ways in which accounting standards, specifically IFRS, affect financial reporting. In general, IFRS adoption has a positive impact on accounting information quality, including the disclosure quality of foreign firms. This is particularly true when firms that previously used home-country domestic GAAP adopt IFRS. Firms applying IFRS report higher net income than firms using US GAAP. Research also suggests that preparers are more opportunistic when applying rules-based standards (US GAAP) than when using principles-based standards (IFRS) (Agoglia et al., 2011). The current research considers whether the pro forma disclosures in the press releases of IFRS firms are similar to the pro forma disclosures of firms reporting results using US GAAP.

The press releases of a matched sample of US firms and US-listed foreign firms (some applying US GAAP and others using IFRS), are examined to observe pro forma disclosure behaviors. Behaviors observed include disclosure frequency, disclosure characteristics and benchmarking tendencies. Furthermore, the study includes an exploratory regional comparison of differences in pro forma disclosures based on reporting standards.

Results of the analysis indicate that US-listed foreign firms that apply IFRS are more likely to disclose a pro forma financial performance measure than US firms and US-listed foreign firms that use US GAAP. Overall, however, disclosure characteristics (adjustment direction and adjustment magnitude) indicate that the pro forma disclosure behavior of foreign firms applying IFRS is similar or less aggressive than the disclosure behavior of firms using US GAAP (US firms and US-listed foreign firms). Similarly, the pro forma disclosures of US-listed foreign firms applying IFRS are less likely to meet or beat a benchmark than the disclosures of US-listed foreign firms using US GAAP.

International pro forma disclosure research is limited. Accordingly, this empirical study explores the association between the pro forma disclosure behavior and the reporting standards (US GAAP and IFRS) of US-listed foreign firms. The current study extends the US-listed foreign firm pro forma disclosure research of Epping and Wilder (2011). Epping and Wilder examined disclosure differences of US-listed foreign firms and US firms. The results of their study indicate that in some cases, not all, proxies for aggressive behavior indicate that US firms behave more opportunistically than US-listed foreign firms. To further explain differences in non-GAAP reporting behavior, the current study explores a factor (reporting standard) that differentiates foreign firms. Prior research shows that the use of IFRS affects information quality and opportunistic behavior. Therefore, the current research investigates non-GAAP disclosure behavior differences for US-listed foreign firms that report result using IFRS compared to US-listed foreign firms and US firms that use US GAAP.

## Background, Motivation and Research Questions

Although convergence of US GAAP and IFRS is in progress, several general differences are current points of discussion. US GAAP is arguably a more rules-based standard, while IFRS is more principles-based. Rules-based standards have more complex rules including some bright-line thresholds. Principles-based standards provide more opportunity for judgment. Some contend that allowing for judgment may lead to diversity in application and reduced comparability. Also, judgment-based standards require more disclosure in support of positions taken. These general distinctions may result in differences in accounting quality and, more specifically, disclosure quality and behavior. While both US GAAP and IFRS are different from the domestic GAAP of foreign countries, we begin by presenting background information regarding the impact that conversion from domestic GAAP to IFRS has had on foreign companies.

The complete information set (including both required and voluntary disclosures) affects accounting quality. Studies that examine the impact of foreign firms' IFRS adoption indicate that accounting quality improves. In a study of 327 firms in 21 countries, Barth *et al.* (2008) find less earnings smoothing, less managing of earnings toward a target, more timely recognition of losses and a higher association of accounting amounts with share prices and returns for firms applying IFRS than for firms that continue to use their home-country domestic GAAP. The Liu *et al.* (2011) study confirms an increase in information quality when adopting IFRS, even when mandated in the regulated market of China.

Further, Daske and Gebhardt (2006) suggest that perceived disclosure quality increased significantly for a sample of German, Austrian and Swiss firms that either voluntarily or mandatorily adopted IFRS. The study measured information quality based on experts' perceptions of the disclosure quality of the financial statements, the notes to financial statements, the report on the current state and future development of the business, supplementary and voluntary information. Brochet *et al.* (2013) found that abnormal returns to insider purchases (a proxy for private information) declined following IFRS adoption in the UK, indicating higher information quality. Chen and Rezaee (2012), using a sample of Chinese listed companies, find that effective internal corporate governance helps companies to be more converged and aligned with IFRS. This, in turn, leads to higher quality financial information.

Research also examines analyst following and forecast accuracy to indicate information quality. Tan *et al.* (2011) report that mandatory IFRS adoption attracts financial analysts. Kim and Shi (2012) suggest that the added disclosure that occurs from IFRS adoption is a factor contributing to analysts' having a more precise information set. The information set referred to in the study includes both public information and private information that is provided to a particular analyst. To further support the benefits of IFRS adoption on the information set, research finds that mandatory IFRS adoption improves analyst forecast accuracy (Tan *et al.*, 2011; Hodgdon *et al.*, 2008). Horton *et al.* (2013) find that the consensus forecast errors of mandatory IFRS adopters decrease in comparison to that of other firms. However, improvements are driven by both information quality increases and greater comparability (Horton *et al.*, 2013; Brochet *et al.*, 2013)[1].

The impact that IFRS implementation has on foreign firms that convert to IFRS from their home-country domestic GAAP may differ from the impact that IFRS use has on foreign firms converting to IFRS from US GAAP (or would potentially have on US firms that converted to IFRS). The SEC's Work Plan for the consideration of incorporating IFRS states that the fundamental difference between US GAAP and IFRS is that "IFRS contains broad principles to account for transactions across industries, with limited specific guidance and stated exceptions to the general guidance" (SEC, 2011). Application of broad principles results in the need for greater disclosure. Therefore, greater disclosure is expected for firms applying IFRS than for those using US GAAP. However, in a survey of 493 US investors (investment managers, asset managers and fund managers), perceptions of disclosure quality differences for IFRS and US GAAP are marginal. The investors, however, that claimed to be more familiar with IFRS rate IFRS disclosure quality higher than that of US GAAP (Association of Chartered Certified Accountants, 2012).

Differences in disclosure levels matter to firms. In general, greater disclosure decreases the cost of capital (Botosan, 1997; Healy *et al.*, 1999). Therefore, there is incentive to provide voluntary disclosures, including pro forma disclosures, to enhance the information available to investors. Standard setters (IFRS Advisory Council, 2011) and research (Bradshaw and Sloan, 2002; Brown and Sivakumar, 2003) support the view that investors find value in the information that pro forma disclosures provide.

Understanding accounting quality and disclosure quality differences and the related motives for disclosure provides a background for understanding pro forma disclosure differences for firms applying IFRS and firms using US GAAP. If increased disclosure reduces the cost of capital, firms applying IFRS and firms using US GAAP benefit from providing voluntary disclosures (such as pro forma disclosures). Although prior research indicates that overall disclosure quality improves for foreign firms that convert from home-country GAAP to IFRS, most US investors do not perceive greater disclosure quality for IFRS firms than for firms using US GAAP (Association of Chartered Certified Accountants, 2012).

The perception of a lack of overall disclosure difference for firms using US GAAP and IFRS leads to the question of whether differences exist in non-GAAP disclosures based on reporting standard. Therefore, the first research question addresses pro forma disclosure frequency as follows:

RQ1.  Are pro forma disclosure frequencies of US-listed foreign firms applying IFRS different from that of US firms and US-listed foreign firms using US GAAP?

Theory on management disclosure suggests two motives for disclosure, informational and opportunistic (Healy and Palepu, 2001). Pro forma disclosures provide relevant information, yet are more unreliable and unverifiable than amounts reported in financial statements. Unaudited pro forma disclosures are subject to managerial opportunism. Curtis *et al.* (2014) find that a significant proportion of firms only disclose pro forma amounts when it increases investors' perceptions of earnings. Prior research provides several examples of questionable pro forma disclosure characteristics. Most pro forma adjustments to GAAP earnings are income increasing rather than balanced (Bhattacharya *et al.*, 2004). Firms place greater emphasis on the performance measure (pro forma earnings or GAAP earnings) that portrays greater improvement (Bowen *et al.*, 2005). Many pro forma adjustments to GAAP earnings are routine expenses that should be included in operating income rather than one-time charges to income (Bhattacharya *et al.*, 2003). Firms lack consistency in excluding the same items in subsequent pro forma announcements (Bhattacharya *et al.*, 2004). Also, Baumker *et al.* (2014) find that many transitory gains are disclosed in the press release, but few firms exclude the gain from the disclosed pro forma amount. Also, the gains are less likely to be excluded from the pro forma amount in the absence of offsetting concurrent transitory losses that are excluded from the pro forma amount.

To develop the background on the effect that reporting standards (rules-based or principles-based) will have on pro forma disclosure, we begin by looking at the effect of reporting standard on recorded accounting transactions. As mentioned previously, rules-based standards have more complex rules including some bright-line thresholds. Principles-based standards provide more opportunity for judgment. The use of judgment causes concern that diversity in application may include opportunistic behavior. However, research findings indicate that preparers are more likely to engage in opportunistic behavior when standards are more precise (more rules-based) than when standards are less precise (more principles-based) (Agoglia *et al.*, 2011).

In a behavioral experiment, Agoglia *et al.* (2011) find that when the term of a lease is subject to interpretation, preparers are more aggressive in lease classification (capital or operating) when applying a more precise standard (SFAS No. 13) than when applying a less precise standard (IAS 17). Collins *et al.* (2012) strengthen the validity of the Agoglia *et al.*'s (2011) study by analyzing the same research question from an archival perspective. Similarly, the findings indicate that IFRS firms are more likely to report a lease as a capital leases than do US GAAP firms. Further, the study finds no greater dispersion in lease classifications for IFRS firms than for US GAAP firms. In a scenario where more aggressive reporting occurs for financial statement purposes, there may be less need to opportunistically use pro forma disclosures. In this case, firms using US GAAP may be less likely than firms applying IFRS to opportunistically report pro forma disclosures.

Another factor that may affect the decision to opportunistically disclose a pro forma amount is a difference in GAAP earnings. Research indicates that there is an income gap for firms applying IFRS when compared to firms using US GAAP. Using data from the time period just prior to the SEC's relaxation of the requirement to reconcile IFRS earnings to US GAAP earnings (2004 to 2006), Henry *et al.* (2009) examined the reconciliations of 75 European Union cross-listed firms and find a significant IFRS/US GAAP net income gap. Although convergence projects continue to reduce the net income gap, the IFRS return on equity (ROE) for the firms in the 2006 sample is an average of 2.11 per cent higher than US GAAP ROE. For many firms (28 per cent) in the study, IFRS ROE is more than 5 per cent higher than US GAAP ROE. Liu (2011) concurs with Henry *et al.* (2009), adding that tangible asset revaluations and business acquisition accounting are the main contributors to the difference in US GAAP and IFRS income. This income gap provides a compelling reason for US firms to have more incentive to opportunistically influence perceptions of firm performance through pro forma disclosures when competing for capital.

The literature provides competing motives for pro forma disclosure tendencies and does not lead to a clear directional hypothesis. Therefore, the *RQ2* is stated as follows:

*RQ2.* Are pro forma disclosure characteristics (adjustment direction and adjustment magnitude) of US-listed foreign firms applying IFRS different from that of US firms and US-listed foreign firms using US GAAP?

Prior literature also shows that firms tend to report pro forma amounts for strategic purposes, such as meeting and earnings target. Lougee and Marquardt (2004) and Bhattacharya *et al.* (2004) find that firms that do not meet analysts' expectations and firms that report earnings decreases are more likely to report pro forma earnings. Eighty per cent of reported pro forma earnings met or beat analysts' expectations, while only thirty-nine per cent of reported GAAP earnings met or beat analysts' expectations (2004). Similarly, pro forma earnings were reported at amounts at least as great as reported GAAP earnings the same quarter a year earlier for 35 per cent of firms confronting earnings decline. Bhattacharya *et al.* (2004) add that 13 per cent of pro forma announcers turn a GAAP loss into a pro forma profit. Barth *et al.* (2012) find that managers exclude stock-based compensation expense in pro forma amounts to smooth earnings and meet earnings benchmarks. They did not find that the pro forma amounts were better able to predict future performance.

The literature provides mixed evidence regarding the impact that transition from domestic GAAP to IFRS has on earnings management (Barth *et al.*, 2008; Ahmed *et al.*, 2013). In one study, Liu *et al.* (2014) look at US GAAP and IFRS differences. Using data from firms listed on the German Frankfurt Stock Exchange from 1999 to 2004, Liu *et al.* (2014) find higher earnings management for IFRS firms through research and development expenses than for US GAAP firms. However, accruals were not different for US GAAP and IFRS firms. Research findings indicate that some firms substitute the use of a pro forma amount for earnings management when it is costlier to use accrual earnings management due to balance sheet constraints (Doyle *et al.*, 2013). The Liu *et al.*'s (2014) study provides some support for the proposition that the US GAAP firms may have a greater need than the IFRS firms to use a non-GAAP amount to meet a benchmark.

However, based on the literature review and discussion (preceding RQ2) regarding competing motives for opportunistic reporting behavior, the *RQ3* is similarly stated as follows:

RQ3.  Are benchmarking tendencies of US-listed foreign firms applying IFRS different from that of US firms and US-listed foreign firms using US GAAP?

## Sample and Data

The annual earnings press releases of a predetermined set of firms are analyzed to compare the effect that reporting standard (specifically IFRS) has on pro forma disclosure frequency, disclosure characteristics and benchmarking[2]. The press releases are primarily obtained from firm websites, with some being found through the LexisNexis Academic database. The press release is initially examined to determine whether a pro forma disclosure exists. For those firms that provide pro forma disclosures, data are collected on disclosure characteristics, such as the size and direction of the adjustment and whether the reported pro forma amount meets or exceeds a benchmark.

All 445 US-listed foreign firms on the New York Stock Exchange in December 2007 and having fiscal years ending during 2007 are included in the initial sample. Using firm data from 2007 provides a sample that consists of a similar number of firms using US GAAP and IFRS. For example, 30 European firms report results using US GAAP and 31 European firms with IFRS. The 123 firms in the financial (SIC code 6000–6799) and utilities (SIC code 4900–4999) industries may disclose pro forma information for regulatory purposes (Johnson and Schwartz, 2005; Marques, 2006; Epping and

Wilder, 2011) and are, therefore, excluded. The 102 firms that report results using domestic GAAP (other than US GAAP and IFRS) are also removed from the sample. Other firms excluded from the sample are 9 firms with multiple equity offerings and 18 firms that did not issue a press release. As shown in Table 6.1, the resulting sample of US-listed foreign firms consists of 193 firms from seven different regions.

Each US-listed foreign firm is matched with a US firm based first on the SIC code and then on firm size to increase the sample size to 386 firms[3]. The pro forma disclosures of these firms are examined in the current research. Of the 193 US firms, 140 (72.5 per cent) report a pro forma financial performance measure. Similarly, 137 of 193 (71.0 per cent) US-listed foreign firms report pro forma financial performance measures. Of the foreign firms that report results using US GAAP (IFRS), 79 of the 125 (63.2 per cent) (58 of 68 [85.3 per cent]) US-listed foreign firms disclose a pro forma financial performance measure.

The number of firms that report a non-GAAP amount differs from the number of non-GAAP disclosures in this study for two reasons. First, pro forma cash flow disclosures are excluded due to the highly differing nature of the adjustments. Second, some firms report more than one pro forma performance measure. Of the firms that report a pro forma earnings-based disclosure, US firms (US-listed foreign firms) report an average of 1.53 (1.73) disclosures per firm. US-listed foreign firms that report results using US GAAP (IFRS) report an average of 1.46 (2.10) disclosures per firm. The pro forma earnings disclosures ($n = 451$ across all firms) are used to test disclosure characteristics and the tendency to meet an earnings benchmark. The 451 earnings disclosures consist of 214 US firm disclosures, 115 disclosures for US-listed foreign firms applying US GAAP and 122 disclosures for US-listed foreign firms using IFRS.

**Table 6.1** Number of US-Listed Foreign Firms by Region

| Region | Total no. of Firms | Firms Using US GAAP | Firms Using IFRS |
|---|---|---|---|
| 1. Asia/Pacific | 59 | 46 | 13 |
| 2. Canada | 13 | 13 | 0 |
| 3. UK | 20 | 2 | 18 |
| 4. Europe | 61 | 30 | 31 |
| 5. Latin America | 17 | 14 | 3 |
| 6. Middle East/Africa | 8 | 5 | 3 |
| 7. Caribbean/Bermuda/Puerto Rico | 15 | 15 | 0 |
| **Total** | **193** | **125** | **68** |

**Note:** This table lists the number of US-listed foreign firms included in this study by region. all of these firms were listed on the New York Stock Exchange in December 2007 and reported results using US GAAP or IFRS

# Results

## Descriptive Results

*Disclosure frequency.* To examine the data associated with the *RQ1* on US and US-listed foreign firms' pro forma, financial performance disclosure tendencies are described and compared. To be considered a pro forma financial performance disclosure, an alternative (pro forma) historical measure of earnings must be located in the headline or body of the press release. The findings in Table 6.2 Panel A reveal differences in pro forma disclosure frequencies. A large segment of US-listed foreign firms that apply IFRS (58 of 68 or 85.3 per cent) disclose a pro forma amount. In comparison, 72.5 per cent (140 of 193) of US firms and 63.2 per cent (79 of 125) of US-listed foreign firms using US GAAP disclose a pro forma amount.

**Table 6.2** Pro Forma Disclosure Behavior by Firm Type (US and US-Listed Foreign Firms) and Reporting Standard (IFRS and US GAAP)

| Measure | US/US GAAP | Foreign/US GAAP | Foreign/IFRS | All firms |
|---|---|---|---|---|
| *Panel A: Pro forma disclosure frequency* | | | | |
| Measure | | | | |
| Disclosure % | 72.5 | 63.2 | 85.3 | 71.8 |
| Disclosure frequency | 140 | 79 | 58 | 277 |
| N | 193 | 125 | 68 | 386 |
| *Panel B: Pro forma disclosure characteristics* | | | | |
| Disclosure characteristic | | | | |
| *Income-increasing adjustments* | | | | |
| Disclosure % | 89.3 | 87.0 | 73.0 | 84.3 |
| Disclosure frequency | 191 | 100 | 89 | 380 |
| N | 214 | 115 | 122 | 451 |
| *Adjustment magnitude* | | | | |
| Mean | 2.81 | 1.14 | 1.14 | 1.93 |
| Median | 0.62 | 0.50 | 0.40 | 0.53 |
| SD | 6.62 | 2.65 | 2.74 | 5.02 |
| N | 214 | 115 | 122 | 451 |
| *Panel C: Benchmarking tendencies* | | | | |
| Measure | | | | |
| Disclosure % | 58.1 | 73.4 | 49.5 | 59.8 |
| Disclosure frequency | 118 | 80 | 55 | 253 |
| N | 203 | 109 | 111 | 423 |

**Notes:** Variables are defined in Table 6.3; the *n* for benchmark = 423 (451 pro forma disclosures less 28 cases with missing benchmark data)

*Disclosure characteristics.* As shown in Table 6.2 Panel B, US-listed foreign firms applying IFRS report an income-increasing pro forma disclosure for 89 of 122 (73 per cent) disclosures. Both US firms and US-listed foreign firms using US GAAP disclose income-increasing pro forma disclosures more frequently than US-listed foreign firms applying IFRS. US firms (US-listed foreign firms) disclose income-increasing pro forma amounts for 191 of 214 (89.3 per cent) [100 of 115 (87.0 per cent)] disclosures. The pro forma disclosure adjustment magnitude, which is measured as (pro forma earnings or GAAP earnings)/|GAAP earnings|, is much greater for US firms than for US-listed foreign firms. The adjustment magnitude is 2.81 for US firms, while it is 1.14 for both US-listed foreign firms using US GAAP and US-listed foreign firms applying IFRS.

*Benchmarking tendencies.* Benchmarking is defined as having met the target when:

- the current pro forma income is greater than the current GAAP income;
- the current pro forma income is greater than the prior year's GAAP income; and
- the current pro forma income is greater than the prior year's pro forma income.

This is a comprehensive measure that includes meeting three benchmarks (current year's GAAP amount, prior year's GAAP amount and prior year's pro forma amount).

Table 6.2 Panel C illustrates the per cent of firms that report a pro forma financial performance measure to meet or beat a benchmark. US-listed foreign firms using US GAAP report 80 of 109 (73.4 per cent) pro forma disclosures that meet the benchmark. US firms and US-listed foreign firms applying IFRS report pro forma disclosures that meet the benchmark for 118 of 203 (58.1 per cent) and 55 of 111 (49.5 per cent) disclosures, respectively.

The sample of US-listed foreign firms consists of companies from diverse regions. To further explore whether the findings are due to the averaging of all US-listed foreign firms' non-GAAP disclosure frequencies and characteristics, descriptive data are presented by region in the additional analysis section.

## Variable Descriptions and Correlation Analysis

The dependent variables, DISC, INCRDISC, ADJMAG and BENCHMARK are used to analyze the data associated with the research questions. DISC represents disclosure frequency and is coded 1 if a pro forma measure is disclosed and 0 if no disclosure is found. INCRDISC and ADJMAG represent disclosure characteristics. INCRDISC is coded 1 if the pro forma amount is greater than GAAP earnings (income increasing) and 0 otherwise. ADJMAG represents the size of the adjustment. Size is measured as the difference between the pro forma amount and GAAP earnings, scaled by the GAAP earnings amount. BENCHMARK represents a pro forma amount that meets or exceeds the current year's earnings (GAAP earnings) and prior year's results (GAAP earnings and the pro forma amount). BENCHMARK is coded 1 if the targets are met and 0 otherwise.

The group dummy variables, USA/USGAAP and FOR/USGAAP, are explanatory variables representing firms applying IFRS (the reference group) and firms using US GAAP (US firms and foreign firms). USA/USGAAP is coded 1 for a US firm and 0 otherwise. FOR/USGAAP is coded 1 for a US-listed foreign firm using US GAAP and 0 otherwise. Control variables used in prior pro forma disclosure research include INDUSTRY, SIZE, LEV, GROWTH and DISCTYPE. Variable definitions are presented in Table 6.3.

Pearson and Spearman correlation coefficients are presented in Table 6.4. Not surprisingly, INCRDISC is positively correlated with ADJMAG (0.631) and BENCHMARK (0.548) indicating that income-increasing disclosures involve larger adjustments to GAAP earnings and are more likely to meet an earnings benchmark[5].

## Regression Analysis

Regression analysis is used to further analyze pro forma disclosure frequency, disclosure characteristics and benchmarking tendencies while controlling for other factors that may impact disclosure behavior. The results of the analysis are provided in the follow sections.

**Table 6.3** Variable Definitions

| | | |
|---|---|---|
| US/USGAAP | = | Coded 1 for a US firm, 0 otherwise (reference group US-listed foreign firm applying IFRS) |
| FOR/USGAAP | = | Coded 1 for a US-listed foreign firm applying US GAAP, 0 otherwise (reference group US-listed foreign firm applying IFRS) |
| DISC | = | Coded 1 if a pro forma financial performance measure was disclosed, 0 otherwise |
| INCRDISC | = | Coded 1 if pro forma earnings – GAAP earnings > 0, 0 otherwise |
| ADJMAG | = | (pro forma earnings – GAAP earnings) / GAAP earnings |
| BENCHMARK | = | Coded 1 if pro forma amount > current year's GAAP amount, prior year's GAAP amount and prior year's pro forma amount, 0 otherwise |
| INDUSTRY | = | Coded 1 for firms in the following industries, 0 otherwise: drugs (283); computer and office equipment (357); electrical machinery and equipment, excluding computers (360); electrical transmissions and distribution equipment (361); electrical industrial apparatus (362); audio, video equipment, audio receiving (365); communication equipment (366); electronic components, semiconductors (367); computer hardware (368); telephone communications (481); computer programming, software, data processing (737); and research, development, testing services (873)[4] |
| SIZE | = | Natural log of total assets |
| LEV | = | Debt-to-equity ratio at fiscal year end |
| GROWTH | = | Market-to-book ratio |
| DISCTYPE | = | Coded 1 for a net-income-related pro forma disclosure, 0 for an operating-income-related pro forma disclosure |

**Table 6.4** Pearson/Spearman Correlation Coefficients

| Spearman/Pearson | Disc | INCRDISC | ADJMAG | Benchmark | US/USGAAP | For/USGAAP | Industry | Size | LEV | Growth | Disctype |
|---|---|---|---|---|---|---|---|---|---|---|---|
| DISC | 1.00 | *** | *** | *** | 0.017 | -0.132** | 0.070 | 0.130* | 0.090 | 0.049 | *** |
| INCRDISC | *** | 1.00 | 0.184** | 0.548** | 0.130** | 0.043 | 0.048 | 0.179** | -0.177** | – | 0.000 |
| ADJMAG | *** | 0.631*** | 1.00 | 0.121* | 0.166** | -0.093* | 0.012 | – | 0.022 | -0.089 | 0.150** |
| BENCHMARK | *** | 0.548*** | 0.258** | 1.00 | -0.033 | 0.163** | -0.019 | -0.121* | -0.101* | -0.033 | -0.090 |
| US/USGAAP | 0.017 | 0.130** | 0.150** | -0.033 | 1.00 | -0.556*** | -0.100* | -0.189*** | 0.036 | -0.169** | -0.030 |
| FOR/USGAAP | -0.132** | 0.0430 | -0.051 | 0.163** | -0.556** | 1.00 | -0.062 | -0.287** | -0.135** | -0.009 | 0.054 |
| INDUSTRY | 0.070 | 0.048 | 0.038 | -0.019 | -0.100* | -0.062 | 1.00 | 0.120* | -0.149** | -0.106* | -0.035 |
| SIZE | 0.137** | -0.168** | -0.188** | -0.115* | -0.191*** | -0.289*** | 0.137** | 1.00 | 0.021 | 0.005 | -0.119* |
| LEV | 0.182** | -0.063 | 0.141** | -0.109* | 0.114* | -0.182** | -0.239** | 0.065 | 1.00 | 0.754*** | -0.087 |
| GROWTH | 0.045 | -0.074 | -0.187** | 0.221** | -0.129** | 0.122* | 0.104* | 0.006 | -0.159** | 1.00 | -0.156** |
| DISCTYPE | *** | 0.000 | 0.141** | -0.090 | -0.030 | 0.054 | -0.035 | -0.122* | 0.060 | -0.136** | 1.00 |

**Notes:** Variables are defined in Table 6.3; pearson (Spearman) correlation coefficients are presented above (below) the diagonal; *** correlations are not provided because disclosure characteristic data are not available for observations that lack a pro forma disclosure; *, ** significant at the 0.05 and 0.01 levels (two-tailed)

*Disclosure frequency.* A binary regression analysis is used to analyze pro forma disclosure frequency. The dependent variable in the model, pro forma disclosure, is coded 1 if the firm discloses a pro forma amount and 0 otherwise. The independent variables include group dummy variables and control variables. Because the sample includes three firm categories, dummy variable are utilized to compare the two groups (US and US-listed foreign firms) using US GAAP with the reference group (US-listed foreign firms) that is applying IFRS. The remaining control variables (industry, size, leverage, growth and disclosure type) are those that prior research has identified as potentially being related to disclosure frequency and characteristics[6].

Table 6.5 presents the results of the binary logistic regression model that examines the association between the likelihood of disclosing a pro forma performance measure and the independent variables of interest, USA/USGAAP and FOR/USGAAP, representing firm type (US and US-listed foreign firms) and reporting standards. The binary regression analysis indicates a negative and statistically significant difference in the disclosure likelihood of US-listed foreign firms using US GAAP and US-listed foreign firms applying IFRS. The regression analysis also finds a negative and statistically significant difference in the pro forma disclosure likelihood of US-listed foreign firms applying IFRS and US firms. Overall, the findings indicate that US-listed foreign firms applying IFRS are more likely to present a pro forma disclosure than US firms and US-listed foreign firms using US GAAP.

*Disclosure characteristics.* Regression analysis is also used to further analyze pro forma disclosure characteristics. As shown in Table 6.5, the binary logistic regression that examines differences in the frequency of reporting income-increasing adjustments finds that firms reporting results using US GAAP (US firms and foreign firms) are on average more likely to report an income-increasing pro forma disclosure than foreign firms applying IFRS. Also, low-growth firms are marginally more likely to report an income-increasing pro forma disclosure than high-growth firms.

The linear regression model examining factors that impact the adjustment magnitude of firms reporting pro forma disclosures indicates that pro forma disclosure adjustment magnitude is greater for US firms than for US-listed foreign firms applying IFRS. The variable USA/USGAAP is a statistically significant indicator of ADJMAG. The analysis fails to find a difference in the pro forma disclosure adjustment magnitude of US-listed foreign firms using US GAAP (FOR/USGAAP) and US-listed foreign firms applying IFRS. Control variables that impact adjustment magnitude are SIZE, LEV, GROWTH and DISCTYPE. Small firms (SIZE), highly leveraged firms (LEV), and low-growth firms (GROWTH) report pro forma disclosures with larger adjustments to GAAP amounts than do large firms, low-leverage firms and high-growth firms. Larger adjustments also occur for net-income-related disclosures than for operating-income-related disclosures (i.e. DISCTYPE is a positive and statistically significant indicator of adjustment magnitude).

*Benchmarking tendencies.* Table 6.5 presents the results of the binary logistic regression model that examines the likelihood of disclosing a pro forma performance measure that meets or beats

**Table 6.5** Regression of Disclosure Behavior on COUNTRY/GAAP (US/USGAAP and FOR/USGAAP)

| Dependent Variable | Disclosure | Income-Increasing Adjustments | Adjustment Magnitude | Benchmark |
|---|---|---|---|---|
| Regression Model | Binary Logistic Beta | Binary Logistic Beta | Linear Beta | Binary Logistic Beta |
| Intercept | 1.819 | 3.187 | 4.475 | 0.082 |
| | 2.481 | 3.670* | 1.721* | 0.005 |
| US/USGAAP | −0.772 | 0.901 | 1.188 | 0.388 |
| | 3.871** | 6.576** | 2.000** | 2.122 |
| FOR/USGAAP | −1.185 | 0.798 | −0.425 | 1.013 |
| | 8.701*** | 3.835* | −0.627 | 10.083*** |
| INDUSTRY | 0.386 | 0.324 | 0.414 | −0.077 |
| | 2.228 | 1.142 | 0.861 | 0.121 |
| SIZE | −0.020 | −0.740 | −0.200 | 0.012 |
| | 0.189 | 1.222 | −1.901* | 0.065 |
| LEV | 0.078 | 0.014 | 0.138 | −0.066 |
| | 1.958 | 0.062 | 1.688* | 3.008* |
| GROWTH | 0.028 | −0.046 | −0.082 | 0.018 |
| | 0.694 | 3.192* | −2.001** | 0.916 |
| DISCTYPE | | −0.422 | 1.580 | −0.363 |
| | | 1.574 | 3.076*** | 2.243 |
| $n$ | 377 | 442 | 442 | 414 |
| Adjusted $R^2$ or Pseudo $R^2$ | 0.060 | 0.115 | 0.055 | 0.066 |

**Notes:** Prob (DISC) = $\beta_0$ + $\beta_1$ US/USGAAP + $\beta_2$ FOR/USGAAP + $\beta_3$ INDUSTRY + $\beta_4$ SIZE + $\beta_5$ LEV + $\beta_6$ GROWTH + $\epsilon$; $\beta_0$ + $\beta_1$ US/USGAAP + $\beta_2$ FOR/USGAAP + $\beta_3$ INDUSTRY + $\beta_4$ SIZE + $\beta_5$ LEV + $\beta_6$ GROWTH + $\beta_7$ DISCTYPE + $\epsilon$; ADJMAG + $\beta_0$ + $\beta_1$ US/USGAAP + $\beta_2$ FOR/USGAAP + $\beta_3$ INDUSTRY + $\beta_4$ SIZE + $\beta_5$ LEV + $\beta_6$ GROWTH + $\beta_7$ DISCTYPE + $\epsilon$; Prob (BENCHMARK) = $\beta_0$ + $\beta_1$ US/USGAAP + $\beta_2$ FOR/USGAAP + $\beta_3$ INDUSTRY + $\beta_4$ SIZE + $\beta_5$ LEV + $\beta_6$ GROWTH + $\beta_7$ DISCTYPE + $\epsilon$; *, **, *** significant at the 0.10, 0.05 and 0.01 levels; all variables are defined in Table 6.3; the $n$ for pro forma disclosure 377 (386 firms less 9 cases with missing data); the $n$ for adjustment magnitude and income-increasing adjustments 442 (451 pro forma disclosures and less than 9 cases with missing data); the $n$ for benchmark 414 (451 pro forma disclosures less 37 cases with missing benchmark and control variable data)

a benchmark and the variables of interest, USA/USGAAP and FOR/USGAAP. Benchmarking is defined as having met the target when:

• current pro forma income is greater than current GAAP income;

• current pro forma income is greater than prior year's GAAP income; and

• current pro forma income is greater than prior year's pro forma income.

The dependent variable in the model, benchmark, is coded 1 if the firm discloses a pro forma amount that meets the target and 0 otherwise.

The regression model indicates that foreign firms using US GAAP are more likely to report a pro forma financial performance measure that meets or exceeds the benchmark than are US-listed foreign firms applying IFRS (i.e. FOR/USGAAP is a positive and statistically significant indicator of BENCHMARK). The regression model fails to find a statistically significant difference in the likelihood of reporting a pro forma disclosure to a meet a benchmark for US firms and US-listed foreign firms applying IFRS. LEV is a negative and marginally statistically significant indicator of benchmarking. Stated another way, highly leveraged firms are less likely to disclose a pro forma amount to meet a benchmark than low-leverage firms.

In summary, the analysis provides an indication that reporting standard impacts pro forma disclosure behavior. The pro forma disclosure behavior of US firms and US-listed foreign firms applying IFRS differs in several ways. Pro forma disclosure frequency is greater for US-listed foreign firms that report results using IFRS than for US firms. Disclosure characteristics (adjustment direction and adjustment magnitude) indicate that foreign firms applying IFRS are less aggressive when reporting pro forma amounts than US firms. No difference is found in the likelihood of benchmarking for US firms and US-listed foreign firms applying IFRS.

The pro forma disclosure behavior of US-listed foreign firms using US GAAP and IFRS differs also. Pro forma disclosure frequency is greater for foreign firms that report results using IFRS than for those using US GAAP. However, income-increasing pro forma adjustments are less likely for foreign firms that apply IFRS than for firms using US GAAP. Also, firms applying IFRS are less likely than firms using US GAAP to use a pro forma amount to meet a benchmark.

# Additional Analysis

## Regional Descriptive Comparisons

The sample of US-listed foreign firms consists of firms from seven different regions. The sample sizes in the various regions are small, limiting the opportunity to statistically analyze the data. However, because prior research on regional pro forma disclosure is very limited, exploratory descriptive analysis is provided for the seven regions.

Table 6.6 presents the pro forma disclosure frequencies of US firms and US-listed foreign firms by region and by reporting standard. Two regions (Canada and Caribbean/Bermuda/Puerto Rico) did not have firms that applied IFRS in 2007. For the five regions that reported results using both US GAAP and IFRS, the frequency of reporting a pro forma disclosure is greater for those firms that report results using IFRS than for those firms using US GAAP. For one region (European firms, other than UK firms), however, pro forma disclosure frequency is similar irrespective of the firm's reporting standards.

**Table 6.6** Pro Forma Disclosure Frequency by Region and Reporting Standard (IFRS and US GAAP)

| Region/Reporting Standards | US | US-Listed Foreign Firms | Asia/Pacific | Canada | Caribbean/Bermuda/Puerto Rico | UK | Other European | Latin America | Middle East/Africa |
|---|---|---|---|---|---|---|---|---|---|
| US GAAP (%) | 72.5 | 63.2 | 52.2 | 61.5 | 53.3 | 0 | 83.3 | 85.7 | 40 |
| Frequency | 140 | 79 | 24 | 8 | 8 | 0 | 25 | 12 | 2 |
| N | 193 | 125 | 46 | 13 | 15 | 2 | 30 | 14 | 5 |
| IFRS (%) | | 85.3 | 69.2 | | | 94.4 | 83.9 | 100 | 100 |
| Frequency | | 58 | 9 | | | 17 | 26 | 3 | 3 |
| N | | 68 | 13 | | | 18 | 31 | 3 | 3 |
| All (%) | 72.5 | 71.8 | 55.9 | 61.5 | 53.3 | 85 | 83.6 | 88.2 | 62.5 |
| Frequency | 140 | 277 | 33 | 8 | 8 | 17 | 51 | 15 | 5 |
| N | 193 | 386 | 59 | 13 | 15 | 20 | 61 | 17 | 8 |

**Note:** Disclosure frequency is defined in Table 6.3

Table 6.7 provides a regional comparison of pro forma disclosure characteristics for firms using US GAAP and IFRS. The comparison reveals some interesting differences. Asian/Pacific firms that report results using US GAAP are more likely (97 per cent) to report income-increasing pro forma amounts than Asian/Pacific firms that apply IFRS (50 per cent). The adjustment magnitude of Asian/Pacific firms is similar for firms reporting results using US GAAP (0.37) and IFRS (0.34).

Only three firms (reporting six pro forma disclosures) in the Latin American region apply IFRS. In this region, firms applying IFRS reported more (100 per cent) income-increasing pro forma disclosures than firms using US GAAP (87.5 per cent). The magnitude of the adjustments, however, is lower for firms applying IFRS (1.00) than for firms using US GAAP (1.83).

Table 6.7 Panel C presents the pro forma benchmarking tendencies for US and US-listed foreign firms by region and by reporting standard to further illustrate disclosure differences. For all regions that report results using US GAAP and IFRS, the frequency of reporting a pro forma disclosure that meets or beats the benchmark is greater for the regions that report results using US GAAP than for firms in the corresponding region that report results using IFRS. The region that stands out as very different is the Asian/Pacific region. The frequency of reporting a pro forma disclosure that meets or beats a benchmark is much greater for firms using US GAAP (81.3 per cent) than for firms applying IFRS (36.8 per cent).

## Discussion and Conclusions

This study extends the research of Epping and Wilder (2011) by providing empirical evidence of the pro forma disclosure behavior of firms reporting results using IFRS. The behavior of US-listed foreign firms applying IFRS is compared to the behavior of firms using US GAAP (US firms and US-listed foreign firms) to provide investors and other readers of press releases a better understanding of differences in pro forma disclosure behavior. The analysis examines disclosure frequency, disclosure characteristics and benchmarking tendencies. The findings are helpful in understanding the impact that reporting standards have on the pro forma disclosure behavior of US-listed foreign firms applying IFRS relative to the pro forma disclosure behavior of US firms and US-listed foreign firms using US GAAP. This understanding is important given the increasing use of IFRS, the number of foreign firms listing on US exchanges and the move toward common global accounting standards.

In prior research, no difference was found in US and US-listed foreign firm pro forma disclosure frequency. The current study grouped foreign firms by reporting standard and finds that US-listed foreign firms applying IFRS are more likely to report a pro forma amount than US-listed foreign firms using US GAAP. Similarly, US-listed foreign firms applying IFRS are more likely than US firms to disclose a pro forma amount. Overall, firms applying IFRS are more likely than firms using US GAAP to disclose a pro forma amount. After grouping firms by reporting standard, the current study finds that foreign firms applying IFRS report fewer income-increasing adjustments than firms using

**Table 6.7** Pro Forma Disclosure Behavior by Region and Reporting Standard (IFRS and US GAAP)

| Region/Reporting Standards | US | US-listed Foreign Firms | Asia/Pacific | Canada | Caribbean/Bermuda/Puerto Rico | UK | Other European | Latin America | Middle East/Africa |
|---|---|---|---|---|---|---|---|---|---|
| *Panel A: income-increasing adjustments* | | | | | | | | | |
| **US GAAP** | | | | | | | | | |
| (%) | 89.3 | 87.0 | 97.0 | 90.0 | 66.7 | | 85.7 | 87.5 | 50.0 |
| Frequency | 191 | 100 | 32 | 9 | 6 | | 30 | 21 | 2 |
| N | 214 | 115 | 33 | 10 | 9 | | 35 | 24 | 4 |
| **IFRS** | | | | | | | | | |
| (%) | | 73.0 | 50.0 | | | 72.3 | 83.7 | 100 | 50.0 |
| Frequency | | 89 | 10 | | | 34 | 36 | 6 | 3 |
| N | | 122 | 20 | | | 47 | 43 | 6 | 6 |
| **All** | | | | | | | | | |
| (%) | 89.3 | 79.7 | 79.2 | 90.0 | 66.7 | 72.3 | 84.6 | 90.0 | 50.0 |
| Frequency | 191 | 189 | 42 | 9 | 6 | 34 | 66 | 27 | 5 |
| N | 214 | 237 | 53 | 10 | 9 | 47 | 78 | 30 | 10 |
| *Panel B: adjustment magnitude* | | | | | | | | | |
| **US GAAP** | | | | | | | | | |
| Mean | 2.81 | 1.14 | 0.37 | 2.59 | 0.97 | | 0.71 | 1.83 | 3.72 |
| SD | 6.62 | 2.65 | 0.51 | 3.87 | 1.52 | | 0.89 | 3.99 | 7.31 |
| N | 214 | 115 | 33 | 10 | 9 | | 35 | 24 | 4 |
| **IFRS** | | | | | | | | | |
| Mean | | 1.14 | 0.34 | | | 0.68 | 2.13 | 1.00 | 0.57 |
| SD | | 2.74 | 0.94 | | | 1.33 | 4.19 | 0.65 | 1.04 |
| N | | 122 | 20 | | | 47 | 43 | 6 | 6 |

# Table 6.7 Pro Forma Disclosure Behavior by Region and Reporting Standard (IFRS and US GAAP) *(Continued)*

| Region/Reporting Standards | US | US-listed Foreign Firms | Asia/Pacific | Canada | Caribbean/Bermuda/Puerto Rico | UK | Other European | Latin America | Middle East/Africa |
|---|---|---|---|---|---|---|---|---|---|
| **All** | | | | | | | | | |
| Mean | 2.81 | 1.14 | 0.36 | 2.59 | 0.97 | 0.68 | 1.49 | 1.67 | 1.83 |
| SD | 6.62 | 2.69 | 0.70 | 3.87 | 1.52 | 1.33 | 3.23 | 3.58 | 4.59 |
| N | 214 | 237 | 53 | 10 | 9 | 47 | 78 | 30 | 10 |
| *Panel C: benchmarking* | | | | | | | | | |
| **US GAAP** | | | | | | | | | |
| (%) | 58.1 | 73.4 | 81.3 | 70.0 | 55.6 | | 71.9 | 81.8 | 25.0 |
| Frequency | 118 | 80 | 26 | 7 | 5 | | 23 | 18 | 1 |
| N | 203 | 109 | 32 | 10 | 9 | | 32 | 22 | 4 |
| **IFRS** | | | | | | | | | |
| (%) | | 49.5 | 36.8 | | | 55.8 | 51.4 | 66.7 | 16.7 |
| Frequency | | 55 | 7 | | | 24 | 19 | 4 | 1 |
| N | | 111 | 19 | | | 43 | 37 | 6 | 6 |
| **All** | | | | | | | | | |
| (%) | 58.1 | 61.4 | 64.7 | 70.0 | 55.6 | 55.8 | 60.9 | 78.6 | 20 |
| Frequency | 118 | 135 | 33 | 7 | 5 | 24 | 42 | 22 | 2 |
| N | 203 | 220 | 51 | 10 | 9 | 43 | 69 | 28 | 10 |

**Note:** Disclosure characteristics (income-increasing adjustments and adjustment magnitude) and benchmarking are defined in Table 6.3

READING 6 Pro forma Disclosure Practices of Firms Applying IFRS ♦ 101

US GAAP (including both US firms as well as US-listed foreign firms using US GAAP). Just as with disclosure frequency, it appears that reporting standard is contributing to the results.

Prior research has found that the adjustment magnitude of pro forma disclosures is smaller for US-listed foreign firms than for US firms. Similarly, the current study finds that US-listed foreign firms applying IFRS report a pro forma amount with a smaller adjustment magnitude than that of US firms. The adjustment magnitude of pro forma disclosures is similar for foreign firms using US GAAP and IFRS. For this measure, the evidence is not as strong that reporting standard is helpful in explaining the result.

US-listed foreign firms have been previously found to be more likely to hit a benchmark than US firms. The current study finds that firms applying IFRS are less likely than foreign firms using US GAAP to meet a benchmark using a pro forma disclosure. However, benchmark tendencies are similar for US-listed foreign firms that apply IFRS and US firms. This measure of opportunistic behavior provides some evidence (but not strong evidence) that reporting standard impacts pro forma disclosure behavior.

In summary, the current research extends the study of Epping and Wilder (2011) and contributes to the pro forma disclosure literature by providing a cross-country analysis of non-GAAP disclosure based on reporting standard (IFRS or US GAAP). Overall, there is evidence that reporting standard is associated with pro forma disclosure behavior. US-listed foreign firms applying IFRS report pro forma disclosures more frequently than firms using US GAAP, but less opportunistically. Understanding the non-GAAP disclosure of firms applying IFRS is useful to investors and regulators as more countries adopt IFRS.

# Notes

1. Although studies indicate that conversion from foreign domestic GAAP to IFRS enhances comparability, Cole *et al.* (2012) find that more improvements are needed. Many respondents in the Cole *et al.'s* (2012) study believe that a lack of industry guidance results in judgment and interpretation differences where comparability is most important, within industries.

2. The data collection technique utilized in the current study has been used in prior research (Entwistle *et al.*, 2005; Marques, 2006; Yi, 2012; Epping and Wilder, 2011). Undertaking a complete reading of the annual earnings press releases of a predetermined set of firms improves the likelihood that all non-GAAP disclosures are detected.

3. The matching design applied in the current study is similar to the design used in the study of Lougee and Marquardt (2004) and Epping and Wilder (2011).

4. The industry measure in the current study follows the one that is used by Bowen *et al.* (2005). Bowen *et al.* (2005) used this measure to control firms in high-tech industries that are more likely to report pro forma earnings.

5. The greatest correlation among independent variables (LEV and GROWTH) is 0.754. To alleviate concerns of multicollinearity, the regression models were rerun after removing LEV and GROWTH, independently. The results are consistent with the original model.

6. Some of the firms in our sample provide more than one non-GAAP disclosure in the sample period. Approximately 80 per cent of the disclosures are net income based with the other 20 per cent based on operating income.

# References

Agoglia, C.P., Doupnik, T.S. and Tsakumis, G.T. (2011), "Principles-based versus rules-based accounting standards: the influence of standard precision and audit committee strength on financial reporting decisions", *Accounting Review*, Vol. 86 No. 3, pp. 747–767.

Ahmed, A.S., Neel, M. and Wang, D. (2013), "Does mandatory adoption of IFRS improve accounting quality? Preliminary evidence", *Contemporary Accounting Research*, Vol. 30 No. 4, pp. 1344–1372.

Association of Chartered Certified Accountants (2012), "IFRS in the US: the investor's perspective", available at: http://images.forbes.com/forbesinsights/StudyPDFs/ACCA_IFRS-Report.pdf (accessed 21 December 2014).

Barth, M., Gow, I. and Taylor, D. (2012), "Why do pro forma and street earnings not reflect changes in GAAP? Evidence from SFAS 123R", *Review of Accounting Studies*, Vol. 17 No. 3, pp. 526–562.

Barth, M.E., Landsman, W.R. and Lang, M.H. (2008), "International accounting standards and accounting quality", *Journal of Accounting Research*, Vol. 46 No. 3, pp. 467–498.

Baumker, M., Biggs, P., McVay, S.E. and Pierce, J. (2014), "The disclosure of non-GAAP earnings following regulation G: an analysis of transitory gains", *Accounting Horizons*, Vol. 28 No. 1, pp. 77–92.

Bhattacharya, N., Black, E.L., Christensen, T.E. and Larson, C.R. (2003), "Assessing the relative informativeness and permanence of pro forma earnings and GAAP operating earnings", *Journal of Accounting & Economics*, Vol. 36 Nos 1/3, pp. 285–319.

Bhattacharya, N., Black, E.L., Christensen, T.E. and Mergenthaler, R.D. (2004), "Empirical evidence on recent trends in pro forma reporting", *Accounting Horizons*, Vol. 18 No. 1, pp. 27–43.

Botosan, C. (1997), "Disclosure level and the cost of equity capital", *The Accounting Review*, Vol. 72 No. 3, pp. 323–349.

Bowen, R.M., Davis, A.K. and Matsumoto, D.A. (2005), "Emphasis on pro forma versus GAAP earnings in quarterly press releases: determinants, SEC intervention, and market reactions", *Accounting Review*, Vol. 80 No. 4, pp. 1011–1038.

Bradshaw, M.T. and Sloan, R. (2002), "GAAP versus the street: an empirical assessment of two alternative definitions of earnings", *Journal of Accounting Research*, Vol. 40 No. 1, pp. 41–66.

Brochet, F., Jagolinzer, A.D. and Riedl, E.J. (2013), "Mandatory IFRS adoption and financial statement comparability", *Contemporary Accounting Research*, Vol. 30 No. 4, pp. 1373–1400.

Brown, L.D. and Sivakumar, K. (2003), "Comparing the value relevance of two operating income measures", *Review of Accounting Studies*, Vol. 8 No. 4, pp. 561–572.

Chen, Y. and Rezaee, Z. (2012), "The role of corporate governance in convergence with IFRS: evidence from China", *International Journal of Accounting and Information Management*, Vol. 20 No. 2, pp. 171–188.

Cole, V., Branson, J. and Breesch, D. (2012), "The uniformity-flexibility dilemma when comparing financial statements: views of auditors, analysts and other users", *International Journal of Accounting & Information Management*, Vol. 20 No. 2, pp. 114–141.

Collins, D.L., Pasewark, W.R. and Riley, M.E. (2012), "Financial reporting outcomes under rules-based and principles-based accounting standards", *Accounting Horizons*, Vol. 26 No. 4, pp. 681–705.

Curtis, A.B., McVay, S.E. and Whipple, B.C. (2014), "The disclosure of non-GAAP earnings information in the presence of transitory gains", *Accounting Review*, Vol. 89 No. 3, pp. 933–958.

Daske, H. and Gebhardt, G. (2006), "International financial reporting standards and experts' perceptions of disclosure quality", *Abacus*, Vol. 42 Nos 3/4, pp. 461–498.

Doyle, J.T., Jennings, J.N. and Soliman, M.T. (2013), "Do managers define non-GAAP earnings to meet or beat analyst forecasts?", *Journal of Accounting & Economics*, Vol. 56 No. 1, pp. 40–56.

Entwistle, G.M., Feltham, G.D. and Mbagwu, C. (2005), "The voluntary disclosure of pro forma earnings: a US-Canada comparison", *Journal of International Accounting Research*, Vol. 4 No. 2, pp. 1–23.

Epping, L.L. and Wilder, W.M. (2011), "US-listed foreign firms' non-GAAP financial performance disclosure behavior", *Journal of International Accounting Research*, Vol. 10 No. 2, pp. 77–96.

Healy, P., Hutton, A. and Palepu, K. (1999), "Stock performance and intermediation changes surrounding increases in disclosure", *Contemporary Accounting Research*, Vol. 16 No. 3, pp. 485–520.

Healy, P.M. and Palepu, K.G. (2001), "Information asymmetry, corporate disclosure, and the capital markets: a review of the empirical disclosure literature", *Journal of Accounting & Economics*, Vol. 31 Nos 1/3, pp. 405–440.

Henry, E., Lin, S. and Yang, Y. (2009), "The European-US 'GAAP gap': IFRS to US GAAP form 20-F reconciliations", *Accounting Horizons*, Vol. 23 No. 2, pp. 121–150.

Hodgdon, C., Tondkar, R.H., Harless, D.W. and Adhikari, A. (2008), "Compliance with IFRS disclosure requirements and individual analysts' forecast errors", *Journal of International Accounting, Auditing & Taxation*, Vol. 17 No. 1, pp. 1–13.

Horton, J., Serafeim, G. and Serafeim, I. (2013), "Does mandatory IFRS adoption improve the information environment?", *Contemporary Accounting Research*, Vol. 30 No. 1, pp. 388–423.

IFRS (2014), "IFRS advisory council meeting", available at: www.ifrs.org/The-organisation/IFRS-Advisory-Council/Documents/IFRS-AC-Meeting-Report-February-2014.pdf (accessed 10 June 2014).

IFRS Advisory Council (2011), "Use of underlying earnings and non-GAAP measures", available at: www.ifrs. org/Meetings/MeetingDocs/Advisory%20Council/2011/June/20th%20and%2021st/AC-0611-AP6.pdf (accessed 10 June 2014).

Johnson, W.B. and Schwartz, W.C. (2005), "Are investors misled by 'pro forma' earnings?", *Contemporary Accounting Research*, Vol. 22 No. 4, pp. 915–963.

Kim, J.B. and Shi, H. (2012), "Voluntary IFRS adoption, analyst coverage, and information quality: international evidence", *Journal of International Accounting Research*, Vol. 11 No. 1, pp. 45–76.

Liu, C. (2011), "IFRS and US-GAAP comparability before release no. 33–8879: some evidence from US-listed Chinese companies", *International Journal of Accounting & Information Management*, Vol. 19 No. 1, pp. 24–33.

Liu, C., Yao, L.J., Hu, N. and Liu, L. (2011), "The impact of IFRS on accounting quality in a regulated market: an empirical study of China", *Journal of Accounting, Auditing & Finance*, Vol. 26 No. 4, pp. 659–676.

Liu, C., Yuen, C.Y., Lee, J. and Yao, S.H.C. (2014), "Differences in earnings management between firms using US GAAP and IAS/IFRS", *Review of Accounting and Finance*, Vol. 13 No. 2, pp. 134–155.

Lougee, B.A. and Marquardt, C.A. (2004), "Earnings informatives and strategic disclosure: an empirical examination of 'pro forma' earnings", *Accounting Review*, Vol. 79 No. 3, pp. 769–795.

Marques, A. (2006), "SEC interventions and the frequency and usefulness of non-GAAP financial measures", *Review of Accounting Studies*, Vol. 11 No. 4, pp. 549–574.

SEC (2003), *Conditions for Use of Non-GAAP Financial Measures: Release No. 33–8176*, Securities and Exchange Commission, Washington, DC.

SEC (2011), *Work Plan for the Consideration of Incorporating International Financial Reporting Standards into the Financial Reporting System for US Issuers: A Comparison of US GAAP and IFRS*, Securities and Exchange Commission Staff Paper, Washington, DC.

Tan, H., Wang, S. and Welker, M. (2011), "Analyst following and forecast accuracy after mandated IFRS adoptions", *Journal of Accounting Research*, Vol. 49 No. 5, pp. 1307–1357.

Yi, H.S. (2012), "Has regulation G improved the information quality of non-GAAP earnings disclosures?", *Seoul Journal of Business*, Vol. 18 No. 2, pp. 95–145.

# The Effect of Managerial Forecasted Financial Statements on Security Analysts' Judgment

By Robert L. Webster and T. Selwyn Ellis

## Introduction

There are three objectives of financial reporting as described by the Financial Accounting Standards Board in its Statement of Financial Accounting Concepts No. 1 (FASB, 1978). The three objectives, in abbreviated form, are:

1. Financial reporting should provide information that is useful to present and potential investors and creditors and other users in making rational investment, credit, and similar decisions.

2. Financial reporting should provide information to help present and potential investors and creditors and other users in assessing the amounts, timing, and uncertainty of prospective cash receipts.

3. Financial reporting should provide information about the economic resources of an enterprise, the claims to those resources, and the effects of transactions, events, and circumstances that change its resources and claims to those resources.

These objectives are derived from the informational needs of external users. External users, however, lack the authority to prescribe what information they want and what format such desired information must take (SFAC No. 1, 1978, para. 28). This lack of user participation in the standard-setting process was noted by the General Accounting Office (GAO) as late as September 1996 (GAO, AIMD-96–98). Therefore, users must rely on the information communicated by management. Currently financial statement information provided by management consists of historical financial information. The second objective of financial reporting (SFAC No. 1, 1978, paragraph 37), however, indicates that financial reporting should provide information that will be beneficial to users in determining the timing, amounts, and uncertainty of prospective cash receipts. This emphasis on future cash flows has led some to conclude that financial forecasts by management would be desirable. This conclusion was recently supported by the GAO (GAO, AIMD-96–98).

The FASB acknowledges in its objectives that the informational needs of users should be considered in design of financial reporting systems. The FASB also recognizes that there are many different types of users of financial reports and that currently designed systems of reporting must attempt to satisfy all. Johnson (1992), however, questions if information needs of users do not differ by user class. Hendriksen (1982) asks how can we be sure that current disclosure rules meet the informational needs of users. Abdel-Khalik (1971) questions if the informational needs of users are not dynamic and therefore subject to change over time. Recognizing the validity of these questions, as well as many others, the Jenkins committee in 1994 (AICPA) recommended numerous proposals to modify the current financial reporting model.

This research sought to determine if a modification to the current data set from historical financial statements to historical data coupled with management forecasted financial statements would have a significant influence on the confidence of users assessing the condition of the firm (a test of content differences).

## Theory and Practice Literature Concerning Forecasts

Accounting theory is divided concerning the desirability and the usefulness of the disclosure by management of financial forecasts and predictions. Summary arguments both for and against the disclosure of financial forecasts by management enumerated by Keiso and Weygandt (1995) are presented below.

### Arguments for Disclosure

1. Investment decisions are based on future performance expectations; therefore forecasts would be helpful to investors.

2. Some forecasts already circulate but because of no control over forecasts, misleading information may be used by investors.

3. The economic environment is too dynamic to rely on historical information only.

4. Others, such as the British, have successfully incorporated forecasts into disclosure.

### Arguments Against Disclosure

1. The economic future is too uncertain to predict with accuracy.

2. Enterprises will limit their performance to the level of their forecasts.

3. If forecasts are not met then lawsuits will follow.

4. Forecasts will aid the competitors of the forecasting enterprise.

This division of thought is likewise incorporated into current accounting and auditing practice. Currently, mandated financial reporting requires only that historical information be contained in the financial reports. This requirement is based in large measure on the accounting principle of reporting financial transactions on the basis of historical cost (Accounting Principles Board Statement No. 4, 1970). An enterprise, though required to report historical data, may at its election decide to disclose financial forecasts. Although this decision is left to management, the Securities Exchange Commission (1978) through its publication guide on the disclosure of future economic performance, supports the release of financial forecasts by management.

The American Institute of Certified Public Accountants (AICPA) has adopted standards for reviewing and reporting on forecasted financial information (AICPA, 1985). These standards are applicable only if an engagement entails the review of voluntarily disclosed financial projections or forecasts.

The current practice of stressing the importance of prospective cash flows while not requiring management predictions seems incongruous to many users of financial statements. Requiring enterprises to forecast their financial position and release such forecasts has been suggested as a remedy.

## Lack of Empirical Evidence on Forecasting

The conflict over whether financial forecasts would be beneficial to users of financial statements is complicated because scant empirical evidence exists to support the position that forecasted management information would actually be beneficial to users in their decision making. Hendriksen (1982, p. 507) comments on the situation offering that management forecasts would likely aid in the investment decision. Hendriksen (1982, p. 103) also says that currently available information may help make markets efficient but that an alternative information set might provide an improvement in market efficiency.

Webster (1993) found, in a pilot study of prospective investors, that respondents were interested in receiving company-generated financial forecasts as well as future cash flow projections.

Walther (1993) argues that the future-oriented information included in the management's discussion and analysis section of the typical annual report is so limited that it precludes the information from being useful. On this same subject, Pava and Epstein (1993) found that while most firms did a good job of describing historical events, few firms provided useful and accurate forecasted information.

Although Nickerson *et al.* (1974) and Penman (1980) found that financial forecasts by management would be beneficial to financial statement users, the actual benefit is difficult to measure. This difficulty in benefit measurement is due to the disclosure environment. The environment is one in which financial forecasts are voluntary and the vast majority of enterprises choose not to disclose financial forecasts.

# Problem Statement

Sufficient evidence does not exist to either confirm or deny that management forecasted financial information would be beneficial and therefore desirable in the decision-making process when assessing the financial condition of the firm.

The central purpose of this study therefore was to test if financial statements that included forecasted financial information were assessed by users to provided information that was different (preferred) from that provided by historically based financial reports.

# Sources of Data

The data collected for this study consisted of responses to a questionnaire applicable to various sets of comparative financial statements of a publicly traded company. The financial statements contained comparative balance sheets, income statements and cash flow statements. The identity of the company was disguised to help eliminate any bias associated with a firm. The control group received nor mal historical reports for analysis. The two treatment groups received the same statements as the control group except a managerial forecast for each statement for the upcoming year was also provided. One of the treatment groups received a management forecast that was constructed to be "optimistic" in nature. The second treatment group received a management forecast than was deemed to be "pessimistic" in nature. Members of the treatment groups, of course, were not informed that the forecasts represented either end of the forecast spectrum. The response instrument provided for a self-assessment of the analysis of the financial condition of the firm in six categories as detailed later. The survey instrument is displayed in Appendix A.

Survey participants were all members of the New York Society of Securities Analysts. Four-hundred and fifty mailed surveys were sent based on a random sample of association members that by self-identification were either pertinent industry specialists or portfolio management specialists. The survey size for the control group and each of the two treatment groups was 150. Of the 450 surveys mailed, 89 usable responses were received back by return mail. The return rate was 20 per cent. Thirty-three responses were from the control group and 28 responses were from each of the treatment groups. After receipt of the returned surveys, potential nonresponse bias was investigated.

Larson and Catton (1959) demonstrated a now commonly used proxy to test for nonresponse bias. A MANOVA model was used to test for differences in early versus late respondents. Results indicated no statistically significant differences between early and late respondents. Additionally, Berdie (1989) found that nonresponse bias in mail surveys typically did not alter the results of the survey findings.

# Hypothesis

$1H_0$: A statistically significant difference in reported self-confidence in assessing the financial condition of a publicly traded company does not exist in comparisons between historical-based financial statements and financial statements that contain financial forecasts.

# Design of the Study

The experimental design for this study was one in which a single categorical independent variable with three classes was measured in order to evaluate its effect on six metric (scaled) dependent variables. The independent variable was financial statement format/content. The three classes of the variable included historical only; historical with optimistic forecast; and historical with pessimistic forecast.

The six scaled dependent variables (described below) were measures of the individual user's confidence levels in assessing the financial condition of the firm. These measurements were obtained from respondent scores in six financial areas, using a seven-point Likert scale for each of the six variables.

These variables were chosen after a review of the financial analysis literature which indicated that analysis should, as a minimum, incorporate measurements of liquidity, both short and longer terms, profitability, and cash flow (Block and Hirt, 1989). Additionally, Hampton (1989) indicates that much of the analysis performed on a firm is done by persons external to the firm, and these analysts must make use of existing financial statements. Kolb and DeMong (1988) state that three of the four types of parties who have a financial interest in a firm and therefore would be involved in financial analysis are external parties to the firm. Kolb and DeMong contend that these parties are most interested in liquidity, profitability, and cash flow. All writers mentioned above agree that in addition to assessing individual financial areas, a combined assessment of the entity should be made prior to reaching a conclusion concerning the overall well being of the firm. The dependent variables were therefore chosen to incorporate the consensus of thought concerning important aspects of financial analysis using financial statements.

The level of confidence expressed by analysts in their analysis was singled out for study in the belief that investment decisions and/or investment advice is materially affected by the level of confidence one attributes to their analysis.

# Data Analysis

The data were analyzed by using MANOVA. MANOVA is concerned with differences between groups, or experimental treatments. MANOVA is termed a multivariate statistical procedure as it is used to determine the effect of categorical independent variables on multiple dependent metric variables simultaneously (Sharma, 1996).

MANOVA is deemed particularly useful when employed in conjunction with experimental designs in which the researcher controls and manipulates one or more independent variables to determine the effect on two or more dependent metric variables (Hair *et al.*, 1992). Additionally, MANOVA does away with the problem of a series of individual *F*-tests (which may lead to increased Type I errors) by testing the linear combination of all dependent variables simultaneously (Hair *et al.*, 1992).

In the study, the six dependent variables are metric variables based on a scaled input. The use of scale based metric variables is a common practice and is demonstrated by Hebert and Freeman (1987) and Johnson and Wichern (1988).

# The Research Model

$$Y_{jk} = U + A_j + E_{jk}$$

where:

$Y_{jk}$ = the vector of responses for each rating category item (six items) from a participant $k$ in group $j$.

$U$ = overall or grand mean effect.

$A_j$ = effect of level $j$ of factor $A$ (format) on the six response items for $j = 1, 2, 3$.

$E_{jk}$ = random error present in response $k$ in cell $j$, for $k = 1, 2, ... nj$.

Practically stated, the model was as follows. Immediately following the model, all variables are defined.

$$Y_1, Y_2, Y_3, Y_4, Y_5, Y_6 = X_1$$

where:

$Y_1$ = confidence in assessing ability of the firm to meet short-term obligations;

$Y_2$ = confidence in assessing ability of the firm to meet long-term obligations;

$Y_3$ = confidence in assessing ability of the firm to continue paying its current cash dividend;

$Y_4$ = confidence in assessing ability of the firm to increase common stock cash dividend in the future;

$Y_5$ = confidence in assessing ability of the firm to increase profitability in the future;

$Y_6$ = confidence in assessing the overall future financial condition of the firm;

$X_1$ = financial statement for mat (three classes; historical, optimistic forecast, pessimistic forecast);

# Results

Table 7.1 displays the mean confidence levels reported by the control group and the two treatment groups for each of the dependent variables.

The results of the multivariate analysis yielded a Wilks' Lambda of 0.5529, an $F$-ratio of 4.655, and a significance of 0.000. Therefore, the null hypothesis was rejected. Rejection of the null hypothesis leads to the alternate hypothesis, e.g. there is a difference in analyst's self-confidence between historical, optimistic forecasted, and pessimistic forecasted statement analysis.

Following the multivariate analysis, univariate analysis of each variable was undertaken. The univariate analysis was conducted using six ANOVA models. This was done to determine if the multivariate results might have been significantly affected by only one or two of the dependent variables. Table 7.2 displays the results of the separate univariate tests. In each case, the variable was found to be significant. These tests add support and credence to the MANOVA results.

**Table 7.1** Mean Scores of Securities Analysts by Financial Statement Format (7-Point Scale)

| Variables | Historical (n = 33) | Optimistic Forecast (n = 28) | Pessimistic Forecast (n = 28) |
|---|---|---|---|
| Self-confidence in assessing whether a firm can meet its short-term financial obligations as they come due | 4.939 | 6.179 | 5.877 |
| Self-confidence in assessing whether a firm can meet its long-term financial obligations as they come due | 4.606 | 5.357 | 5.536 |
| Self-confidence in assessing whether a firm can continue paying its current cash dividend in the future | 4.727 | 5.571 | 5.607 |
| Self-confidence in assessing whether a firm can increase its common stock cash dividend in the future | 4.030 | 4.536 | 4.786 |
| Self-confidence in assessing whether a firm can increase its profitability in the future | 3.606 | 4.357 | 4.750 |
| Self-confidence in assessing the overall future financial condition of the firm | 3.909 | 5.000 | 4.821 |

Table 7.3 displays that when compared to historical based statements, forecasted statements show a statistical difference in 11 of 12 separate tests. The Table also shows that no differences exist between the forecasted groups themselves. The mean scores reported in Table 7.1 show that the forecasted statements always provided higher levels of confidence in analysis than did the historical based statements.

If forecasted financial statements were commonplace or mandatory, the range of forecasts would represent a continuum from the most pessimistic to the most optimistic. To test if a difference exists between groups of historical financial statements and mixed forecasted statements, the optimistic and pessimistic forecast groups were combined into a single group, named "forecasted". This group,

**Table 7.2** Individual ANOVA tests of no Differences Between Financial Statement Formats

| Variables | F Ratio | Significance of F |
|---|---|---|
| Self-confidence in assessing whether a firm can meet its short-term financial obligations as they come due | 15.412 | 0.0000 |
| Self-confidence in assessing whether a firm can meet its long-term financial obligations as they come due | 7.278 | 0.0012 |
| Self-confidence in assessing whether a firm can continue paying its current cash dividend in the future | 7.724 | 0.0004 |
| Self-confidence in assessing whether a firm can increase its common stock cash dividend in the future | 4.529 | 0.0135 |
| Self-confidence in assessing whether a firm can increase its profitability in the future | 9.770 | 0.0002 |
| Self-confidence in assessing the overall future financial condition of the firm | 10.230 | 0.0001 |

**Table 7.3** Results of *Post Hoc* Univariate Tests of Differences Between Groups

| | Historical Versus Optimistic Forecast | Historical Versus Pessimistic Forecast | Optimistic Versus Pessimistic Forecast |
|---|---|---|---|
| Self-confidence in assessing whether a firm can meet its short-term financial obligations as they come due | yes | yes | no |
| Self-confidence in assessing whether a firm can meet its long-term financial obligations as they come due | yes | yes | no |
| Self-confidence in assessing whether a firm can continue paying its current cash dividend in the future | yes | yes | no |
| Self-confidence in assessing whether a firm can increase its common stock cash divedend in the future | no | yes | no |
| Self-confidence in assessing whether a firm can increase its profitability in the future | yes | yes | no |
| Self-confidence in assessing the overall future financial condition of the firm | yes | yes | no |

comprising 56 forecasted observations, was compared with the historical group which contained 33 observations. A MANOVA was used to test if differences existed between the two groups. The results of the multivariate test produced a Wilks' Lambda of 0.68466, an $F$-ratio of 6.2947, and a significance of 0.000. Table 7.4 shows response means by financial statement format for the two groups, historical and forecasted. Table 7.5 displays the results of the individual analysis of variance test conducted on the dependent variables by group.

**Table 7.4** Response Means of Securities Analysts by Financial Statement Format (7 Point Scale)

| Variables | Historical (n = 33) | Forecasted (n = 56) |
|---|---|---|
| Self-confidence in assessing whether a firm can meet its short-term financial obligations as they come due | 4.939 | 6.018 |
| Self-confidence in assessing whether a firm can meet its long-term financial obligations as they come due | 4.606 | 5.446 |
| Self-confidence in assessing whether a firm can continue paying its current cash dividend in the future | 4.727 | 5.589 |
| Self-confidence in assessing whether a firm can increase its common stock cash dividend in the future | 4.030 | 4.661 |
| Self-confidence in assessing whether a firm can increase its profitability in the future | 3.606 | 4.554 |
| Self-confidence in assessing the overall future financial condition of the firm | 3.909 | 4.911 |

**Table 7.5** ANOVA Results for Hypotheses of no Difference in Confidence Assessments Between Formats

| Variables | F Ratio | Significance of F |
|---|---|---|
| Self-confidence in assessing whether a firm can meet its short-term financial obligations as they come due | 28.837 | 0.000 |
| Self-confidence in assessing whether a firm can meet its long-term financial obligations as they come due | 14.220 | 0.000 |
| Self-confidence in assessing whether a firm can continue paying its current cash dividend in the future | 17.188 | 0.000 |
| Self-confidence in assessing whether a firm can increase its common stock cash dividend in the future | 8.203 | 0.005 |
| Self-confidence in assessing whether a firm can increase its profitability in the future | 17.305 | 0.000 |
| Self-confidence in assessing the overall future financial condition of the firm | 20.299 | 0.000 |

# Summary of Findings

The results showed that the use of management forecasted financial statements used in conjunction with historical statements, *vice* historical statements, produced consistently higher levels of reported confidence in assessing the financial condition of the firm. The results demonstrated that the vector of means for the forecasted group(s) were statistically different (higher) from the historical group. Additionally, for each of the dependent variables, the mean was higher for the groups using the forecasted financial statements as a basis of assessment.

# Implications

The finding that financial statements containing management forecasts enhance the confidence of analysts should be of particular interest to organizations that promulgate accounting and reporting requirements such as the FASB, the SEC, and the AICPA. The findings supported the recommendation of the 1996 General Accounting Office Report 96–98 calling for a set of management forecasted financial statements (GAO,AIMD-96–98). Additionally, these findings should be of particular interest to those who are involved in research concerning accounting disclosure. Finally, these findings should be tested in a broader environment using other groups of financial statement users.

# References

Abdel-Khalik, A.R. (1971), "User preference ordering value: a model", *The Accounting Review*, pp. 457–71.

Accounting Principles Board (1970), "Statement No. 4".

American Institute of Certified Public Accountants (1985), *Statement on Standards for Accountants' Services on Prospective Financial Information, Financial Forecasts Projections*, AICPA, New York, NY.

American Institute of Certified Public Accountants (1994), *Improving Business Reporting–A Customer Focus: Meeting the Information Needs of Investors and Creditors. Comprehensive Report of the Special Committee on Financial Reporting* (Jenkins Committee), New York, NY.

Berdie, D. (1989), "Reassessing the value of high response rates to mail surveys", *Market Research*, pp. 52–63.

Block, S.B. and Hirt, G.A. (1989), *Foundations of Financial Management*, 5th ed., Irwin, Homewood, IL, pp. 56–8.

Financial Accounting Standards Board (1978), "Objectives of financial reporting by business enterprises", *Statement of Financial Accounting Concepts No. 1*, Stamford, CT.

Hair, J.F., Anderson, R.E., Tatham, R.L. and Black, W.C. (1992), *Multivariate Data Analysis with Readings*, 3rd ed., Macmillan, New York, NY.

Hampton, J.J. (1989), *Financial Decision Making: Concepts, Problems, and Cases*, 4th ed., Prentice-Hall, Englewood Cliffs, NJ, pp. 98–9.

Hebert, M.G. and Freeman, R.J. (1987), "Governmental fund operating statements: should the format be standardized?", *Accounting Horizons*, pp. 17–35.

Hendriksen, E.S. (1982), *Accounting Theory*, 4th ed., Irwin Press, Homewood, IL, pp. 103, 504, 507.

Johnson, R.A. and Wichern, D.W. (1988), *Applied Multivariate Statistical Analysis*, 2nd ed., Prentice-Hall, Englewood Cliffs, NJ.

Johnson, T.L. (1992), "Research on disclosure", *Accounting Horizons*, pp. 101–03.

Kieso, D.E. and Weygandt, J.J. (1995), *Intermediate Accounting*, 8th ed., John Wiley, New York, NY, pp. 1368–70.

Kolb, B.A. and DeMong, R.F. (1988), *Principles of Financial Management*, 2nd ed., Business Publications, Plano, TX, pp. 88–90.

Larson, R., and Catton, W. Jr (1959), "Can the mail-back bias contribute to a study's validity?", *American Sociological Review*, Vol. XXIV, February, pp. 243–5.

Nickerson, C.A., Pointer, L.G. and Strawser, R.H. (1974), "Published forecasts: choice or obligation?", *Financial Executive*, pp. 70–3.

Pava, M.L. and Epstein, M.J. (1993), "How good is MD&A as an investment tool?", *Journal of Accountancy*, pp. 51–3.

Penman, S.H. (1980), "An empirical investigation of the voluntary disclosure of corporate earnings forecasts", *Journal of Accounting Research*, Vol. 18 No. 1, pp. 157–8.

Securities Exchange Commission (1978), "Guides for disclosure of projections of future economic performance", SAR 5992, EAR 34-15305 and Guide 62, Washington, DC, p. 7.

Sharma, S. (1996), *Applied Multivariate Techniques*, John Wiley, New York, NY.

(GAO/AID-96–98) United States General Accounting Office (1996), "The accounting profession, major issues: progress and concerns", (GAO/AID-96-98), Washington, DC.

Walther, L.M. (1993), "A case for required public forecasts", *Management Accountant*, pp. 46–9.

Webster, R.L. (1993), "Toward a normative model for financial reporting", in Amin, S.G. (Ed.), *Business Science: Theory and Practice, Proceedings of the 1993 National Conference of the Academy of Business Administration*, Maryland, pp. 27–34.

# Appendix: Financial Statement Analysis Survey Response Sheet

For each of the six items below, conduct your analytical assessment of the company based on the enclosed financial statements. Then, after conducting your analysis, indicate your level of confidence in your assessment using the scale below.

Self-confidence response scale:

Low                                                                High

1        2        3        4        5        6        7

*Circle your level of assessment/confidence for each item*

(1)  Ability of the firm to meet its short-term obligations as they come due

    1        2        3        4        5        6        7

    My confidence in making the above assessment is:

    1        2        3        4        5        6        7

(2)  Ability of the firm to meet its long-term obligations as they come due

    1        2        3        4        5        6        7

    My confidence in making the above assessment is:

    1        2        3        4        5        6        7

(3)  Ability of the firm to maintain its current cash dividend on common stock

    1        2        3        4        5        6        7

    My confidence in making the above assessment is:

    1        2        3        4        5        6        7

(4)  Ability of the firm to increase its cash dividend on common stock in the future

    1        2        3        4        5        6        7

    My confidence in making the above assessment is:

    1        2        3        4        5        6        7

(5)  Ability of the firm to increase its level of profitability in the future

    1        2        3        4        5        6        7

    My confidence in making the above assessment is:

    1        2        3        4        5        6        7

(6)  The overall future financial condition of the firm

    1        2        3        4        5        6        7

    My confidence in making the above assessment is:

    1        2        3        4        5        6        7

# MODULE 5

# Time Value of Money— Mathematics of Finance

*If you would know the value of money, go and try to borrow some.*

**Benjamin Franklin**

The foundation and perhaps most important concept in the study of financial management is time value of money, alternatively known as the mathematics of finance. This material should perhaps be stressed not just as a business or financial management concept but also as a topic of importance to all as a matter of personal survival.

In "Time Value of Money Made Simple: A Graphic Teaching Method" (2013), Valeria Martinez provides an integrated and graphic approach to presenting time value concepts. Martinez argues that the method, as discussed, provides students with a better understanding of the concept.

The arguments presented include the simple requirement that the applications of time value are varied and range in coverage over a variety of chapters in the basic introductory finance texts, which "makes it hard for students to grasp the concepts and find a structured method to solve these types of problems ..."

The Martinez paper presented in the *Journal of Financial Education* includes a "graphic template" for students to use as a means of visualizing time value of money problems. Such an approach, the author argues, provides a way for students to "consistently solve problems correctly in a timely manner."

It has often been said that a dollar today is worth more than a dollar tomorrow. Students often mistakenly assume that the only reason for this statement is that inflation causes a devaluation of the dollar's purchasing power. While inflation does, in fact, cause a dollar tomorrow to be worth less than today's dollar, that is not the primary reason that a dollar now is worth more than a dollar in the future. The real reason lies in the fact that dollars held today can be invested to earn interest. As a result, the present value of today's dollar is worth more than a dollar in the future because it has its own initial value plus any interest accumulated over the time the dollar has been invested, and that interest earned should include compensation for expected inflation over the investment period.

The recommended goal of business firms is the maximization of shareholder wealth or value. In order to make decisions to run a business effectively, management should therefore understand what shareholders require as compensation for their investment funds.

Financial theory suggests that when shareholders provide funding to business organizations, the compensation they require should provide compensation for both time and risk. Time value of money, therefore, deals with the compensation provided to investors for both the postponement of consumption and the acceptance of risk. Since an investor gives up the opportunity to immediately satisfy consumption needs, that investor requires a return for that consumption-postponement decision. The concept of the time value of money comes from this opportunity to invest that money obtained from foregone consumption.

In dealing with time value problems, it is important to realize that there are really only three basic dollar variables that are involved. These are the present value of a sum of money, the future value of a sum of money, or some annuity of money—a stream of money flows. In addition to the three dollar amounts that may be involved in a time value problem, there are also the variables of time and rate of interest.

To solve a time value problem, consider the following factors: first, the cash flows involved in the problem; second, the term or span of time covered by the problem; and third, the interest rate that must be paid per period to provide a return to the funding source.

The interest involved may be one of two types. It may be either simple interest, in which interest is paid on the principal amount only, or it may be compound interest, in which interest is paid not only on the principal amount but also on all interest earned since the beginning of the investment.

If our problem involves solving for the future value of a given present amount or principal, if we know that the term of investment spans $n$ periods and that the interest rate is $k$ percent, we can then solve for the future value of that investment.

It is possible to adjust the equations or the interest table factors for situations in which interest is compounded more than once per year or when we are investing for periods of less than one year. Simply adjust both the interest and the term for the amount of compounding that takes place. Calculators and spreadsheet macros will provide a way to do this automatically, but it is simple to just manually adjust the rates, times, and even the flows where necessary.

When interest is compounded more than once per year, it is implied that an investor will receive a rate of return that is actually greater than the stated annual rate or a borrower will actually be paying a rate of interest that is greater than the stated rate on a loan. This actual rate is referred to as the effective rate of interest. To determine the effective rate of interest, we simply allow for the number of periods of compounding that take place within a given year.

Since there are only three monetary or unit values that may be possible, there are six possible permutations or combinations of these three monetary or unit variables that may provide a problem format. The six possibilities include:

1. present value, given the future value
2. present value, given the annuity value
3. future value, given the present value
4. future value, given the annuity value
5. annuity value, given the present value
6. annuity value, given the future value

Many monetary decisions, both of an individual and business nature, involve determining the present value of some future or compound sum of money. In other words, we want to know what the future value or equivalent value is today. This process of finding the present value of a future sum is referred to as discounting. It should be noted that as long as the interest rate involved in the discounting process is a positive rate, the future value of the amount involved will always be greater than the present value.

Annuities, which are streams of level payments or withdrawals, are really only special cases of present value or future value computation. In the present value or future value problems examined previously, we always considered situations in which there were lump sum payments presented as either present values or future values. Now, however, we are considering the situation in which additional equal payments or withdrawals are made after the first period of investment. An annuity takes place for a specified number of periods, and the annuities themselves are the equal or level payments or withdrawals made each period.

There are basically two different types of annuities that may be encountered. These are the ordinary, or deferred, annuity and the annuity due. Ordinary annuities are annuities in which the initial payment or withdrawal in a stream of payments or withdrawals takes place at the end of the period. This is the most common situation. In an annuity due, the stream of payments or withdrawals takes place at the beginning of each period involved. The future value of an annuity is the amount the stream of payments would accumulate to if each and every investment were left to earn the stated interest for the total term of the investment as stated.

An annuity due situation, as previously stated, is exactly the same as an ordinary annuity situation in terms of computation, with the exception that each of the annuities takes place at the beginning of the period. This implies that interest earned or interest paid, as the case may be, must be greater for the annuity due situation than for the ordinary annuity.

This is related to the fact that the interest begins earning on every annuity at a faster rate than it does for an ordinary annuity. Why does the annuity due earn more interest? This is because the annuity stream begins at the beginning of the period rather than at the end of the period. Therefore, each annuity earns interest for one period more than in an ordinary annuity case.

The present value of an annuity is the lump sum payment that is required today as an equivalent of either the annuity itself or the future value of that annuity after $n$ periods of time.

Occasionally, we encounter situations in which the annuity to be received or to be paid is a perpetuity. A perpetuity is simply an annuity that will continue into infinity. Consol bonds, which have no maturity date and promise to pay interest into infinity, are an example of a perpetuity. In "Time Value of Money and Its Applications in Corporate Finance: A Technical Note on Linking Relationships between Formulas" (2009), Jeng-Hong Chen first stresses the importance of time value of money (TVM), noting that it is "the most important chapter in the basic corporate finance course in business education." Chen further notes that "students who really understand TVM concepts and formulas can learn better in TVM applications, such as bond valuation, stock valuation, cost of capital, and capital budgeting."

Chen then describes growing annuities and links the growing annuity formula with other related time value of money formulas. The intent of the discussion is to clarify and to stress the fact that time value of money equations are not independent of each other but rather are related.

In many individual and business dealings, we do not have the luxury of analyzing level annuities. Instead, we have series of cash inflows or outflows that vary from period to period.

In order to solve for the present or future value of these nonlevel or variable cash flows, we must approach the problem as a series of present value or future value problems rather than as an annuity. Each individual cash flow either must be compounded to the terminal date of the problem for a future value computation or, alternatively, must be discounted to the beginning of the term of investment to solve the problem for a present value.

Often, as in the case of loan payments, it is desirable to determine the annuity, given that we know the present or the future value of that annuity. Loans present just such a situation.

The amount of the annuities or the payments can be determined based on the loan amount, the number of payments required, the term of the loan, and the interest rate charged.

A unique time value problem occurs when we encounter compounding that takes place continuously. In such a situation, it is necessary to use an adaption of the time value table. Specifically, the problem encountered here is that as the number of compounding periods per annum increases, the effective rate of interest increases. In the case of continuous compounding and/or discounting, the period of compounding is so small that it approaches zero.

## Selected Readings

Chen, Jeng-Hong. "Time Value of Money and Its Applications in Corporate Finance: A Technical Note on Linking Relationships between Formulas." *American Journal of Business Education* 2, no. 6 (2009): 77–88.

Martinez, Valeria. "Time Value of Money Made Simple: A Graphic Teaching Method." *Journal of Financial Education* (Spring/Summer 2013): 96–117.

# Time Value of Money and its Applications in Corporate Finance

## A Technical Note on Linking Relationships Between Formulas

By Jeng-Hong Chen

...........................................................................................................................

## Abstract

Time Value of Money (TVM) is the most important chapter in the basic corporate finance course. It is imperative to understand TVM formulas because they imply important TVM concepts. Students who really understand TVM concepts and formulas can learn better in chapters of TVM applications. This technical note intends to present more complete TVM formulas and link their relationships from the growing annuity perspective to assist instructors in teaching and students in learning. Although TVM formulas are already available in the textbooks, this technical note provides another perspective of presenting and summarizing TVM formulas. The simplification or extension of the growing annuity formula to reach other TVM formulas is discussed in this note.

**Keywords:** Time Value of Money Formulas, The Growing Annuity

## 1. Introduction

Time Value of Money (TVM) is the most important chapter in the basic corporate finance course in business education.[1] Students who really understand TVM concepts and formulas can learn better in TVM applications, such as bond valuation, stock valuation, cost of capital, and capital budgeting. Due to the technological advancement, TVM formulas are built in the financial calculator and students can utilize its function keys to work TVM calculations efficiently. Although financial calculators help students compute answers faster, understanding TVM formulas is still imperative because these formulas imply important TVM concepts. With solid understanding of TVM formulas, students are able to identify what the questions ask and compute the correct answers by using either formulas or function keys.

Jeng-Hong Chen, "Time Value of Money and Its Applications in Corporate Finance: A Technical Note on Linking Relationships Between Formulas," *American Journal of Business Education*, vol. 2, no. 6, pp. 77–87. Copyright © 2009 by The Clute Institute. Reprinted with permission.

When learning TVM, students may see many formulas listed in the textbook. Some students may think these formulas are difficult to understand because they are confused with these formulas. In fact, most of TVM formulas are closely related. When introducing TVM formulas, the instructor can classify them under different conditions and link their relationships to organize them. This way is easier for students to better understand these formulas and the essence of TVM. Moreover, students can learn better in TVM applications, taught in later chapters.

TVM formulas are available in the textbooks. Some textbooks only list frequently used formulas while others include more formulas. In addition, different textbooks present and organize TVM formulas in different ways. This technical note intends to present more complete TVM formulas and link their relationships from the growing annuity perspective to assist instructors in teaching and students in learning. Although many TVM formulas listed in this technical note can be found in the textbooks, it provides another perspective of presenting and summarizing TVM formulas. The simplification or extension of the growing annuity formula to reach other TVM formulas is discussed in this note.

The remainder of this technical note is organized as follows. Section 2 describes the growing annuity. Section 3 simplifies or extends the growing annuity formula to reach other TVM formulas and links their relationships. Section 4 concludes this note with tables summarizing TVM formulas discussed in section 3.

## 2. The Growing Annuity

For the growing annuity, the payment is expected to grow at a constant rate for a finite number of periods. The formulas for the present value (PV) of growing annuity and the future value (FV) of growing annuity are shown as follows and derived in Appendix A.

$$PV_{growing\ annuity} = \frac{PMT\left(1 - \left(\frac{1+g}{1+i}\right)^n\right)}{i - g} \tag{1}$$

$$FV_{growing\ annuity} = \frac{PMT((1+i)^n - (1+g)^n)}{i - g} \tag{2}$$

Where

$PMT$: Payment at end of the first period (Payment one period from today)

$g$: the payment growth rate per period

$i$: the interest rate per period[2]

$n$: number of periods

# 3. Other TVM Formulas

Other TVM formulas can be achieved by simplifying or extending equation (1) or (2), the formula for the PV or FV of growing annuity.

## 3.1. Present Value Interest Factor Annuity (PVIFA$_{i,n}$)

Present value interest factor annuity (PVIFA$_{i,n}$) represents the PV of $1 payment (PMT = $1) occurred at end of each period for a finite number of periods. PVIFA$_{i,n}$, which requires PMT = $1 and g = 0 (zero growth rate because of the same amount of PMT each period), is a special case of PV of growing annuity. When PMT = $1 and g = 0, equation (1) will be simplified to the following equation (3).

$$PVIFA_{i,n} = \frac{\left(1 - \frac{1}{(1+i)^n}\right)}{i} \tag{3}$$

Many finance and accounting textbooks put PVIFA$_{i,n}$ table in the appendix. The numbers in table are made based on equation (3).

### 3.1.1. Present Value (PV) of Ordinary Annuity

PV of ordinary annuity means the PV of same PMT (PMT > $0) occurred at end of each period for a finite number of periods. PV of ordinary annuity, which requires g = 0 (zero growth rate because of the same amount of PMT each period), is a special case of PV of growing annuity. To get PV of ordinary annuity, we can either simplify equation (1) by assuming g = 0 or use PMT to multiply by equation (3).

So, let g = 0 in equation (1) or use PMT to multiply by equation (3). PV of ordinary annuity can be reached as follow.

$$PV_{ordinary\ annuity} = \frac{PMT\left(1 - \frac{1}{(1+i)^n}\right)}{i} = PMT \times PVIFA_{i,r} \tag{4}$$

### 3.1.2. Present Value (PV) of Annuity Due

Comparing annuity due with ordinary annuity, we can find the following relationship.

$$PV_{annuity\ due} = PV_{ordinary\ annuity} \times (1+i) \tag{5}$$

The detailed proof of equation (5) is shown in Appendix B.

Use equation (3) to multiply by (1 + i). We get

$$PVIFA_{i,n} \times (1+i) = \frac{\left(1 - \frac{1}{(1+i)^n}\right)}{i} \times (1+i) = \frac{\left((1+i) - \frac{1}{(1+i)^{n-1}}\right)}{i} = \frac{\left(1 - \frac{1}{(1+i)^{n-1}}\right)}{i} + 1 = PVIFA_{i,n-1} + 1 \qquad (6)$$

Combine equation (4), (5), and (6). PV of annuity due can be written as follow.

$$PV_{annuity\ due} = PMT \times PVIFA_{i,n} \times (1+i) = PMT \times (PVIFA_{i,n-1} + 1) \qquad (7)$$

## 3.2. Future Value Interest Factor Annuity (FVIFA$_{i,n}$)

Future value interest factor annuity (FVIFA$_{i,n}$) represents the future value (FV) of $1 payment (PMT = $1) occurred at end of each period for a finite number of periods. FVIFA$_{i,n}$, which requires PMT = $1 and g = 0 (zero growth rate because of the same amount of PMT each period), is a special case of FV of growing annuity. When PMT = $1 and g = 0, equation (2) will be simplified to the following equation (8).[3]

$$FVIFA_{i,n} = \frac{((1+i)^n - 1)}{i} \qquad (8)$$

Many finance and accounting textbooks also put FVIFA$_{i,n}$ table in the appendix. The numbers in table are made based on equation (8).

### 3.2.1. Future Value (FV) of Ordinary Annuity

FV of ordinary annuity means the FV of same PMT (PMT > $0) occurred at end of each period for a finite number of periods. FV of ordinary annuity, which requires g = 0 (zero growth rate because of the same amount of PMT each period), is a special case of FV of growing annuity. To get FV of ordinary annuity, we can either simplify equation (2) by assuming g = 0 or use PMT to multiply by equation (8).

So, let g = 0 in equation (2) or use PMT to multiply by equation (8). FV of ordinary annuity can be reached as follow.

$$FV_{ordinary\ annuity} = \frac{PMT((1+i)^n - 1)}{i} = PMT \times FVIFA_{i,n} \qquad (9)$$

### 3.2.2. Future Value (FV) of Annuity Due

Comparing annuity due with ordinary annuity, we can find the following relationship.

$$FV_{annuity\ due} = FV_{ordinary\ annuity} \times (1+i) \qquad (10)$$

The detailed proof of equation (10) is also shown in Appendix B.

Use equation (8) to multiply by $(1 + i)$. We get

$$FVIFA_{i,n} \times (1+i) = \frac{((1+i)^n - 1)}{i} \times (1+i) = \frac{((1+i)^{n+1} - (1+i))}{i} = \frac{((1+i)^{n+1} - 1)}{i} - 1 = FVIFA_{i,n+1} - 1 \quad (11)$$

Combine equation (9), (10), and (11). FV of annuity due can be written as follow.

$$FV_{annuity\ due} = PMT \times FVIFA_{i,n} \times (1+i) = PMT \times (FVIFA_{i,n+1} - 1) \quad (12)$$

## 3.3. Perpetuity and Stock Valuation
## (Zero Growth Common Stock and Preferred Stock)

### 3.3.1. Perpetuity

Perpetuity defines that the same amount of PMT per period occurs forever. Therefore, PMT is the same for each period ($g = 0$, zero growth rate) and the number of periods is infinite ($n \rightarrow \infty$).

Again, based on equation (1), when $g = 0$ and $n \rightarrow \infty$, $\left(\frac{1+g}{1+i}\right)^n = \frac{1}{(1+i)^n} \rightarrow 0$.[4] So, the present value of perpetuity will become

$$PV_{perpetuity} = \frac{PMT}{i} \quad (13)$$

### 3.3.2. Stock Valuation: Common Stock (Zero Growth Model)

Zero growth common stock assumes that the expected future dividend per period will be the same and it will last forever. Actually, this is the same situation as what we discussed for perpetuity. The formula to calculate the value of stock today ($P_0$) should be the same as equation (13) except using different notations.

$$P_0 = \frac{D}{k_s} \quad (14)$$

In equation (14), D, the expected future dividend per share per period, is like PMT in equation (13) and $k_s$, the required rate of return on common stock per period, is like i in equation (13).

### 3.3.3. Stock Valuation: Preferred Stock

Preferred stock has the same situation as perpetuity and zero growth common stock. The fixed amount of dividend is expected to last forever. Again, the formula to calculate the value of preferred stock today ($V_p$) should be the same as equation (13) and (14) except using different notations.

$$V_p = \frac{D_p}{k_p} \qquad (15)$$

In equation (15), $D_p$, the fixed amount of preferred stock dividend per share per period, is like PMT in equation (13) and D in equation (14). $k_p$, the required rate of return on preferred stock per period, is like i in equation (13) and $k_s$ in equation (14).[5]

## 3.4. Stock Valuation: Common Stock (Constant Growth Model)

The constant growth model assumes that the stock dividend per period is expected to grow at the constant rate (g) forever (n → ∞) and the required rate of return should be greater than the dividend growth rate ($k_s$ > g). The constant growth model is like the growing perpetuity.

Again, based on equation (1) and use $D_1$ $(= D_0(1 + g))$ and $k_s$ to substitute for PMT and i, respectively.

When $k_s$ > g and n → ∞, $\left(\dfrac{1+g}{1+k_s}\right)^n \to 0$. The value of stock today ($P_0$) will be as follow.

$$P_0 = \frac{D_1}{k_s - g} = \frac{D_0(1+g)}{k_s - g} \qquad (16)$$

Where

$D_0$: Today's (just paid) dividend

$D_1$: Dividend at the end of period 1 (Dividend one period from today)[6]

Equation (16) can be extended to the following equation (17) to calculate the value of stock t periods from today, $P_t$.

$$P_t = \frac{D_{t+1}}{k_s - g} = \frac{D_0(1+g)^{t+1}}{k_s - g} = \frac{D_0(1+g)}{k_s - g} \times (1+g)^t = P_0(1+ \qquad (17)$$

## 3.5. Two-Stage Growth Stock Valuation

Some firms have supernormal growth rate for the first few years due to rapid expansion and later go back to the normal growth rate, which continues forever. This is the case of two-stage growth stock. For two-stage growth stock, the dividend growth rate is $g_1$ for the first stage (finite number of t periods). The dividend growth rate for the second stage is constant at $g_2$ from period t + 1 until infinity. The situation in the first stage is like the growing annuity so equation (1) can be used in the first stage to compute the PV. The constant growth model can be applied to the second stage. $P_t$, the value of stock t periods from today, is $D_{t+1}/(k_s - g_2)$ based on equation (17). $D_{t+1}$, the dividend per share at period t + 1, should be $D_0(1 + g_1)^t(1 + g_2)$ in this two-stage growth case. To find the PV of $P_t$, we need to discount $P_t$ back t periods. The formula for the value of two-stage growth stock today ($P_0$) can be written as follow.

$$P_0 = \frac{D_1\left[1 - \left(\frac{1+g_1}{1+k_s}\right)^t\right]}{k_s - g_1} + \frac{P_t}{(1+k_s)^t}$$

$$= \frac{D_1\left[1 - \left(\frac{1+g_1}{1+k_s}\right)^t\right]}{k_s - g_1} + \frac{\frac{D_{t+1}}{k_s - g_2}}{(1+k_s)^t} \tag{18}$$

$$= \frac{D_0(1+g_1)\left[1 - \left(\frac{1+g_1}{1+k_s}\right)^t\right]}{k_s - g_1} + \frac{\frac{D_0(1+g_1)^t(1+g_2)}{k_s - g_2}}{(1+k_s)^t}$$

In equation (18), $g_1$ can be greater than $k_s$ but $g_2$ must be less than $k_s$. This means the supernormal growth rate of the first stage can be greater than the required rate of return but the normal growth rate of the second stage must be less than the required rate of return.

## 3.6. Bond Valuation

The value of bond is the sum of present value of future coupon payments at end of each period and the present value of face value (par value) at maturity. The yield (yield to maturity) represents the annual rate of return an investor can earn if he or she holds the bond until maturity. The annual coupon bond makes the coupon payment at end of each year and the face value (par value) payment at maturity. The value of annual coupon bond ($V_B$) is calculated as follow.[7]

$$V_B = \sum_{t=1}^{N} \frac{PMT}{(1+y)^t} + \frac{F}{(1+y)^N} = PMT \times (PVIFA_{y,N}) + \frac{F}{(1+y)^N}$$

$$= \frac{PMT\left[1 - \frac{1}{(1+y)^N}\right]}{y} + \frac{F}{(1+y)^N} \tag{19}$$

Where

N = Number of years

PMT = Annual coupon payment (= annual coupon rate × face value)

y = Bond's yield (or called yield to maturity)

F = Bond's face value (par value), which is generally assumed $1,000

The present value of future coupon payments at end of each year is like the present value of ordinary annuity so equation (4) can be used in this part. The present value of face value (par value) at maturity is like the present value of a lump sum, which is rearranged from equation (C1).

### 3.6.1. Internal Rate of Return (IRR)

Again, bond valuation formula can be written as follow.

$$
\begin{aligned}
V_B &= \sum_{t=1}^{N} \frac{PMT}{(1+y)^t} + \frac{F}{(1+y)^N} \\
&= \frac{PMT}{1+y} + \frac{PMT}{(1+y)^2} + \frac{PMT}{(1+y)^3} + \cdots + \frac{PMT}{(1+y)^{N-1}} + \frac{(PMT+F)}{(1+y)^N}
\end{aligned}
\tag{20}
$$

Rearrange equation (20) by moving $V_B$ to the right of "=" to get

$$
0 = -V_B + \frac{PMT}{1+y} + \frac{PMT}{(1+y)^2} + \frac{PMT}{(1+y)^3} + \cdots + \frac{PMT}{(1+y)^{N-1}} + \frac{(PMT+F)}{(1+y)^N}
\tag{21}
$$

The internal rate of return (IRR) method, often used in the capital budgeting, defines that IRR is the discount rate, which makes the net present value (NPV) equal to zero. Based on its definition, IRR can be expressed as follow.

$$
0 = CF_0 + \frac{CF_1}{1+IRR} + \frac{CF_2}{(1+IRR)^2} + \frac{CF_3}{(1+IRR)^3} + \cdots + \frac{CF_{N-1}}{(1+IRR)^{N-1}} + \frac{CF_N}{(1+IRR)^N}
\tag{22}
$$

Comparing equation (21) and (22), we see that the initial investment ($CF_0$, negative (cash outflow)) is like the value of bond that investors pay for today ($-V_B$) and IRR is like the yield (y) in bond valuation. It is tedious and time consuming to find y manually since we need to use trial and error method. We usually use the financial calculator's function keys to find y. In addition to using $\boxed{I/Y}$ key to find y, we can use $\boxed{IRR}$ key to find y because the yield is like the internal rate of return.

# 4. Conclusion

From the discussion in the previous section, we can know that TVM formulas are closely related. Based on different conditions, we can simplify or extend the formula of growing annuity to reach other formulas. The following tables summarize TVM formulas and link their relationships discussed in the previous section.

**Table 8.1** Summary of PV Formulas

| Under the Condition of | PV of Growing Annuity [eq (1)] becomes | Extension |
|---|---|---|
| PMT = $1, g = 0, and n is finite | • $PVIFA_{i, n}$ [eq (3)] | • $PVIFA_{i, n} \times (1 + i) = PVIFA_{i, n-1} + 1$ [eq (6)] |
| PMT > $0 (PMT ≠ $1), g = 0, and n is finite | • PV of Ordinary Annuity [eq (4)] | • PV of Ordinary Annuity × (1 + i) = PV of Annuity Due [eq (5)] <br> • PV of Annuity Due = PMT × $PVIFA_{i, n} \times (1 + i)$ = PMT × $(PVIFA_{i, n-1} + 1)$ [eq (7)] |
| PMT > $0, g = 0, and n is infinite (n → ∞) | • PV of Perpetuity [eq (13)] <br> • Zero Growth Model [eq (14)] <br> • Value of Preferred Stock [eq (15)] | |
| PMT > $0, and n is infinite (n → ∞) | • Constant Growth Model [eq (16)] | • $P_t = D_{t+1}/(k_s - g) = P_0(1 + g)^t$ [eq (17)] |

The equation number for each formula, eq (#), is shown in the bracket [ ].

**Table 8.2** Summary of FV Formulas

| Under the Condition of | FV of Growing Annuity [eq (2)] becomes | Extension |
|---|---|---|
| PMT = $1, g = 0, and n is finite | • $FVIFA_{i,n}$ [eq (8)] | • $FVIFA_{i, n} \times (1 + i) = FVIFA_{i, n+1} - 1$ [eq (11)] |
| PMT > $0 (PMT ≠ $1), g = 0, and n is finite | • FV of Ordinary Annuity [eq (9)] | • FV of Ordinary Annuity × (1 + i) = FV of Annuity Due [eq (10)] <br> • FV of Annuity Due = PMT × $FVIFA_{i, n} \times$ (1 + i) = PMT × $(FVIFA_{i, n+1} - 1)$ [eq (12)] |

The equation number for each formula, eq (#), is shown in the bracket [ ].

**Table 8.3** Two-Stage Growth Stock Valuation and Bond Valuation

| Combination | Valuation |
|---|---|
| 1st Stage: PV of Growing Annuity<br>2nd Stage: Constant Growth Model (Extension) | Two-Stage Growth Stock Valuation [eq (18)] |
| 1st Part: PV of Ordinary Annuity<br>2nd Part: PV of a Lump Sum | Bond Valuation [eq (19)]<br>(Implication: Yield is the IRR.) [eq (20), (21), (22)] |

The equation number for each formula, eq (#), is shown in the bracket [ ].

## Author Information

**Jeng-Hong Chen** is a faculty member at College of Business, Albany State University. He has experience of teaching corporate finance, business statistics, and principles of microeconomics. His recent research interests include fixed income securities and international finance.

## References

Brigham, Eugene F. and Joel F. Houston, *Fundamentals of Financial Management, Concise 5th Edition*, Thomson South-Western, Mason, Ohio, 2006.

Ross, Stephen A., Randolph W. Westerfield, and Bradford D. Jordan, *Fundamentals of Corporate Finance*, 8th, McGraw-Hill/Irwin, New York, New York, 2008.

# Appendix A: Derivation of the Present Value (PV) of Growing Annuity and the Future Value (FV) of Growing Annuity

A simple way learned in high school mathematics to derive a geometric series can be as follows.

Suppose a geometric sequence is $a, ar, ar^2, ar^3, \ldots, ar^{n-1}$ ($n$ terms and $r$ as common ratio). Let $S$ be a geometric series, which is the sum of terms of a geometric sequence.

$$S = a + ar + ar^2 + ar^3 + \ldots + ar^{n-1} \tag{A1}$$

$$rS = ar + ar^2 + ar^3 + \ldots + ar^{n-1} + a \qquad (A2)$$

(A1) – (A2) [Subtract equation (A2) from equation (A1)], then gives

$$(1-r)S = a(1-r^n)$$

Therefore, $S = \dfrac{a(1-r^n)}{1-r}$ \qquad (A3)

For the growing annuity, the payment (PMT), occurred at the end of each period, is expected to grow at the constant rate (g) for a finite number of periods (n is finite). i is the interest rate per period. Therefore, the PV of growing annuity is calculated as follow.

$$PV_{growing\ annuity} = \frac{PMT}{1+i} + \frac{PMT(1+g)}{(1+i)^2} + \frac{PMT(1+g)^2}{(1+i)^3} + \ldots + \frac{PMT(1+g)}{(1+i)^n}$$

Since $PV_{growing\ annuity}$ is a geometric series, we can apply it to equation (A3).

Substitute $S = PV_{growing\ annuity}$ $a = \dfrac{PMT}{1+i}$, and $r = \dfrac{1+g}{1+i}$ in equation (A3). Then, equation (1) is derived as follow.

$$PV_{growing\ annuity} = \frac{\dfrac{PMT}{1+i} \times \left[1 - \left(\dfrac{1+g}{1+i}\right)^n\right]}{1 - \dfrac{1+g}{1+i}} = \frac{\dfrac{PMT}{1+i} \times \left[1 - \left(\dfrac{1+g}{1+i}\right)^n\right]}{\dfrac{i-g}{1+i}} = \frac{PMT\left[1 - \left(\dfrac{1+g}{1+i}\right)^n\right]}{i-g}$$

The FV of growing annuity is calculated as follow.

$$FV_{growing\ annuity} = PMT(1+i)^{n-1} + PMT(1+g)(1+i)^{n-2} + PMT(1+g)^2(1+i)^{n-3} + \ldots + PMT(1+g)^{n-1}$$

Since $FV_{growing\ annuity}$ is a geometric series as well, we can apply it to equation (A3).

Substitute $S = FV_{growing\ annuity}$, $a = PMT(1+i)^{n-1}$, and $r = \dfrac{1+g}{1+i}$ in equation (A3). Then, equation (2) is derived as follow.

$$FV_{growing\ annuity} = \frac{PMT(1+i)^{n-1}\left[1-\left(\dfrac{1+g}{1+i}\right)^n\right]}{1-\dfrac{1+g}{1+i}} = \frac{PMT(1+i)^{n-1}\left[1-\left(\dfrac{1+g}{1+i}\right)^n\right]}{\dfrac{i-g}{1+i}}$$

$$= \frac{PMT(1+i)^{n}\left[1-\left(\dfrac{1+g}{1+i}\right)^n\right]}{i-g} = \frac{PMT((1+i)^n - (1+g)^n)}{i-g}$$

# Appendix B: Relationships between Ordinary Annuity and Annuity Due

Ordinary annuity represents the same amount of payment (PMT) at end of each period for a finite number of periods (n). The time line of ordinary annuity is as follow.

```
0                1                2                3        ...    n − 1              n
|----------------|----------------|----------------|---------------|----------------|
              PMT              PMT              PMT       ...     PMT              PMT
```

Based on the above time line, PV of ordinary annuity and FV of ordinary annuity can be expressed as follows.

$$PV_{ordinary\ annuity} = \frac{PMT}{1+i} + \frac{PMT}{(1+i)^2} + \frac{PMT}{(1+i)^3} + ... + \frac{PMT}{(1+i)^{n-1}} + \frac{PMT}{(1+i)^n} \qquad (B1)$$

$$FV_{ordinary\ annuity} = PMT(1+i)^{n-1} + PMT(1+i)^{n-2} + PMT(1+i)^{n-3} + ... + PMT(1+i) + PMT \qquad (B2)$$

Annuity due represents the same amount of payment (PMT) at beginning of each period for a finite number of periods (n). The time line of annuity due is as follow.

```
0                1                2                3        ...    n − 1              n
|----------------|----------------|----------------|---------------|----------------|
PMT            PMT              PMT              PMT       ...     PMT
```

Based on the above time line, PV of annuity due and FV of annuity due can be expressed as follows.

$$PV_{annuity\ due} = PMT + \frac{PMT}{1+i} + \frac{PMT}{(1+i)^2} + \frac{PMT}{(1+i)^3} + \ldots + \frac{PMT}{(1+i)^{n-1}} \qquad (B3)$$

$$FV_{annuity\ due} = PMT(1+i)^n + PMT(1+i)^{n-1} + PMT(1+i)^{n-2} + PMT(1+i)^{n-3} + \ldots + PMT(1+i) \quad (B4)$$

Comparing equation (B1) with (B3), we can find that if (B1) × (1 + i), it will be (B3).
$PV_{annuity\ due} = PV_{ordinary\ annuity} \times (1+i)$      Thus, equation (5) is proved.
Comparing equation (B2) with (B4), we can find that if (B2) × (1 + i), it will be (B4).
$PV_{annuity\ due} = PV_{ordinary\ annuity} \times (1+i)$      Thus, equation (10) is proved.

## Appendix C: Find FVIFA$_{i,n}$ by Compounding PVIFA$_{i,n}$ for n Periods

The most basic TVM formula is

$$FV = PV(1+i)^t \qquad (C1)^{[8]}$$

To find FVIFA$_{i,n}$, we can utilize equation (C1) to compound PVIFA$_{i,n}$ for n periods. Substitute PVIFA$_{i,n}$ (equation (3)) for PV and plug in equation (C1). Therefore,

$$FVIFA_{i,n} = \frac{\left(1 - \dfrac{1}{(1+i)^n}\right)}{i} \times (1+i)^n = \frac{\left((1+i)^n - \dfrac{(1+i)^n}{(1+i)^n}\right)}{i} = \frac{((1+i)^n - 1)}{i}$$

## Endnotes

1. To emphasize the importance of TVM, Brigham and Houston (2006) move TVM from Chapter 6 to Chapter 2 to allow students longer time to digest TVM materials before learning TVM application chapters and add more sections in the content of TVM chapter to help students better understand TVM. Ross et al. (2008) use two chapters to introduce TVM and add real world examples and end-of-chapter minicase to enhance TVM content.

2. When PV (FV) of growing annuity is calculated, $i$ is the discount (compound) rate.

3. Another way to find FVIFA$_{i,n}$ is to compound PVIFA$_{i,n}$ for n periods. See the details in Appendix C.

4. Similarly, equation (13) can be achieved based on equation (4). When $n \to \infty$, $\dfrac{1}{(1+i)^n} \to 0$. Then, equation (4) will become equation (13).

5. Equation (15) can be rearranged as $k_p = \dfrac{D_p}{V_p}$. $k_p$ is the required rate of return on preferred stock from the investors' perspective and it is the cost of preferred stock from the firm's perspective. This formula can be used as a component for calculating the firm's weighted average cost of capital if the firm issues the preferred stock.

6. Equation (16) can be rearranged as $k_s = \dfrac{D_1}{P_0} + g \cdot k_s$, which consists of the dividend yield ($D_1/P_0$) and the capital gains yield (g), is the required rate of return on common equity from the investors' perspective. $k_s$ is the cost of common equity from the firm's perspective. This formula can be used as a component for calculating the firm's weighted average cost of capital.

7. Although most bonds are semiannual coupon bonds, for simplicity the annual coupon bond is used for demonstration. We can modify equation (19) by replacing N with 2N, replacing PMT with PMT/2, and replacing y with y/2 to find the value of semiannual coupon bond.

8. We can rearrange equation (C1) to get $PV = \dfrac{FV}{(1+i)^n}$, $i = \left(\dfrac{FV}{PV}\right)^{\frac{1}{n}} - 1$, or $n = \dfrac{\ln\left(\dfrac{FV}{PV}\right)}{\ln(1+i)}$.

# Time Value of Money Made Simple

## A Graphic Teaching Method

By Valeria Martinez

..........................................................................................................................................

A presented integrated time value of money graphic method helps students visualize and achieve a clearer understanding of time value of money. This tool helps students determine what type of time value of money problem they are dealing with as well as identify the variables involved in the problem. This method can be used as a visual aid to help students solve a problem when working with formulas or a financial calculator, or it can be used as the basis for a personalized time value of money spreadsheet template. This allows the students to understand the intuition behind time value of money concepts and problems and also helps them become proficient in the use of a financial calculator and/or spreadsheets to solve the problems. The tool developed [...] will help our students be better prepared for careers in the fields of finance and accounting.

## Introduction

Time value of money is a very important topic in finance because it represents the building block and basic tool for many other fundamental topics such as bond valuation, stock valuation, capital budgeting, and options valuation. Unfortunately it is also a very challenging topic for students.

For many of our students, understanding what the time value of money problem is asking and what variables are involved in the problem can be a daunting task. And even though they may cover time value of money in more than one course, for many of them it continues to be a challenging theme.

Valeria Martinez, "Time Value of Money Made Simple: A Graphic Teaching Method," *Journal of Financial Education*, vol. 39, no. 1/2, pp. 96–117. Copyright © 2013 by Valeria Martinez. Reprinted with permission.

Time value of money is commonly covered in introductory or basic finance courses, and is the stepping stone for more advanced topics. Most introductory finance books currently address the topic using a combination of formulas, time lines, and boxes of spreadsheet and financial calculator examples. However, time value of money problems are presented in a disintegrated manner, and sometimes they are spread out in more than one chapter or topic of the book (Jalbert, 2002). This makes it hard for the students to grasp the concepts and find a structured method to solve these types of problems, as well as understand the differences and similarities between solving annuity, lump sum, perpetuity or mixed cash flow stream problems.

The purpose of this work is to provide a graphic template to help students visualize the problem at hand and achieve a clearer understanding of time value of money so they can consistently solve problems correctly in a timely manner. The tool that I develop throughout this paper is a visual aid that helps students determine what type of time value of money problem they are dealing with and also helps them identify the variables involved in the problem.

The time value of money graphic method can be used as a visual aid to help students solve a time value of money problem when working with a financial calculator or formulas, or it can be used as the basis for a spreadsheet template for students to build their personalized time value of money spreadsheet.

## Literature Review

Very little work has been done on the topic of alternative ways to teach time value of money. Eddie and Swanson (1996) develop a methodology to teach time value of money which focuses on the use of timelines and the concept of inflows and outflows of funds. Their method avoids any type of memorization or use of algebraic formulas. Jalbert (2002) finds that the most popular finance books lack precise definitions and organization of time value of money topics throughout the texts. He develops a technique to help students better grasp time value of money. His technique involves the use of time lines, a flow chart, and a matrix.

Jalbert, Jalbert, and Chan (2004) continue the discussion from Jalbert (2002) and offer a simplified version of the technique presented in Jalbert (2002) targeted to students who have difficulty understanding the annuity concept.

While Eddie and Swanson (1996), Jalbert (2002), and Jalbert et al. (2004) are useful alternative techniques, they are not fully integrated approaches because they rely on a combination of tools to explain time value of money. In addition, these methods do not address variable identification. And while their conceptual approach may be useful to some students, these methods do not support the use of financial calculators or spreadsheets, a necessary skill in today's business world.

I add value to existing literature by proposing an integrated time value of money graphic method that will help students identify the type of time value of money technique as well as the variables involved in a time value of money problem. This chart can be used as a visual aid in conjunction with the time value of money formulas which help students understand the time value of money concepts and solve problems. The chart can also be used along with financial calculators, or as a spreadsheet template for students to solve their time value of money problems in. This allows the students to understand the intuition behind time value of money concepts and problems and also become proficient in the use of a financial calculator and/or spreadsheets to solve the problems. The tool developed [...] will help to better equip students for a career in the fields of finance and accounting.

## Time Value of Money

Time value of money is an essential stepping stone for more advanced finance topics and also one of the most challenging and confusing topics for the introductory course students. Personally I like to introduce the topic using both a visual aid—the time value of money tree—along with the basic formulas for time value of money. Once students have a basic understanding of these concepts, then I introduce spreadsheets and financial calculators as a more efficient tool for solving time value of money problems.

There are variations of some of these formulas, but as an example, I enlist the basic lump sum, annuity, and perpetuity formulas [...].

Future value of a lump sum:

$$FV = PV \times (1+i)^n \tag{1}$$

Present value of a lump sum:

$$PV = \frac{FV}{(1+i)^n} \tag{2}$$

Future value of an annuity:

$$FV = \left( \frac{(1+i)^n - 1}{i} \right) \times PMT \tag{3}$$

Present value of an annuity:

$$PV = \left( \frac{1 - \frac{1}{(1+i)^n}}{i} \right) \times PMT \tag{4}$$

Perpetuity:

$$PV = \frac{PMT}{i} \tag{5}$$

Where:
FV = future value, PV = present value, i = interest rate, n = number of time periods, and PMT = payment.

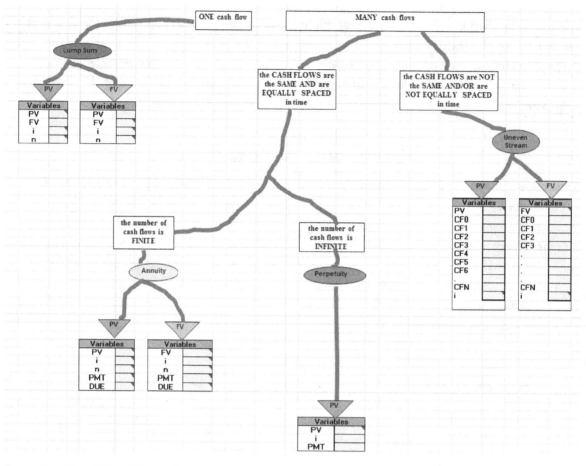

**Figure 9.1:** Time Value of Money Tree

In order to give some structure and breakdown a time value of money problem into simple steps, we will use the time value of money tree (Figure 9.1) to guide us to the specific time value of money situation we are dealing with and help us determine what variables we have information on. The basis of the analysis is a set of five questions which will lead us down the different branches of the time value of money tree:

1. Does the problem involve one or many cash flows?

2. Are the cash flows the same or different? Are the cash flows equally spaced in time?

3. Are the cash flows finite or infinite?

4. Is this a present value or a future value problem?

5. What variables do we have information on?

In the following sections we will discuss five different classifications for time value of money problems: lump sums, annuities, perpetuities, mixed streams of cash flows, and combination problems.

## Lump Sums

This is a time value of money problem that involves moving a single cash flow in time. Assume the following situation: Jane has saved $1,000 for her college graduation trip. With this money, Jane will purchase a certificate of deposit (CD) that earns 5% interest annually. She plans to graduate from college in 2 years. How much money will Jane have in the bank when she graduates? We now start answering our set of questions which take us through the branches of our time value of money tree.

1. Does the problem involve one or many cash flows? The problem involves moving a single cash flow in time. Based on this answer, we move down the left branch of the tree and can skip to question 4.

4. Is this a present value or a future value problem? The problem talks about a future purchase so we infer it is a future value problem. We now find ourselves on the right side of the left branch of the tree. Here we can see that a future value of a lump sum problem involves four variables. Since we have only one equation to find our answer, we can only solve for one unknown at a time. This means that we have information about three of the four variables.

5. What variables do we have information on? Today Jane has $1,000; this is our present value (PV). She can earn 5% on her CD; this is the interest rate (i). She will invest her money for two years, so n = 2. We want to find the future value of her money (FV).

At this point students can solve the problem using the formula for future value of a lump sum, a financial calculator, or a spreadsheet.[1] In sum, PV = 1,000, FV = ?, i = 5%, and n = 2, so FV = $1,102.50. If Jane invests $1,000 for 2 years at a 5% interest rate, at the end of the second year she'll have $1,102.50 in her bank account.

The time value of money tree makes it easy for the students to identify the type of problem it is and variables used in it so they can find a solution with any of the mentioned tools.

A similar procedure follows when we deal with present value lump sum problems. Nonetheless it is important to point out to the students that time value of money not only involves finding future

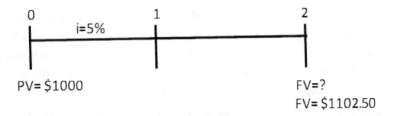

**Figure 9.2:** Time Line for Future Value of a Lump Sum

values and present values, but also finding the interest rate or time periods in which we will save or receive a cash flow(s). To do this we apply the same procedure.[2]

## Annuities

Annuities represent a stream of identical cash flows equally spaced out in time. A lot of the cash flows we deal with in real life are annuities. Examples of outflows include rent, tuition, loan payments, and systematic investment plans like a 401K; while examples of inflows include salaries, pensions, dividends and regular investment withdrawals. All of these can be identical cash flows we pay or receive at equal intervals of time.

A big difference between annuities and lump sums is that in addition to the four variables we have been talking about: future value (FV), present value (PV), interest rate (i) and number of time periods (n), we now have an additional variable called payment (PMT), which represents the annuity amount. If we look at our annuity formula we can see we are still in a situation where we have a single equation to find our answer, thus we can solve for any of our variables, but only one at a time. In looking at the formulas for future value and present value of an annuity, we should also note that when dealing with a present value of an annuity problem, the future value (FV) is not involved. And when solving a future value of an annuity problem, the present value (PV) is not involved in the problem. So, in an annuity problem we will be dealing with 4 variables at a time. PV, i, n and PMT, if it is the present value of an annuity and FV, i, n, and PMT, if it is the future value of an annuity.

Example: Mary will invest $200 each year for the next 3 years in a mutual fund that has an expected annual return of 10%. How much will Mary have saved by the end of three years?

1. Does the problem involve one or many cash flows? This problem involves many cash flows, since Mary will invest money for multiple years. This takes us to the right branch of our tree.

2. Are the cash flows the same or different? Are the cash flows equally space out in time? The cash flows are the same, $200 every year, and they are equally spaced out in time, one cash flow per year. Therefore we take the left side of the "many cash flows" branch.

3. Are the cash flows finite or infinite? The cash flows are finite; they are 3, since Mary will save money for 3 years. At this point we know we are talking about an annuity problem. But we still need to find out more information to determine the answer

4. Is this a present value or a future value problem? This is a future value problem. We want to know how much money Mary will have in the *future*-in 3 years. We are on the lowest right hand side of the annuity branch-or future value. The branch confirms the four variables involved in the problem: FV, i, n, and PMT. We need to find information on three of these variables to be able to solve for the fourth.

5. What variables do we have information on? i = 10%, n = 3, PMT = $200. Thus we are solving for future value (FV). Using the future value of annuity formula, A spreadsheet or a financial calculator we find that FV = 662. If Mary saves $200 every year for the next 3 years at a 10% interest rate, at the end of the 3rd year she will have $662 dollars.

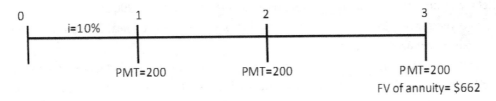

**Figure 9.3:** Time Line for Future Value of Annuity

## Annuities Due

So far we've implicitly assumed that the cash flows take place at the end of the year. Thus, Mary will be putting $200 into her investment account at the end of each year. But what happens if she decides to save her money at the beginning of each year instead? Let's take the first year's cash flow as an example. If Mary invests this cash flow at the end of the first year by the end of the third year she will have earned two years of interest on this cash flow (interest in the second and third years). On the other hand if Mary invests the first year's cash flow at the beginning of the first year, by the end of the 3rd year she'll have earned three years of interest (interest for years one, two, and three). This means that by investing at the beginning of the year, she will receive an extra year of interest. The same thing will happen with the cash flows in years 2 and 3. Mary will earn one extra period of interest on the year 2 and year 3 cash flows as compared to a regular annuity.

When we have an annuity with cash flows taking place at the beginning of the time period, it is called an annuity due. In this case, we use the same formulas and procedures as for regular annuities but we must adjust them to reflect the fact that the cash flows take place at the beginning of the time periods. From the example above it is clear to see the adjustment involves adding an extra period of interest to each of the annuity cash flows. Thus our annuity formulas for future and present value must be multiplied by $(1 + i)$ to adjust for this extra period of interest.[3] When using a financial calculator or spreadsheet we can apply this same adjustment.[4] We must multiply our present value of annuity or future value of annuity by $(1 + i)$ to account for the fact that the cash flows take place at the beginning of the year and not at the end of the time period.

Future value of an annuity due:

$$FV = \left( \frac{(1+i)^n - 1}{i} \right) \times PMT \times (1+i) \tag{3a}$$

Present value of an annuity due:

$$PV = \left( \frac{1 - \dfrac{1}{(1+i)^n}}{i} \right) \times PMT \times (1+i) \tag{4a}$$

Let's take our previous example and assume that instead of saving $200 at the end of the year for the next 3 years, Mary saves $200 at the beginning of the year for the next 3 years. How does this change our procedure? Our answer?

Note that the steps and information used to solve an annuity due problem are the same as those needed to solve a regular annuity problem. We are located at exactly the same branch of our time value of money tree as in the case of a regular annuity. The difference is that in the case of an annuity due, we must adjust our answer by multiplying the future value of a regular annuity by $(1 + i)$ to turn it into the future value of an annuity due. In our time value of money tree, the adjustment occurs in the annuity variable cell titled "DUE." This is where we include the term $(1 + i)$. In this example, DUE = $(1.10)$. Then, using the future value of annuity formula, a spreadsheet or a financial calculator we find that the future value of the annuity due is: FV annuity × DUE = $662 \times (1.10) = 728.20$. If Mary saves $200 every year at the beginning of the year, for the next 3 years at a 10% interest rate at the end of the 3rd year she will have $728.20.

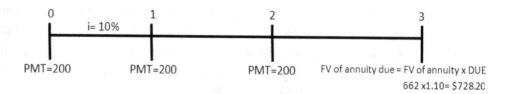

**Figure 9.4:** Time Line for Future Value of Annuity Due

Thus when comparing an annuity and an annuity due we can see the procedure involved in solving the problem is the same until the last stage, where we adjust our results for the annuity due to reflect beginning of the year cash flows. This adjustment accounts for the difference in our results.

Just like in the case of lump sums, in the case of annuities we have one equation to find our answer and four variables involved (PV or FV, i, n, and PMT). Thus we are not limited to finding only future and present values of annuities. Using the same formulas and procedures, we can also solve for payment, number of time periods or interest rate.[5]

## Perpetuities

Perpetuities represent never-ending annuities. This means they represent multiple cash flows that are the same and equally spaced in time but are never-ending. Since perpetuities represent an infinite stream of cash flows it is natural that we can only calculate their present value.[6]

Note that to solve a perpetuity problem we always use the perpetuity formula. Since the computation is quite simple, there are no spreadsheet or financial calculator functions specific for perpetuities.

## Mixed Stream of Cash Flows

So far we have discussed time value of money situations in which we have a single cash flow (lump sums) or situations where we have multiple cash flows that are the same and are equally spaced in time. Nonetheless it is evident that many real life situations that deal with time value of money involve many cash flows that are not the same and/or are not equally spaced in time. This type of time value of money problem is called mixed stream of cash flows. We will learn how to deal with this type of time value of money problem, using the following example.

Martin just bought a doughnut franchise for $200 million. He wants to recover this money in 3 years. Martin expects to earn $60m the first year, $75m the second year, and $100m the third year from his franchise. If the appropriate discount rate is 7%, can Martin recover his initial investment in 3 years?

1. Does the problem involve one or many cash flows? It involves many cash flows. Martin expects to have multiple cash flows from the franchise. We move down the right branch of the tree.

2. Are the cash flows the same or different? Are the cash flows equally spaced out in time? The cash flows are different and they are equally spaced out. Then we move down the far right side of this branch. And we can skip to question 4.

3. Is this a present value or a future value problem? This is a present value problem. Martin just purchased a doughnut franchise (today). We want to determine whether the present value of the cash flows in the next 3 years is enough for him to recover this initial investment. Then we are looking for the present value of these three cash flows.

4. What variables do we have information on? We have information on cash flows (CF) for the first three years: CF1= 60, CF2 = 75, CF3 = 100, as well as n = 3 and i = 7%. We are looking for the present value of these cash flows (PV).

To solve for this uneven cash flow stream problem we can use the spreadsheet net present value function (NPV), the cash flow function of a financial calculator or treat each cash flow in the stream as an individual lump sum and use the lump sum formulas.[7] We find that PV = 203.21.

Since Martin's initial investment is $200m, and the present value of his earnings in the first 3 years is $203.21m, this means that Martin will be able to recover his initial investment by the third year of the doughnut franchise's operation. The present value of his earnings over the next 3 years exceeds his initial investment.[8]

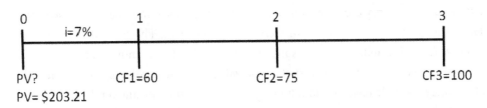

**Figure 9.5:** Time Line for Present Value of Mixed Stream of Cash Flows

## Combination Problems

[...] we've talked about how to master the basic time value of money tools and proficiently solve time value of money problems using the time value of money tree. Nonetheless, real life situations and advanced finance topics typically involve a combination of the time value of money tools here described. So how do we use the tree in these situations? Simple!

We break down our problem into the basic tools found in the tree and solve for each part of the problem. Once we have answers to each part of the problem we combine these results to find the final answer.

For example, in the case of a coupon bond, we can break down the problem into an annuity to represent the bond's interest paid periodically and a lump sum to represent the principal payment. Or we can treat the bond's cash flows as a mixed stream of cash flows.[9]

# Expanding the Tree

So far we have talked about the basic time value of money tools used in finance. Nonetheless, topics like stock valuation include additional tools such as growing perpetuities and growing annuities. Once the students master the simpler version of the tree, growing perpetuities and growing annuities can be added as another branch in the tree (Figure 9.6). This allows us to build on the basic time value of money tools in moving on to more advanced topics such as stock valuation.

# Fruits from the Tree

The Association to Advance Collegiate Schools of Businesses' (AACSB) assurance of learning (AoL) requires that we assess how successful we are in reaching our learning objectives by assessing these. To conform to AACSB's assurance of learning requirement, I created a questionnaire on time value of money using spreadsheets, to evaluate if there is an increase in students' understanding of the topic and of time value of money spreadsheet skills when using the Time Value of Money Tree here presented. For those interested in using the Time Value of Money Tree and assessing AoL, the questionnaire can be found in Appendix II.

I applied the questionnaire to 60 students. 23 of those were taught time value of money using the time value of money tree and 37 students were taught without the tree. The questionnaire consisted of three time value of money problems (one lump sum, one annuity and one uneven stream problem). Students were asked to submit their answers in a spreadsheet. The students were tested on their quantitative reasoning ability and their spreadsheet skills. For the quantitative reasoning assessment, I analyzed how well they could identify the time value of money problem, whether it was a present or future value, variable identification, finding and interpreting the answer. In addition I evaluated whether student were able to use time value of money spreadsheet functions or not.

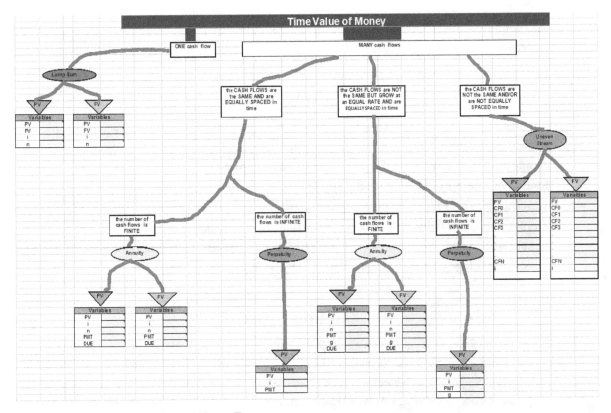

**Figure 9.6:** Expanded Time Value of Money Tree

I found that the group that was taught using the tree was better able to identify the type of time value of money problem they were dealing with in the case of lump sums (91.3% vs. 64.9%) and annuities (100% vs. 81.08%). In the case of annuities, the group taught with the tree was also better able to identify the variables involved in the problem (100% vs. 75.7%) and correctly solve the problem (100% vs. 54.05%). Both groups had trouble finding the answers for uneven cash flow streams (47.8% vs. 32.43%). However, students taught with the tree were better able to identify the variables involved in the uneven stream problem (100% vs. 75.7%).[5]

As far as their ability to use spreadsheet time value of money functions, only 2 of the 23 students (8.7%) that were taught time value of money functions using the TVM tree were able to use the time value of money functions in the survey. In comparison 4 out of 37 students (10.8%) that were taught time value of money without the tree used spreadsheet time value of money functions.

In sum, results indicate the tree does help them better understand time value of money problems or improve their quantitative reasoning. Nonetheless, the time value of money spreadsheet applications need to be emphasized more so students can learn to use them. Perhaps with more spreadsheet examples, homework and tests, we can improve our students' proficiency of time value of money using spreadsheets.

# Conclusion

The present work provides information on a visual aid to help students learn time value of money. I add value to existing research by proposing a time value of money tree that not only helps identify the type of time value of money problem we are dealing with but also the variables we are using in the problem. In addition, the tree can help students learn how to use the time value of money spreadsheet formulas as well as the time value of money and cash flow functions in a financial calculator. Understanding the intuition and variables involved in a time value of money situation as well as learning how to use a financial calculator and the financial functions in a spreadsheet are essential tools that any business student needs to master to thrive in today's business world.

# Endnotes

1. Using a financial calculator or a spreadsheet it is important to mention that cash flows need to be treated as inflows and outflows. The money Jane invests in the bank is an outflow from her pocket and has a negative sign. The cash flow she receives from the bank at the end of the two years is an inflow for Jane and carries a positive sign. As is well known, without the recognition of inflows and outflows, a financial calculator and spreadsheets will provide erroneous answers.

2. See appendix for examples on solving for other variables in a lump sum problem.

3. To estimate a present value of annuity due the adjustment is the same as for the future value of an annuity due. We must multiply the present value of the annuity by $(1 + i)$. In this case, when compared to cash flows occurring at the end of the time period, cash flows occurring at the beginning of the time period have been discounted one period too many. We need to add back one period of interest to each cash flow so our annuity formula can account for the fact that they take place at the beginning of the year and not at the end of the year.

4. When using a financial calculator we can adjust our answer for an annuity due by changing the cash flow mode to "beg" or beginning of period cash flows. Note that if you are solving for an annuity due in a spreadsheet, you can use the FV or PV formula in mode 1, to account for cash flows at the beginning of the time period, instead of using the DUE cell. Nonetheless, using the DUE cell adjustment allows us to find our results regardless of the method we use to solve.

5. See appendix section II for an example on using the time value of money tree to solve for payment (PMT) in an annuity problem.

6. See appendix section III for an example on using the time value of money tree to solve for perpetuities.

7.  If we are solving for the future value of a mixed stream of cash flows, we can use our formulas and treat each cash flow as a lump sum, use the net present value (NPV) function in a spreadsheet or the cash flow function in a financial calculator. For the latter two we are finding the present value of the stream of cash flows. To turn this into the future value we must use the present value answer as a lump sum and solve for the future value of this lump sum.

8.  See appendix section IV for an example on using the time value of money tree to solve for uneven cash flow stream problems where cash flows are not equally spaced in time.

9.  See appendix section V, for an example on using the time value of money tree to solve for combination problems.

10. Differences presented between the two student groups are statistically significant at the 5% or 1% level. The odds of getting the correct answer are not significantly affected by major (accounting or finance vs. all others in the business school), sex (male/female), standing (sophomore, junior or senior), grade point average, prior time value of money knowledge, or personal use of spreadsheets in class. A detailed analysis of this survey is available from the author upon request.

# References

Eddie, A. and G. Swanson, 1996. A hierarchy of skills approach to teaching accounting present value, *Journal of Accounting Education* 14 (1), 123–131.

Jalbert, T., 2002. A new method for teaching the time value of money, *Journal of American Academy of Business* 2, 73–79.

Jalbert, T., M. Jalbert, and C. Chan, 2004. Advances in teaching the time value of money, *Journal of College Teaching and Learning* 1, 7–12.

# Appendix I

### I. Lump Sum Example: Finding the interest rate

Assume the following situation: Margo has $1,000 invested in a mutual fund that pays a 9% average annual return. How long will it take Margo to double her money? We start off with our set of questions:

1.  Does the problem involve one or many cash flows? One cash flow, Margo has $1,000 to invest. Since we are dealing with a lump sum problem then we skip questions 2 and 3 and move on to question 4.

4.  Is this a present value or a future value problem? Margo wants to know how much her money will grow to in the future. So this is a future value problem

5.  What variables do we have information on? Margo has $1,000 to invest today (PV = 1,000). She can invest her money at a 9% rate ($i = 9\%$), and she would like to double her money, such that the

future value is $2,000 (FV = $2,000). We need to know how long Margo must have her money invested at a 9% rate so that it can grow from $1,000, to $2,000. This means we are solving for "n". Using your lump sum formula, spreadsheet or a financial calculator we find that n = 8.04 years.

## II. Annuity Example: Mortgage Example-solving for payment

Bob is buying a new house for $100,000. He will be paying the house in monthly equal installments, and no money down. Bob will be charged a 14% nominal rate on a 30 year mortgage loan. However, he has decided to pay down 2 percentage points reducing the nominal rate to 12%. Each point reduction will cost Bob $1,000 which are added to the cost of the house, increasing it from $100,000 to $102,000.

1.  Does the problem involve one or many cash flows? Many cash flows.

Bob owes $102,000 today and he will pay this in monthly installments over 30 years. We move down the right branch of the tree.

2.  Are the cash flows the same or different? Are the cash flows equally spaced out in time? The cash flows are the same, they are monthly mortgage payments. The cash flows are equally spaced in time, occurring every month.

3.  Are the cash flows finite or infinite? The cash flows are finite. Bob will finish paying off the house in 30 years. This leads us down the left side of the "same cash flows" branch. At this point we know we are dealing with an annuity problem.

Is this a present value or a future value problem? This is a present value problem. Note that annuity problems involve a series of payments *and* a future value *or* a present value that is obtained precisely through these payments. In this example Bob is incurring in a mortgage *today*. Therefore, we are talking about a present value of annuity problem. Not convinced? Read step 5.

5.  What variables do we have information on? We have information on the following variables: PV = $102,000 (what we owe today), i = 12% nominal annual rate, n = 30 years. Annuity problems involve four variables: PV *or* FV, i, PMT and n. We have information on PV, i and n. We are missing information on PMT, so we are solving for PMT. Since we have information on PV, we reiterate this is a present value of annuity problem. Note that in this problem, the payments are monthly. Therefore the rest of the variables (n and i) must be converted from annual terms to monthly terms such that n = 360 months and i = 1% monthly rate, consistent with a 12% nominal rate and a 12.68% effective rate.

Thus our variables expressed in monthly terms are: i = 1% and n = 360, PV = $102,000 and we solve for PMT. PMT = $1,049.18

Bob must pay $1,049.18 every month for the next 30 years to pay off his mortgage.

## III. Perpetuity Example

Your broker offers you a perpetuity of $2000 a year. Considering an interest rate of 4%, how much are you willing to pay for the perpetuity today?

1. Does the problem involve one or many cash flows? Many cash flows. We will receive $2,000 every year forever from this investment. Then we move down the right branch of the tree.

2. Are the cash flows the same or different? Are the cash flows equally spaced out in time? The cash flows are the same and are equally spaced out in time, they are $2000 every year. So we move down the left side of the tree's right branch.

3. Are the cash flows finite or infinite? The cash flows are infinite. This leads us down the right side of the "same cash flows" branch. At this point we know we are dealing with a perpetuity problem.

4. Is this a present value or a future value problem? Since we are dealing with a perpetuity problem, then we must be solving for the present value.

   In the case of a perpetuity we have only three variables involved in the problem: present value (PV), payment (PMT), and interest rate (i). So we must be able to find information on two of these variables to solve for the third.

5. What variables do we have information on? PMT = 2000, i = 4%. So we are solving for present value (PV).

With the above information we find that PV = $50,000. The present value of this investment is $50,000. Then, this is the maximum amount of money we are willing to pay for it.

## IV. Mixed Stream of Cash Flows: Example for cash flows spaced at different time intervals

[...] we dealt with an uneven cash flow stream problem where the cash flows were equally spaced in time. What happens when the cash flows are different and they are also spaced at different time intervals? The cash flows continue to represent an uneven stream and we find ourselves on exactly the same part of the tree. Nonetheless in solving the problem we must consider smaller time intervals that allow us to measure the distance between these cash flows in time. For example, if our cash flows occur one year from now, fifteen months from now and three years from now. Then we can use monthly time intervals to measure the distance between our cash flows. If we solve the uneven cash flow stream problem again but now assume the cash flows take place 12 months from now, 15 months from now and 36 months from now, we will still find ourselves in the same part of the tree, solving for the present value of a mixed stream of cash flows. However, in this modified example our variables are measured in monthly intervals. Next, we follow our set for questions for this modified problem.

Martin just bought a doughnut franchise for $200 million. He wants to recover this money in 3 years. Martin expects to earn $60m the first year, $75m in 15 months and $100m the third year from his franchise. If the appropriate discount rate is 7%, can Martin recover his initial investment in 3 years?

1. Does the problem involve one or many cash flows? It involves many cash flows. We move down the right branch of the tree.

2. Are the cash flows the same or different? Are the cash flows equally spaced out in time? The cash flows are different and they are not equally spaced out. We skip to question 4.

4. Is this a present value or a future value problem? This is a present value problem.

5. What variables do we have information on? We will use months as our measurement unit. The cash flows are stated as follows: $CF12 = 60$, $CF15 = 75$, $CF36 = 100$. All other cash flows from CF1 to CF35 not mentioned above are zero.

Considering cash flows every month then, n = 36 and our interest rate must also be expressed in a monthly time frame so i = 0.5654%, assuming an effective annual rate of 7%.[1]

PV = $206.62. The higher present value of these cash flows compared to our original example is because in this case, the second cash flow occurs in 15 months, instead of in 2 years like in our original example.

### V. Combination Problems: A Bond Example

Jack's broker is offering him a coupon bond that pays a 3% annual coupon, has a 2.5% yield to maturity, matures in 10 years and has a $1,000 par value. He is selling this bond for $1,100.00. Should Jack purchase this bond?

1. Does the problem involve one or many cash flows? Many cash flows.

This problem is about a coupon bond that pays interest annually. So we have cash flows every year for 10 years.

2. Are the cash flows the same or different? Are the cash flows equally spaced out in time? There are two types of cash flows here. First, we have the annual coupon which is the same every year. Then, we have the principal payment which is a single payment in 10 years. The cash flows are equally spaced in time, occurring every year.

3. Are the cash flows finite or infinite? The cash flows are finite.

At this point we know we are dealing with an annuity problem. However, we must not forget that besides the annuity we have a single payment in year 10. This is a lump sum. Thus we have both an annuity represented by the annual coupon and a lump sum which is the principal bond payment at maturity.

4. Is this a present value or a future value problem? We want to know what the value of the bond is today so we are dealing with a present value. This is, the present value of an annuity and the present value of a lump sum.

5. What variables do we have information on?

For the annuity we have information on:

PMT = 30, i = 2.5%, n = 10, so we are solving for PV of an annuity.

For the lump sum we have information on: FV = 1000, i = 2.5%, and n = 10. So we are solving for PV of a lump sum.

Note that we are solving a single problem with two time value of money tools: an annuity and a lump sum.

Using formulas we solve for each and add the answers to get the bond's present value. However, using a spreadsheet or a financial calculator, we can combine both tools (annuity and lump sum) into a single function. Note that for both financial calculators and spreadsheets, lump sums and annuities are solved with the same function.

For example with a spreadsheet, the variables for the problem combining the information for the lump sum and the annuity are: FV = 1000, PMT = 30, i = 2.5% and n = 10. We solve for PV.

$$PV = \$1,043.76$$

This is not a good purchase for Jack. Jack estimated the bond to be worth $1043.76 and the broker is selling the bond for $1,100.00. The bond is too expensive.

[1]We use an effective rate of 7% to be consistent with the original uneven cash flow example which has a 7% effective interest rate.

# Appendix II Time Value of Money Survey

## Background Data

1. State your major(s) and minor(s): Major(s)       Minor(s)

2. Highlight what best applies to you:
   Freshman _____ Sophmore _____ Junior _____ Senior _____

3. Choose one: Male _____ Female _____

4. What is your GPA?

5. Did you use spreadsheets in class to solve TVM problems?
   Yes _____ No _____

6. Have you covered the topic of TVM in previous courses before taking Introduction to Finance? Yes _____ No _____

7. Do you use the TVM tree to help guide you through TVM problems? Yes _____ No _____

Susan is a College Freshman who plans to graduate in 4 years. When she graduates she would like to take a three month trip to Europe and Asia. Susan estimates she will need to have $20,000 for the trip and wants to explore different ways in which to raise this money in 4 years.

I. Susan recently received a high school graduation gift of $1000 from her grandmother. If she can invest this amount of money for 4 years in a bond mutual fund that gives her a 3% return annually how much will she have at the end of the 4 years?

1. Determine and clearly state whether the problem is a lump sum, annuity, uneven stream or perpetuity.

2. Are you looking for the future value or the present value?

3. Clearly identify the variables you have information on (pv = present value, fv = future value, pmt = payment, i = interest rate, n = number of time periods, or cf1, cf2.etc.. For an uneven stream of cash flows).

4. What variables are you looking for?

5. Estimate your final answer(preferably) using spreadsheet time value of money functions.

6. What does your final answer mean?

II. Susan also plans to save money by selling cookies during her time at college. She has estimated that she can generate the following cash flows per year from her cookie business. Assuming the appropriate discount rate is 5%, how much money will Susan be able to raise by the end of 4 years from her cookie business?

| year 1 | year2 | year3 | year 4 |
|--------|-------|-------|--------|
| 1000 | 1500 | 2000 | 2000 |

1. Determine and clearly state whether the problem is a lump sum, annuity, uneven stream or perpetuity.

2. Are you looking for the future value or the present value?

3. Clearly identify the variables you have information on (pv = present value, fv = future value, pmt = payment, i = interest rate, n = number of time periods, or cf1, cf2.etc.. For an uneven stream of cash flows).

4. What variables are you looking for?

5. Estimate your final answer(preferably) using spreadsheet time value of money functions.

6. What does your final answer mean?

III. Susan also plans to save part of her allowance. She has estimated that she can save $2500 by the end of every year she is in college in a stock fund that pays a 6% per year. How much money will Susan be able to save in this fund by the end of 4 years?

1. Determine and clearly state whether the problem is a lump sum, annuity, uneven stream or perpetuity.

2. Are you looking for the future value or the present value?

3. Clearly identify the variables you have information on (pv = present value, fv = future value, pmt = payment, i = interest rate, n = number of time periods, or cf1, cf2.etc.. For an uneven stream of cash flows).

4. What variables are you looking for?

5. Estimate your final answer(preferably) using spreadsheet time value of money functions.

6. What does your final answer mean?

IV. Considering your answers in I, II and III, do you think Susan met her savings goal? Why or why not.

# MODULE 6

# Financial Management Decisions in a Risk-Return Environment

*It seems to be a law of nature, inflexible and inexorable, that those who will not risk cannot win.*

**John Paul Jones**

All the decisions made by a financial manager require consideration of the relevant trade-off of risk and return. For most decision makers, the more risk accepted with a given decision, the greater the required return. This is to be accepted, since most managers (and investors as well) are risk averse. While some individuals are risk-takers, willing to accept more risk without relative increases in required return, and some are risk neutral, focusing more attention on the returns expected than the risks taken to obtain those returns, the norm is to be risk averse. It is important, therefore, to understand the concepts and components of risk and to fully evaluate the risk and return characteristics of a decision.

In the article "Rethinking Risk Management" (1996), the author, René Stulz, discusses the differences found via a survey of corporate managers on the subject of risk management in corporate firms. One finding was that despite the fact that small firms had cash flows that were understandably more volatile than those of larger firms and had less access to new funding, they were less likely to use derivative securities to reduce their risk exposure. As Stulz phrased it, "even more puzzling, however, is that many companies appear to be using risk management to pursue goals other than reducing variance."

Stulz, in the *Journal of Applied Corporate Finance* article, further notes that the "primary goal of risk management is to eliminate the probability of costly lower-tail outcomes—those that would cause financial distress or make a company unable to carry out its investment strategy ..." He further notes that "by eliminating downside risk and reducing the expected costs of financial trouble, risk management can also help move companies toward their optimal capital and ownership structure."

Since the rate of return is defined as the rate of profit from holding an asset over a period of time, we can see that there is one more element to be considered in the risk and return trade-off. This is the element of time. Not only must the decision be examined in terms of the risk and return characteristics of that decision but also in terms of the time or duration for which that decision is made. The effect of inflation on the rate of return is also an extremely important consideration. The Fisher equation, which states that the observed rate of return is equal to the real rate of return plus the expected rate of inflation, takes into account the effect of inflation on earned rates of return.

One commonly ignored fact about risk is that it is a two-sided coin. While downside risk, the possibility of an undesirable result, is generally considered, there is also the possibility of upside risk. Upside risk is the possibility of a result that is even better than that which is expected. All investment and managerial decisions have the potential for both.

Risk can take many forms and has been segmented in a variety of ways. Managers often view risk as being either internal, something over which they have some control, or external, issues over which they have no control. Internal risk includes the risk characteristics of a firm's business operations and its financial structure. External risk is risk that a manager cannot control; it is possible, however, with foresight, to prepare for alternative external risk possibilities. Some of the external risk factors to be considered include the inflation rate, exchange rates, tax laws and regulations, and political events.

Risks have also been categorized as unsystematic and systematic. Unsystematic risk factors are those unique to a firm, business, or industry and are diversifiable for investors. Systematic risk, also referred to as market risk, is not diversifiable, as it refers to the risks extant in the overall market within which a firm must operate.

The rate of inflation, is an example of a market or systematic risk factor. Some firms will be affected positively by a change in the rate of inflation, while others will be affected negatively. Similarly, some will be affected more, others less.

Returns provide the expected payoff for accepting risk. Since risk has both an upside and a downside, the decision-related returns are sometimes greater and sometimes lower than the return expected. Returns required to make a decision acceptable should be commensurate with the expected risks of that decision.

The basic components of any return are compensation for simply delaying consumption, the real rate of return; compensation to protect against possible losses in purchasing power, an inflation premium; and compensation for the level of anticipated risk accompanying the decision. The combination of the real rate of return and the inflation premium provide a return for taking zero risk. That return is commonly referred to as the risk-free rate of return.

Both risk and return characteristics related to a managerial or investment decision must be quantifiable to be of real use in making those decisions. Returns are calculated on an arithmetic or geometric averaging basis based on a simple weighting of actual holdings or on probabilities of occurrence for potential investments. This is true regardless of whether the assessment is for specified potential or actual investments, for specified holding periods, or to determine realized versus unrealized returns. The same is not true for risk assessment measures.

The most common risk measures are the standard deviation and beta. While beta is a measure of the volatility of an investment relative to a market variable, the standard deviation, the square root of the variance measure of the returns dispersion, is a measure of returns variation around the expected mean of those returns.

The beta characteristic of volatility is perhaps most well known for its use in the application of the capital asset pricing model, also known as (CAPM). CAPM is a market-based model for forecasting the expected returns on investments and/or portfolios and includes the beta risk characteristic as well as the risk-free rate and a measure of market return.

The CAPM market return variable is determined from a market proxy, often the Standard and Poor's 500 or some other large asset index considered large enough to be a proxy for the market. CAPM is used by investors of all types—individual, institutional, and business—and is based on the idea that unsystematic or unique risk can be diversified away, while systematic or market risk, measured by beta, cannot. Thus, the model provides a method of evaluating the returns that can be expected by the acceptance of various levels of market risk.

In "Components of Market Risk and Return" (2007), John M. Maheu and Thomas H. McCurdy address the issue of the market portfolio and its accompanying level of market return and risk. The importance of these market measures, they note, is the fact that they are useful for making "accurate measures or forecasts of the equity premium," and this premium is "important for computing risk-adjusted discount rates, capital budgeting decisions involving the cost-of-equity capital, as well as optimal investment allocations."

The authors further discuss in their study the use of "historical average market excess return," addressing the issue by directly incorporating "the information governing changes in risk." Maheu and McCurdy present an alternative approach to determining a "market premium for equity risk" with a model that includes information based on historical realized volatility in the market.

# Recommended Readings

Stulz, René M. "Rethinking Risk Management." *Journal of Applied Corporate Finance* 9, no. 3 (1996): 8–24.

Fama, E., and K. French, "Common Risk Factors in the Returns on Stocks and Bonds." *Journal of Financial Economics* 33 (1993): 3–56.

Carhart, M. "On Persistence in Mutual Fund Performance." *Journal of Finance* 52 (1997): 57–82.

# Selected Readings

Maheu, John M., and Thomas H. McCurdy. "Components of Market Risk and Return" *Journal of Financial Econometrics* 5, no. 4 (2007): 560–90.

# Components of Market Risk and Return

By John M. Maheu and Thomas H. McCurdy

······································································································

## Abstract

[This reading] proposes a flexible but parsimonious specification of the joint dynamics of market risk and return to produce forecasts of a time-varying market equity premium. Our parsimonious volatility model allows components to decay at different rates, generates mean-reverting forecasts, and allows variance targeting. These features contribute to realistic equity premium forecasts for the U.S. market over the 1840–2006 period. For example, the premium forecast was low in the mid-1990s but has recently increased. Although the market's total conditional variance has a positive effect on returns, the smooth long-run component of volatility is more important for capturing the dynamics of the premium. This result is robust to univariate specifications that condition on either levels or logs of past realized volatility (RV), as well as to a new bivariate model of returns and RV.

**KEYWORDS:** volatility components, long-run market risk premium, realized volatility

The expected return on the market portfolio is an important input for many decisions in finance. For example, accurate measures or forecasts of the equity premium are important for computing risk-adjusted discount rates, capital budgeting decisions involving the cost-of-equity capital, as well as optimal investment allocations.

The simplest approach to measuring the market premium is to use the historical average market excess return. Unfortunately, this assumes that the premium is constant over time. If the premium is time varying, as asset pricing theory suggests, then a historical average will be sensitive to the time period used. For example, if the level of market risk were higher in some subperiods than others, then the average excess return will be sensitive to the subsample chosen.

John M. Maheu and Thomas H. McCurdy, "Components of Market Risk and Return," *Journal of Financial Econometrics,* vol. 5, no. 4, pp. 560–590. Copyright © 2007 by Oxford University Press. Reprinted with permission.

A better approach to estimating the premium is to directly incorporate the information governing changes in risk. For example, the Merton (1980) model implies that the market equity premium is a positive function of market risk, where risk is measured by the variance of the premium. Under certain conditions discussed in the next section, intertemporal asset pricing models (IAPM) reduce to a conditional version of Merton (1980). That is, if the conditional variance of the market portfolio return is larger, investors will demand a higher premium to compensate for the increase in risk.[1]

This positive risk–return relationship for the market portfolio has generated a large literature which investigates the empirical evidence. Historically, authors have found mixed evidence concerning the relationship between the expected return on the market and its conditional variance. In some cases a significant positive relationship is found, in others it is insignificant, and still others report it as being significantly negative.[2]

Recent empirical work investigating the relationship between market risk and return offers some resolution to the conflicting results in the early literature. Scruggs (1998) includes an additional risk factor implied by the model of Merton (1973), arguing that ignoring it in an empirical test of the risk–return relationship results in a misspecified model. Including a second factor, measured by long-term government bond returns, restores a positive relationship between expected return and risk. Campbell and Hentschel (1992), Guo and Whitelaw (2006) and Kim, et al. (2004) report a positive relationship between market risk and return when volatility feedbacks are incorporated. Using a latent VAR process to model the conditional mean and volatility of stock returns, Brandt and Kang (2004) find a negative conditional correlation between innovations to those conditional moments but a positive unconditional correlation due to significant lead–lag correlations. Lundblad (2007) reports a positive trade-off over a long time period, Engle and Lee (1999) find a positive relationship between return and the permanent volatility component, and Ghysels, et al. (2005) find a positive trade-off using a mixed data sampling (MIDAS) approach to estimate variance. Pastor and Stambaugh (2001) find evidence of structural breaks in the risk–return relationship.[3]

[Our reading] investigates a conditional version[4] of the risk–return specification. We exploit improved measures of *ex post* variance and incorporate them into a new component forecasting model in order to implement a time-varying risk model of the equity premium.

---

1 There are many other models of asset premiums, many of which can be thought of as versions of a multi-factor approach, such as the three-factor model of Fama and French (1992), or the arbitrage pricing theory of Ross (1976). For example, Claus and Thomas (2001), Fama and French (2002), and Donaldson, et al. (2004) use earnings or dividend growth to estimate the market premium. Pastor, et al. (2007) use implied cost of capital as a measure of expected return.

2 Early examples include Campbell (1987), Engle, et al. (1987), French, et al. (1987), Chou (1988), Harvey (1989), Turner et al. (1989), Baillie and DeGennaro (1990), Glosten, et al. (1993) and Whitelaw (1994). Table 1 of Scruggs (1998) summarizes that empirical evidence.

3 There is also a literature which investigates a nonlinear relationship between market risk and return, for example, Pagan and Hong (1990), Backus and Gregory (1993), Whitelaw (2000) and Linton and Perron (2003).

4 As discussed below, our conditional parameterization is motivated by the IAPM of Campbell (1993) and Merton (1973), as well as the component model of Engle and Lee (1999).

How do we achieve better forecasts of a time-varying market equity premium? First, we use a nonparametric measure of *ex post* variance, referred to as realized volatility (RV). Andersen and Bollerslev (1998) show that RV is considerably more accurate than traditional measures of *ex post* latent variance. Due to the data constraints of our long historical sample, in this article we construct annual RV using daily squared excess returns.[5]

Second, as in Andersen, et al. (2003), French, et al. (1987) and Maheu and McCurdy (2002), our volatility forecasts condition on past RV. Since RV is less noisy than traditional proxies for latent volatility, it is also a better information variable with which to forecast future volatility.

Third, we propose a new volatility forecasting function which is based on exponential smoothing. Our model inherits the good performance of the popular exponential smoothing filter but allows for mean reversion of volatility forecasts and targeting of a well-defined long-run (unconditional) variance. This feature adds to the parsimony of our forecasting function, which is important in our case given the relatively low frequency data necessary to allow estimation over a long time period. It also allows for multiperiod forecasts.

Fourth, motivated by the component-GARCH approach of Engle and Lee (1999) applied to squared returns, we extend our conditional variance specification, which conditions on past RV, to a component-forecasting model. This flexible conditioning function allows different decay rates for different volatility components. We also investigate whether or not total market risk or just some component of it is priced, that is, we allow our risk–return model to determine which components of the volatility best explain the dynamics of the equity risk premium.

Finally, in one of our parameterizations, we generalize the univariate risk–return model for the market equity premium by estimating a bivariate stochastic specification of annual excess returns and the logarithm of RV. In this case, the conditional variance of excess returns is obtained as the conditional expectation of the RV process. Again, multiperiod forecasts are available from the assumed dynamics of the bivariate process.

We focus on the dynamics of the premium over the 1840–2006 period. Our volatility specification, which only requires one parameter per volatility component, produces precise estimates of the risk–return relationship. The forecasts of a time-varying premium match important features of the data. For example, our Figure 10.9 shows how well our forecasts captured the declining equity premium in the mid-1990s.

In summary, we use improved measures of volatility in a parsimonious forecasting model which allows components of volatility with different decay rates to be priced in a conditional risk–return model. This involves several new contributions. We introduce a new weighting function on past RV, and show how mean reversion can be imposed in the model to target the unconditional mean of RV. Building on Engle and Lee (1999), we focus on a multiple component formulation of our

---

5 Early empirical applications of this measure at low frequencies, for example, using daily squared returns to compute monthly volatility, included Poterba and Summers (1986), French, et al. (1987), Schwert (1989), Schwert and Seguin (1990) and Hsieh (1991).

new-volatility forecasting function in order to allow components of volatility to decay at different rates and to investigate which component is priced. Exploiting our mean-reverting multiperiod variance forecasts, our models can generate multiperiod premium forecasts. We analyze a long, low-frequency dataset and show that our models produce realistic time-varying premium forecasts over the entire 1840–2006 time period.

Our empirical results show that for 167 years of the U.S. equity market, there is a significant positive relationship between market risk and the market-wide equity premium. The equity premium varies considerably over time and confirms that the average excess return associated with subperiods can be misleading as a forecast. Nevertheless, long samples of historical information are useful as conditioning information and contribute to improved estimates of the time-varying market premium.

In our two-component specifications of the conditional variance, one component tracks long-run moves in volatility while another captures the short-run dynamics. The two-component conditional variance specification provides a superior variance forecast. Furthermore, it is the long-run component in the variance that provides a stronger risk–return relationship.

[...] Section 1 introduces the models that motivate our empirical study, and discusses the importance of the measurement and modeling of the variance of market returns. Section 2 details our results on the significance of the risk–return relationship for several model specifications. We discuss the importance of volatility components, and the range of implied premiums that the models produce. Finally, Section 3 summarizes the results and future work.

# 1 The Risk–Return Model

## 1.1 Background

Both static and intertemporal models of asset pricing imply a risk–return relationship. Examples of intertemporal models which do not require consumption data are the IAPM proposed by Merton (1973) and Campbell (1993), and also the conditional capital asset pricing model(CAPM).

The IAPM of Merton (1973) relates the expected market return and variance through a representative agent's coefficient of relative risk aversion and also allows sensitivity of the market premium to a vector of state variables (or hedge portfolios) which capture changing investment opportunities. Under some assumptions, the intertemporal model implies a market risk–return relationship with no additional factors, that is, market risk is captured by the variance of the market portfolio. Merton (1980) argues that this case will be a close approximation to the intertemporal asset pricing model in Merton (1973) if either the variance of the change in wealth is much larger than the variance of the change in the other factor(s), or if the change in consumption in response to a change in wealth is much larger than that associated with a change in other state variable(s). Sufficient conditions are if the investment opportunity set is essentially constant, or if the representative investor has logarithmic utility.

Campbell (1993) provides a discrete-time intertemporal model which substitutes out consumption. In this case, the expected market premium is a function of its variance as well as its covariance with news (revisions in expectations) about future returns on the market. As in Merton (1973), if the coefficient of relative risk aversion is equal to 1 or if the investment opportunity set is constant or uncorrelated with news about future market returns, the expected market premium will only be a function of the market return variance. However, the Campbell (1993) derivation provides an alternative, empirically plausible, condition under which that market risk–return relationship obtains. If the covariance of the market return with news about future investment opportunities is proportional to the variance of the market return, then the latter will be a sufficient statistic for market risk.[6] Section III of Campbell (1993) provides conditions that produce this conditional market risk–return relationship.

This motivates a risk–return model

$$E_{t-1}(r_{M,t}) = \gamma_1 \sigma^2_{M,tt} \qquad (1)$$

where $E_{t-1}(r_{M,t})$ is the conditional expectation of the excess return on the market, and $\sigma^2_{M,t}$ is the conditional variance of the market excess return (that is, the forecast of the variance conditional on time $t-1$ information). This model implies a proportional relationship between the market equity premium and its conditional variance. As discussed in introduction above, Merton (1980) argues that one should impose the prior that the *expected* equity premium is nonnegative. If Equation (1) were the risk–return model, this would be satisfied as long as $\gamma_1 > 0$.

## 1.2 Measuring and Forecasting Volatility

In this section, we discuss how we measure and then forecast the volatility which drives the time-varying risk premiums. Note that [...] we use the term volatility to refer generically to either the variance or standard deviation. Where necessary for clarity, we refer specifically to whether it is an *ex post* (realized) measure or a conditional estimate (forecast); and whether we are referring to a variance or a standard deviation. For ease of notation, we also drop the subscript $M$ on the market excess return and its conditional variance so that henceforth $r_t \equiv r_{M,t}$ and $\sigma^2_t \equiv \sigma^2_{M,t}$.

---

6 Campbell (1996) reports empirical evidence in support of an analogous condition in a cross-sectional application for which the restriction is that covariances of all asset returns with news about future returns on invested wealth are proportional to their covariances with the current return on wealth. In this case, most of the explained cross-sectional variation in returns is explained by cross-sectional variation in the assets' covariances with the market return.

### 1.2.1 Measuring Volatility

[...], we employ a nonparametric measure of volatility. A traditional proxy for *ex post* latent volatility has been squared returns or squared residuals from a regression model. As shown by Andersen and Bollerslev (1998), this measure of volatility is very noisy and of limited use in assessing features of volatility such as its time-series properties.

Better measures of *ex post* latent volatility are available. [...] we use a measure of *ex post* variance, termed (RV), developed in a series of papers by Andersen, Bollerslev, Diebold and co-authors, and Barndorff-Nielsen and Shephard. The increment of quadratic variation is a natural measure of *ex post* variance over a time interval. RV is computed as the sum of squared returns over this time interval. As shown by Andersen, et al. (2001b), as the sampling frequency is increased, the sum of squared returns converges to the quadratic variation over a fixed time interval for a broad class of models. Thus RV is a consistent estimate of *ex post* variance for that period. The asymptotic distribution of RV has been studied by Barndorff-Nielsen and Shephard (2002b) who provide conditions under which RV is also an unbiased estimate. Recent reviews of this growing literature are by Andersen, et al. (2004) and Barndorff-Nielsen, et al. (2004).

Defining RV of the market return for year $t$ as $RV_t$, we construct annual RV as

$$RV_t = \sum_{j=1}^{D_t} r_{t,j}^2 \qquad (2)$$

where $r_{t,j}$ is the continuously compounded return for the $j$th day in year $t$, and $D_t$ is the number of days in year $t$ for which market equity returns were available. Prior to 1886, $RV_t$ is computed from squared monthly continuously compounded returns since we only have monthly data for that early part of our sample. This allows us to use a longer time period. We analyze whether computing annual $RV$ prior to 1886 from lower frequency intra-period observations has any effect on our results.

### 1.2.2 Forecasting Volatility

Our time-varying risk model of the equity premium is forward looking. That is, the expected market equity premium is a function of market equity risk. According to our test equations, the latter is measured by the conditional variance of market excess returns. Therefore, we need a forecast of the time $t$ volatility, conditional on information at time $t - 1$. Our volatility forecasts condition on past RV. Given that RV has a superior signal-to-noise ratio for measuring latent volatility, it should be a superior conditioning variable for forecasting future volatility.

What functional form should be used to summarize information in past RV? Given our objective to model risk and return at annual frequencies, parsimony is an obvious objective. One candidate is the infinite exponential smoothing function. In this case, estimates can be derived from the recursion

$$\sigma_t^2 = (1-\alpha)RV_{t-1} + \alpha\sigma_{t-1}^2 \qquad (3)$$

in which $0 \le \alpha < 1$, $\alpha$ is the smoothing parameter, and $\sigma_t^2$ is the conditional variance. A small value of $\alpha$ puts more weight on the most recent observable value of RV, that is $RV_{t-1}$, and less weight on the past forecast $\sigma_{t-1}^2$. Conversely, an $\alpha$ close to 1 puts less weight on recent observations and more weight on past forecasts which smooths the data. This model is analogous to the popular *RiskMetrics* filter, except for the fact that the standard practice is to smooth on lagged squared returns rather than on lagged RV. The recursion in Equation (3) implies the following weighting function on past RV,

$$\sigma_t^2 = (1-\alpha)\sum_{j=0}^{\infty} \alpha^j RV_{t-j-1} \qquad (4)$$

in which the weights sum to one.

Although infinite exponential smoothing provides parsimonious estimates, it possesses several drawbacks. Given our long time period and low sampling frequency, we prefer to estimate the smoothing parameter $\alpha$ rather than taking it as given as is common practice with filtering approaches such as *RiskMetrics*. The smoothing parameter $\alpha$ can be estimated using an objective criterion, such as maximum likelihood. However, as Nelson (1990) has shown in the case of squared returns or squared innovations to returns, filters with no intercept and whose weights sum to one are degenerate in the asymptotic limit in the sense that the distribution of the variance process collapses to zero variance asymptotically. This is problematic for maximum-likelihood estimation of the smoothing parameter. To circumvent these problems, but still retain the parsimony and accuracy of exponential smoothing, we propose the following volatility specification,

$$\sigma_t^2 = \omega + (1-\alpha)\sum_{j=0}^{\tau-1} \alpha^j RV_{t-j-1}, \qquad (5)$$

where we truncate the expansion at the finite number $\tau$.[7] In this specification the weights sum to less than one allowing mean reversion in volatility forecasts as shown below.

Based on Corollary 1 of Andersen, et al. (2003), we assume that the conditional expectation of annual quadratic variation $(QV_t)$ is equal to the conditional variance of annual returns,[8] that

---

7 In the empirical applications below, we fixed $\tau = 40$ due to presample data requirements. We provide some robustness checks for alternative choices of $\tau$.

8 Barndorff-Nielsen and Shephard (2002a) also discuss the theoretical relationship between integrated volatility and RV.

is, $E_{t-1}(QV_t) = \text{Var}_{t-1}(r_t) \equiv \sigma_t^2$.[9] Assuming that RV is a unbiased estimator of quadratic variation it follows that $E_{t-1}(RV_t) = \sigma_t^2$, and we can derive the unconditional variance associated with specification (5) as[10]

$$E(\sigma_t^2) = \frac{\omega}{1-(1-\alpha)\sum_{j=0}^{\tau-1}\alpha^j} \qquad (6)$$

This unconditional variance leads to our strategy of variance targeting by setting $\sigma^2$ from the data and using

$$\omega = \sigma^2\left[1-(1-\alpha)\sum_{j=0}^{\tau-1}\alpha^j\right]. \qquad (7)$$

In summary, this new specification is similar in spirit to exponential smoothing but allows for mean reversion in volatility forecasts. In addition, the finite unconditional variance allows for variance targeting which means that only one parameter needs to be estimated. Our specification is also more parsimonious than the covariance-stationary GARCH(1,1) model.[11] As discussed later in the text, at least for our sample of annual data the more parsimonious specification is critical for precision of the estimates of the risk–return relationship and also for generating reasonable premium estimates.

As is evident from Equation (5), past data receive an exponentially declining weight. As we will see below, this is not flexible enough to capture the time-series dynamics of RV. A simple approach to providing a more flexible model is to allow different components of volatility to decay at different rates.[12] This can be achieved with a component volatility function which estimates the conditional

---

9 We assume that any stochastic component in the intraperiod conditional mean is negligible compared to the total conditional variance.

10 To make the mean reversion in variance forecasts clear, note that with the assumption $E_{t-1}(RV_t) = \sigma_t^2$, the dynamics of RV implied by Equation (5) follow the ARCH-like AR representation, $RV_t = \omega + \sum_{j=1}^{\tau}\beta_j RV_{t-j} + \upsilon_t$, where $\upsilon_t = RV_t - \sigma_t^2$, with $E_{t-1}\upsilon_t = 0$ and $\beta_j = (1-\alpha)\alpha^{j-1}$. Conditional variance forecasts can be derived from $E_t\sigma_{t+1}^2 = E_t RV_{t+1}$; and, as $i \to \infty$, we have Equation (6).

11 The covariance-stationary GARCH (1,1) model, $\sigma_t^2 = \omega + \alpha \in_{t-1}^2 + \beta\sigma_{t-1}^2$, with $\in_{t-1} \equiv r_{t-1} - E_{t-1}r_{t-1}$ can be written as $\sigma_t^2 = \omega/(1-\beta) + \alpha\sum_{i=0}^{\infty}\beta^i \in_{t-1-}^2$ which requires an extra parameter compared to (5).

12 Several papers, for example, long memory, mixtures of regimes, mixtures of jumps and stochastic volatility, have highlighted that a single exponential decay rate is inadequate to capture volatility dynamics over time. Examples include Engle and Lee (1999), Maheu and McCurdy (2000), Alizadeh, et al. (2002), Bollerslev and Zhou (2002), Chernov, et al. (2003), Chacko and Viceira (2003) and Ghysels, et al. (2006a). Engle and Rangel (2004) develop a two-component volatility specification with a GARCH(1,1) model for short-run volatility dynamics which mean revert to a nonparametrically estimated time-varying unconditional volatility.

variance as the average of two or more components. Formally, define the $k$-component volatility model as

$$\sigma^2_{t,(k)} = \omega + \frac{1}{k}\sum_{i=1}^{k}\sigma^2_{t,i},\qquad(8)$$

where

$$\sigma^2_{t,i} = (1-\alpha_i)\sum_{j=0}^{\tau-1}\sigma^j_i RV_{t-j-1},\quad i=1,\ldots,k\qquad(9)$$

Note that the conditional variance components are projections on past RV. We do not specify the high-frequency dynamics of spot volatility. Indeed, one of the attractions of using RV, besides being an efficient estimate of *ex post* volatility, is that it will be a consistent estimate of volatility for a very large class of empirically realistic models. Therefore, our modeling assumptions are on the annual conditional variance process given observations on RV.

Related work on volatility modeling includes the component model of Engle and Lee (1999) and Ghysels, et al. (2005). Relative to component-GARCH models, our parameterization only requires 1 parameter per component rather than two. Another difference is that we smooth on past annual RV. Ghysels, et al. (2005) use a MIDAS approach to estimate volatility. In that paper, using data from 1928 to 2000, the monthly conditional variance of returns is modeled using a flexible functional form to estimate the weight given to each lagged daily squared return. They find that a two- parameter filter works well.[13] Our decay rates are additive. That is, in our case with two components, the coefficient on $RV_{t-j-1}$ is $(1-\alpha_1)\alpha_1^j/2+(1-\alpha_2)\alpha_2^j/2$, allowing us to separate out and price short-lived versus slower-decaying components. In contrast, the smoothing coefficients in Ghysels, et al. (2005) interact (multiplicatively) in a way that makes it difficult to isolate their separate effects on pricing.[14]

Our conditional variance specification maintains the parsimony of smoothing models but allows mean reversion. This allows us to use variance targeting which may be important to gain precision in our application. In the next section, we extend the existing literature to investigate a bivariate risk–return specification. This joint stochastic specification of returns and RV allows for multiperiod forecasts of the premium.

Our objective is to have a parsimonious and flexible function that summarizes information in past RV that might be useful for forecasting changes in the market equity risk premium. We allow for alternative components of volatility with different decay rates. Not only is this a more flexible way to capture the time-series dynamics of volatility, but it also allows us to investigate whether a particular component, rather than the full conditional variance, is more important in driving the market premium.

---

13 Their monthly variance is $V_t = 22\sum_{j=0}^{251} w_j r^2_{t-j}, w_j(\kappa_1,\kappa_2) = \dfrac{\exp(\kappa_1 j+\kappa_2 j^2)}{\sum_{j=0}^{251}\exp(\kappa_1 j+\kappa_2 j^2)}.$

14 Note that their weight on past squared returns is proportional to $\exp(\kappa_1 j+\kappa_2 j^2)=\tilde{\kappa}_1^j\tilde{\kappa}_2^{j^2}$ with $\tilde{\kappa}_1=\exp(\kappa_1)$ and $\tilde{\kappa}_2=\exp(\kappa_2)$.

# 1.3 The Empirical Risk–Return Models

As discussed in Section 1.1, our empirical models based on Equation (1) are motivated as special cases of an IAPM. Each of the empirical models implies a time-varying equity premium which is a function of its own conditional second moment, that is, a forecast of the equity premium's time $t$ variance conditional on time $t - 1$ information.

The conventional univariate test equation for (1) is a linear model,

$$r_t = \gamma_0 + \gamma_1 \sigma_t^2 + \epsilon_t \tag{10}$$

For example, Scruggs (1998) motivates the addition of an intercept to account for market imperfections, such as differential tax treatment of equity versus Treasury-bill returns, which might account for a constant equity premium unrelated to risk.

In this subsection we introduce two alternative empirical specifications of the risk–return relationship. Each of our models jointly estimate the conditional mean and conditional variance parameters using maximum likelihood. We label the first specification univariate since it fits the stochastic excess return process by conditioning on variance forecasts which are estimated using a projection on past RV as in Equation (8).[15] The second specification is bivariate since we estimate a bivariate stochastic specification of annual excess returns and log(RV). In that case, the conditional variance of excess returns is obtained as the conditional expectation of the RV process.

## 1.3.1 Univariate Risk–Return Specifications

The Conditional Mean is,

$$r_t = \gamma_0 + \gamma_1 \sigma_{t,(q)}^2 + \epsilon_t, \quad \epsilon_t = \sigma_{t,(k)} z_t, \quad z_t \sim N(0, 1); \tag{11}$$

and the conditional variance is either applied to levels of RV, as in Equations (8) and (9), or applied to log(RV) as in

$$\log \sigma_{t,(k)}^2 = \omega + \frac{1}{k} \sum_{i-1}^{k} \log \sigma_{t,i}^2, \tag{12}$$

$$\log \sigma_{t,i}^2 = (1 - \alpha_i) \sum_{j=0}^{\tau-1} \alpha_i^j \log RV_{t-j-1}, \quad i = 1, \ldots, k, \tag{13}$$

where $k$ indexes the total number of variance components and $q$ indexes the number of variance components that affect the conditional mean. That is, we specify $\sigma_{t,(q)}^2$ in the conditional mean, in which $q$ denotes the number of volatility components that affect the market premium when the conditional variance follows a $k$-component model. Note that $q \leq k$. For example, where we want

---

15 The risk–return regressions in Ghysels, et al. (2006b) also estimate market risk based on past RV.

the total variance to enter the mean, we set $q = k$. On the other hand, for models in which $q = 1$, $k = 2$, we let the maximum likelihood estimator determine which component of the variance is optimal in the mean specification.

The $t$th contribution to the loglikelihood is

$$l_t = \frac{1}{2}\log(2\pi) - \frac{1}{2}\log(\sigma_{t,(k)}^2) - \frac{(r_t - \gamma_0 - \gamma_1\sigma_{t,(q)}^2)^2}{2\sigma_{t,(k)}^2}, \tag{14}$$

where $\sigma_{t,(\cdot)}^2$ depends on the levels or log specification. The loglikelihood $\sum_{t=1}^{T} l_t$ is maximized with respect to the parameters $\gamma_0, \gamma_1, \alpha_1, \cdots, \alpha_k$.

## 1.3.2 Bivariate Risk–Return Specification

In this case, we estimate a bivariate stochastic specification of annual excess returns and $\log(RV)$. The parameterization has conditional mean

$$r_t = \gamma_0 + \gamma_1\sigma_{t,(q)}^2 + \epsilon_t = \sigma_{t,(k)}z_t, \quad z_t \sim N(0, 1) \tag{15}$$

and the following conditional variance specification

$$\sigma_{t,(k)}^2 \equiv E_{t-1}(RV_t \mid k) = \exp(E_{t-1}(\log RV_t \mid k) + .5\mathrm{Var}_{t-1}(\log RV_t \mid k) \tag{16}$$

$$\log RV_t = \omega + \frac{1}{k}\sum_{i=1}^{k}\log\sigma_{t,1}^2 + \eta_t, \quad \eta_t \sim N(0, \phi^2) \tag{17}$$

$$\log\sigma_{t,i}^2 = (1 - \alpha_i)\sum_{j=0}^{\tau-1}\alpha_i^j \log RV_{t-j-1}, \quad i = 1, \ldots, k. \tag{18}$$

Again, $\sigma_{t,(q)}^2 \equiv E_{t-1}(RV_t \mid q), \quad q \leq k$, represents the conditional variance component(s) that affect the conditional mean. $l_t$ consists of contributions from the return and volatility equation,

$$l_t = -\log(2\pi) - \frac{1}{2}\log(\sigma_{t,(k)}^2) - \frac{1}{2}\log(\phi^2) - \frac{(r_t - \gamma_0 - \gamma_1\sigma_{t,(q)}^2)^2}{2\sigma_{t,(k)}^2} - \frac{\left(\log RV_t - \omega - \frac{1}{k}\sum_{i=1}^{k}\log\sigma_{t,i}^2\right)^2}{2\phi^2}. \tag{19}$$

In this case, by parameterizing the joint density of annual excess returns and $\log(RV)$, we explicitly model the annual $\log(RV)$ process as stochastic given the most recent information. However, making a conditional log-normal assumption for RV allows for a convenient calculation of the conditional variance as in Equation (16).

# 2 Results

## 2.1 Data and Descriptive Statistics

We are evaluating the risk–return relationship associated with equity for the market as a whole. Therefore, we require data on a broad equity market index and on a riskfree security so that we can construct returns on the equity index in excess of the riskfree rate.

There are two considerations. First, as shown by Merton (1980) for i.i.d. returns, we can only increase the precision of expected return estimates by increasing the length of the time period (calendar span) covered by our historical sample. In other words, sampling more frequently (for example, collecting daily instead of monthly data) will not improve the precision of the market premium estimates. For this reason we want our historical sample to be as long as possible. Second, since we use a nonparametric measure of RV which is constructed as the sum of squared *intraperiod* returns, we will need data at a higher frequency than our estimation frequency in order to compute RV as in Equation (2). As noted in Section 1.2.1 above, we use monthly returns from 1802–1885 and daily returns from 1886–2006 to compute annual RV.

The U.S. market equity returns from 1802–1925 are from Schwert (1990). The Schwert equity index was constructed from various sources: railway and financial companies up to 1862 from Smith and Cole (1935); the Macaulay (1938) railway index (1863–1870); the value-weighted market index published by the Cowles Commission for the time period 1871–1885; and the Dow Jones index of industrial and railway stocks for 1885–1925.[16] For the 1926–2006 period, we use returns (including distributions) for the value-weighted portfolio of NYSE, NASDAQ and AMEX stocks compiled by the Center for Research in Security Prices (CRSP). The equity return data are converted to continuously compounded returns by taking the natural logarithm of one plus the monthly or daily equity return.

Annual bill yield data (riskfree rate) for the 1802–1925 period are from Jeremy Siegel. Siegel (1992) describes how these annual yields were constructed to remove the very variable risk premiums on commercial paper rates in the 19th century.[17] For the period 1926–2006, we use monthly bid yields associated with U.S. 3-month Treasury Bills from the Fama monthly riskfree file provided by CRSP. The annual riskfree yield was obtained by summing the 12 monthly yields.

Annual continuously compounded equity returns are computed as the sum of the monthly continuously compounded returns. Annual excess returns are then computed by subtracting the annual riskfree rate. Henceforth, unless otherwise indicated, returns and excess returns refer to continuously compounded rates.[18]

---

16 Schwert adjusts for the time averaging in the original series for 1863–1885 and adds an estimate of dividends for the period 1802–1870.

17 The market excess return is often measured with respect to a long-term (for example, 30 year) Treasury yield rather than the Treasury Bill yield used [...]. Although this choice depends on investment horizon and the purpose of the calculation, for example, capital budgeting versus asset pricing, our focus is on forecasting the market equity premium over a (approximately) riskfree rate rather than over an alternative risky asset. Booth (1999) compares several approaches and shows that for certain periods the risk associated with long-term Treasuries was almost as large as that associated with market equity.

18 We use continuously compounded returns to conform with our estimate of RV.

Figure 10.1 plots annual market excess returns for the entire sample from 1803–2006. Figures 10.2 and 10.3 plot two alternative measures of *ex post* volatility, the absolute value of the excess returns and the square root of RV, respectively. Notice how much smoother the square root of RV is than the absolute value of annual excess returns. It is also clear from these plots that the data for the

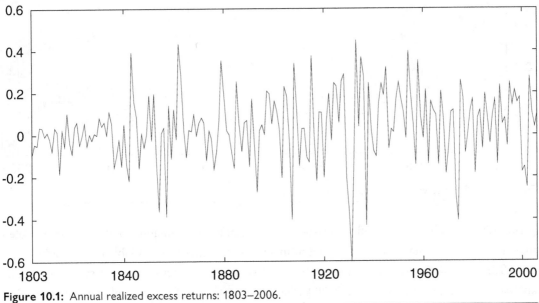

**Figure 10.1:** Annual realized excess returns: 1803–2006.

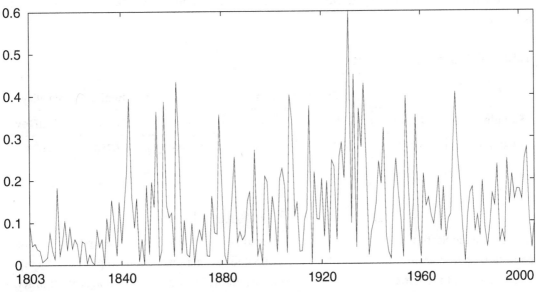

**Figure 10.2:** Annual absolute value measure of *ex post* volatility.

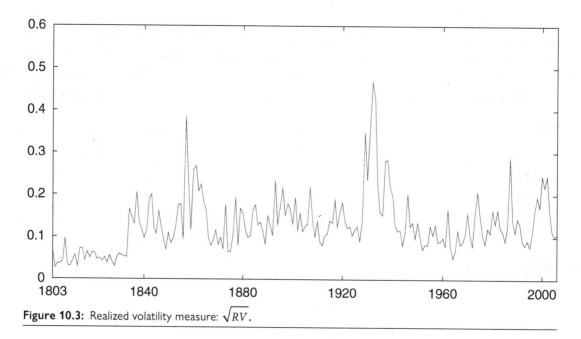

**Figure 10.3:** Realized volatility measure: $\sqrt{RV}$.

period 1803–1834 have a very different structure than that for the remainder of the sample. As noted in Schwert (1990), data from only a small number of companies was available for that subperiod. Both Schwert (1989) and Pastor and Stambaugh (2001) drop this period. For the same reason, our analyses focus on the time period 1840–2006. Starting in 1840 provides presample values to condition our time-varying volatility model.

Table 10.1 reports summary statistics for the time period, 1840–2006. The average excess return is 4.27%.

**Table 10.1** Summary statistics.

|  | Excess Return | | | | Realized Volatility | |
| --- | --- | --- | --- | --- | --- | --- |
| Sample | Mean | StdDev | Min | Max | Mean | StdDev |
| 1840–2006 | 0.0427 | 0.1824 | −0.6017 | 0.4490 | 0.0250 | 0.0293 |

## 2.2 Univariate Risk–Return Results

As discussed in Section 1.3.1, the univariate specifications fit the stochastic excess return process by conditioning on variance forecasts which are estimated using a projection on past RV. We report results using both the levels of RV, as in Equations (8) and (11), and the natural logarithm of RV, as in Equations (12) and (11).[19] Due to the importance of the length of the time period necessary for efficient conditional mean forecasts, we use all of our data and thus forecasts are in-sample.

See Inoue and Kilian (2004) for evidence in favor of using in-sample forecasts for model evaluation.

### 2.2.1 Using RV Levels

Table 10.2 reports parameter estimates and likelihood ratio test (LRT) results associated with the risk–return relationship estimated using the alternative component volatility models applied to levels of RV. Note that $\omega$ is computed, as in Equation (7). To avoid influential observations in our small

**Table 10.2** Parameter Estimates: Univariate Risk–Return Using RV Levels

$$r_t = \gamma_0 + \gamma_1 \sigma^2_{t,(q)} + \epsilon_t, \quad \epsilon_t = \sigma_{t,(k)} z_t, \quad z_t \sim N(0,I)$$

$$\sigma^2_{t,(k)} = \omega + \frac{1}{k} \sum_{i=1}^{k} \sigma^2_{t,i}; \quad \sigma^2_{t,i} = (1-\alpha_i) \sum_{j=0}^{\tau-1} \alpha_i^j RV_{t-j-1}, \quad i = 1,\dots,k$$

Model Labels: $U(k)$ ≡ univariate risk–return model with $k$-component model of $RV$; $U(2s)$ ≡ univariate risk–return model with two-component volatility but the conditional mean prices the smooth volatility component.

| | $\gamma_0$ | $\gamma_1$ | $\omega$ | $\alpha_1$ | $\alpha_2$ | L | $LRT_{\gamma_0=0}$ | $LRT_{\gamma_1=0}$ |
|---|---|---|---|---|---|---|---|---|
| U(1) | −0.032 | 3.122 | 0.0003 | 0.910 | | 38.14 | 1.08 | 5.24 |
| (q = k = 1) | [−1.027] | [2.197] | | (0.024) | | | (0.30) | (0.02) |
| Proportional Model | | 1.768 | 0.0002 | 0.903 | | 37.60 | | 12.58 |
| | | [3.543] | | (0.027) | | | | (0.00) |
| U(2) | −0.012 | 2.314 | 0.0009 | 0.950 | 0.396 | 39.71 | 0.24 | 3.68 |
| (q = k = 2) | [−0.479] | [1.930] | | (0.020) | (0.294) | | (0.62) | (0.06) |
| Proportional Model | | 1.794 | 0.0009 | 0.950 | 0.406 | 39.59 | | 12.76 |
| | | [3.557] | | (0.021) | (0.282) | | | (0.00) |
| U(2$_s$) | −0.052 | 4.338 | 0.0009 | 0.951 | 0.408 | 41.64 | 2.50 | 7.54 |
| (q = 1, k = 2) | [−1.573] | [2.624] | | (0.019) | (0.256) | | (0.11) | (0.01) |
| Proportional Model | | 1.986 | 0.0009 | 0.950 | 0.438 | 40.39 | | 14.36 |
| | | [3.580] | | (0.021) | (0.242) | | | (0.00) |

**Notes:** Conditional mean coefficient estimates of $\gamma_i$ with $t$-statistics in brackets; $\omega$ is the volatility function intercept which is consistent with targeting the median of RV; volatility function coefficient estimates $\alpha_i$ have standard errors in parenthesis; L is the log-likelihood function; and LRT are likelihood ratio test statistics with $p$-values in parenthesis.

---

19 Andersen, et al. (2001a) show that for equity returns the natural logarithm of RV is more normally distributed than the level of RV.

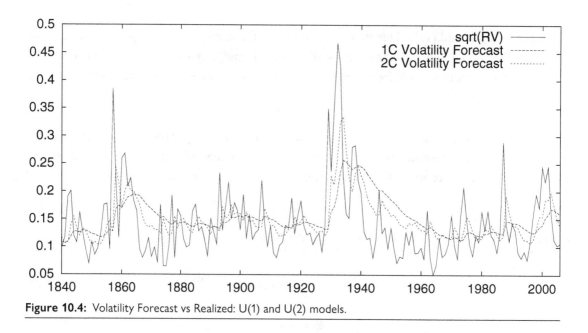

**Figure 10.4:** Volatility Forecast vs Realized: U(1) and U(2) models.

sample, we set the long-run target volatility, $\sigma^2$, to the sample median of annual RV over the period 1802–2006. For each model, U(1), U(2) and U($2_s$), we report both the linear parameterization of the risk–return relationship, Equation (11), and the proportional parameterization with $\gamma_0 = 0$, as motivated by Equation (1).[20] Models U(2) and U($2_s$) have the same volatility specification but U($2_s$) allows the risk–return model to determine which volatility component has the most explanatory power for the dynamics of the equity premium. We find that, when given the choice, the maximum likelihood estimator always chooses to price the long-run or smooth component.

It is clear from Figure 10.4 that the two-component volatility specification tracks RV better than the one-component version.[21] Figure 10.5 plots the individual components of volatility from the U(2) specification, that is, Equation (9) for $k = 1, 2$. This shows that the smooth component is persistent, as expected from the smoothing coefficient estimate $\hat{\alpha}_1 = .950$ reported in Table 10.2. Note in particular how long it takes the smooth component to decay from its high level in the 1930s. On the other hand, the second component has much lower persistence, $\hat{\alpha}_2 = .396$, which implies that it is more influenced by the most recent RV.

Table 10.2 reveals that the risk–return relationship is positive for all specifications. For linear parameterizations of the premium, the LRT results reveal a statistically significant relationship between

---

20  See Lanne and Saikkonen (2006) and Bandi and Perron (2006) for statistical arguments in favor of estimating the proportional model when the estimated intercept is insignificant. For example, based on results showing low power of a Wald test when an unnecessary intercept is included, Lanne and Saikkonen (2006) conclude with a recommendation to always restrict the intercept to zero if it is implied by the theory being tested. Note that our models with an intercept all have a positive slope parameter so that restricting the statistically insignificant intercept to zero does not force the slope parameter to be positive but rather allows us to estimate it with more precision.

21  Note that these volatility plots are square roots of the volatility forecasts versus $\sqrt{RV_t}$.

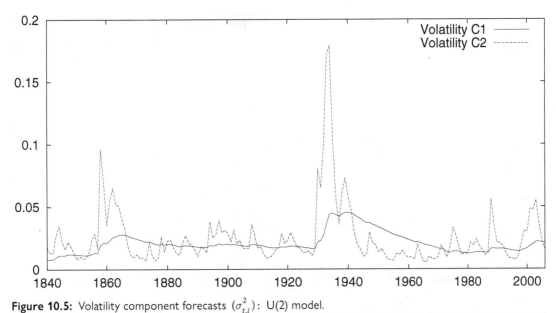

**Figure 10.5:** Volatility component forecasts $(\sigma^2_{t,i})$: U(2) model.

excess market returns and their conditional variance, although it is marginal ($p$-value = 0.06) for the U(2) case. For these linear parameterizations, the $t$-statistic on the risk–return slope coefficient, $\gamma_1$, is highest (2.624) for the U($2_s$) model. That version also has the highest log-likelihood, 41.64, and a LRT statistic of 7.54 which rejects the hypothesis that $\gamma_1 = 0$.

However, for all volatility specifications, the more parsimonious proportional premium model cannot be rejected by the data. That is, the intercept in the conditional mean is statistically insignificant, both from the perspective of $t$-tests on $\gamma_0$ and from the LRT reported in the second-last column of Table 10.2. As noted above, by restricting the intercept to be zero, the precision of the estimate $\hat{\gamma}_1$ improves. For instance, the $t$-statistics associated with the hypothesis $\gamma_1 = 0$ increase, as do the LRT statistics which are more than twice as large for the proportional as opposed to the linear model. The one exception is the U($2_s$) model which reveals a strongly positive market risk–return relationship for both the linear and the proportional parameterization of the premium.

The LRT statistics in the final column of the table all reject the null hypothesis that $\gamma_1 = 0$. This result is particularly strong for the proportional parameterizaton of the risk premium in which case the test statistics are all greater than 12 so that the $p$-value associated with the null hypothesis is very small. The $t$-statistic for $\gamma_1$ also supports this conclusion in that it is greater than 3.5 for the proportional model for all of the alternative volatility specifications.

Figure 10.6, plots the market equity premium forecast for the proportional risk premium parameterization. When total volatility from the two-component volatility specification is priced (the U(2) model), there is a high peak in the forecasted market equity premium which lasts for 2 years, 1933 and 1934. In contrast, pricing the smooth component of volatility (the U($2_s$) model) results in a lower

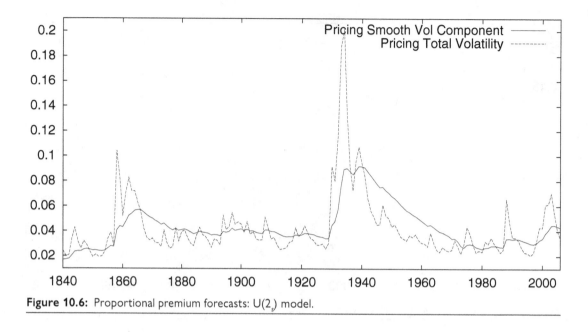

**Figure 10.6:** Proportional premium forecasts: U(2$_s$) model.

peak which decays more slowly. In this case, the premium forecast ranges from 1.7% to 9.2% with the average forecasted premium over the 1840–2006 sample equal to 4.29 percent.

Table 10.3 reports model diagnostics and statistics for volatility and premium fit. These include mean absolute error (MAE) and root mean squared error (RMSE), as well as the $R^2$ from Mincer and Zarnowitz (1969) forecast regressions for a particular model's premium and volatility forecasts.[22] The results in Table 10.3 support the two-component models U(2) and U(2$_s$) over the more restrictive one-component version U(1). For example, as suggested by Figure 10.4, the $R^2$ increases from about 7% to 26% by adding a second volatility component. Note that the U(2$_s$) model, which had the highest log-likelihood, also has the best premium fit whether measured from the perspective of MAE, RMSE, or $R^2$.

### 2.2.2 Using Log(RV)

We also fit the univariate risk–return model (11) using variance forecasts which are estimated from a projection on the natural logarithm (rather than levels) of past RV, that is, Equations (12) and (13). Tables 10.4 and 10.5 report these results. Again, $\omega$ is computed to target long-run volatility, for which log $\sigma^2$ is set to the 1802–2006 average of log(RV).[23]

The parameter estimates using log(RV), reported in Table 10.4, reveal that the risk–return relationship is again positive for all specifications and, with two exceptions, is very significant—even

---

22  For example for the volatility forecasts, the regression is $RV_t^{.5} = a + b\hat{\sigma}_t + u_t$ is the square root of the particular model's volatility forecast for time t given information up to time t – 1.

23  The log transformation reduced the outliers present in the levels of RV.

**Table 10.3** Model Comparisons and Diagnostics: Univariate Risk–Return Using RV Levels

$$r_t = \gamma_0 + \gamma_1 \sigma^2_{t,(q)} + \epsilon_t, \quad \epsilon_t = \sigma_{t,(k)} z_t, \quad z_t \sim N(0,1)$$

$$\sigma^2_{t,(k)} = \omega + \frac{1}{k}\sum_{i=1}^{k} \sigma^2_{t,i}; \quad \sigma^2_{t,i} = (1-\alpha_i)\sum_{j=0}^{\tau-1} \alpha_i^j RV_{t-j-1}, \quad i = 1,\dots,$$

Model Labels: $U(k) \equiv$ univariate risk–return model with $k$-component model of $RV$; $U(2_s) \equiv$ univariate risk–return model with two-component volatility but the conditional mean prices the smooth volatility component.

| Model | L | Diagnostics | | | Volatility Fit | | | Premium Fit | | |
|---|---|---|---|---|---|---|---|---|---|---|
| | | $LB^2(10)$ | $LB(10)$ | KS | MAE | RMSE | $R^2$ | MAE | RMSE | $R^2$ |
| U(1) ($q = k = 1$) | 38.14 | (0.54) | (0.19) | (0.03) | 0.0165 | 0.0284 | 0.0727 | 0.1410 | 0.1800 | 0.0224 |
| U(2) ($q = k = 2$) | 39.71 | (0.57) | (0.23) | (0.09) | 0.0147 | 0.0250 | 0.2656 | 0.1410 | 0.1807 | 0.0162 |
| U(2$_s$) ($q = 1, k = 2$) | 41.63 | (0.87) | (0.15) | (0.16) | 0.0147 | 0.0251 | 0.2639 | 0.1405 | 0.1795 | 0.0272 |

$L$ is the log-likelihood function. $LB^2(10)$ is the Ljung and Box (1978) heteroskedastic-robust portmanteau test statistic for serial correlation in the squared standardized residuals up to 10 lags; $LB(10)$ is the same for conditional mean residuals; and $KS$ is the Kiefer and Salmon (1983) test for departures from the normal distribution for standardized residuals. We report $p$-values for these diagnostic tests. MAE $\equiv$ mean absolute error; RMSE $\equiv$ square root of the mean-squared error; $R^2$ from Mincer-Zarnowitz regressions applied to the volatility and premium forecasts.

more so than when projecting on the levels of past RV. The two exceptions, with $p$-values of 0.08 and 0.05 respectively for the LR test of the restriction $\gamma_1 = 0$, are the linear parameterizations of the premium with one-component and two-component volatility specifications. However, the proportional parameterizations of the premium do result in very statistically significant positive risk–return relationships for all cases. The LRT statistics in the final column range from 16.00 to 18.42, even larger than in Table 10.2. The $t$-statistics associated with the risk–return slope parameter estimates, $\hat{\gamma}_1$, range from 3.97 to 4.15 in this case.

Table 10.5 shows that the two-component parameterizations of volatility dominate the one-component version from the perspective of all three criteria, MAE, RMSE, or $R^2$, for volatility fit. As in the levels case, the $U_{log}(2_s)$ model, which prices the smooth component of volatility, has the best overall fit.

Figure 10.8 shows that the smooth proportional premium forecasts using the univariate model that conditions on log(RV), that is, the $U_{log}(2_s)$ model, range from 1.6% to 9.5% with an average of 4.33% over the period 1840 to 2006. This figure also shows that these premium forecasts are similar

**Table 10.4** Parameter Estimates: Univariate Risk–Return Using Log(RV)

$$r_t = \gamma_0 + \gamma_1 \sigma^2_{t,(q)} + \epsilon_t, \quad \epsilon_t = \sigma_{t,(k)} z_t, \quad z_t \sim N(0,1)$$

$$\log \sigma^2_{t,(k)} = \omega + \frac{1}{k}\sum_{i=1}^{k}\log \sigma^2_{t,i}; \quad \log \sigma^2_{t,i} = (1-\alpha_i)\sum_{j=0}^{\tau-1}\alpha_i^j \log RV_{t-j-1}, \quad i = 1,\ldots,k$$

Model Labels: $U_{log}(k)$ ≡ univariate risk–return model with $k$-component model of the natural logarithm of RV; $U_{log}(2_s)$ ≡ univariate risk–return model with two-component volatility but the conditional mean prices the smooth volatility component.

| | $\gamma_0$ | $\gamma_1$ | $\omega$ | $\alpha_1$ | $\alpha_2$ | L | $LRT_{\gamma_0=0}$ | $LRT_{\gamma_1=0}$ |
|---|---|---|---|---|---|---|---|---|
| $U_{log}(1)$ | −0.007 | 2.617 | −0.0025 | 0.830 | | 20.81 | 0.60 | 3.01 |
| ($q = k = 1$) | [−0.231] | [1.576] | | (0.056) | | | (0.81) | (0.08) |
| Proportional | | 2.259 | −0.0018 | 0.823 | | 20.78 | | 16.00 |
| Model | | [3.966] | | (0.051) | | | | (0.00) |
| $U_{log}(2)$ | −0.008 | 2.734 | −0.0931 | 0.924 | 0.309 | 23.04 | 0.12 | 3.98 |
| ($q = k = 2$) | [−0.348] | [1.931] | | (0.032) | (0.235) | | (0.73) | (0.05) |
| Proportional | | 2.287 | −0.0812 | 0.921 | 0.311 | 22.98 | | 16.20 |
| Model | | [3.987] | | (0.032) | (0.238) | | | (0.00) |
| $U_{log}(2_s)$ | −0.067 | 5.631 | −0.1688 | 0.938 | 0.236 | 26.07 | 3.96 | 10.04 |
| ($q = 1, k = 2$) | [−1.940] | [3.294] | | (0.021) | (0.207) | | (0.05) | (0.00) |
| Proportional | | 2.355 | −0.0796 | 0.921 | 0.308 | 24.09 | | 18.42 |
| Model | | [4.149] | | (0.029) | (0.230) | | | (0.00) |

**Notes:** Conditional mean coefficient estimates of $\gamma_i$ with $t$-statistics in brackets; $\omega$ is the volatility function intercept which is consistent with targeting the mean of log($RV$); volatility function coefficient estimates $\alpha_i$ have standard errors in parenthesis; L is the log-likelihood function; and $LRT$ are likelihood ratio test statistics with $p$-values in parenthesis.

to the univariate case in which volatility forecasts were estimated from past levels of RV rather than log(RV), except that in the log(RV) case the peaks are slightly higher with faster decay.[24]

## 2.3 Bivariate Risk–Return Results

In this section, we generalize our risk–return model for the market equity premium by estimating a joint stochastic specification of the conditional mean and annual log(RV) of market excess returns. The logarithmic specification of RV ensures that volatility is nonnegative during estimation of the joint stochastic process. The system of test equations is (15) and (16) to (18); and the results are summarized in Tables 10.6 and 10.7, as well as Figures 10.7 to 10.8.

---

24 The plots of the premium forecasts for all specifications show that the premiums are increasing from a low level over the first few years of the estimation period. This is partly due to the low volatility of the presample data from 1802 to 1834 which the initial part of our estimation period require as conditioning information when $\tau = 40$.

**Table 10.5** Model Comparisons and Diagnostics: Univariate Risk–Return Using Log(RV)

· · · · · · · · · · · · · · · · · · · · · · · · · · · · · · · · · · · · · · · · · · · · · · · · · · · · · · · · · · · · · · · · · · · · · · · · · · · · · · · ·

$$r_t = \gamma_0 + \gamma_1 \sigma^2_{t,(q)} + \epsilon_t, \quad \epsilon_t = \sigma_{t,(k)} z_t, \quad z_t \sim N(0,1)$$

$$\log \sigma^2_{t,(k)} = \omega + \frac{1}{k}\sum_{i=1}^{k} \log \sigma^2_{t,i}; \quad \log \sigma^2_{t,i} = (1-\alpha_i)\sum_{j=0}^{\tau-1} \alpha_i^j \log RV_{t-j-1}, \quad i = 1,\dots,k$$

Model Labels: $U_{log}(k)$ ≡ univariate risk–return model with $k$-component model of the natural logarithm of RV; $U_{log}(2_s)$ ≡ univariate risk–return model with two-component volatility but the conditional mean prices the smooth volatility component.

| Model | L | Diagnostics | | | Volatility Fit | | | Premium Fit | | |
|---|---|---|---|---|---|---|---|---|---|---|
| | | LB²(10) | LB(10) | KS | MAE | RMSE | R² | MAE | RMSE | R² |
| $U_{log}(1)$ ($q = k = 1$) | 20.81 | (0.23) | (0.12) | (0.10) | 0.0145 | 0.0281 | 0.1179 | 0.1414 | 0.1807 | 0.0133 |
| $U_{log}(2)$ ($q = k = 2$) | 23.05 | (0.36) | (0.19) | (0.19) | 0.0136 | 0.0263 | 0.2608 | 0.1415 | 0.1809 | 0.0119 |
| $U_{log}(2_s)$ ($q = 1, k = 2$) | 26.07 | (0.69) | (0.15) | (0.26) | 0.0135 | 0.0263 | 0.2737 | 0.1406 | 0.1803 | 0.0199 |

L is the log-likelihood function. LB²(10) is the Ljung and Box (1978) heteroskedastic-robust portmanteau test for serial correlation in the squared standardized residuals up to 10 lags; LB(10) is the same for the conditional mean residuals; and KS is the Kiefer and Salmon (1983) test for departures from the normal distribution for standardized residuals. We report p-values for these diagnostic tests. MAE ≡ mean absolute error; RMSE ≡ square root of the mean-squared error; R² from Mincer-Zarnowitz regressions applied to the volatility and premium forecasts.

The results are very comparable to the univariate results reported above. Figure 10.7 plots the individual components of log volatility from the B(2) specification, that is, Equation (18) for $k = 1, 2$. Table 10.7 shows that the two-component volatility specification fits log(RV) better. For example, the $R^2$ for volatility fit increases from about 23% to 28% by adding the second volatility component.

Table 10.6 reports that the risk–return relationship is positive for all models and statistically significant for all of the models except two. As in the log(RV) univariate case, the $t$-statistic associated with $\gamma_1$ is smaller for the linear risk premium parameterizations B(1) and B(2). However, since we are unable to reject that $\gamma_0 = 0$, either by $t$-tests or by the LR tests reported in the second-last column of the table, the data support a proportional parameterization of the risk premium. In that case, the risk–return relationship is significantly positive for all volatility specifications. Again, as in Tables 10.2 and 10.4, the LRT results in the final column indicate that the relationship between excess market returns and their conditional variance is very strong for proportional parameterizations of the risk premium.

## Table 10.6 Parameter Estimates: Bivariate Return and Log(RV) model

$$r_t = \gamma_0 + \gamma_1 \sigma^2_{t,(q)} + \epsilon_t, \quad \epsilon_t = \sigma_{t,(k)} z_t, \quad z_t \sim N(0, I)$$

$$\sigma^2_{t,(k)} \equiv E_{t-1}(RV_t \mid k) = \exp(E_{t-1}(\log RV_t \mid k) + .5 Var_{t-1}(\log RV_t \mid k));$$

$$\sigma^2_{t,(q)} \equiv E_{t-1}(RV_t \mid q), \quad q \leq k$$

$$\log RV_t = \omega + \frac{1}{k} \sum_{i=1}^{k} \log \sigma^2_{t,i} + \eta_t, \quad \eta_t \sim N(0, \phi^2)$$

$$\log \sigma^2_{t,i} = (1 - \alpha_i) \sum_{j=0}^{\tau-1} \alpha_i^j \log RV_{t-j-1}, \quad i = 1, \ldots, k$$

Model Labels: $B(k)$ ≡ bivariate model of returns and the natural logarithm of $RV$ with $k$-component volatility. $B(2_s)$ ≡ bivariate model with two-component volatility but the conditional mean prices the smooth volatility component.

|  | $\gamma_0$ | $\gamma_1$ | $\omega$ | $\alpha_1$ | $\alpha_2$ | $\phi$ | L | $LRT_{\gamma_0=0}$ | $LRT_{\gamma_1=0}$ |
|---|---|---|---|---|---|---|---|---|---|
| B(1) | 0.019 | 0.861 | −0.2e-7 | 0.621 |  | 0.763 | −143.72 | 0.74 | 0.94 |
| (q = k = 1) | [0.874] | [0.963] |  | (0.079) |  | (0.046) |  | (0.39) | (0.33) |
| Proportional |  | 1.533 | −0.7e-7 | 0.638 |  | 0.765 | −144.09 |  | 10.88 |
| Model |  | [3.272] |  | (0.078) |  | (0.046) |  |  | (0.00) |
| B(2) | −0.006 | 1.954 | −0.0653 | 0.916 | 0.176 | 0.745 | −136.60 | 0.04 | 4.48 |
| (q = k = 2) | [−0.239] | [1.693] |  | (0.034) | (0.140) | (0.045) |  | (0.84) | (0.03) |
| Proportional |  | 1.706 | −0.0596 | 0.914 | 0.175 | 0.745 | −136.62 |  | 12.08 |
| Model |  | [3.440] |  | (0.034) | (0.141) | (0.045) |  |  | (0.00) |
| B(2_s) | −0.066 | 4.289 | −0.1429 | 0.934 | 0.159 | 0.745 | −134.30 | 2.94 | 9.08 |
| (q = 1, k = 2) | [−1.648] | [2.859] |  | (0.027) | (0.140) | (0.045) |  | (0.09) | (0.00) |
| Proportional |  | 1.791 | −0.0612 | 0.915 | 0.171 | 0.744 | −135.77 |  | 13.78 |
| Model |  | [3.645] |  | (0.031) | (0.145) | (0.045) |  |  | (0.00) |

**Notes:** Conditional mean coefficient estimates of $\gamma_i$ with $t$-statistics in brackets; $\omega$ is the volatility function intercept which is consistent with targeting the mean of log($RV$); volatility function coefficient estimates $\alpha_i$ have standard errors in parenthesis; L is the log-likelihood function; and $LRT$ are likelihood ratio test statistics with $p$-values in parenthesis.

Table 10.7 reports that the preferred model is, once again, the $2_s$ specification, that is, two volatility components with the smooth component being priced in the conditional mean.[25] As in the univariate cases, all of the premium fit statistics, MAE, RMSE, or $R^2$, support this conclusion; as does the log

---

25 Given our relatively small number of annual observations, we investigated potential small-sample bias for the maximum-likelihood estimator by simulating 1000 bootstrap samples using the parameter estimates for the B(2s) model in Table 10.6 as the DGP. The bias for all of the parameters was small. This suggests that the maximum-likelihood estimator is reliable for our sample which addresses one of the issues raised by Stambaugh (1999) in our context.

**Table 10.7** Model Comparisons and Diagnostics: Bivariate Return and Log(RV) Model

$$r_t = \gamma_0 + \gamma_1 \sigma^2_{t,(q)} + \epsilon_t, \quad \epsilon_t = \sigma_{t,(k)} z_t, \quad z_t \sim N(0,1)$$

$$\sigma^2_{t,(k)} \equiv E_{t-1}(RV_t \mid k) = \exp(E_{t-1}(\log RV_t \mid k) + .5 \text{Var}_{t-1}(\log RV_t \mid k))$$

$$\sigma^2_{t,(q)} \equiv E_{t-1}(RV_t \mid q), \quad q \leq k$$

$$\log RV_t = \omega + \frac{1}{k}\sum_{i=1}^{k}\log\sigma^2_{t,i} + \eta_t, \quad \eta_t \sim N(0, \phi^2)$$

$$\log\sigma^2_{t,i} = (1-\alpha_i)\sum_{j=0}^{\tau-1}\alpha_i^j \log RV_{t-j-1}, \quad i = 1,\dots,k$$

Model Labels: $B(k)$ ≡ bivariate model of returns and the natural logarithm of $RV$ with $k$-component volatility. $B(2_s)$ ≡ bivariate model with two-component volatility but the conditional mean prices the smooth volatility component.

| Model | L | Diagnostics | | | Volatility Fit | | | Premium Fit | | |
|---|---|---|---|---|---|---|---|---|---|---|
| | | $LB^2(10)$ | $LB(10)$ | KS | MAE | RMSE | $R^2$ | MAE | RMSE | $R^2$ |
| B(1) <br> ($q = k = 1$) | −143.72 | (0.12) | (0.21) | (0.33) | 0.0165 | 0.0268 | 0.2330 | 0.1413 | 0.1806 | 0.0133 |
| B(2) <br> ($q = k = 2$) | −136.60 | (0.34) | (0.17) | (0.20) | 0.0149 | 0.0248 | 0.2771 | 0.1415 | 0.1810 | 0.0115 |
| B(2$_s$) <br> ($q = 1, k = 2$) | −134.30 | (0.67) | (0.15) | (0.26) | 0.0148 | 0.0248 | 0.2809 | 0.1407 | 0.1804 | 0.0196 |

L is the log-likelihood function. $LB^2(10)$ is the Ljung and Box (1978) heteroskedastic-robust portmanteau test for serial correlation in the squared standardized residuals up to 10 lags; $LB(10)$ is the same for the conditional mean residuals; and KS is the Kiefer and Salmon (1983) test for departures from the normal distribution for standardized residuals. We report p-values for these diagnostic tests. MAE ≡ mean absolute error; RMSE ≡ square root of the mean-squared error; $R^2$ from Mincer-Zarnowitz regressions applied to the volatility and premium forecasts.

likelihood which is −134.30 for the B(2$_s$) model, as opposed to −143.72 for the B(1) model which has a one-component volatility specification.

As displayed in Figure 10.8, the proportional premium for the preferred B(2$_s$) specification is similar to that for the univariate case which conditions on past log(RV). The premium forecasts from this bivariate stochastic model range from 1.6% to 9.7% with an average of 4.31%. Note that all of our specifications deliver reasonable estimates of the market premium.[26]

---

26 We do not have enough annual data to get reliable estimates from a conventional GARCH-in-Mean parameterization using squared returns.

**Table 10.8** Robustness Checks: Bivariate Return and Log(RV) Model

$$\log RV_t = \omega + \frac{1}{2}\sum_{i=1}^{2}\log \sigma_{t,i}^2 + \eta_t, \qquad \eta_t \sim N(0, \phi^2);$$

$$\log \sigma_{t,i}^2 = (1-\alpha_i)\sum_{j=0}^{\tau-1}\alpha_i^j \log RV_{t-j-1}, \qquad i = 1, 2$$

Model B(2$_s$) : $r_t = \gamma_0 + \gamma_1 \exp\left[\omega + \log \sigma_{t,1}^2 + .5 Var_{t-1}(\log RV_t)\right] + \epsilon_t,$
$$\epsilon_t = \sigma_{t,}(2)z_t, \qquad z_t \sim N(0, 1)$$

Model B(2$_a$) : $r_t = \gamma_0 + \gamma_1 \exp\left[\omega + \gamma_2 \log \sigma_{t,1}^2 + (1-\gamma_2)\log \sigma_{t,2}^2 + .5 Var_{t-1}(\log RV_t)\right] + \epsilon_t,$
$$\epsilon_t = \sigma_{t,}(2)z_t, \qquad z_t \sim N(0, 1)$$

| | $\gamma_0$ | $\gamma_1$ | $\gamma_2$ | $\omega$ | $\alpha_1$ | $\alpha_2$ | $\phi$ | L |
|---|---|---|---|---|---|---|---|---|
| Model B(2$_a$) | −0.064 [−1.569] | 4.188 [2.603] | 1.035 [5.149] | −0.1325 | 0.932 (0.028) | 0.161 (0.142) | 0.744 (0.045) | −134.29 |
| Model B(2$_s$) | −0.066 [−1.648] | 4.289 [2.859] | | −0.1429 | 0.934 (0.027) | 0.159 (0.140) | 0.745 (0.045) | −134.30 |
| $\tau = 5$ | −0.024 [−0.365] | 0.826 [1.042] | | −1.437 | 0.920 (0.043) | 0.229 (0.148) | 0.741 (0.046) | −135.94 |
| $\tau = 15$ | −0.080 [−0.994] | 1.924 [2.007] | | −1.184 | 0.960 (0.025) | 0.185 (0.140) | 0.741 (0.045) | −134.56 |
| 1886–2006 | −0.088 [−1.257] | 4.636 [2.314] | | −0.3689 | 0.957 (0.018) | 0.1e−7 (0.167) | 0.677 (0.047) | −87.87 |
| 1928–2006 | −0.073 [−1.000] | 4.224 [2.127] | | −0.3882 | 0.958 (0.020) | 0.1e−8 (0.225) | 0.745 (0.067) | −65.67 |
| 1945–2006 | −0.149 [−1.736] | 7.483 [2.154] | | −0.4059 | 0.959 (0.028) | 0.2e−8 (0.365) | 0.658 (0.064) | −34.56 |
| RV from monthly (1840–2006) | −0.071 [−1.758] | 3.804 [2.868] | | −0.1281 | 0.932 (0.033) | 0.269 (0.141) | 0.771 (0.043) | −139.97 |

**Notes:** Conditional mean coefficient estimates of $\gamma_i$ with $t$-statistics in brackets; $\omega$ is the volatility function intercept which is consistent with targeting the mean of log(RV); volatility function coefficient estimates $\alpha_i$ have standard errors in parenthesis; L is the log-likelihood function.

Figure 10.9 illustrates the premium for the 1990–2006 period generated by our bivariate specification B(2$_s$). The time-varying premium estimates for the period 1990 to 2000 were below the long-run average of 4.27%, reaching a low of 3.15% in 1997. In addition, they are considerably lower than the 1980–2006 average continuously compounded excess return of 6.2%. This graphically illustrates

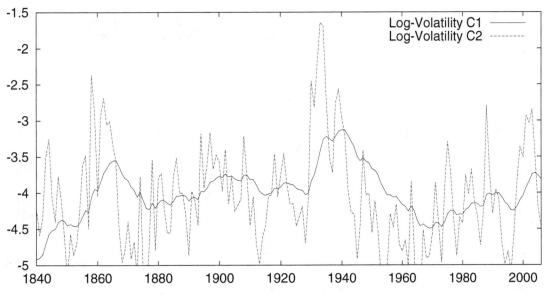

**Figure 10.7:** Log-Volatility component forecasts $(\log \sigma_{t,i}^2)$: B(2) model.

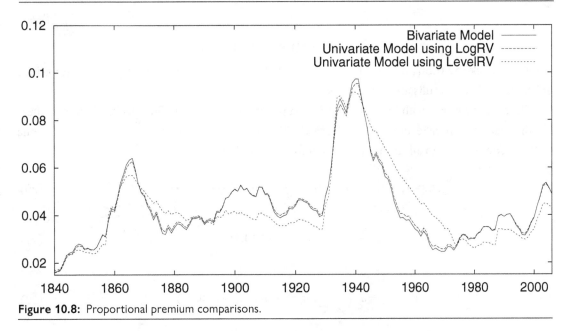

**Figure 10.8:** Proportional premium comparisons.

the point, discussed in the introduction, that the average realized excess return is not a very reliable forecast of the market equity premium since it will be sensitive to the subsample chosen. Finally, the forecasted continuously compounded premium increased from the low of 3.15% in 1997 to 5.4% in 2004 then back down to 4.9% in 2006.

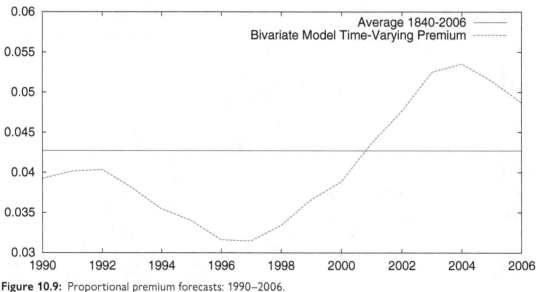

**Figure 10.9:** Proportional premium forecasts: 1990–2006.

## 2.4 Robustness Analyses

We now check the robustness of the above results to alternative parameterizations and various subsamples. These results are summarized in Table 10.8.

The bivariate model with the most empirical support is labeled B($2_s$). This specification specializes the bivariate system in Section 1.3.2 to the case with two volatility components ($k = 2$); allowing one of those components to affect the conditional mean ($q = 1$). That is,

$$r_t = \gamma_0 + \gamma_1 \exp\left[\omega + \log \sigma_{t,1}^2 + .5\mathrm{Var}_{t-1}(\log RV_t)\right] + \in_t, \tag{20}$$

$$\in_t = \sigma_{t,(2)} z_t, \quad z_t \sim N(0,1) \tag{21}$$

$$\log RV_t = \omega + \frac{1}{2}\sum_{i=1}^{2}\log \sigma_{t,i}^2 + \eta_t, \quad \eta_t \sim N(0, \phi^2) \tag{22}$$

$$\log \sigma_{t,i}^2 = (1-\alpha_i)\sum_{j=0}^{\tau-1}\alpha_i^j \log RV_{t-j-1} \quad i=1,2 \tag{23}$$

The results for this model for the sample 1840–2006 are repeated in the second panel of Table 10.8, labeled Model B($2_s$).

To check that our parsimonious B($2_s$) specification is able to adequately capture the potential differential effect of the smooth long-run volatility component on the dynamics of the premium, we introduce a new bivariate specification that replaces Equation (20) with

$$r_t = \gamma_0 + \gamma_1 \exp\left[\omega + \gamma_2 \log \sigma_{t,1}^2 + (1-\gamma_2)\log \sigma_{t,2}^2 + .5\text{Var}_{t-1}(\log RV_t)\right] + \in_t \quad (24)$$

Imposing $\gamma_2 = 1/2$ corresponds to the total variance being priced, while restricting $\gamma_2 = 1$ is one component being priced. These cases were discussed in the previous subsection and Table 10.6 as models B(2) and B($2_s$) respectively.

The results for the less parsimonious specification in Equation (24) are reported in the first panel of Table 10.8, labeled Model B($2_a$). The estimate for parameter $\gamma_2$ is 1.035 with a standard error of 0.201. Therefore, we can reject that it is zero (the $t$-statistic is 5.149) which confirms the results from all of our earlier $2_s$ specifications that the persistent volatility component has a positive and very significant effect on the dynamics of excess returns. On the other hand, the coefficient on the second, less persistent volatility component is not significantly different from zero. While it is useful to see how the two volatility components are separately priced, notice that our more parsimonious model B($2_s$) has an almost identical fit which confirms the robustness of the $2_s$ parameterizations reported earlier.

The third and fourth panels of Table 10.8 report results for the B($2_s$) model with alternative values of $\tau$, the number of lags used in the exponential smoother components. As compared to the default value, $\tau = 40$, the $\tau = 5$ case results in an insignificant risk–return relationship. As $\tau$ is increased, the $t$-statistic on the slope parameter $\gamma_1$ increases. We have found that the optimal $\tau$ is somewhat model and criterion specific. For example, a $\tau = 25$ produces a significantly better loglikelihood ($-131.57$) and higher $t$-statistic (3.153) associated with $\gamma_1$ than our base B($2_s$) which has $\tau = 40$. However, the univariate specifications favored higher values of $\tau$. Therefore, we chose a common value that was high enough to capture the smooth volatility component with our limited number of data.

The next three panels of Table 10.8 report subsample results for model B($2_s$). This specification which prices the smooth volatility component of a two-component volatility model was able to deliver a positive and statistically significant risk–return relationship for subsamples such as 1886–2006, 1928–2006 and 1945–2006. Note that as the sample gets shorter, the persistence, $\alpha_2$, of the second volatility component goes to zero. Nevertheless, the B($2_s$) parameterization still always dominates a one-component volatility specification.

Finally, the last panel of Table 10.8 reports results for model B($2_s$) for which annual RV is computed using monthly squared returns for the entire 1840–2006 sample, rather than daily squared returns when they became available in 1886. Our default model which uses the latter has a higher loglikelihood but otherwise the results are similar. We also tried using an indicator variable in the volatility function for the 1840–1885 part of the sample for which daily data were not available. Again, although that indicator variable was significantly different from zero indicating that annual RV was slightly lower over that first part of the sample, the risk–return results were similar. Also, note that the results for the 1886–2006 subsample refer to the period over which annual RV is always computed from daily squared returns. Again, the positive and significant risk–return relationship still obtains.

# 3 Summary and Future Directions

[This reading] evaluates the market risk–return relationship for U.S. equity over the period 1840–2006 using a time-varying market premium for equity risk. We begin with a univariate specification of the risk–return relationship. This application models the stochastic market excess returns by conditioning on variance forecasts which are estimated by projecting onto past RV. We assess the robustness of those results by also estimating a univariate version which projects onto past log(RV).

We propose a parsimonious and flexible function that summarizes information in past RV that might be useful for forecasting changes in the market equity risk premium. We allow for alternative components of volatility with different decay rates. Not only is this a flexible way to capture the time-series dynamics of volatility, but it also allows us to investigate whether a particular component, rather than the full conditional variance, is more important in driving the market premium.

Our conditional variance specification maintains the parsimony of exponential smoothing functions but allows mean reversion in forecasts, and targets the implied long-run variance. In addition, we allow for increased flexibility by explicitly modeling more than one volatility component.

Finally, we generalize the risk–return model for the market equity premium by estimating a bivariate stochastic specification of annual excess returns and log(RV). In this case, the conditional variance of excess returns is obtained as the conditional expectation of the RV process.

In summary, in addition to our volatility specification, we consider two additional contributions to the literature. First, unlike the univariate specifications that dominate the literature, we extend the analysis to a bivariate risk–return model of returns and RV. Second, we investigate whether or not one volatility component is more important than total volatility in driving the dynamics of the equity premium.

All of the empirical specifications support a conclusion that the relationship between risk and return for the market equity premium is positive. The higher the expected market risk, the higher the market equity premium. This relationship is strongest for a two-component specification of volatility with the long-run smooth component being priced in the conditional mean.[27] In fact, the preferred model from the perspective of overall as well as equity premium fit, for both the univariate and bivariate specifications, is the $2_s$ model which uses a two-component volatility specification and prices the smooth component of volatility in the conditional mean. In future work, as in Engle and

---

27  A persistent component in also shown to be important for asset pricing in Bansal and Yaron (2004). Also, see Bansal, et al. (2007) who investigate the implications for risk and return of risks in the long run versus the short run.

Rangel (2004) and Engle, et al. (2006), we plan to explore potential sources of this smooth component of volatility.

*Received January 18, 2007; revised May 16, 2007; accepted June 20, 2007.*

# References

Alizadeh, S., M. Brandt, and F. X. Diebold. (2002). "Range-Based Estimation of Stochastic Volatility Models." *Journal of Finance 57*, 1047–1092.

Andersen, T. G., and T. Bollerslev. (1998). "Answering the Skeptics: Yes, Standard Volatility Models Do Provide Accurate Forecasts." *International Economic Review 39*(4), 885–905.

Andersen, T. G., T. Bollerslev, and F. X. Diebold. (2004). "Parametric and Nonparametric Volatility Measurement." In L. Hansen and Y. Ait-Sahalia (eds.), *Handbook of Financial Econometrics*: North Holland.

Andersen, T. G., T. Bollerslev, F. X. Diebold, and H. Ebens. (2001a). "The Distribution of Realized Stock Return Volatility." *Journal of Financial Economics 61*, 43–76.

Andersen, T. G., T. Bollerslev, F. X. Diebold, and P. Labys. (2001b). "The Distribution of Exchange Rate Volatility." *Journal of the American Statistical Association 96*, 42–55.

Andersen, T., T. Bollerslev, F. X. Diebold, and P. Labys. (2003). "Modeling and Forecasting Realized Volatility." *Econometrica 71*, 529–626.

Backus, D. K., and A. W. Gregory. (1993). "Theoretical Relations Between Risk Premiums and Conditional Variances." *Journal of Business & Economic Statistics 11*, 177–185.

Baillie, R. T., and R. P. DeGennaro. (1990). "Stock Returns and Volatility." *Journal of Financial and Quantitative Analysis 25*, 203–214.

Bandi, F. M., and B. Perron. (2006). Long-Run Risk–Return Trade-Offs, University of Chicago, manuscript.

Bansal, R., and A. Yaron. (2004). "Risks for the Long Run: A Potential Resolution of Asset Pricing Puzzles." *Journal of Finance 59*(4), 1481–1509.

Bansal, R., R. Dittmar, and D. Kiku. (2007). "Cointegration and Consumption Risks in Asset Returns." Forthcoming in *Review of Financial Studies*.

Barndorff-Nielsen, O. E., and N. Shephard. (2002a). "Econometric Analysis of Realised Volatility and its Use in Estimating Stochastic Volatility Models." *Journal of the Royal Statistical Society, Series B 64*, 253–280.

Barndorff-Nielsen, O. E., and N. Shephard. (2002b). "Estimating Quadratic Variation Using Realized Variance." *Journal of Applied Econometrics 17*, 457–477.

Barndorff-Nielsen, O. E., S. E. Graversen, and N. Shephard. (2004). "Power Variation and Stochastic Volatility: a Review and some New Results." *Journal of Applied Probability 41A*, 133–143.

Bollerslev, T., and H. Zhou. (2002). "Estimating Stochastic Volatility Diffusion using Conditional Moments of Integrated Volatility." *Journal of Econometrics 109*, 33–65.

Booth, L. (1999). "Estimating the Equity Risk Premium and Equity Costs: New Ways of Looking at Old Data." *Journal of Applied Corporate Finance 12*, 100–112.

Brandt, M. W., and Q. Kang. (2004). "On the relationship between the conditional mean and volatility of stock returns: A latent VAR approach." *Journal of Financial Economics 72*, 217–257.

Campbell, J. Y. (1987). "Stock Returns and the Term Structure." *Journal of Financial Economics 18*, 373–399.

Campbell, J. Y. (1993). "Intertemporal Asset Pricing without Consumption Data." *American Economic Review 83*, 487–512.

Campbell, J. Y. (1996). "Understanding Risk and Return." *Journal of Political Economy 104*, 298–345.

Campbell, J. Y., and L. Hentschel. (1992). "No News is Good News: An Asymmetric Model of Changing Volatility in Stock Returns." *Journal of Financial Economics 31*, 281–318.

Chacko, G., and L. Viceira. (2003). "Spectral GMM estimation of continuous-time processes." *Journal of Econometrics 116*, 259–292.

Chernov, M., R. A. Gallant, E. Ghysels, and G. Tauchen. (2003). "Alternative Models for Stock Price Dynamics." *Journal of Econometrics 116*, 225–257.

Chou, R. Y. (1988). "Volatility Persistence and Stock Valuations: Some Empirical Evidence Using GARCH." *Journal of Applied Econometrics 3*, 279–294.

Claus, J., and J. Thomas. (2001). "Equity Premium as Low as Three Percent? Evidence from Analysts' Earnings Forecasts for Domestic and International Stock Markets." *Journal of Finance 56*(5), 1629–1666.

Donaldson, R. G., M. Kamstra and L. Kramer. (2006). Estimating the Ex Ante Equity Premium, University of Toronto, manuscript.

Engle, R. F., and G. G. L. Lee. (1999). "A Long-Run and Short-Run Component Model of Stock Return Volatility." In R. F. Engle and H. White (eds.), *Cointegration, Causality, and Forecasting*: Oxford University Press.

Engle, R. F., and J. G. Rangel. (2004). The Spline GARCH model for Unconditional Volatility and its Global Macroeconomic Causes. NYU and UCSD, Manuscript.

Engle, R. F., D. M. Lilen, and R. P. Robins. (1987). "Estimating Time Varying Risk Premia in the Term Structure: The ARCH-M Model." *Econometrica 55*, 391–407.

Engle, R. F., E. Ghysels, and B. Sohn. (2006). On the Economic Sources of Stock Market Volatility, University of North Carolina at Chapel Hill, Manuscript.

Fama, E. F., and K. R. French. (1992). "The Cross-Section of Expected Stock Returns." *Journal of Finance 47*, 427–465.

Fama, E. F., and K. R. French. (2002). "The Equity Premium." *Journal of Finance 57*(2), 637–659.

French, K. R., G. W. Schwert, and R. F. Stambaugh. (1987). "Expected Stock Returns and Volatility." *Journal of Financial Economics 19*, 3–29.

Ghysels, E., P. Santa-Clara, and R. Valkanov. (2005). "There is a Risk–Return Tradeoff After All." *Journal of Financial Economics 76*, 509–548.

Ghysels, E., P. Santa-Clara, and R. Valkanov. (2006a). "Predicting Volatility: How to Get the Most Out of Returns Data Sampled at Different Frequencies." *Journal of Econometrics 131*, 59–95.

Ghysels, E., A. Sinko, and R. Valkanov. (2006b). "MIDAS Regressions: Further Results and New Directions." Forthcoming in *Econometric Reviews*.

Glosten, L. R., R. Jagannathan, and D. E. Runkle. (1993). "On the Relation between the Expected Value and the Volatility of the Nominal Excess Return on Stocks." *Journal of Finance 48*(5), 1779–1801.

Guo, H., and R. F. Whitelaw. (2006). "Uncovering the Risk–Return Relation in the Stock Market." *Journal of Finance 61*(3), 1433–1463.

Harvey, C. R. (1989). "Time-varying conditional covariances in tests of asset pricing models." *Journal of Financial Economics 24*, 289–317.

Hsieh, D. (1991). "Chaos and Nonlinear Dynamics: Applications to Financial Markets." *Journal of Finance 46*, 1839–1877.

Inoue, A., and L. Kilian. (2004). "In-sample or out-of-sample tests of predictability: Which one should we use?." *Econometric Reviews 23*(4), 371–402.

Kiefer, N., and M. Salmon. (1983). "Testing Normality in Econometric Models." *Economics Letters 11*, 123–127.

Kim, C.-J., J. C. Morley, and C. R. Nelson. (2004). "Is there a Positive Relationship Between Stock Market Volatility and the Equity Premium?." *Journal of Money Credit and Banking 36*(3), 339–360.

Lanne, M., and P. Saikkonen. (2006). "Why is it so Difficult to Uncover the Risk–Return Tradeoff in Stock Returns?." *Economics Letters 92*, 118–125.

Linton, O., and B. Perron. (2003). "The Shape of the Risk Premium: Evidence from a Semiparametric Generalized Conditional Heteroscedasticity Model?." *Journal of Business & Economic Statistics 21*(3), 354–367.

Ljung, L., and G. Box. (1978). "On a Measure of Lack of Fit in Time-Series Models." *Biometrika 67*, 297–303.

Lundblad, C. (2007). "The Risk Return Tradeoff in the Long-Run: 1836–2003." *Journal of Financial Economics 85*, 123–150.

Macaulay, R. (1938). *The Movements of Interest Rates, Bond Yields and Stock Prices in the United States since 1856*. NBER.

Maheu, J. M., and T. H. McCurdy. (2000). "Volatility Dynamics under Duration-Dependent Mixing." *Journal of Empirical Finance 7*(3–4), 345–372.

Maheu, J. M., and T. H. McCurdy. (2002). "Nonlinear Features of FX Realized Volatility." *Review of Economics and Statistics 84*(4), 668–681.

Merton, R. C. (1973). "An Intertemporal Asset Pricing Model." *Econometrica 41*, 867–888.

Merton, R. C. (1980). "On Estimating the Expected Return on the Market: An Exploratory Investigation." *Journal of Financial Economics 8*, 323–361.

Mincer, J., and V. Zarnowitz. (1969). "The Evaluation of Economic Forecasts and Expectations." In J. Mincer (ed.), *Economic Forecasts and Expectations*. New York: National Bureau of Economic Research.

Nelson, D. B. (1990). "ARCH Models as Diffusion Approximations." *Journal of Econometrics 45*, 7–39.

Pagan, A., and Y. Hong. (1990). "Non-Parametric Estimation and the Risk Premium." In W. Barnett, J. Powell and G. Tauchen (eds.), *Nonparametric and Semiparametric Methods in Econometrics and Statistics*: Cambridge University Press.

Pastor, L., and R. F. Stambaugh. (2001). "The Equity Premium and Structural Breaks." *Journal of Finance 4*, 1207–1231.

Pastor, L., M. Sinha, and B. Swaminathan. (2007). "Estimating the Intertemporal Risk–Return Tradeoff using the Implied Cost of Capital." Forthcoming in *Journal of Finance*.

Poterba, J., and L. Summers. (1986). "The Persistence of Volatility and Stock Market Fluctuations." *American Economic Review 76*, 1142–1151.

Ross, S. (1976). "The Arbitrage Theory of Capital Asset Pricing." *Journal of Economic Theory 13*, 341–360.

Schwert, G. (1989). "Why Does Stock Market Volatility Change Over Time?." *Journal of Finance 44*, 1115–1154.

Schwert, G. W. (1990). "Indexes of U.S. Stock Prices from 1802 to 1987." *Journal of Business 63*(3), 399–426.

Schwert, G. W., and P. J. Seguin. (1990). "Heteroskedasticity in Stock Returns." *Journal of Finance 45*, 1129–1155.

Scruggs, J. T. (1998). "Resolving the Puzzling Intertemporal Relation between the Market Risk Premium and Conditional Market Variance: A Two-Factor Approach." *Journal of Finance 53*, 575–603.

Siegel, J. (1992). "The Real Rate of Interest from 1800–1990: A Study of the U.S. and the U.K." *Journal of Monetary Economics 29*, 227–252.

Smith, W., and A. Cole. (1935). *Fluctuations in American Busines, 1790–1860*: Harvard University Press.

Stambaugh, R. F. (1999). "Predictive Regressions." *Journal of Financial Economics 54*, 375–421.

Turner, C. M., R. Startz, and C. R. Nelson. (1989). "A Markov Model of Heteroskedasticity, Risk, and Learning in the Stock Market." *Journal of Financial Economics 25*, 3–22.

Whitelaw, R. F. (1994). "Time Variations and Covariations in the Expectation and Volatility of Stock Market Returns." *Journal of Finance 49*, 515–541.

Whitelaw, R. (2000). "Stock Market Risk and Return: An Equilibrium Approach." *Review of Financial Studies 13*, 521–547.

# MODULE 7

# Financial Markets

*The efficiency, credibility, and liquidity of the financial markets have been foundational to the largest economy in the world.*

### Dan Gilbert

*Developments in financial markets can have broad economic effects felt by many outside the markets.*

### Ben Bernanke

M arkets can be defined simply as places where buyers and sellers of some good or service transact business. Business organizations often must buy funds by securing loans or selling stock. This occurs when their internal supply of funding from operations is less than their need. The financial manager is concerned with the procurement of such necessary external financing at the lowest cost to the firm.

The financial marketplace is classified into distinct categories. These are the primary and secondary markets and the formal or organized exchanges and the over-the-counter-markets. The financial markets can also be further classified into the money market, capital market, spot market, futures market, and the mortgage market subcategories.

Within our society, there are always individuals, organizations, or governments that are either net savers or net users. Net savers may be defined as those individuals, organizations, or governments that have an excess of funding. Net users are defined as those individuals, organizations, or governments that have an excess of uses or, alternatively, deficit funding. The financial marketplace provides a location for the transfer of excess funds from net savers to net users.

Since net savers or investors generally have small or limited amounts of financing available, and since net users generally require large amounts of financing, an important member of the financial marketplace is the financial intermediary. Financial intermediaries, to include banks, savings and loans, insurance companies, and mutual funds, are important players in the financial markets, as they help to provide for the transfer of funds in the proper dollar unit size in the proper time frame, and they also provide for quick transfer.

Financial intermediaries provide this service by pooling the funds provided by many savers and funneling these individual small savings amounts in large units to the net users. Since financial intermediaries obtain economies of scale from their operations, the efficiency of the marketplace is enhanced by their activity.

The financial marketplace is comprised of two separate markets: the money market and the capital market. The money market includes securities or financial claims that have less than or equal to one year to maturity. The capital marketplace includes financial claims or securities that have more than one year to maturity. The money market is primarily made up of debt securities, while the capital market is made up of both debt and equity securities.

The financial marketplace, as previously noted, may be further segmented into the primary and the secondary markets. The primary marketplace is that market in which an issuer offers for sale securities that have never been previously sold. The secondary market is the market in which securities that have already been sold by the issuer and are currently outstanding and held by investors are traded to other investors.

The key to whether a transaction is taking place in the primary or the secondary market is identifying the final location of the funds involved in the trade. In the case of the primary market, all or most of the funds used to purchase securities end up in the hands of the issuer of that security. In the secondary market, the funds used for the purchase of securities end up in the hands of another investor rather than the issuer. The primary market is composed of two types of issues: initial public offerings (IPOs) and seasoned or additional issues. Seasoned issues are simply additional issues of the same securities previously issued to the public. Since similar securities are already trading in the secondary markets, they have an initial market price on which to base the offering.

Initial public offerings are offerings of securities to the public for the first time. The issuers may be start-up type firms, or they may be firms that were privately held and in business for many years. IPOs provide an additional inflow of cash for firms, and this cash may be earmarked for any number of uses, to include expansion, reduction of debt, growth-oriented investments, or any number of other uses.

In a 2010 paper entitled "Going Public to Acquire? The Acquisition Motive in IPOs," the authors (Celikyurt, Sevilir, and Shivdasani) expand on the benefits of IPOs, noting that

> in theory, an IPO creates liquidity for the firm's shares, provides an infusion of capital to fund growth, allows insiders to cash out, provides cheaper and ongoing access to capital, facilitates the sale of the company, gives founders the ability to diversify their risk, allows venture capitalists and other early-stage investors to exit their investment, and increases the transparency of the firm by subjecting it to capital market discipline.

In a 2015 paper in the *American Journal of Entrepreneurship*, Brandi and Kemelgor note that, the positive motives associated with IPOs aside, a number of negative aspects are also related to IPOs. They suggest that "going public," aside from the positive benefits, requires "control to be relinquished ... reduced flexibility is further constrained" and "due to disclosure requirements mandated by federal and state regulatory requirements, accountability as well as public scrutiny of actions and results increases."

With regard to state securities regulations, in "Chapter 7A, Merit Regulation" (1985), Brandi notes that state securities regulations do restrict some of the benefits noted in the Celikyurt paper. One area of restriction, for example, can come in the area of escrow or restrictions on insider stock. To this issue, the author notes that

> when a disparity of substantial proportion exists between the promoter or inside price paid for securities and the price paid by the new public investor, an escrow or lettering of all or part of the promotional or cheap securities may be required. Certain jurisdictions may require promoter or insider stock to be escrowed or lettered regardless of whether there is a disparity in price.

Two formal marketplaces exist for the trading of financial claims or securities. These are the exchange and the over-the-counter markets. Some exchanges, such as the New York Stock Exchange and the

American Stock Exchange, have formal geographical locations for the trading of financial claims. Others, such as the Bats exchange, are located solely on the Internet. Some players—NASDAQ (originally the National Association of Securities Dealers Automated Quotation System), for example—provide trading platforms for both exchange and over-the-counter (OTC) issues. NASDAQ is the second-largest trading system player in the world and is now known only as NASDAQ.

All individuals executing trades on the formal exchanges must meet specific requirements and are required to be licensed by those exchanges. Individuals executing trades in the over-the-counter market must be registered as brokers or dealers but do not have to meet specific requirements as set down by the exchanges. Similarly, all issues of securities traded on the formal exchanges must meet specific listing requirements. Over-the-counter issues of securities are not required to meet the same stringent requirements for trading as exchange-listed issues.

In the literature review paper "Ethics and Financial Markets: The Role of the Analyst" (2013), the author, Marianne M. Jennings, provides a lengthy and thorough review of ethics issues and remedies in the financial markets. While the study focus is on "the ethical dilemmas faced by security analysts in contrasts to other types of investment professionals, such as portfolio managers, traders, financial planners, and pension plan sponsors," the basic discussion is applicable to all of the players in the financial marketplace.

Jennings begins the story with Hammurabi's code (circa 1800 BC), making the point that ethical issues are not new. Two of the most interesting points made in the paper are her observations that

> (1) history does repeat itself, and (2) when analysts depart from three simple questions, complex issues are resolved through a thicket of codes, laws, and regulations that encourage further interpretations and exceptions and cloud ethical judgement.

The three simple questions noted include: "Does this violate the law? Is this honest? What if I were on the other side?" She notes that when ethical concerns arise in the financial marketplace, regulation is usually the result, then new ethical issues arise and, regrettably, history repeats itself, like a dog chasing its tail. The article deals with numerous ethical stories and results, providing a strong foundation in not only ethics and ethical behaviors but also in the operations of the financial markets.

## Recommended Readings

Brandi, Jay T. "Chapter 7A Merit Regulation." In *Business Organizations: Blue Sky Regulation*, by H. Sowards and N. Hirsch, 11C-Part I. New York: Matthew Bender Corp., 1985.

Brandi, Jay T. "Securities Practitioner and Blue Sky Laws: A Survey of Comments and a Ranking of States by Stringency of Regulation." *Journal of Corporation Law* 10, no. 3 (1985): 689–710.

Jennings, Marianne M. "Ethics and Financial Markets: The Role of the Analyst." Arizona State University, CFA Institute Research Foundation, 2013.

Loughran, T., and J. Ritter. "The New Issues Puzzle." *Journal of Finance* 50 (1995): 23–51.

Loughran, T., and J. Ritter. "Why Has IPO Underpricing Changed Over Time?" *Financial Management* 33 (2004): 5–37.

## Selected Readings

Brandi, Jay T., and Bruce Kemelgor. "An Expectancy Theory Model of Initial Public Offerings." *American Journal of Entrepreneurship* 8, no. 1 (2015): 44–70.

# An Expectancy Theory Model of Initial Public Offerings

By Jay T. Brandi and Bruce Kemelgor

## Abstract

[...] we present an argument for the application of expectancy theory to the decision take a privately held firm public. Expectancy theory is well suited as the foundation for the creation of a theory to describe or understand the motivation for a privately held firm to go public.

It is clear that going public is not best for every small firm desiring additional funding. Where raising cash is the primary objective, alternative sources of financing such as borrowing at financial institutions, equipment leasing, strategic partnering, securing private investors, employee stock ownership plans, government assistance programs, or the use of venture capitalists may prove to be better avenues of pursuit.

**Keywords:** Expectancy Theory, Initial Public Offering, Start Up

**JEL Codes:** G32, G34, L26, M13

## Introduction

Well established over the last fifty years, expectancy theory, although controversial, suggests that when individuals perceive that a given activity will obtain a probable beneficial result, that belief will result in the individuals taking action to accomplish the desired outcome. [...] we present an expectancy theory model as a means of explaining the entrepreneurial motivation and process of going public with an IPO.

Deeds, DeCarolis and Coombs (1998, 56) noted that "While entrepreneurs may create organizations for reasons other than economic gain, such as personal challenge or lifestyle choices, from an economic perspective the goal of entrepreneurship remains the creation of wealth through innovative activity." Contributions to wealth creation principally occur as a result of the entrepreneur's

Jay T. Brandi and Bruce Kemelgor, "An Expectancy Theory Model of Initial Public Offerings," *American Journal of Entrepreneurship*, vol. 8, no. 1, pp. 44–70. Copyright © 2015 by Addleton Academic Publishers. Reprinted with permission. Provided by ProQuest LLC. All rights reserved.

involvement in the organizational founding and growth processes (Certo, Colvin, Daily & Dalton, 2001). The resultant level of satisfaction enjoyed by the owners of privately held firms will vary from individual to individual (Brockner, Higgins & Low, 2004). Such satisfaction may evolve over time as a result of life-cycle changes (Shepherd & Haynie, 2009) and the effects of both endogenous and exogenous variables. For a variety of reasons, at some point, owners may determine that the decision to go public is a plausible alternative for the future.

As described by several researchers (Cooper & Artz, 1995; Cardon, Vincent, Singh & Drnovsek, 2009; Fauchert & Gruber, 2011), entrepreneurs are unique in that they are not motivated in the same manner as hired employees, and are not simply involved, but rather are committed to their organization. A founder/CEO will have greater personal identification with a firm, greater commitment to it and greater trust from the employees (Fischer & Pollack, 2004). The Fisher and Pollack (2004) study cites additional research which indicates that the personal assumptions and perceptions of founders play a central role in both the formulation of strategy and the manner in which influence will be shared within the firm (Fischer, et al., 2004). To further clarify, the entrepreneur as founder of a firm organizes, takes initiative, and ownership of the organizational founding process through realizing the firm as operational (Nelson, 2003). Nelson (2003) further notes, as a result of her research, that founders exercise strong strategic leadership which is valuable at the time of transition to public ownership.

The goals driving entrepreneurs to found a new venture can be either economic or non-economic. Economic goals vary, but may include the desire for enhancing wealth, providing security for family members, or funding for retirement. Success or satisfaction can be more easily identified for those seeking such financial goals as these are more readily identified and measured than non-economic goals such as a sense of achievement, satisfaction from ownership, control, or flexibility. Wennberg, Wiklund, DeTienne and Cardon (2010), citing several studies, advance the idea that people enter entrepreneurship to exploit a perceived opportunity, seek autonomy or self-realization, or for lack of alternative employment. Becoming an entrepreneur is effectively exercising a real option, which incurs both the business start-up cost and the opportunity costs of giving up an alternative career/job (Wang, Wang & Yang, 2012). Cooper, Woo and Dunkleberg (1988) and others (e.g. Baker, Miner & Eesley, 2003; Forbes, 2005) have reported that expectations tend to be higher for entrepreneurial than for non-entrepreneurial individuals. Ireland and Webb (2007) argue that in many respects, entrepreneurship is an identity construction process. The individual's needs are embraced within entrepreneurial pursuits. Gatewood, Shaver and Gartner (1995) and Krueger, Reilly and Carsrud (2000) suggest that the cognitive process of entrepreneurs can significantly affect their propensities to pursue entrepreneurial activity even in difficult periods. Brockhaus and Horwitz (1986) further suggest that the more an entrepreneur perceives control over the environment the more likely is the individual to persevere in entrepreneurial activities.

Given that entrepreneurs may have both economic and non-economic goals, have high expectations and are committed to their companies, why do some privately held firms choose to go public? IPO firms are typically cash-poor, not firms with free cash flow (Certo, et al., 2001) and, as Rock (1986) has suggested, a major reason to undertake an IPO is to produce funding for new projects.

Pastor, Taylor and Veronesi (2008) suggest the decision to take a firm public can be made to help diversify one's holdings, raise capital for investment, exploit market conditions, facilitate acquisitions, better define the firm's market value and make the firm more visible. Chod and Lyandres (2011) stress the market benefits by finding that public firms adopt riskier and more aggressive output market strategies than private firms, thus improving their competitive position. They further suggest that performing an IPO allows the firm to commit to a product market strategy that reduces the aggressiveness of its industry rivals. Shepherd and Zacharakis (2001) and Latham and Braun (2010) suggest that aside from providing additional capital, an IPO provides a means for early-stage investors to cash out.

"In theory, an IPO creates liquidity for the firm's shares, provides an infusion of capital to fund growth, allows insiders to cash out, provides cheaper and ongoing access to capital, facilitates the sale of the company, gives founders the ability to diversify their risk, allows venture capitalists and other early-stage investors to exit their investment, and increases the transparency of the firm by subjecting it to capital market discipline" (Celikyurt, Sevilir & Shivdasani, 2010, p. 345).

Yet, despite the theoretical arguments, the process of going public lacks any models to help define the motivational process over time as the firm evolves to an IPO stage.

Naffziger, Hornsby and Kuratko (1994) propose that while entrepreneurs enter the start-up process with expectations of extrinsic and intrinsic outcomes, these vary for individuals. More importantly for our purposes, they posit that such expectations evolve over time as new opportunities present themselves or as the realities of operation and competition emerge. For example, research identifies founders primarily in the context of business start-ups, but significant discussions in the literature question whether a founders' entrepreneurial management style is compatible with growing and establishing a sustainable firm (Nelson, 2003). Owner-managers have been found to become more risk-averse since they cannot diversify their firm-coupled wealth and, as such, they may opt to extract private benefits at the expense of overall firm value (Latham & Braun, 2010). For example, Bodnaruk, Kandel, Massa and Simonov (2008) found that risk-averse entrepreneurs can benefit from an IPO because diversified investors assign higher valuations to a risky asset. This can improve profitability because risk considerations generally prevent profit maximization.

[...] we present a cognitive process model adapted from the Vroom (1964) expectancy theory model as a means of explaining the entrepreneurial motivation and process of going public.

## The Intent to Launch a New Venture

Entrepreneurs have a set of goals they seek to accomplish when they decide to initiate a new venture. These goals vary for each entrepreneur. Some may seek to rapidly grow a firm, cash out, retire or move on while others may simply seek to be their own boss. Still others may attempt to provide financial security for current and future family generations.

Bird (1988, p 444) commented that "the founder's intentions determine the form and direction of an organization at its inception. Subsequent organizational success, development (including written plans), growth, and change are based on these intentions, which are modified, elaborated, embodied, or transformed." Katz and Gartner (1988, p. 431) included "intentionality" in their model of properties of emerging organizations. They stated "organizational intentionality at the time of creation reflects the goals of the agents or founding entrepreneurs." Greenberger and Sexton (1988) identify the entrepreneur's "vision" as a significant guiding force in the development of the new venture. Furthermore, Learned (1992) included intentionality and propensity to found a venture as key variables in the entrepreneurial process, while Herron and Sapiencza (1992) demonstrated the importance of the entrepreneur's "level of aspirations" in their venture initiation model. Finally, Brockner, et al., (2004) suggest that achievement oriented individuals are apt to pursue entrepreneurial tasks as a means to realize happiness. Thus, the entrepreneur's goal set should be included in any model of the venture creation process. However, it must be stated that each entrepreneur may have a goal set unique to his or her particular business and molded by his or her individual situation.

Another key factor is identified as the individual's perception that the outcomes of the envisioned organization will meet or exceed expectations. It is proposed that the entrepreneur enters the process with expectations of extrinsic and intrinsic outcomes that will result from the inception and operation of the venture. The specific expectations may vary for each individual. The expectations may evolve over time as new opportunities present themselves or as the reality of operation and competition emerges (Naffziger, et al., 1994).

Outcomes will be either intrinsic or extrinsic (psychological or tangible) in nature. Extrinsic outcomes will include financial or other tangible rewards made possible by the financial performance of the firm. Intrinsic rewards, often cited by entrepreneurs, center around the satisfaction of being one's own boss, being more in control of your own destiny, and having ultimate responsibility for the success of the venture. All outcomes will have some level of perceived value to the owner. Each owner will have his or her own system of valuing outcomes. The actual outcomes accruing as a result of ownership will then be compared with the individual's expectations in the manner discussed above. The outcome of that comparison will then influence the individual's decision to sustain entrepreneurial behavior. According to the model, the entrepreneur's expectations are then compared with the actual or perceived outcomes of the firm.

Future entrepreneurial behavior is based on the results of these comparisons. When outcomes meet or exceed expectations, the entrepreneurial behavior is positively reinforced and the individual is motivated to continue to behave entrepreneurially, either within the current venture or possibly through the initiation of additional ventures, depending on the existing entrepreneurial goal set. When outcomes fail to meet expectations, the motivation of the entrepreneur will be lower and thus will have a corresponding impact on the decision to continue to act entrepreneurially. It is important to note that these expectations will change over time. They may be modified as the venture evolves or as the entrepreneur enters succeeding individual life-cycle stages.

For example, self-employment or survival may be the overriding goals in the early stages of the venture, while later on growth and success, market share, or family succession may take precedence. This shift must be taken into account when trying to determine the strength of entrepreneurial motivation. It can be argued that when the firm ceases to achieve the goals of the entrepreneur to a satisfactory degree, the owner will terminate the organization by closing it down or terminate his or her association with it by selling the firm. Following the Porter and Lawler (1968) theory, entrepreneurs will be motivated to continue to behave entrepreneurially as long as they view that behavior as instrumental in leading to goal accomplishment, i.e. as long as they view that behavior as being effective, or as long as they see entrepreneurship as the alternative with the highest expected outcome. Performance will always be linked to successful entrepreneurship because at least some of an entrepreneur's goals will be performance oriented.

## Motivation to Take the Firm Public

The process of going public begins with some motivational impetus. For privately held firms, the decision to go public is a critical and key event in the history of the organization. As a result of a public offering of securities, many of the cultural and even operational aspects of the firm, not just the financial, may be affected.

## Positive Aspects of Going Public—Second Level Outcomes

Entrepreneurs may choose to take a firm public for any of a variety of reasons. For entrepreneurs who thrive on the thrill of battle, for example, the funds may be for the sale of their own stock thus enabling them to begin new ventures. Other owners may simply be looking to retire or diversify wealth. Finally, the entrepreneur may wish to expand the business, pay off other sources of financing, finance research and development, or acquire other firms. These motives, if acted upon, can ultimately result in the realization of the initial public offering.

While the need for cash from a public offering is often necessitated by the previously discussed motives, other uses for the equity are also available to the issuer. If expansion is to be pursued via the acquisition of other firms, the authorized stock may be more easily utilized for the acquisition if the firm is publicly traded as opposed to privately held. The additional benefit in such situations is the ability to acquire another firm without utilizing existing cash.

Perhaps the most important outcome is the inflow of funding, which unlike debt financing, requires no repayment. In addition, unlike the interest required on debt financing, the firm is under no obligation to pay dividends where profits are low or non-existent. The economic utility related to raising additional capital can outweigh the noneconomic utility of remaining private (Leitterstorf & Rau, 2014).

As a result, and perhaps ironically, additional equity funding improves the financial condition of the organization such that debt financing, probably with better terms than previously available, will in fact be easier to obtain in the future. Future debt or preferred equity issues can also be enhanced with warrants on the new publicly traded stock.

Chemmanur and He (2011) advocate that going public not only allows a firm to raise capital at a lower cost than if it were a private firm, but may also allow it to take market share from competitors who remain private. This can lead to gaining additional credibility with customers and suppliers, hiring more qualified employees, creating better reward systems and even being able to acquire related firms in the industry through use of their stock (Chemmanur & He, 2011).

Further, the success of the firm's operations and its subsequent market performance can, if positive, provide a market for future additional issues of public securities. Equity, once publicly issued, can also be used for employee incentive and executive compensation packages via stock options, stock appreciation rights, and stock bonuses.

The valuation of privately held firms can be a difficult task and buyers and sellers often are unable to agree on a fair price without significant and sometimes costly negotiation. The public trading of the firm's stock can provide a publicly determined market value (Pastor, et al., 2008).

Similarly, the public trading of the firm's securities provides a market-based value for estate, and for gifting purposes. Additionally, the ability to liquidate estate-related shares to pay estate taxes and to settle disputes is greatly improved due to the enhanced marketability and liquidity derived from going public. Going public through an IPO is optimal when the market value of the firm (value to investors) exceeds the private value of the firm (value to the entrepreneur) (Pastor, et al., 2008).

By going public a firm may also obtain an intangible benefit in the form of enhanced prestige. The firm's public trading status may improve not only its ability to raise funds, but may also improve product or service sales and supplier interest due to the increased notoriety achieved via the financial markets. Suppliers and customers are more likely to commit resources to firms that they perceive as more likely to succeed (Gompers, Kovner, Lerner & Scharfstein, 2010). Customers and suppliers may even take a more active approach by acquiring shares in the firm.

Finally, an increase in the level of insider or private owner satisfaction may result from a successful public offering. Completing such an offering can provide a psychological feeling of accomplishment and verification of one's worth. The resultant belief that "success breeds success" can lead to increased firm performance and the desire to explore further opportunities (Gompers, et al., 2010). This payoff for previous hard work and effort may, in fact, be of more value to some owners than the financial or managerial benefits that result.

# Negative Aspects of Going Public

Regardless of the motive, going public is far from a risk-free proposition. As such there are both positive and negative aspects to the "going-public" decision.

Several negative aspects or disadvantages likely accrue when a firm goes public. From a cultural perspective, the ability to control the organization and to operate flexibly and autonomously with a minimum of external reporting responsibility is lost when a firm obtains public financing. As a result of both legal and practical constraints, for example, the ability to employ relatives and friends, and to provide unique compensation deals is significantly reduced following a public offering.

The extent to which control is relinquished is dependent on the number and percentage of shares to be offered to investors. Further dilution of ownership can occur as a result of subsequent additional offerings, the exercise of warrants and options, and acquisitions with stock.

Reduced flexibility is further constrained by a necessary concern for the publicly determined market price of the firm's stock. Where decisions were previously made without such concerns, managers must now undertake a thorough assessment of the potential for return, risk, and the ultimate effect of decisions on firm value. Many firms may in fact take this assessment responsibility to the extreme, subjecting not just significant but also minor decisions to such analysis.

Due to the disclosure requirements mandated by federal and state regulatory requirements, accountability as well as public scrutiny of actions and results increases. A common but seldom realized fear of private owners is the loss of a competitive advantage when disclosure becomes a necessity. The continuing reporting requirements of securities laws further serve to increase annual accounting and legal costs.

The speed with which management can act or react can also be affected when a firm becomes publicly held. The ability of the firm to react quickly may, for example, be reduced when decisions must go to a board of directors, or to public shareholders. Taking a firm public requires a large amount of time, effort and resources on behalf of the filing organization, with the typical IPO taking anywhere from 9 to 18 months and costing an average of approximately 7% to 14% of the gross proceeds (Latham, et al., 2010). As Ritter (1987) observed, the costs to go public can differ between firmly underwritten and best efforts basis offerings. Ritter (1987) found that firm underwriting costs averaged about 21.22% while best efforts underwritings averaged about 31.87%.

On average, direct investment banking costs can reach 10% of the offering total, while the additional costs of printing prospectuses and certificates, filing registrations with federal and state agencies, and various legal and accounting fees can often amount to another 10% of the total offering. Indirect costs can also be incurred by going public. Ritter's (1987) study provided evidence that underpricing or "money left on the table" when "defined as the percentage price change from the offer price to the first day's closing bid price is 14.80% for firm commitment offers and 47.78% for best efforts offers." The positive side of this, however, is that firm offerings raise an average of $8.88 million as opposed to the $2.37 million raised, on average, in a best efforts underwriting.

Many privately held firms provide monetary compensation or other perquisites at higher levels than publicly held firms in an effort to reduce or eliminate double taxation by keeping taxable dividend payments to a minimum. While, by arrangement with underwriters, some non-dividend paying stock can be provided to the insiders going public, the need to pay dividends becomes a stock valuation rather than a tax decision in publicly traded firms.

Further, as a result of state securities regulations, insiders and promoters of IPO stock are often also subject to stock resale restrictions (Brandi, 1985). Such restrictions are required to provide a level of safety to new investors, and to ensure a continued interest by the affected parties in the success of the firm after the public offering. These restrictions, commonly known as an IPO lockup, are typically for a period of up to 6 months during which certain insiders are prohibited from selling their holdings in an open market (Tolia & Yip, 2003). Lock-ups are also a signal to investors that insiders are not seeking to cash out in advance of imminent bad news (Arthurs, Busenitz, Hoskisson & Johnson, 2009).

While the ability to use publicly traded stock to pay estate taxes can be cited as an advantage to going public, and the ready market based valuation alleviates the need to have a costly business valuation performed, there is a negative aspect to this issue. The market often values stocks at significantly high multiples of book value, earnings, or sales. Too often these market values are inflated and not founded on strong fundamentals which may result in an unwarranted high estate tax burden.

## Previous Findings on the Effects of IPOs

Jensen and Meckling (1976), Jain and Kini (1994), and Holthausen and Larcker (1996) suggest that as the ownership interests of founders decline, these stockholders become more estranged from their organizations, and firm performance is negatively affected. Jain and Kini (1994) attribute the reduction to a decrease in incentives to improve firm performance. Similarly, Morck, Shleifer, and Vishny (1988) find that lower measures of corporate value accompany lower percentages of ownership. Thus, the type of owner with concentrated holdings in a firm will be an important influence on the selection of objectives, governance, and conduct of the firm in addition to performance (Sur & Martens, 2013).

In a 1997 study, however, Mikkelson, Partch and Shah conclude that the changes in equity ownership that result from going public do not lead to changes in incentives that affect operating performance. They rationalize that a substitution of compensation and other benefits realized after going public replace the benefits of significant ownership positions.

Nelson (2003) revealed that the presence of a founder-CEO at the time of an IPO results in higher firm valuation. And the significant personal investments of time, energy and money a founder typically expends in getting the company to an IPO stage results in a founder-CEO being more committed to completing the transformation and seeing the company through the IPO transition (Nelson, 2003). Aldrich (1999) also found that the presence of a founder-CEO at the time of an IPO helps the continuation or extension of the firm's existing strategy (which resulted in the firm getting to the

IPO stage in the first place), thus reducing risks associated with major strategic shifts requiring skills the firm does not possess. Fischer, et al. (2004), commenting upon their earlier research, suggest that direct CEO ownership of the company's stock is more effective than stock options and other forms of incentive compensation in aligning management and shareholder interests and insuring that the newly public firm does not fail.

In their study, Certo, et al., (2001) found that entrepreneurs create wealth for first day investors through their very presence as CEOs (i.e. founder-manager) of IPO-stage firms. Yet, citing other research, they note that a large majority of founder-managers do not make the transition to a professional style of management, largely because they do not make changes in management style in response to the demands of an evolving organization (Certo, et al., 2001). Fischer, et al. (2004) also found that the presence of a founder-CEO who retained a high level of direct ownership was most beneficial to a firm that initiated an IPO. Thus, it is suggested that the founder-CEO has a key role in advancing an IPO and in initial wealth generation, but may become somewhat of a liability if he or she retains significant ownership as the organization evolves.

The question remains as to what motivates the decision to go public and how such a decision is reached.

## Expectancy Theory

Expectancy theory, separately introduced by Atkinson (1958) and Lewin (1958) is based on the assumption that individuals take action to realize desired value-providing outcomes after assessing the probabilities of outcome success. Vroom (1964) is often credited with proposing two separate models of expectancy. One model for predicting valence outcomes and the second, the behavioral choice or job effort model, predicting the amount of force necessary for individuals to actively pursue an end outcome.

A number of models, with their roots in the expectancy models presented by Vroom (1964) have been proposed over time. The Vroom model is essentially a theory of the cognitive process of motivation suggesting that individuals will or will not be motivated to act based on their perceptions of the potential outcomes of those acts.

According to the theory, individuals are motivated to act when they form a belief that beneficial objectives can be achieved as the result of performance and that performance provides the specified beneficial objectives or rewards. The theory allows for both first- and second-level outcomes. Second-level outcomes are dependent on attaining the first-level objectives and, according to the theory, the choice to act in a manner geared to realizing the desired objectives is voluntary.

Expectancy theory as originally proposed is a multiplicative theory comprised of three essential components—expectancy, instrumentality, and valence. Each of the components can individually affect motivation, but when combined can provide a magnified level of motivation. As presented

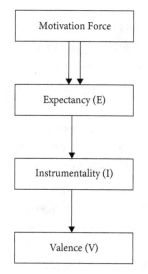

**Figure 11.1:** Basic Expectancy Model: Expectation-Performance-Reward

by Vroom (1964), this magnifying or multiplicative version of the theory (Figure 11.1) can be presented as:

$$\text{Motivation Force} = \text{Expectancy} \times \text{Instrumentality} \times \text{Valence}.$$

Expectancy (E) can best be described as simply the level of confidence that engaging in a specific act or effort can result in attaining a specified objective or first-level outcome or performance. Instrumentality (I) is best defined here as the probability that achieving the first-level outcome or performance will lead to the desired end result or second-level outcome. Both Expectancy and Instrumentality can range in value from zero to plus one. As Mitchell (1974) points out, however, expectancies differ from instrumentalities in that expectancies are based on an action-outcome relationship, while instrumentality is an outcome-outcome relationship. Instrumentalities are therefore "perceived correlations" while expectancies are "perceived probabilities."

The Valence (V) can be considered a value-adding factor or reward representing the importance of the final outcome or reward to be gained by the first-level outcome or initial performance. The value of an action's outcome as perceived by the individual, not the actual outcome of that activity, defines the valence of performance expectancy. In essence, this aspect of expectancy theory is based on the simple assumption that value perception varies across individuals and thus provides variable incentives to performance. The actual value, or achieved utility of the outcome to the individual may differ from valence, however, because of the possible variation between perceived and realized value. The Valence can have a value ranging from minus one to plus one.

Because the model as presented is multiplicative, if any of the model elements has a value of zero, no motivation exists. Locke and Latham (1990) further propose that the theory predicts that when instrumentality and valence are held constant, expectancy will be positively associated with performance level. Various studies substantiate the Locke and Latham (1990) hypothesis, (Garland, 1984; Locke, Motowidlo, & Bobko, 1986).

The expectations theory model requires effort and performance (P) to attain an outcome (O) or reward. The expectations model links these with the basic factors of expectation (E), instrumentality (I), and valence (V) as presented in Figure 11.2 to provide the motivation to act.

The general application of expectancy theory consists of the two linking factors often presented as shown in Figure 11.3. The specified factors include effort-performance expectancy (E-P), and the performance-outcome expectancy (P-O) linkages. The impetus to act, however, must come from a perceived and favorable outcome. The expected value of the benefit to be derived should therefore dictate whether an individual is prompted to consider the effort required to achieve the result. That factor is simply the valence or reward as defined earlier.

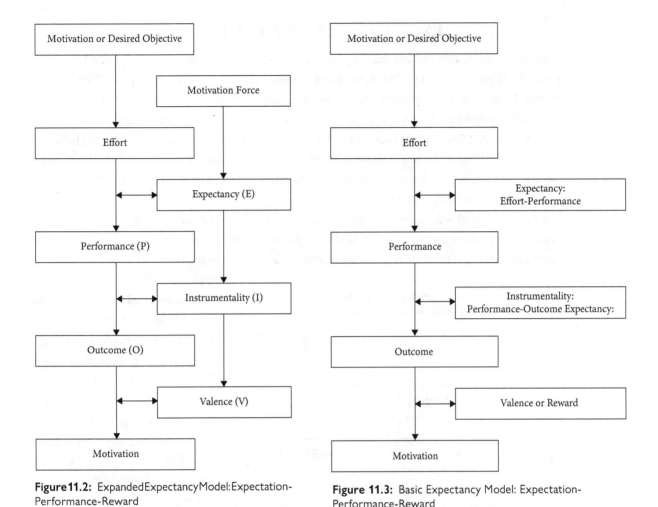

**Figure 11.2:** Expanded Expectancy Model: Expectation-Performance-Reward

**Figure 11.3:** Basic Expectancy Model: Expectation-Performance-Reward

Essentially an input-output relationship, effort-performance (E-P) expectancy is based on the assumption that an individual perceives the level of performance and effort necessary to achieve a desired outcome. It further depends on the assumption that the individual believes that the effort expended will actually result in the necessary level of performance required to attain a desired outcome.

Belief in the direct relationship between satisfactorily completing the necessary functions (via effort) and achieving the ultimate outcome is defined as performance-outcome (P-O) expectancy. The P-O linkage may be defined as the determined probability that the necessary performance will lead to the desired outcome while the I-P link provides insight as to the level of reward or benefit to be derived from achieving the objective. Scholl (2002) includes these linkages for a restatement of the original multiplicative Vroom (1964) model where R is designated as the desired reward or outcome as:

$$\text{Motivation Force} = (\text{E-P}) \times (\text{P-R}) \times \text{V(R)}.$$

# Expectancy Theory and The IPO

Particularly important when considering the application of the expectancy model for an IPO is the work of Fishbein and Ajzen (1975), Ajzen and Fishbein, (1980), and Miller and Grush (1988) which expanded expectancy theory by including environmental effects and individuality. Fishbein and Ajzen (1975) point out that individual attitude provides the impetus or motivation to take action. Further, Miller and Grush (1988) note that while early expectancy theories suggested that the behavior of all individuals was rationally determined by the perceived likelihood and desirability of outcomes associated with various behaviors, later studies found that expectancy theory may not be applicable to all individuals or in all situations.

An abundance of work in organizational behavior and occupational choice has been done with the expectancy theory framework as a foundation. Weiner (1986), however, posits that most cognitive theories include expectancy theory in some way to explain actions, thus setting the foundation for our application of expectancy theory to explain why individuals choose to go public with offerings of securities of privately-held companies.

As adapted from Gatewood (1993) and Mitchell (1974) a simple restatement of Figure 11.3 is presented in Figure 11.4 with the inclusion of the process application for a firm considering an IPO. Expected or desired outcomes may be categorized as either level one or level two.

First level outcomes are considered to be the basic or fundamental outcome desired or, in this case, the offering via an IPO. Second level outcomes are more indirect and result from the attainment of first level outcomes. Second level outcomes for an IPO would be the ability to use the funds from a successful IPO for the necessary uses providing the initial motivation to undertake the offering.

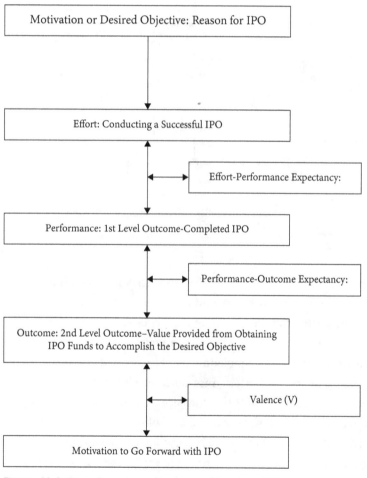

**Figure 11.4:** Basic Expectancy Model as Adapted for IPO

The end reward or valence concerns actual value to the firm of a successful process, in this case a successful IPO and funds available for desired purposes The basic motivation or desired objectives of the entrepreneur or privately held firm provide the basic rationale for considering an IPO.

## Motivation and Perceived Outcomes

An expanded presentation of the application of expectancy theory is provided in Figure 11.5. For owners considering an initial public offering (IPO), their motivation, as previously noted, may come from a variety of perceived second-level objectives or goals. One objective prompting a privately held firm to consider an IPO might be to improve the firm's finances to include increasing working capital or reducing the firm's debt. Alternatively a firm might use IPO funding for research and

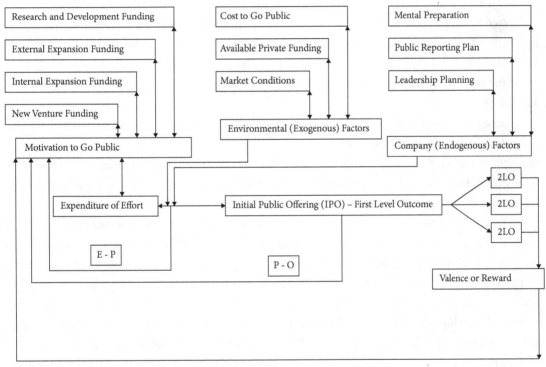

Legend:

Motivation to Go Public: Reason for IPO
Instrumentality or Performance: Actions to Complete IPO
Valence or Reward: Funds for Desired Use
E - P: Effort – Performance Expectancy Linkage
P - O: Performance – Outcome Expectancy Linkage
Initial Public Offering: First Level Outcome
2LO: Second Level Outcomes

**Figure 11.5:** In-Depth Expectancy Model of the IPO Process

development or expansion, or simply to improve net worth thereby enhancing the firm's ability to borrow funds in the future. Additional reasons may include gaining the prestige of being a publicly traded company, improving the liquidity of shares for current stockholders or developing a market-derived stock price.

## Effort and Performance Required to Go Public

Once a firm's leadership is convinced that the outcome of obtaining public financing is in fact a desirable outcome, and that the environment is favorable to successful financing, management must take action (effort and performance or E-P) to achieve the result. The decision to go public should not be short-term in nature. To ensure that the firm is adequately prepared, some believe as noted by Fischer and Pollack (2004) that the organization should prepare as much as two years in advance.

The effect of both endogenous and exogenous environmental variables on the decision to go public is significant. To go public a firm must first ensure that it is, in fact, ready for such an undertaking. The size of the firm, credibility and capability of the management team, growth prospects, and the use of the proceeds must be considered to ensure that the firm will be appealing to both underwriters and the market.

Management should recognize the probability of a successful offering by realizing that generally, firms going public are often expected to have at least $10 million in annual revenues, $1 million of net income, and growth anticipated in the range of 25% to 50 % at least for the next two to five years. If the firm does not meet these criteria, working towards those goals should become a priority before an offering is attempted.

The effort expended towards a public offering must include assembling a registration team to include attorneys, independent accountants, and most importantly, an underwriter—although this route can be circumvented via internal underwriting, underwriter's counsel and the appropriate company representatives. The choice of an investment banker is extremely important. While second tier bankers may be cheaper than those considered first tier, the name of the underwriter can carry a troubled offering. The idea here is that if the offering or underlying firm is questionable, investors may still choose to participate because of a reliance on the knowledge and integrity of the sponsoring underwriter.

The team, once assembled, must have the necessary information to successfully accomplish the task of taking the firm public. The information required should include five years of financial data, as well as data on growth prospects, competitors, and product markets.

The effort required to realize the desired outcomes is the completion of a successful IPO. For an IPO, the E-P linkage or Expectation is the confidence that the IPO will be successful. The IPO itself is the result of the effort expended and is defined as a first-order outcome.

# Exogenous and Endogenous Factors

The cost to go public, for example, is an initial consideration of primary importance when the basic objective is cash financing. If the cost of non-public funding is fair and acceptable, the decision to go public may not be appropriate in such situations. Provided that private funding is available, the organization's value and growth prospects might be better served using those sources than by issuing a public offering. This can be viewed as delaying the public financing until a later date with the issuance of a lesser number of shares.

The question of motivation becomes important when determining if the timing is correct from a market perspective. If one motive is to provide funding to buy out existing insiders, the market may view this as a negative and question the reduction of insider investment when the offering goes to the public. Similar concerns pertain to offerings in which the funds are to be used for payment of debt or insider dividends, neither of which contributes to the growth of the firm.

Often a firm may have negative working capital, a fact that can be circumvented by an adequately disclosed explanation. Liquidity issues such as increasing inventories or accounts receivable may also be challenges to a firm going public. Concentration of sales in one or a few customers, or similar reliance on one or a few suppliers of necessary resources can also be concerns for new investors.

To go public, it is important that both the firm and the marketplace be ripe for investment interest in the stock to be offered. If the firm does not have an adequate history of profitability and success, or if the marketplace is not conducive to initial public offerings, the offering may fail. Revenues and margins should be growing, not be in decline for an offering to be successful.

Timing is a critical entrepreneurial skill; market timing skill is a component of success that comes from starting a company at an opportune time and place (Gompers, et al., 2010; Chemmanur, et al., 2011). Entrepreneurs who have good market timing skill will have an easier time attracting high quality resources (Gompers, et al., 2010). New faddish or limelight firms, or industries can beat the odds here, but such is the exception, not the rule. The offering success of internet firms in the late nineties can be looked upon as an example of this deviation from the norm.

Similarly, the market must be open to initial public offerings in general. If the market is weak, prices are suffering, and investors are wary, the offering may be doomed to failure regardless of the firm's strengths. The external factors affecting the success of the issue include the political climate, interest rate movement, inflation forecasts, the economic outlook, foreign affairs as well as a myriad of other influences. When the market is not ready for a public offering, failure can be costly and leave an unnecessary and unwarranted stigma attached to the organization.

Numerous issues must be addressed to include determining if the firm wishes to utilize a capital structure that includes preferred stock or classes of common stock; the number of shares to be authorized for public sale; whether privately held stock should be split before the offering; verifying that company stock records are current; clearing up or altering contractual, compensation, and loan arrangements with insiders, suppliers, and customers prior to going public; altering articles of incorporation or bylaws; determining if affiliated companies should be combined to make the firm more attractive and thus more valuable; and finally, determining if the current management team is credible and capable of managing a publicly held company. Once the team has verified that the firm is ready to go public, the type of offering, the underwriting arrangement—to include a pricing agreement-and whether the offering will include "kickers"—to enhance its' appeal to investors must be determined.

Paramount to the successful public offering is the preparation and filing of registration statements for both federal and appropriate state regulators, and prospectuses for use in the sale of the securities to be offered. Adequate financial and organizational information must be obtained and provided to the registration team. One necessary decision is whether the offering will be a full public offering or a smaller Regulation A, Intrastate, private, or limited offering. Such smaller offerings are exempt from the registration requirements of the Securities Act of 1933 thereby reducing costs and some disclosure requirements.

Related to the filing of registration statements is the decision as to the states in which to offer the securities. A number of states utilize a substantive form of regulation in addition to the disclosure form of the federal government. This substantive or merit regulation (Brandi, 1985; Brandi 1987, pp 699–702; Brandi, 1987, pp 713–714), often referred to as Blue Sky Law, further constrains insiders and promoters via requirements on the offering price and dilution to new investors; the issuance of cheap stock; the amount of required promoters investment; the escrow of promoter stock; the issuance of options and warrants to promoters and insiders; voting rights; and the amount of offering expenses and commissions which can be paid to underwriters in an offering.

Working with the underwriters, an initial offering price must be identified and approved by regulators (Brandi, 1985; Brandi, 1987, pp 701–702). The offering price has several implications from the desirability of the issue to the underwriter, and the number of shares to be offered, to the psychological effect the price may provide in the investing market. The minimum price for IPO shares is generally considered to be around $5 to $10. The minimum number of shares to be offered is generally around the 300,000 to 400,000 share range.

Prior to going public it will be necessary for management to create a well thought out and clearly articulated business plan. The creation of such a strategic game plan can serve to advise interested investors, regulators, and media of critical issues and objectives, and can provide the standards against which the organization's performance can be measured. Post-IPO firms are already introduced to additional risk as they attempt to overcome vulnerabilities stemming from their newness and they must adapt their structures and processes, attaining new skills and routines, and learning to deal with an expanded shareholder base with often conflicting demands (Latham, et al., 2010).

The mental preparation of the firm's owners and management must also be complete prior to going public. Mental preparation is necessary due to the culture shock that can follow the move from private to public status. Not only is there a loss of free and flexible control, but the need to publicly account for actions and results is a stressful and sometimes distasteful necessity. Management and board members alike must be ready to undergo public inquiry and criticism.

A related concern is the preparation the firm has placed on leadership planning and grooming. When key entrepreneurs are present, retaining them usually increases the chances that the venture will continue to grow and create value for its investors (Arthurs, et al., 2009). In addition, prestigious top management teams have also been found to help certify IPO firms in the eyes of shareholders (Certo, et al., 2007). Taken together, these studies and others indicate that growth-oriented changes undertaken by an experienced and capable leader or management team are much more acceptable to stakeholders (Florin, et al., 2003). However, if credible and capable leadership does not appear to exist within the firm, there may be a push by the public owners to replace current managers or board members with new external leaders. The firm must plan to avoid this, or gear up to cope with the change if mandated.

As the move to public funding carries the need for accountability and financial reporting, the need for appropriate information systems increases as well. The organization must be prepared to provide timely and accurate information, and must be capable of dealing with inquisitive media and regulators as well as investors, both friendly and hostile. The negative valuation or legal repercussions which can result from an inability to handle financial reporting needs quickly and efficiently can be devastating to an otherwise efficient and profitable firm.

For the IPO, the P-O linkage between the performance or successful IPO and the second-level outcomes or reward is the Instrumentality or confidence that the IPO will provide the funding necessary to realize the initial objectives which provided the initial motivation to consider an IPO. As discussed earlier, the end reward or valence concerns the actual value to the firm of the realized second-level outcomes.

## Conclusions

[...] we present an argument for the application of expectancy theory to the decision take a privately held firm public. Expectancy theory is well suited as the foundation for the creation of a theory to describe or understand the motivation for a privately held firm to go public.

It is clear that going public is not best for every small firm desiring additional funding. Where raising cash is the primary objective, alternative sources of financing such as borrowing at financial institutions, equipment leasing, strategic partnering, securing private investors, employee stock ownership plans, government assistance programs, or the use of venture capitalists may prove to be better avenues of pursuit.

While going public provides a new beginning, it also signifies the end of the business as the private owners knew it. While, for example, image and funding possibilities may be enhanced, a new fiduciary responsibility is created, public scrutiny of disclosed information and managerial decisions is ensured, and varying amounts of control are lost. The application of the expectancy theory to initial public offerings is a new approach to describing the motivation, rationale, process and rewards of moving from a privately held firm to a publicly held one.

A variety of reasons exist for an entrepreneur to consider taking a privately held firm public. A number of possible negative results for entrepreneurs are present as well. The model suggests that entrepreneurs will be motivated to take a firm public if the rewards, either extrinsic or intrinsic, provide enough value. The process and factors contributing to the success or failure of an IPO can be specified within the expectancy model as can the potential rewards to be derived. We posit, therefore, that the expectancy model provides a logical framework for the process, but requires validation.

While the model appears to be applicable to the IPO decision, several avenues of consideration warrant further review. Further work is necessary, for example, to determine the specific motives of entrepreneurs moving from private to publicly-held firm status is necessary and to what degree the entrepreneur was actually aware of all the procedural considerations and factors affecting an initial public offering. How well prepared was the entrepreneur, the firm, and the management team, to deal with all the endogenous and exogenous factors affecting an initial offering?

Aside from studies seeking a basic understanding of entrepreneurial considerations as outlined in the IPO expectancy model, we suggest that future longitudinal studies should seek to determine, for example, if gender, age, educational, or industry differences exist and to what extent they may affect the motivation for a "going-public" decision.

Additional study should also be geared to ascertaining the ability of entrepreneurs, to time the marketplace for initial public offerings relative to their degree of understanding and preparation as revealed by an expectancy model analysis. Finally, as a number of studies have indicated previously, operating performance and IPO activity appear to be related, another area of possible research should consider the after-IPO success of a firm relative to the expectancy model description of an entrepreneur prior to the IPO.

# References

Arthurs, J.D., Busenitz, L.W., Hoskisson, R.E. and Johnson, R.A. (2009). Firm-specific capital and governance in IPO firms: Addressing agency and resource dependence concerns. *Entrepreneurship Theory and Practice.* 34(3): 845–865.

Ajzen, I., & Fishbein, M. (1980). *Understanding Attitudes and Predicting Social Behavior.* Englewood Cliffs, NJ: Prentice Hall.

Aldrich, H. (1999). *Organizations Evolving.* Thousand Oaks, CA: Sage.

Atkinson, J. W. (1958). Motivational determinants of risk-taking behavior. *Psychological Review,* 64(6), 359–372.

Baker, T., Miner, A. and Eesley, D. (2003). Improvising firms: Bricolage, account giving and improvisational competencies in the founding process. *Research Policy.* 32: 255–276.

Bird, B.J. (1988). Implementing entrepreneurial ideas: the case for intention, *Academy of Management Review,* 13(3): 442–453.

Brandi, J.T. (1985). *Chapter 7A, Merit Regulation,* 11C-Part 1 Business Organizations, Sowards and Hirsch, Blue Sky Regulation, Matthew Bender Corp., New York.

Brandi, J.T. (1987). Merit securities regulation, market efficiency, and new issue stock performance. *Journal of Corporation Law.* 12(4); 699–712.

Brandi, J.T. (1987). The silver lining in blue sky laws: the effect of merit regulation on common stock returns and market efficiency. *Journal of Corporation Law.* 12(4); 713–734.

Brockhaus, R.H. and Horwitz, P.S. (1986). The psychology of the entrepreneur. In D.L. Sexton and R.W. Smilor, eds., *The Art and Science of Entrepreneurship.* Cambridge, MA: Ballinger: 25–48.

Brockner, J., Higgins, E.T. and Low, M.B. (2004) Regulatory focus theory and the entrepreneurial process. *Journal of Business Venturing.* 19 (2), 203–220.

Cardon, M.S., Vincent, J., Singh, J. and Drnovsek, M. (2009). The nature and experience of entrepreneurial passion. *The Academy of Management Review.* 34(3), 511–532.

Celikyurt, U., Sevilir, M. and Shivdasani, A. (2010). Going public to acquire? The acquisition motive in IPOs. *Journal of Financial Economics.* 96: 345–363.

Certo, S.T., Covin, J.G., Daily, C.M. and Dalton, D.R. (2001). Wealth and the effects of founder management among IPO-Stage new ventures. *Strategic Management Journal,* 22 (6/7): 641–658.

Certo, S.T., Holmes, R.M. and Holcomb, T.R. (2007). The influence of people on the performance of IPO firms. *Business Horizons.* 50: 271–276.

Chemmanur, T. J. and He, J. (2011). IPO waves, product market competition and the going public decision: Theory and evidence. *Journal of Financial Economics,* 101, 382–412.

Chod, J. and Lyandres, E. (2011). Strategic IPOs and product market competition. *Journal of Financial Economics.* 100, 45–67.

Cooper, A.C, and Artz, K.W. (1995). Determinants of satisfaction for entrepreneurs. *Journal of Business Venturing,* 10(6): 439–457.

Cooper, A.C., Woo, C.W. and Dunkelberg, W.C. (1988). Entrepreneurs' perceived chances for success. *Journal of Business Venturing,* 3(2): 97–108.

Deeds, D.L., DeCarolis, D. and Coombs, J.E. (1998). Firm-specific resources and wealth creation in high-technology ventures: Evidence from newly public biotechnology firms. *Entrepreneurship Theory and Practice,* 22(3): 55–73.

Fauchart, E. and Gruber, M. (2011). Darwinians, communitarians and missionaries: the role of founder identity in entrepreneurship. *Academy of Management Journal,* 54(5), 935–957.

Fischer, H.M. and Pollock, T.G. (2004). Effects of social capital and power on surviving transformational change: The case of Initial Public Offerings. *Academy of Management Journal,* 47(4): 463–481.

Fishbein, M and Ajzen, I. (1975). *Belief, Attitude, Intention, and Behavior: An Introduction to theory and research.* Reading, MA.: Addison-Wesley.

Florin, J., Lubatkin, M., and Schulze, W. (2003). A social capital model of high-growth ventures. *Academy of Management Journal.* 46(3): 374–384.

Forbes, D.P. (2005). The effects of strategic decision making on entrepreneurial self-efficacy. *Entrepreneurship Theory and Practice.* 29: 599–626.

Gatewood, E. (1993). The expectancies in public sector venture assistance. *Entrepreneurship Theory and Practice.* 18(1): 91–95.

Gatewood, E.J., Shaver, K.G, and Gartner, W.B. (1995). A longitudinal study of cognitive factors influencing start-up behaviors and success at venture creation. *Journal of Business Venturing*, 10: 371–391.

Gompers, P., Kovner, A., Lerner, J. and Scharfstein, D. (2010). Performance persistence in entrepreneurship. *Journal of Financial Economics.* 96, 18–32.

Greenberger, D.B. & Sexton, D.L. (1988). An interactive model for new venture creation. *Journal of Small Business Management.* 26(3): 107–118.

Holthausen, R. and D. Larker. (1996). The financial performance of reverse leveraged buyouts. *Journal of Financial Economics.* 24(3): 293–332.

Jain, B.A. and Kini, O. (1994). The post-issue operating performance of IPO firms. *Journal of Finance.* 49(5): 1699–1726.

Jensen, M., and W. Meckling. (1976). The theory of the firm: managerial behavior, agency costs, and ownership structure. *Journal of Financial Economics.* 3(4): 305–360.

Katz, J.A, and Gartner, W.B. (1988). Properties of Emerging Organizations, *Academy of Management Review*, 13(3): 429–441.

Latham, S. and Braun, M.R. (2010). To IPO or to not IPO: Risks, uncertainty and the decision to go public. *British Journal of Management*, 21, 666–683.

Learned, K.E. (1992). What happened before the organization? A model of organization formation, *Entrepreneurship Theory & Practice*, 17(1): 39–48.

Leitterstorf, M.P. and Rau, S.B. (2014). Socioemotional wealth and IPO underpricing of family firms. *Strategic Management Journal*, 35, 751–760.

Lewin, K. (1958). Group decision and social change. In E. E. Maccoby, T. M. Newcomb, and E. L. Hartley, eds. *Readings in Social Psychology.* New York: Holt, Rinehart & Winston, 197–211.

Locke, E., Frederick, E. Lee, C., and Bobko, P. (1984). Effects of self-efficacy, goals and task strategies on task performance. *Journal of Applied Psychology,* 69 (2), 241–251.

Locke, E.A. & Latham, G.P. (1990). Work motivation and satisfaction: Light at the End of the Tunnel. *Psychological Science,* 1(2), 240–246.

Locke, E.A., Motowidlo, S. J. and Bobko, P. (1986). Using self-efficacy theory to resolve the conflict between goal setting theory and expectancy theory in organizational behavior in industrial/organizational psychology, *Journal of Social and Clinical Psychology,* 4, 328–338.

Miller, L.E. and Grush, J.E. (1988). Improving predictions in expectancy theory research: effects of personality, expectancies, and norms. *The Academy of Management Journal.* 31(1): 107–122.

Mikkelson, W., Partch, M. and K. Shah. (1997). Ownership and operating performance of companies that go public. *Journal of Financial Economics.* 44: 281–307.

Mitchell, T. R. (1974). Expectancy models of job satisfaction, occupational preference, and effort: a theoretical, and methodological appraisal. *Psychological Bulletin.* 81(12): 1053–1077.

Morck, R., A. Shleifer, and R. Vishny. (1988). Management ownership and market valuation: an empirical analysis. *Journal of Financial Economics.* 20: 293–315.

Naffziger, D.W., Hornsby, J.S., and Kuratko, D.F. (1994). A proposed research model of entrepreneurial motivation. *Entrepreneurship Theory and Practice.* 19: 29–42.

Nelson, T. (2003). The persistence of founder influence: Management, ownership and performance effects at Initial Public Offering. *Strategic Management Journal.* 24(8): 707–724.

Pastor, L., Taylor, L.A. and Veronesi, P. (2008). Entrepreneurial learning, the IPO decision, and the post-IPO drop in firm profitability. *The Review of Financial Studies,* 22(8), 3005–3046.

Porter, L.W., & Lawler, E. E.(1968). *Managerial attitudes and performance.* Homewood, IL: Irwin.

Ritter, J.R. (1987). The Costs of Going Public. *Journal of Financial Economics.* 19: 269–281.

Rock, K. (1986). Why new issues are underpriced. *Journal of Financial Economics.* 15: 187–212.

Scholl, R.W. (2002). *Motivation: Expectancy theory.* The University of Rhode Island Website. (http://www.uri.edu/research/irc/scholl/webnotes/Motivation Expectancy.htm.

Shepherd, D.A. and Zacharakis, A. (2001). Speed to initial public offering of VC-backed companies. *Entrepreneurship Theory and Practice.* 26: 59–70.

Sur, S. and Martens, M. L. (2013). Whose firm is it anyway? Analyzing ownership effects on IPO performance. *Canadian Journal of Administrative Sciences,* 30(4), 264–279.

Tolia, B. and Yip, Y.M. (2003). Hot IPOs and lock-up expiration—an anomaly? *Competitiveness Review.* 13(2): 53–59.

Vroom, V. H. (1964). *Work and Motivation.* San Francisco: Jossey-Bass.

Wang, C., Wang, N. and Yang, J. (2012). A unified model of entrepreneurial dynamics. *Journal of Financial Economics,* 106, 1–23.

Weiner, B. (1985). An attributional theory of achievement motivation and emotion. *Psychological Review.* 92: 548–573.

Wennberg, K., Wiklund, J., DeTienne, D.T. and Cardon, M.S. (2010). Reconceptualizing entrepreneurial exit: Divergent exit routes and their drivers. *Journal of Business Venturing,* 25, 361–375.

# MODULE 8

# Bonds, Bond Valuation, and Interest Rates

*Gentlemen prefer bonds.*

**Andrew Mellon**

*What I put in the stock market, I don't have to touch in my lifetime.*
*I want to live off my bonds. I want to be that safe.*

**Monica Seles**

*It is very difficult to predict when a bond crisis could happen.*

**Alan Greenspan**

To insure continuity and growth, business firms must continuously buy and sell assets or resources. Recalling the basic accounting equation, it is necessary that all assets be financed with some form of debt or equity capital. The only other alternative methods of financing new assets are gifts (not likely) or the sale of existing assets. As a result, the basic fundamental value of a business organization is the present value of the firm's assets. Present values or prices may also be placed on both the debt and equity issues of the firm. Placing a value on the assets, debt, or equity of a firm is nothing more than an application of time value of money.

The discounted cash flow (DCF) technique of valuation incorporates the time, risk factors, required returns, and expected cash flows related to the financial asset investment. In this way, a price or appropriate present value for the asset can be derived. No investment should be undertaken without considering the amount of risk being accepted. The time frame of the investment is a second major consideration. Risk and return are related, and the various yields related to bond investment—to include the current, interest, and capital gains yields as well as the yield to maturity—all have risk implications.

The DCF model also provides a method for determining the yield to maturity (YTM) or market yield when the present value or price of a debt instrument is a known value. This application of the model is extremely helpful in comparing alternative investments. Once the yield of the investment is determined, it can be compared to alternative investment returns in consideration of the amount of risk undertaken in that investment. The derived YTM provides management with an indication of the return required by investors in the current market and thus an indication of the required coupon rate and other characteristics necessary for the issuance of new bonds in the current marketplace.

Bonds as issued by corporations are technically long-term debt obligations of the firm. These obligations generally have three basic values of concern to the financial manager. These are the par value, the terminal or face value, and the market value of the bond. The par value is the value that the owner of the bond will receive at the time of maturity. The terminal value is the value of the bond to be paid to investors holding the bond at maturity. The market value or price is a value that is dependent on the cash flows to be received from ownership of the bond as discounted by a risk-appropriate discount rate, or required rate of return.

Most bonds pay two different types of return to investors. The first return is an income return, which occurs periodically over the life of the bond. The second return comes in the form of principal repayment or face value payment at the time of the bond's maturity.

In the case of zero-coupon bonds, or bonds which pay no coupon interest, there is no interest payment portion to the equation required to determine the price of that bond. Thus, the model that can be used is very similar to the normal bond pricing equation except that it has no interest payment section. This is because the bond is considered to be fully reinvested at the time of purchase. For zero coupon bonds, the only return comes in the form of principal repayment and that will occur, at the time of maturity.

How do bond prices change in the marketplace? We know that most bonds offer fixed coupon or interest payments over a specified period of time and that they also offer a stated maturity value at the termination or maturity of the bond's life. As a result, the only way bonds can adjust to ensure the bond will provide a market required rate of return (rather than a historic rate of return) is for the bond price to change as interest rates change. As a result, the bond's price will rise as interest rates fall, and it will decrease as interest rates rise.

As a result, new investors must pay a premium to obtain bonds with higher coupon interest rates than are required via the current interest rate versus coupon rate relationship. The converse is true where bonds have coupon rates that are lower than current required interest rates. In those cases, new bond holders have less desire for the old bonds and, therefore, to be induced to purchase those older bonds, the bonds must be sold at a discount.

Bond price volatility is another issue of concern to investors and issuers as well. Three basic axioms regarding volatility in bond prices are that first, the lower the coupon, the more volatile a bond's price will be, given a change in required interest rates in the market. Second, as with low coupon bonds, bonds with longer terms to maturity will have a greater pricing response to interest rate changes than will shorter-term bonds. Finally, all bonds will have larger changes in price—that is, they will be more volatile when interest rates fall than when they rise.

The total yield on a bond is made up of two components: the current yield and the capital gains yield. Together, these provide the total yield on a bond investment. When bonds are selling at a discount, the capital gain to be obtained from bond investment offsets a loss of interest income to provide the required market rate of return if the bond is held to maturity. Similarly, when a bond is selling at a premium, the increased interest income to be received from the bond investment offsets the loss of capital at maturity when the terminal value will be less than the price paid to obtain the bond.

Israel, Palhares, and Richardson, in their 2018 paper "Common Factors in Corporate Bond Returns," address the issue of excess returns earned on bond investments. Their paper first clarifies that while both the bonds and equity issues of companies are reliant on the "underlying value of the assets of the firm" for their fundamental values, they do not, in fact, react in the same way in terms of pricing. The authors are careful to point out that the prices of bonds are "not independent from equity prices, but nor are they simply a mirror image." They further note that even if the value of the issuer does not change, their prices may.

The 2018 study focuses on four characteristics or factors considered to be useful in predicting returns in other markets, finding that the characteristics "explain a significant portion of the cross-sectional variation in corporate bond excess returns." The factors in these positive relationships to excess return include carry, defensive, momentum, and value.

By definition, carry refers to the performance of investments providing high returns to be greater than the returns of lower-return-yielding investments. The value characteristic is similar but with respect to pricing rather than yields. This characteristic suggests that lower-cost investments also tend to provide better performance for investors than that provided by more pricey investments. Defensive quality is, as might be expected, related to the potential risk faced in an investment. This characteristic is based on the expectation that the lower the risk (alternatively interpret this as higher quality) of an investment, the better or greater the resulting risk-adjusted return will be to the investor. Finally, the momentum quality relates to the performance of the investment. The momentum characteristic is simply an expectation that performance in current periods will continue as similar performance in future periods.

Bonds exhibit four major risk types. These are default risk, interest rate risk, liquidity risk, and purchasing power risk. Default risk is that risk associated with the potential or possibility that the bond issuer will not be able to make required interest payments or face value payment at maturity.

As a result of fluctuating changes in the supply and demand for credit, interest rates in the marketplace vary widely over time. As a result, the required rate of return on bond investments will also change over time. The risk that bond prices will fluctuate as a result of changes in required interest rates in the marketplace is referred to as interest rate risk.

Liquidity risk actually has two component parts. First is the marketability portion of liquidity risk. Marketability refers to the ease with which an investment may be purchased or sold in the marketplace. As this ease of investment increases, marketability increases. Conversely, as ease of investment, or disinvestment, decreases, marketability decreases.

The second component or portion is the actual liquidity portion. Liquidity deals with the change in price from transaction to transaction. If the market is truly liquid with regard to an investment, the change in price from one transaction in the investment to the next transaction in the investment will be very small. On occasion, of course, these changes will not be small, but the majority of time, changes in investment price from transaction to transaction will be small if the investment is a liquid investment.

In the article "Bonds, Jammed Bonds" (2017), author Ed McCarthy provides his own observations and conclusions as well as those of other market experts in the area of bond trading and markets. He notes that increasing investor interest over time has caused more bond-structured exchange-traded funds (ETFs) to be created for bond investors. The primary cause of the ETF growth spurt in bond holdings has been a concern for historical illiquidity in bond markets. As an indication of that illiquidity, McCarthy notes that "less than 20% of investment-grade corporate bonds trade every day. Consequently, corporate bond investors are less likely 'to be successful in finding someone to trade with and finding a price at which [they] want to transact' ..."

Another interesting observation is that because of the liquidity issue facing investors, they are apparently taking the time to "consider how they will sell a position before completing the buy transaction." The obvious concern is not just for return and pricing but also for simple liquidation problems when determining that a bond needs to be sold.

The road to the creation of a broad spectrum of bond ETFs for investing is not without its bumps. There are a variety of hurdles and restrictions that must be resolved, but the future seems to be headed in that direction as a way to encourage bond investment and issuance while also providing a better perspective on bond investment liquidity.

Purchasing power risk is the last type of risk associated with bond investment. Purchasing power risk, of course, affects all types of investments and is related to inflation rates. If the expected inflation rate that is a part of the required rate of return at the time of purchase is higher than anticipated, a loss of purchasing power occurs. If, on the other hand, the expected inflation rate is lower than the rate of inflation that has been included in the required rate of return at the time of purchase, a gain in purchasing power is obtained.

Remember that the basic required rate of return for any investment is comprised of three subsections or three component returns. These are the real rate of return, the inflation premium, and the risk premium. As a result, over- or underexpectation of inflation rates can affect the rate of return that we actually earn on any investment.

## Recommended Reading

Cook, D., X. Fu, and T. Tang. "The Effect of Liquidity and Solvency Risk on the Inclusion of Bond Covenants." *Journal of Banking and Finance* 48 (2014): 120–136.

## Selected Reading

Israel, Ronen, Diogo Palhares, and Scott Richardson. "Common Factors in Corporate Bond Returns." *Journal of Investment Management* 16, no. 2 (2018): 17–46.

McCarthy, Ed. "Bonds, Jammed Bonds." *CFA Institute Magazine* 28, no. 1 (2017): 46–47.

# Common Factors in Corporate Bond Returns

By Ronen Israel, Diogo Palhares, Scott Richardson

## 1. Introduction

Corporate bonds are an enormous—and growing—source of financing for companies around the world. As of the first quarter of 2016, there was $8.36 trillion of U.S. corporate debt outstanding, and from 1996 to 2015 corporate bond issuance grew from $343 billion to $1.49 trillion (Securities Industry and Financial Markets Association). Surprisingly little research, however, has investigated the cross-sectional determinants of corporate bond returns.

We study the drivers of the cross-section of corporate bond expected returns. To do so we focus on a set of characteristics that has been shown to predict returns in other markets, yet researchers have not studied the viability of all these characteristics to predict returns in credit markets. The characteristics are carry, quality, momentum and value (Koijen et al. (2014) for carry; Frazzini and Pedersen (2014) for quality; Asness et al. (2013) for momentum and value). Our contribution includes (i) applying these concepts to credit markets (ii) studying them together in a way that shines light on their joint relevance or lack thereof; (iii) evaluating their economic significance by examining both long-and-short, transaction-costs-oblivious portfolios, and also long-only, transaction-costs aware portfolios; and (iv) exploring the source of the return premia by testing both risk- and mispricing explanations.

Using traditional long-and-short portfolio analysis and cross-sectional regressions we find positive risk premiums that are highly significant (*t*-statistics of 3 or more) for all characteristics but carry. These premia are distinct from traditional credit, bond and equity market risk premia, as well as from the premium earned by long-and-short equity anomalies based on value, momentum and defensive. The strong relation between carry, defensive, value and momentum and future credit excess returns can be interpreted as out-of-sample evidence for the broader efficacy of these characteristics.

We also make a methodological contribution to long-and-short portfolio analysis for credit markets. The volatility and market beta of corporate bonds is tightly related to credit spreads and

Ronen Israel, Diogo Palhares, and Scott Richardson, "Common Factors in Corporate Bond Returns," *Journal of Investment Management*, vol. 16, no. 2, pp. 17–46. Copyright © 2018 by Journal of Investment Management. Reprinted with permission.

durations. Many return predictors are also correlated with credit spreads. As a consequence, if one just creates portfolios by sorting on these measures, the long-and-short portfolios will have very different risk profiles, making their expected returns hard to compare and the long-high-short-low portfolio far from market neutral. In the end, contrary to what happens in equity long-and-short portfolios that end up with small market exposures, simple long-and-short credit portfolios do not. Furthermore, credit spread itself is a return predictor so it is important to understand whether a candidate variable simply predicts returns because of its correlation with spreads or whether it has any extra forecasting power. To solve these general issues, we use a double sort on an ex-ante measure of beta (duration times spread) and the candidate characteristic.

Trading costs and liquidity are also very different in credit markets relative to equity markets. Corporate bonds are difficult to trade and the expected trading cost is high relative to the underlying volatility of the asset class (see e.g., Harris, 2015). Thus, simple analyses of Sharpe ratios based on 'academic' quintile long/short portfolios may substantially overstate the economic significance of any characteristic. Thus, when studying credit portfolios, we explicitly account for transaction costs and other potential trading restrictions.

To establish more realistic returns we also study long-only portfolios of relatively liquid corporate bonds with exposure to carry, defensive, momentum and value themes. We show that these portfolios generate high risk-adjusted returns, net of trading costs. Relative to a value-weighted benchmark of corporate bonds, the long-only portfolio yields a net (of transaction cost) active return of 2.20 percent annualized, which translates to an information ratio of 0.86. While the number is a point estimate out of a roughly 20-year sample, its exact magnitude is less important than the fact that it is well above zero.

We explore possible explanations for the observed return's patterns. We examine both risk explanations—characteristic portfolios expose the aggregate investor to losses at times in which those losses are particularly tough to bear—and mispricing theories—investors deviate from rationality because of mistakes or agency problems and limits-to-arbitrage stop arbitrageurs from fully correcting these mistakes and their impact on asset prices.

We examine the risk hypothesis with two tests. First we measure the exposure of each individual characteristic and a combination of all of them to traditional macroeconomic factors (e.g., Chen et al., 1986). While the coefficients are statistically significant, they suggest that the characteristics have a hedging profile. That is, the returns of the combined portfolio are higher when growth expectations are lower, volatility increases and inflation expectations increase. In the second test, we replace the traditional macroeconomic factors with changes in broker-dealer leverage. Adrian et al. (2014) found that exposures to broker-dealer balance sheet can explain equity anomalies as well as government bond returns. We do not find evidence that broker-dealer leverage can explain credit characteristic returns. In particular, the combined portfolio, exposed to all individual characteristics, has a positive (hedging), but indistinguishable from zero loading on leverage shocks.

We break down the drivers of mispricing into (i) factors that influence the likelihood that noise traders (Grossman and Stiglitz (1980)) are important for a given security and (ii) factors that limit the activity of arbitrageurs (Shleifer and Vishny (1997)). We proxy for the likelihood of noise traders with (i) a measure of the investor base sophistication (institutional ownership of the bond), and (ii) a measure of firm transparency (analyst coverage of the issuing firm equity). For limits to arbitrage we measure liquidity (bond amount outstanding) and ease of shorting (as reflected by the shorting fee).

We run two tests using with those proxies. In the first test we examine whether the bonds most attractive to an arbitrageur—those with extreme values for the anomalies—are particularly hard to arbitrage or more vulnerable to investor's errors. For the shorting fee the test is one sided: are bonds that represent the most attractive short from the point of view of arbitrageurs—those with unusually low anomaly scores—unusually hard to short? We do not find evidence of this pattern for any of the characteristics.

In the second test we look at long-and-short portfolios built on security universes which differ in expected mispricing and limits to arbitrage. The hypothesis here is that anomaly returns should be stronger among the hard-to-arbitrage-or-high-error bonds. Momentum returns are indeed larger among harder-to-arbitrage-or-high-error bonds and the result is statistically significant. The other anomalies perform similarly across the different universes.

Finally, the last test focuses on the investor mistake hypothesis. We test whether the returns can be explained by investors' errors in forecasting sales (e.g., Bradshaw et al. (2001)). To proxy for investors' expectations, which are unobservable, we use equity analyst forecasts. If these forecasts were rational and unfettered by agency conflicts, analyst revisions should not be predictable by public information. On the other hand, if they underestimate the sales of firms with high scores and overestimate the sales of those with low scores, the correction of those expectations may explain the anomaly premium. The evidence is in the right direction, statistically significant and quantitatively important for momentum, but not for the remaining characteristics. Overall, returns to the momentum characteristic seem to be the most tightly linked to mispricing, with the evidence being less clear about the source of the returns of other characteristics.

[...] Section 2 discusses a simple framework for corporate bond excess returns and links our analysis to earlier papers exploring determinants of cross-sectional variation in corporate bond expected excess returns. Section 3 explains our data sources, sample-selection criteria, characteristic measures and research design. Section 4 describes our empirical analyses and section 5 concludes.

## 2. A Framework for Expected Corporate Bond Excess Returns

Unlike equity markets with variants of dividend discount model to guide empiricists in their measurement of expected returns, there is not an agreed upon framework for estimating excess credit returns. Ex post, researchers agree that credit excess returns can, and should, be measured as the difference between the returns to a corporate bond and an appropriately cash flow matched treasury bond (see e.g., Hallerbach and Houweling, 2013; Asvanunt and Richardson, 2017). Ex ante, as credit and equity are related securities, one approach would be to simply explore whether characteristics known to explain cross-sectional variation in equity excess returns also explain credit excess returns. Indeed, some recent research has followed this approach (e.g., Chordia et al., 2016). This approach amounts to testing whether priced sources of risk span across markets (e.g., Fama and French, 1993). Whilst this approach is useful in commenting on whether characteristics share similar returns across equity and credit markets, this approach misses an important point that the relevant risk across credit and equity markets are not identical. After all, simply documenting that (i) X is correlated with equity excess returns, (ii) equity excess returns and credit excess returns are correlated, and hence (iii) X is therefore correlated with credit excess returns is not that exciting (see e.g., Lok and Richardson, 2011).

Prices of corporate bonds are not independent from equity prices, but nor are they simply a mirror image. First, while the fundamental value of bonds and equities both depend on the underlying value of the assets of the firm (e.g., Merton, 1974), the way these two assets respond to changes in properties of asset values is not identical. Second equity and bond values can change even when the underlying value of the firm business does not. Corporate events such as leverage buyouts, for example, tend to benefit shareholders at the expense of debtholders. Third, bonds and equities are traded in different 2 markets and typically held by different investors. This can make stock and bond prices diverge, as they are anchored to the risk aversion, liquidity demands and sentiment of different investor clienteles. As a consequence, knowledge about the cross-section of expected stock returns do not translate one-to-one to bond returns (see e.g., Chordia et al. 2016, and Choi and Kim, 2015).

Our approach is to directly measure characteristics that could inform about expected credit excess returns. A natural candidate is the spread of the corporate bond, which we call 'carry'. This is a suitable measure of expected returns if, and only if, there is no change in either default expectations or aggregate risk premium. To complement a measure of spread we also look to multiple characteristics that could potentially inform about future changes in spreads. Such measures include dimensions of value, momentum and quality that have been examined in equity markets. But we need to tailor these measures to reflect the type of risk priced in the credit market (notably the risk of default). As such, [...] is related to some prior research exploring cross-sectional determinants of corporate bond excess returns.

Correia et al. (2012) study value investing in corporate bond markets by comparing market spreads to model-implied spreads estimated using fundamental and market-based inputs. Kwan (1996) and Gebhardt et al. (2005b) document strong evidence for equity momentum in corporate bond markets by showing that past equity returns strongly predict future corporate bond returns of the same issuer, even after controlling for corporate bond momentum. Jostova et al. (2013) examine credit momentum and show that it is profitable when used to trade high-yield US corporate bonds—even when controlling for equity momentum.

Koijen et al. (2014) evaluate carry factors across several markets: for credit markets, they test corporate bond indices of varying durations, maturities and rating categories. Carvalho et al. (2014) identify a low-risk anomaly across a broad universe of fixed income assets for various measures of risk. Similarly, Frazzini and Pedersen (2014) document positive risk-adjusted returns for portfolios that take long positions for short duration and higher-rated corporate bonds and take short positions for long duration and lower-rated corporate bonds. In contrast, Ng and Phelps (2014) note that the low risk anomaly in corporate bonds is sensitive to the selected measure of risk.

Our work extends this literature. First, we study the standalone performance of characteristics and investigate the relation between them and their combined efficacy. Second, we consider simple unconstrained long-short portfolios and also more realistically investable long-only portfolios, which account for transaction costs and shorting constraints typical for corporate bonds. The investable portfolios show that our results are economically meaningful. Third we investigate the sources of return predictability. We explore risk-based and non-risk-based explanations and find that macroeconomic exposures are not consistent with a positive premia for the anomalies, whereas limits to arbitrage and investor errors seem to play a role in momentum strategies, though not the others.

# 3. Data and Methodology

## 3.1 Corporate Bond Data

Our analysis is based on a comprehensive panel of U.S. corporate bonds between January 1997 and April 2015 measured at a monthly frequency. This panel includes all constituents of the Bank of America Merrill Lynch ("BAML") investment-grade ("US Corporate Master") and high-yield ("US High Yield Master") corporate bond indices. The BAML dataset relies on the industry standard for valuations, aggregating data from TRACE as well as other sources. For an academic use of the data see Schaefer and Strebulaev (2008).

Following the criteria of Haesen et al. (2013), we select a representative bond for each issuer every month. The criteria used for identifying the representative bond are selected so as to create a sample of liquid and cross-sectionally comparable bonds. Specifically, we select representative bonds on the basis of (i) seniority, (ii) maturity, (iii) age and (iv) size.

First, we filter bonds on the basis of seniority, limiting ourselves to only senior debt. We then select only the bonds corresponding to the most prevalent rating of the issuer. To do this, we first compute the amount of bonds outstanding for each rating category for a given issuer. We keep only those bonds that belong to the rating category that contains the largest fraction of debt outstanding. This category of bonds tends to have the same rating as the issuer. Second, we filter bonds on the basis of maturity. If the issuer has bonds with time to maturity between five and 15 years, we remove all other bonds for that issuer from the sample. If not, we keep all bonds in the sample. Third, we filter bonds on the basis of time since issuance. If the issuer has any bonds that are at most two years old, we remove all other bonds for that issuer in the sample. If not, we keep all bonds from that issuer in the sample. Finally, we filter on the basis of size. Of the remaining bonds, we pick the one with the largest amount outstanding. A deliberate consequence of our bond selection criteria is that we will not be exploring a liquidity premium (such as issue size) for our primary empirical analyses.

Our resulting sample includes 274,665 unique bond-month observations, corresponding to 11,804 bonds issued by 4,296 unique firms. Table 12.1 reports annual statistics describing the composition of our sample over time. The average month in the sample consists of 1,247 bonds representing

**Table 12.1** Universe Statistics (January 1997–April 2015)

The table below reports annual summary statistics of the Bank of America Merrill Lynch (BAML) bond sample. Each column statistic is computed monthly and averaged within the specified year. Investment grade (IG) and high yield (HY) classifications are based on S&P ratings. Bond issues are linked to Compustat based on CUSIPs and Tickers as described in the text. Total notional is reported in billions of dollars.

| Year | Count | Total Notional | % IG | % HY | % Linked to Compustat |
|------|-------|----------------|------|------|------------------------|
| 1997 | 1,096 | 239 | 60% | 40% | 54% |
| 1998 | 1,188 | 278 | 61% | 39% | 53% |
| 1999 | 1,104 | 306 | 63% | 37% | 52% |
| 2000 | 1,026 | 335 | 65% | 35% | 50% |
| 2001 | 1,026 | 375 | 70% | 30% | 49% |
| 2002 | 1,099 | 443 | 70% | 30% | 49% |
| 2003 | 1,263 | 511 | 63% | 37% | 49% |
| 2004 | 1,398 | 562 | 60% | 40% | 47% |
| 2005 | 1,291 | 569 | 59% | 41% | 45% |
| 2006 | 1,268 | 560 | 58% | 42% | 43% |
| 2007 | 1,256 | 578 | 56% | 44% | 43% |
| 2008 | 1,046 | 553 | 64% | 36% | 47% |
| 2009 | 967 | 540 | 66% | 34% | 49% |
| 2010 | 1,269 | 689 | 56% | 44% | 46% |
| 2011 | 1,380 | 768 | 53% | 47% | 46% |
| 2012 | 1,406 | 812 | 53% | 47% | 46% |
| 2013 | 1,521 | 893 | 51% | 49% | 45% |
| 2014 | 1,564 | 936 | 50% | 50% | 45% |
| 2015 | 1,533 | 948 | 51% | 49% | 46% |
| Average | 1,247 | 573 | 59% | 41% | 48% |

$573 billion of total notional outstanding, of which 59% (41%) corresponds to investment grade (high yield) issues. To construct variables requiring financial statement information, we can link 48% of our universe to the Compustat database (using CUSIP and Ticker identifiers contained in the BAML dataset).

Next we describe a few key variables contained in the BAML dataset. Option-adjusted-spread (OAS) is the fixed spread that needs to be added to the Treasury curve such that the corporate bond's discounted payments match its traded market price (accounting for embedded options). Duration, which measures a bond's sensitivity to interest rates, is also adjusted for embedded optionality. BAML provides total returns as well as excess returns, which are equal to total returns minus the return of a duration-matched Treasury. Credit ratings are based on Standard & Poor's ratings classification system. To construct numerical ratings that can be used in our regressions, we map ratings of AAA, AA, A, BBB, BB, B, CCC, CC, C and D to scores of 1, 2, 3, 4, 5, 6, 7, 8, 9 and 10, respectively. A rating less (greater) than or equal to 4 (5) therefore corresponds to investment grade (high yield). As newly issued bonds tend to be more liquid, we define a measure of bond illiquidity labelled "age percent," which is computed as time-since-issuance (in days) divided by original maturity (in days).

Table 10.2 provides a description of several issue and issuer characteristics. All of our variable definitions are contained in Table A.1. For each characteristic, we compute several statistics (e.g.,

**Table 12.2** Issue and Issuer Characteristics (January 1997–April 2015)

The table below reports summary statistics of bond issue and issuer characteristics (as defined in Table A.1). For each characteristic, the column statistic is computed on a monthly basis and then averaged over the full sample period.

|  | Mean | Std | 5% | 10% | 25% | 50% | 75% | 90% | 95% |
|---|---|---|---|---|---|---|---|---|---|
| OAS | 386 | 308 | 85 | 107 | 161 | 302 | 512 | 783 | 1,002 |
| Duration | 5.1 | 2.2 | 1.6 | 2.4 | 3.8 | 5.0 | 6.3 | 7.3 | 8.2 |
| Total Ret. | 0.6% | 3.1% | □2.9% | □1.6% | □0.4% | 0.6% | 1.7% | 3.0% | 4.2% |
| Excess Ret. | 0.2% | 3.0% | □3.2% | □1.9% | □0.7% | 0.2% | 1.2% | 2.4% | 3.6% |
| Amt. Out. | 437 | 442 | 134 | 159 | 208 | 309 | 495 | 811 | 1,123 |
| Time to Mat. | 7.8 | 5.1 | 2.7 | 3.9 | 5.5 | 7.1 | 8.7 | 10.4 | 15.5 |
| Age Percent | 28% | 19% | 5% | 7% | 12% | 24% | 39% | 54% | 67% |
| Rating | 4.7 | 1.4 | 2.5 | 3.0 | 3.8 | 4.7 | 6.0 | 6.6 | 6.9 |
| Dist. to Def. | 6.0 | 3.5 | 1.4 | 2.0 | 3.4 | 5.5 | 8.0 | 10.6 | 12.2 |
| Momentum | 5% | 16% | □16% | □10% | □3% | 2% | 11% | 24% | 36% |
| Leverage | 0.31 | 0.41 | □0.02 | 0.03 | 0.13 | 0.28 | 0.47 | 0.66 | 0.77 |

**Table A.1** Variable Definitions

| | Variable | Definition |
|---|---|---|
| | Duration | Option-adjusted duration as reported by BAML. |
| | Total Return | Monthly total return on the corporate bond, inclusive of coupons and accrued interest. |
| | Excess Return | Monthly excess return on the corporate bond, computed as the difference between the monthly total return on the corporate bond and the monthly return of a duration-matched US Treasury bond. |
| | Amt. Out. | The face value of the corporate bond measured in USD millions. |
| | Time to Maturity | Number of years before bond matures. |
| | Age Percent | Fraction of bond life that has expired (time since issuance divided by original maturity). |
| | Rating | Standard & Poor's issuer-level rating, coded from 1 (AAA) to 10 (D). |
| | Market Beta | Slope from 12-month rolling regression of credit excess returns on the credit market excess return (see CREDIT below). |
| Carry | OAS | Option-adjusted spread as reported in the Bank of America Merrill Lynch (BAML) bond database. |
| Value | Empirical | The residual from a cross-sectional regression of the log of OAS onto the log of duration, rating and bond excess return volatility (12 month). |
| | Structural | The residual from a cross-sectional regression of the log of OAS onto the log of the default probability implied by a structural model (Shumway 2001). |
| Momentum | Credit | The most recent six-month cumulative corporate-bond excess return. |
| | Equity | Equity momentum, defined as the most recent six-month cumulative issuer equity return. |
| Defensive | Leverage | Market leverage, measured as the ratio of net debt (book debt + minority interest + preferred stocks–cash) to the sum of net debt and market capitalization. Measured using data available at the start of each month (assuming a six-month lag for the release of financial statement information). |
| | Duration | Effective duration as reported in the Bank of America Merrill Lynch (BAML) bond database. |
| | Profitability | Gross profits over assets. |

| Variable | Definition |
|---|---|
| CONST_VOL_ CHAR | Credit excess returns of a characteristic portfolio that goes long bonds in the top characteristic quintile and short those in the bottom. Every month the portfolio is scaled to have an ex-ante volatility of 5%, where the ex-ante volatility is the realized volatility over the last 2 years. |
| TSY | Excess returns to long-term government bonds, measured as the difference between monthly total returns on the Bank of America Merrill Lynch US Treasuries seven–10 year index and one-month U.S. Treasury bills. |
| CREDIT | Excess returns to corporate bonds, measured as the difference between the value-weighted monthly total returns of corporate bonds included in the BAML dataset and a portfolio of duration-matched US Treasury bonds. |
| EQUITY | Excess returns to the S&P 500 Index, measured as the difference between monthly total returns to the S&P 500 and one-month US Treasury bills. |
| SMB | Monthly mimicking-factor portfolio return to the size factor, obtained from Ken French's website. |
| HML | Monthly mimicking-factor portfolio return to the value factor, obtained from Ken French's website. |
| UMD | Monthly mimicking-factor portfolio return to the momentum factor, obtained from Ken French's website. |
| QMJ | Monthly mimicking-factor portfolio return to the quality factor, obtained from AQR's library website. |
| ΔLOGVIX | One-month change in log VIX (VIXCLS) from FRED website. |
| ΔLOGINDPRO | One-month change in log seasonally adjusted industrial production Index (INDPRO) from FRED website. |
| ΔLOGCPI | One-month change in log seasonally adjusted CPI (CPIAUCSL) from FRED website. |
| ΔLEV | Change in log broker-dealers $leverage = \dfrac{financial\ assets}{financial\ assets - total\ liabilities}$. From FED's flow of funds data and seasonally adjusted (Adrian et al. (2014)) |
| Equity Analyst Coverage | The number of analysts covering the issuer equity, from I/B/E/S. |
| Credit Institutional Ownership | Fraction of bond amount outstanding owned by non-retail investors, from Lipper emaxx database. |
| Bond shorting score | Score between 0 and 5 from Markit: 0 represents lowest cost to borrow and 5 represents the highest. |
| Equity Analyst Revisions in Sales Expectations | Weighted average change in the next fiscal year (FY1) and the one after (FY2) sales forecasts. The weights are chosen such that the forecast is refers to a number that is on average 12 months into the future. |

mean, standard deviation and various percentiles) on a monthly basis and report the average of these monthly statistics in the table. The average issue in our sample has an OAS of 386 basis points, duration of 5.1 years, $437 million of notional outstanding, 7.8 years to maturity, and age percent of 28%. The average issuer in our sample has a six-month average credit and equity excess return of 5% and market leverage of 0.31.

## 3.2 Characteristic Measures

In this section, we define the four key characteristics that we use to explain cross-sectional variation in corporate bond excess returns. Our choices are driven by the desire to have intuitive and, to the extent possible, standard measures that span both public and private issuers of corporate bonds. When multiple measures satisfy that criteria, we combine them using equal-risk weights to obtain a more robust portfolio and make the results less susceptible to a specific variable selection.[1] We deliberately do not select size as a characteristic, as the corporate bond market is notoriously expensive to trade. Our interest is in the identification of characteristics that explain excess returns of large and liquid corporate bonds.

Carry is the return of a security if time passes but market conditions do not change and we measure it using the option adjusted spread (OAS). We use OAS rather than bond yield because we are interested in credit returns in excess of key-rate-duration-matched treasuries. Bond yield reflects both the credit component and the Treasury component.

OAS also has its problems. It is a perfect measure of carry only if the credit curve is flat. If the curve has a positive or negative slope, OAS will underestimate and overestimate carry respectively. Most issuers have upward sloping credit spread term structures, implying the OAS will be an imperfect measure of carry. The alternative, however, is to estimate credit spread curves for each issuer. While potentially more precise, the curve interpolation exercise is model dependent and adds considerable complexity and opaqueness to the carry measure. In our view, OAS strikes a reasonable balance between precision on one hand and simplicity and transparency on the other.

Past research has identified a tendency for safer low-risk assets to deliver a higher risk-adjusted return (e.g., Frazzini and Pedersen (2014); Carvalho et al. (2014)). We apply this idea to corporate bonds by building a *defensive* (or low-risk) measure using multiple variables. Our first measure is market leverage, measured as the value of net debt (book debt + minority interest + preferred stocks − cash) divided by the sum of the value of net debt and market value of equity. Both intuitively and theoretically speaking, firms with higher levels of leverage (or greater use of debt) are more likely to default and are hence fundamentally riskier (e.g., Altman 1968; Shumway 2001).

Our second measure of safety is gross profitability as defined in Novy-Marx (2013). Unlike other profitability measures, such as net income over equity value, gross profitability speaks to the quality

---

1 If one of the standardized measures is missing, we assign a zero score such that the combination will have a non-missing score for the union of names which have at least one non-missing score.

of the overall assets owned by the firm. As such, it reasonably proxies for the safety of the enterprise, covering both equity and debt claims.

Our third measure of safety is simply low duration. Binsbergen and Koijen (2015) document that short maturity securities across different asset classes tend to have higher risk-adjusted returns. Palhares (2013) has shown that this also holds among single-name credit default swaps. Here we apply the same concept to corporate cash bonds.

For financial instruments that trade in cash markets (i.e., government bonds and equities), there is reliable evidence of a negative relation between beta and future excess returns (e.g., Frazzini and Pedersen (2014)). One reason for this negative relation is the prevalence of leverage-averse investors in cash markets who seek higher returns by buying higher beta assets as opposed to levering up the mean-variant efficient portfolio. Indeed, evidence from holdings of equity mutual fund shows that the average stock held has a beta of about 1.08 (see Table 11 of Frazzini and Pedersen (2014)).

For credit markets, both systematic and idiosyncratic volatility can be captured by the product of duration and spread, or DTS (e.g., Ben Dor et al. (2007)). The first component, duration, has been shown to be negatively associated with risk-adjusted returns in equities, bonds and several other asset classes (e.g., Palhares 2013; Binsbergen and Koijen 2015). The second component, credit spread, simply measures carry in credit markets. Beta and idiosyncratic volatility, therefore, implicitly combine two measures that have confounding effects on expected returns, leading to their inadequacy as suitable characteristics to explain corporate bond excess returns. As a consequence we have excluded beta and volatility as measures of the defensive theme.

For our *momentum* characteristic, we use two widely studied momentum measures. The first is credit momentum defined as the trailing six-month bond excess return. Jostova (2013) shows that, in a broad sample of corporate bonds, including both high-yield and investment-grade securities, past winners tend to outperform past losers. The second momentum measure is the six-month equity momentum of the bond issuer. Kwan (1996) and Gebhardt et al. (2005b) show that stock returns tend to lead corporate bond returns.

To construct a value signal, we need a market value measure (price, yield, spread, etc.), a fundamental value measure and a way to compare the two. For example, Fama and French (2003) use the price of a stock for the market measure, the book value for the fundamental measure and the ratio to make a comparison. For credit markets we use the spread of the bond and credible measures of default risk as the fundamental anchor. A cheap bond has high spread relative to default risk.

We use two proxies for default risk. First, we follow Correia et al. (2012) and use the issuer default probability. We measure the default probability as in Bharath and Shumway (2008). One drawback of this approach is that it can only be computed for issuers with publicly traded equity. To increase coverage, we use a second value anchor that combines three broadly available fundamental measures: credit rating, bond duration and the volatility of bond excess return returns in the last 12 months.

## 3.3 Portfolio Construction

The traditional way of examining the relationship between expected returns and a candidate predictor in the equity literature consists of constructing portfolios based on the cross-sectional rank of the characteristic, averaging the returns within the portfolio and then averaging those over time (e.g., Fama and French (1993)). This approach does not guarantee that the different quantile portfolios will have similar ex-ante volatilities and beta, and, as consequence, that the long-top-minus-short-bottom portfolios will be market neutral. In spite of that, in the equity literature, the different anomaly portfolios do tend to have similar risk and the long-and-short risk factors tend to have moderate betas—though not zero, for example, the SMB and HML factors are notorious for their positive and negative betas respectively (e.g., Fama and French (1993)) and the betting-against-beta factor (e.g., Frazzini and Pedersen (2014)) has negative beta.

This quirk of the traditional portfolio construction methodology is important [...] because the cross-section of corporate bonds has a much larger dispersion in beta and risk than equity markets. Furthermore, many of the characteristic we examine correlate with beta. As a consequence, the long-and-short portfolios formed using those characteristics will not be beta neutral, complicating the interpretation of their expected returns and time-series properties as the reflection of something other than their embedded market exposure. To obtain long-and-short portfolios that are closer to market neutrality we demean characteristics within five ex-ante beta quintiles, with beta being measured as duration times spread (DTS). We exclude duration and carry from that step because, mechanically, that would induce a portfolio that mixes high carry and low duration together.

We construct two types of characteristic portfolios. First, we follow the standard convention of computing a zero-cost portfolio that is long corporate bonds in the highest quintile of a given characteristic and short corporate bonds in the lowest quintile of a given characteristic. Within quintiles, we report excess returns based on value-weighted returns. Our inferences are unaffected if we instead use equal weighting. We also display a constant-5-percent volatility version of each long-and-short portfolio (Muir and Moreira (2016)). We use the 24-month realized volatility of the unscaled portfolio as the measure of ex-ante risk.[2]

We construct the quintiles and long-and-short portfolios for each characteristic individually and for a combination of them all. The combination sorting variable is an inverse-of-risk-weighted sum of the four characteristics. More precisely, for each characteristic we form a portfolio that is linear in ranks (Asness et al. (2014)) and then multiply it by 5% and divide it by its 24-month realized volatility—the outcome is an alternative constant-volatility portfolio with linear weights instead of just having non-zero values for the most extreme quintiles. The combined characteristic is them just an equal weighted average of those single-characteristic, linear-in-ranks portfolio weights.

A critical part [of this reading] is to examine the return-forecasting characteristics jointly. Each single characteristic informs us about properties of the stochastic discount factor that prices corporate

---

2 Between January 1997 and December 1998, we set the scalar equal to its value as of January 1999.

credit securities, but the single portfolio that makes optimal use of the multiple characteristics goes beyond: it alone is sufficient to fully characterize that discount factor (e.g., Cochrane (2009)). From the point of view of an investor, that single portfolio is also interesting. For example, for a mean-variance investor allocating between these long-and-short credit strategies and cash, the allocation to that optimal portfolio would be sufficient to summarize its asset allocation policy.

The question is then how to build this optimal portfolio. Without observing expected returns and covariance matrices, one cannot observe the optimal portfolio weights. Using sample moments is problematic because of look-ahead bias and the relative shortness of a 20-year sample to estimate expected return. Our answer to the problem is an equal weighted portfolio. It generalizes the robustness of the 1/N portfolio (e.g., DeMiguel et al. (2009)) by applying it to similarly risky characteristic portfolios rather than underlying assets.

For the combination of characteristics, we also analyse a second type of portfolio: a long-only portfolio that takes into consideration realistic implementation by solving a linear optimization problem. The analysis of a long-only portfolio is unusual when studying cross-sectional return predictability. But given the well-known challenges in shorting corporate bonds (e.g., Asquith et al. 2013) and the significant costs in trading corporate bonds relative to their underlying volatility (e.g., Bessembinder et al. (2006); Edwards et al. (2007)), it is important to test whether the characteristic's premia survives difficult but realistic real-world constraints.

# 4. Results

## 4.1 Regression Analysis

Before reporting the performance of our portfolios, we first report Fama-Macbeth regressions of monthly corporate-bond excess returns regressed onto lagged characteristics along with control variables. Each month, we run cross-sectional regressions of the form:

$$R_{i,t+1} = \alpha + \beta_1 CARRY_{i,t} + \beta_2 DEF_{i,t} + \beta_3 MOM_{i,t} + \beta_4 VALUE_{i,t} + \gamma Z + \varepsilon_{i,t+1}, \tag{1}$$

where $R_{i,t+1}$ denotes the duration-hedged excess return of bond i over month t + 1. Each of the four characteristics is converted to a normalized variable. Specifically, for each characteristic, for every month, we rank issues by their characteristic values, subtract the mean rank and then divide by the standard deviation of the ranks. We also fill missing values with zero, but the results are robust if we do not. As a result, estimated coefficients may be interpreted as the future one-month excess return difference for a one standard deviation difference in characteristic ranking. To rule out the hypothesis that the characteristics predict returns because they proxy for traditional measures of risk, we include control variables in the regression. The first variable is a market beta, where the market is defined as the credit return of the cap-weighted portfolio of all bonds in our database and the beta is computed using a 12-month rolling regression. For robustness, we also include two other traditional measures of risk in credit markets—rating and duration—as well as a proxy for illiquidity, age percent (e.g. Gebhardt et al. (2005a)).

Table 12.3 reports our Fama-Macbeth regression estimates for the monthly sample period from January 1997 to April 2015. Regression (1) includes just an intercept and beta, and regression (2) adds our control variables, which reduce the average numbers of bonds in the cross-section from 723 to 671. Regressions (3) through (6) evaluate the predictive ability of each of our characteristics

**Table 12.3** Fama-Macbeth Regressions (January 1997–April 2015)

The table below reports Fama-Macbeth regressions of monthly bond excess returns regressed onto normalized carry, defensive, momentum, and value style measures along with controls for market beta, rating, duration, and age percent variables (as defined in Table A.1).

|  | (1) | (2) | (3) | (4) | (5) | (6) | (7) |
|---|---|---|---|---|---|---|---|
| Intercept | 0.10 [1.5] | −0.02 −[0.2] | 0.04 [0.5] | −0.01 −[0.1] | 0.05 [0.5] | −0.10 −[1.2] | −0.02 −[0.2] |
| Carry |  |  | 0.00 [1.0] |  |  |  | 0.14 [2.3] |
| Defensive |  |  |  | 0.15 [5.0] |  |  | 0.03 [0.9] |
| Momentum |  |  |  |  | 0.15 [3.3] |  | 0.22 [7.1] |
| Value |  |  |  |  |  | 0.26 [5.8] | 0.30 [10.7] |
| Mkt Beta | 0.05 [0.7] | 0.04 [0.6] | 0.10 [1.6] | 0.04 [0.7] | 0.06 [0.9] | 0.08 [1.2] | 0.14 [2.3] |
| Rating |  | 0.02 [0.8] | −0.03 −[1.0] | 0.02 [0.6] | 0.00 [0.1] | 0.03 [1.0] | 0.00 −[0.1] |
| Duration |  | −0.01 −[0.5] | −0.01 −[0.5] | 0.01 [0.8] | 0.00 −[0.4] | 0.01 [1.1] | 0.01 [1.1] |
| Age Percent |  | 0.25 [2.2] | 0.23 [2.0] | 0.22 [1.9] | 0.23 [2.0] | 0.14 [1.2] | 0.09 [0.9] |
| Avg. R-squared | 0.07 | 0.10 | 0.14 | 0.10 | 0.11 | 0.11 | 0.15 |
| Avg. Num. Obs. | 723 | 671 | 671 | 671 | 671 | 671 | 671 |

on a standalone basis. Both individually and combined, the value and momentum characteristics have explanatory power for corporate bond excess returns. The carry characteristic does not exhibit a reliable association with future bond excess returns as a standalone variable but is marginally significant when controlling for the remaining characteristics. The opposite is true with defensive: it is highly significant as a standalone variable but loses significance when controlling for value and momentum. This suggests that the defensive theme in credit may be spanned by the value and momentum themes. This is not surprising as the value factors we build for credit make explicit use of fundamental information. Our value measures identify a bond as cheap when its spread is wide relative to default probabilities. Our measures of default probabilities include distance to default and rating information. These fundamental anchors incorporate measures of leverage and expected profitability. As a consequence it is not surprising that they help explain the defensive premium.

The average R-squared of the Fama-Macbeth cross-sectional regressions is 15 percent, suggesting that our characteristics collectively explain a nontrivial portion of the cross-sectional variation in bond excess returns. The interpretation of the 15 percent average explanatory power is not that we can predict 15 percent of the variation in corporate bond excess returns but rather that knowledge of the four characteristics combined with (unknown ex ante) time-varying loadings to our four characteristics can explain 15 percent of the variation in corporate bond excess returns. To put that number in context, Lewellen (2015) finds that 15 equity characteristics explain 7.6% of the cross-sectional variation of equity returns. The value and momentum characteristics have the strongest statistical relation with future excess returns, as indicated by the large positive Fama-Macbeth test statistics in the final column.

## 4.2 Long-Short Quintile Portfolios

Table 12.4 reports performance statistics of our long-short quintile portfolios. Consistent with the Fama-Macbeth results, we see the strongest positive association between characteristics and returns for defensive, momentum and value. A portfolio that combines all of the factors at an equal-risk weight ("combined") performs even better, with an annualized Sharpe Ratio of 2.19, indicating that the different characteristics are weakly correlated amongst themselves. Note also that the realized volatilities of the constant-volatility portfolios are close to the targeted value of 5%, confirming that our simple scalar methodology succeeds reasonably in estimating the volatility of the combined portfolio.

Across all characteristics, we can see that the long-short returns are driven by positive performance on the long-side and negative (or weaker) performance on the short-side. In fact, reading Sharpe ratios across each of the rows clearly illustrates that performance is generally monotonically increasing across quintiles for each of the characteristics.

Figure 12.1 plots cumulative excess characteristic returns over time. We can see that performance, especially for the combination of characteristics, is not driven by any particular sub-period and has not changed substantially over time. While different characteristics performed better and worse over different sub-periods, it is clear that the combined portfolio has been relatively stable in its

**Table 12.4** Quintile Portfolio Tests (January 1997–April 2015)

The table below reports performance annualized performance statistics for value-weighted quintile portfolios formed on carry, defensive, momentum, value, and combined style factors (as described in the text). "ConstVol" corresponds to quintile long-short portfolios targeting a constant volatility of 5% per annum (as described in the text).

| | | Q1 | Q2 | Q3 | Q4 | Q5 | Q5–Q1 | ConstVol |
|---|---|---|---|---|---|---|---|---|
| Carry | Ret. | ⏑0.4% | 1.1% | 1.5% | 3.7% | 3.7% | 4.1% | 1.1% |
| | Vol. | 2.9% | 4.4% | 6.6% | 8.7% | 13.9% | 11.7% | 5.8% |
| | S.R. | ⏑0.12 | 0.26 | 0.22 | 0.43 | 0.27 | 0.35 | 0.19 |
| Defensive | Ret. | 0.0% | 1.4% | 2.0% | 1.9% | 2.7% | 2.7% | 8.3% |
| | Vol. | 6.0% | 5.8% | 6.4% | 6.2% | 5.6% | 2.4% | 6.9% |
| | S.R. | 0.00 | 0.24 | 0.31 | 0.32 | 0.49 | 1.11 | 1.21 |
| Momentum | Ret. | ⏑0.2% | 1.3% | 1.5% | 1.4% | 2.7% | 2.9% | 7.5% |
| | Vol. | 7.2% | 6.1% | 5.2% | 5.3% | 6.5% | 3.4% | 6.7% |
| | S.R. | ⏑0.03 | 0.21 | 0.28 | 0.27 | 0.41 | 0.85 | 1.12 |
| Value | Ret. | ⏑0.4% | 0.7% | 1.6% | 2.4% | 3.5% | 3.9% | 10.7% |
| | Vol. | 5.5% | 5.8% | 6.3% | 6.8% | 5.6% | 2.2% | 6.0% |
| | S.R. | ⏑0.07 | 0.13 | 0.25 | 0.35 | 0.62 | 1.75 | 1.80 |
| Combined | Ret. | ⏑0.5% | 1.0% | 1.5% | 2.3% | 4.9% | 5.4% | 14.0% |
| | Vol. | 5.6% | 5.6% | 6.3% | 6.8% | 6.0% | 2.5% | 6.0% |
| | S.R. | ⏑0.09 | 0.18 | 0.24 | 0.34 | 0.81 | 2.19 | 2.32 |

outperformance. Not surprisingly the most visible drawdown is carry during the Global Financial Crisis, when investors sought safe assets and shunned riskier ones like high-yield bonds (e.g., Koijen et al. (2014)). Whilst we are hesitant to draw too strong inferences from a relatively short time period, the relative smoothness of the returns of the combined portfolio is initial evidence that risk-based explanations will be challenging to support.

To better understand the source of the characteristic's premia we report return correlations for the various constant-volatility, long-and-short characteristic portfolios and well-known sources of risk premia. We report the various pairwise return correlations in Table 12.5 using the full time series of data for the period January 1997 through to April 2015, inclusive. We consider the following traditional risk premia: (i) credit risk premium ('CREDIT'), measured as the value-weighted corporate-bond excess returns; (ii) equity risk premium, measured as the difference between the total returns on the S&P500 index and one-month U.S. Treasury bills ('EQUITY'); (iii) Treasury term premium ('TSY'), measured as the difference between total returns on 10-year U.S. Treasury bonds and one-month U.S. Treasury bills.

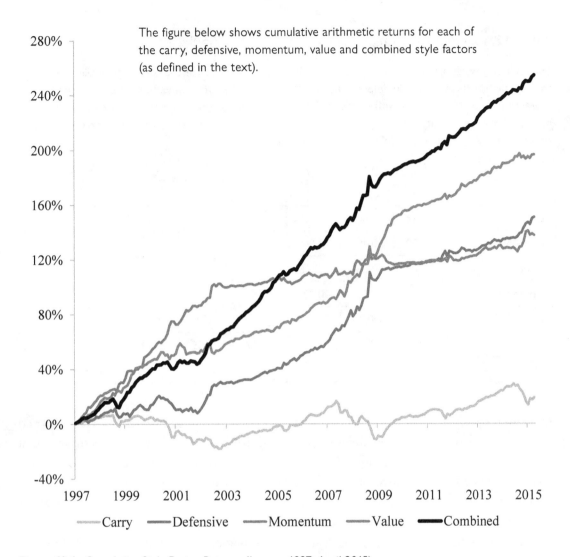

The figure below shows cumulative arithmetic returns for each of the carry, defensive, momentum, value and combined style factors (as defined in the text).

Carry ——Defensive ——Momentum ——Value ——Combined

**Figure 12.1:** Cumulative Style Factor Returns (January 1997–April 2015)

Several of the correlations in Table 12.5 are worth discussing. First, among the four characteristics, we see negative correlations between carry and the other three measures. This is not surprising as issuers with higher spreads will typically have considerable leverage and low profit margins (part of defensive), will have experienced poor recent performance (poor momentum) or both. The correlations reported here are still negative even after our attempt to mitigate the negative correlation with carry by first ranking bonds into duration-times-spread groups and then ranking on characteristic measures within those groups. But they are considerably less negative than without this adjustment. While the carry characteristic is relatively less attractive on a stand-alone basis, it has low correlation with the other characteristics (see the correlations reported in Table 12.5). Conditional on each characteristic

**Table 12.5** Return Correlation Matrix (January 1997–April 2015)

The table below reports monthly excess return correlations for each of the constant-volatility, long-top-quintile-short-bottom-quintile portfolios for the carry, defensive, momentum, value, and combined characteristic portfolios along with market indices corresponding to credit returns in excess of duration matched treasuries, equity returns in excess of the risk-free rate and treasury returns in excess of the risk-free rate. All variables are defined in the appendix.

|           | (1)    | (2)    | (3)    | (4)    | (5)    | (6)    | (7)    | (8)  |
|-----------|--------|--------|--------|--------|--------|--------|--------|------|
| Carry     | 1.00   |        |        |        |        |        |        |      |
| Defensive | −0.18  | 1.00   |        |        |        |        |        |      |
| Momentum  | −0.30  | 0.40   | 1.00   |        |        |        |        |      |
| Value     | −0.09  | 0.28   | −0.16  | 1.00   |        |        |        |      |
| Combined  | 0.15   | 0.79   | 0.43   | 0.38   | 1.00   |        |        |      |
| CREDIT    | 0.80   | −0.24  | −0.17  | −0.10  | 0.01   | 1.00   |        |      |
| EQUITY    | 0.55   | −0.27  | −0.05  | −0.17  | −0.05  | 0.59   | 1.00   |      |
| TSY       | −0.49  | 0.02   | 0.03   | 0.10   | −0.16  | −0.50  | −0.25  | 1.00 |

generating a positive risk-adjusted return on a stand-alone basis as was evident in tables 12.3 and 12.4, the relatively low (and sometimes negative) correlations across characteristics suggests that characteristics do not span each other. Second, the correlations between the various characteristic measures and well-known sources of risk premia show that the characteristic premia are not simply a manifestation of these other well-known risk premia. With the exception of carry, the return correlations between the characteristic factors and risk premia are all less than 0.30 and are often *negative*.

We next test the hypothesis that the characteristic's long-and-short portfolio expected returns cannot be explained by loadings on traditional sources of market risk premia (CREDIT, EQUITY and TSY) as well as exposures to well-known equity anomalies (SMB, HML and UMD from Ken French's data library and QMJ from Asness et al.'s (2014)). The latter test examines whether stocks and bonds with a certain characteristic both earn their expected return due to a common exposure. For example, do cheap stocks (high book-to-market) and cheap bonds (high spread in relation to default risk) earn high average returns due to a common, shared exposure or are the two expected return sources distinct? To answer those questions, we run regressions of constant-volatility, long-and-short characteristic portfolio returns on market and equity anomaly returns as follows:

$$CONST\_VOL\_CHAR_t = \alpha + \beta_0 EQUITY_t + \beta_1 TSY_t + \beta_2 CREDIT_t$$
$$+ \beta_3 SMB_t + \beta_4 HML_t + \beta_5 UMD_t + \beta_6 QMJ_t + \varepsilon_{i,t}. \qquad (2)$$

Consistent with the simple correlations reported in Table 12.5, we see in Table 12.6 that the carry characteristic has a significant positive exposure to credit risk premium. After controlling for other well-known sources of return, the intercept is not significant for carry. The defensive characteristic is negatively correlated with market risk premia (e.g. credit risk premium), consistent with it reflecting a flight to quality or a risk-on/risk-off tendency of investors.

Momentum has a positive correlation with UMD and nothing else. Credit value exhibits a negative loading on SMB and QMJ, −2.0 and −2.3 t-statistics respectively. Interestingly, the value characteristic in credit markets is mildly negatively associated with the HML factor, a result consistent with the evidence that characteristic portfolios in one asset class have limited correlations with those in other asset classes (Asness et al. 2015). In the 5th column of Table 12.6, we regress the combined

**Table 12.6** Long-and-Short Portfolio Alphas and Betas with Respect to Market and Equity Factors (January 1997–April 2015)

The table reports monthly excess return regressions of the carry, defensive, momentum, value, and combined characteristic long-top-quintile-short-bottom-quintile, constant-volatility factors onto (i) market excess returns for treasuries, credit and equity; (ii) equity anomaly factors SMB, HML and UMD from Ken French's website and QMJ from Asness et. al. (2014). All variables are defined in the appendix.

|  | Carry | Defensive | Momentum | Value | Combined |
|---|---|---|---|---|---|
| Intercept | 0.05% | 0.75% | 0.55% | 1.02% | 1.23% |
|  | [0.7] | [5.3] | [3.9] | [8.1] | [9.6] |
| CREDIT | 0.58 | −0.22 | −0.19 | −0.02 | −0.07 |
|  | [10.5] | −[2.1] | −[1.8] | −[0.2] | −[0.7] |
| EQUITY | 0.04 | −0.07 | 0.09 | −0.11 | −0.02 |
|  | [0.0] | [0.0] | [0.0] | [0.0] | [0.0] |
| TSY | −0.12 | −0.12 | −0.10 | 0.05 | −0.18 |
|  | −[2.9] | −[1.4] | −[1.2] | [0.7] | −[2.4] |
| SMB | 0.01 | 0.06 | 0.01 | −0.08 | 0.02 |
|  | [0.4] | [1.3] | [0.2] | −[2.0] | [0.5] |
| HML | −0.02 | 0.05 | 0.06 | −0.02 | 0.06 |
|  | −[0.7] | [1.2] | [1.4] | −[0.6] | [1.4] |
| UMD | 0.00 | −0.01 | 0.06 | −0.01 | 0.04 |
|  | [0.1] | −[0.2] | [2.3] | −[0.4] | [1.6] |
| QMJ | −0.04 | 0.03 | 0.11 | −0.14 | −0.06 |
|  | −[1.2] | [0.4] | [1.6] | −[2.3] | −[0.9] |
| R-squared | 0.67 | 0.10 | 0.09 | 0.07 | 0.05 |

characteristic long-short portfolio return onto the various market risk premia and equity factor returns. The combined portfolio does not have a statistically significant loading on any of the equity factors and a mildly negative relation with term premium. As a consequence, its intercept is a significant 123 basis points per month with a *t*-statistic of 9.6 and an information ratio of 2.25. The combination portfolio is superior to any individual characteristic portfolio reassuring us that the equal-risk approach is a sensible way to combine the different characteristics. Furthermore, the fact that the combination portfolio does not load on traditional market risk premia and equity anomalies suggests that the source of return predictability is distinct from those.

The economic magnitude of the intercept requires further discussion. The literal interpretation would suggest that a 2.25 information ratio is available for investors. Such a statement needs to be interpreted very cautiously. Corporate bond and equity markets differ substantially in terms of their trading costs.

For example, Chen et al. (2007) show that the average bid-mid spread for BBB-rated and B-rated medium maturity bonds are 22 bps and 30 bps, respectively. Frazzini et al. (2012) report average value-weighted trading costs for global equities of 20 bps. These numbers, however, severely understate the impact of transaction costs, as stocks are much more volatile than bonds. Andersen et al. (2001) find that the median stock volatility is 22%, whereas the median bond in our sample has an excess return volatility close to 7%. More importantly, whereas our combined one-dollar-long-and-one-dollar-short portfolio from Table 12.4 has a 2.5% annualized volatility, Fama-French HML's factor—long 1 dollar of cheap stocks and short 1 dollar of expensive stocks—achieves 11.6% annual volatility over the same period.

Given the similarity in dollar transaction costs estimates across bonds and stocks, and similar turnover across bond and stock portfolios, the bond portfolio transaction cost per unit of risk is more than four times larger than that of equity. As a consequence, if a long-and-short portfolio of stocks and bonds are to have similar net-of-transaction costs Sharpe ratios, the bond portfolio must have a much larger gross-of-transaction cost Sharpe ratio.

To illustrate any time-varying performance across the various characteristics (in Figure 12.2), we use the full-sample regression coefficients from Table 12.6 to compute 36-month rolling average alphas for each respective long-and-short, constant-volatility characteristic portfolio. While outperformance has been marginally attenuated in recent years, it is clear that excess returns have been relatively stable and positive. Again the smoothness of the returns, albeit over a short time series, is difficult to reconcile with a risk-based explanation. We formally examine this issue in section 4.4.

## 4.3 Long-Only Optimized Portfolio

While our long-short characteristic portfolios suggest a robust relation between credit excess returns and each of the considered characteristics, they do not take into account actual portfolio implementation considerations. To more realistically address the hypothetical performance of our characteristic portfolios, we build and test optimized long-only portfolios with explicit portfolio implementation

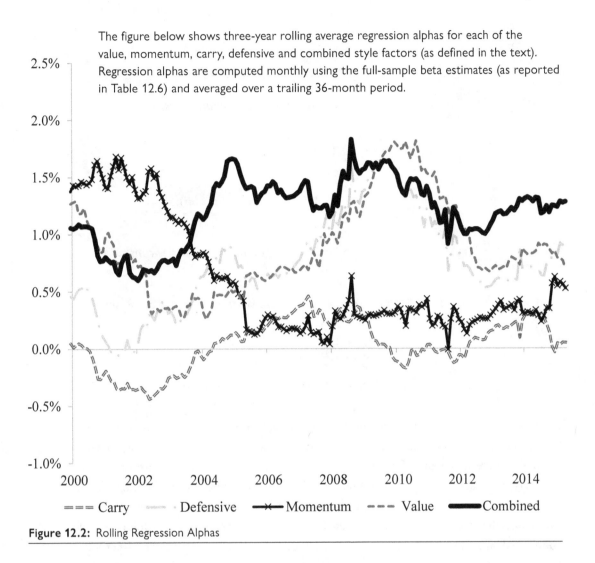

The figure below shows three-year rolling average regression alphas for each of the value, momentum, carry, defensive and combined style factors (as defined in the text). Regression alphas are computed monthly using the full-sample beta estimates (as reported in Table 12.6) and averaged over a trailing 36-month period.

**Figure 12.2:** Rolling Regression Alphas

constraints. Hence our optimized portfolios are designed to be comparable to traditional actively managed corporate bond portfolios, which tend to be long-only (as individual bonds are difficult to short).

We build and rebalance long-only portfolios on a monthly frequency by solving a linear optimization problem. While mean-variance optimization is a commonly utilized objective function in portfolio construction, here we build our portfolios using a simpler objective function that does not require estimation of an asset-by-asset covariance matrix (i.e., an asset-level risk model). Our optimization problem is specified as follows:

$$Maximize: \sum_{i=1}^{I} w_i \cdot COMBO_i$$

*subject to:*

$$w_i \geq 0, \forall i \ (\textit{no shorting constraint})$$

$$|w_i - b_i| \leq 0.25\%, \forall i \ (\textit{deviation from benchmark constraint})$$

$$\sum_{i=1}^{I} w_i = 1 \ (\textit{fully invested constraint})$$

$$\sum_{i=1}^{I} |w_{i,t} - w_{i,t-1}| \leq 10\% \ (\textit{turnover constraint})$$

$$\sum_{i=1}^{I} |(w_{i,t} - w_{i,t-1}) \cdot PRICE_{i,t}| \geq \$100,000, \forall i \ (\textit{minimum trade size constraint})$$

$$\sum_{i=1}^{I} |(w_i - b_i) \cdot OAS_i| \leq 0.50\% \ (\textit{deviation from benchmark spread constraint})$$

$$\sum_{i=1}^{I} |(w_i - b_i) \cdot Duration_i| \leq$$

0.50 (*deviation from benchmark duration constraint*),

where $w_i$ is the portfolio weight for a given bond, and $COMBO_i$ is an equal-weighted combination of the carry, defensive, momentum, and value long-short characteristic portfolios for a given bond. When computing the realized returns from our optimal portfolio holdings, we subtract an estimate of transaction costs based on each bond's rating and maturity in line with Table 12.1 of Chen, Lesmond, and Wei (2007). $PRICE_i$ is the bond price for a given bond, $OAS_i$ is the option adjusted spread for a given bond, $Duration_i$ is the effective duration for a given bond, and $b_i$ is the benchmark portfolio weight for a given bond based on a value-weighted benchmark of all corporate bonds in our one-bond-per-issuer dataset.

The solution to this optimization problem is a long-only corporate bond portfolio that has maximal exposure to the combined characteristic portfolio while taking into consideration the challenges of trading corporate bonds as well as the risk contribution of individual positions to the final portfolio. Importantly, we limit the portfolio's differences from (or tracking error to) the benchmark by limiting the portfolio's active weights relative to the benchmark (i.e., at most 25 bps), limit the portfolio's aggregate OAS exposure to be within 50 bps of the benchmark, and limit the portfolio's aggregate duration exposure to be within 0.50 years of the benchmark. As discussed earlier, Ben Dor et al. (2007) document that spread and duration are the key determinants of volatility in credit markets. Hence constraining the aggregate active weights on these two dimensions is a simple and transparent way to control the active risk of the long-only portfolio. We also constrain turnover to at most 10% per month and force trades to be at least $100,000 (small trades are much more costly, e.g., Edwards et al. (2007)). Despite our best efforts to incorporate constraints and transaction costs, the trading of corporate bonds is challenging. Thus we add the caveat to our empirical results that dynamic trading strategies in corporate bonds are not as implementable as those in more liquid assets.

Table 12.7 reports performance statistics for the optimized long-only portfolio as well as the benchmark. The portfolio earned an annual average excess return of 5.72% per year (and 5.26%

**Table 12.7** Long-Only Backtest Portfolio Performance (January 1997–April 2015)

The table below reports performance statistics for the long-only optimized backtest portfolio based on the optimization problem outlined below. The optimized portfolio refers to the stream of returns generated by the optimized long-only portfolio that maximizes the score of the bonds held as explained in the text. Benchmark is a cap-weighted portfolio of all the corporate bonds in our database; i.e., it includes both investment-grade and high-yield bonds. The active returns reported below are the returns from the optimized portfolio less the benchmark using a 24-month rolling beta. Gross returns are returns in excess of the risk free-rate only. Net returns subtract estimated transaction costs from gross returns.

$$\text{Maximize} : \sum_{i=t}^{I} w_i \cdot COMBO_t$$

subject to:

$$w_i \geq 0, \forall i \ \text{(no shorting constraint)}$$

$$|w_i - b_i| \leq 0.25\%, \forall i \ \text{(deviation from benchmark constraint)}$$

$$\sum_{i=t}^{I} w_i = 1 \ \text{(fully invested constraint)}$$

$$\sum_{i=t}^{I} |w_{i,t} - w_{i,t-1}| \leq 10\% \ \text{(turnover constraint)}$$

$$\sum_{i=1}^{I} |(w_{i,t} - w_{i,t-1}) \cdot PRICE_{i,t}| \geq \$1 000,000, \forall i \ \text{(minimum trade size constraint)}$$

$$\sum_{i=1}^{I} |(w_i - b_i) \cdot OAS_i| \leq 0.50\% \ \text{(deviation from benchmark spread constraint)}$$

$$\sum_{i=1}^{I} |(w_i - b_i) \cdot Duration_i| \leq 0.50 \ \text{(deviation from benchmark duration constraint)}$$

|  | Optimized Portfolio | Benchmark | Active: Portfolio-Beta * Benchmark |
|---|---|---|---|
| Excess Return (gross) | 5.72 | 4.14 | 2.45 |
| Excess Return (net) | 5.26 | 3.84 | 2.20 |
| Volatility (net) | 5.10 | 5.59 | 2.56 |
| Sharpe Ratio (net) | 1.03 | 0.69 | 0.86 |

after taking into account estimated transaction costs). Given its realized annualized volatility of 5.1%, the net Sharpe ratio over this period was 1.03. By comparison, the gross (net) benchmark earned a 4.14% (3.84%) annualized excess return with a Sharpe ratio of 0.69. The active portfolio (i.e., portfolio minus beta times the benchmark) realized an annualized net information ratio of 0.86 with a tracking error of 2.56%. Figure 12.3 shows the cumulative performance of the portfolio and the benchmark.

## 4.4 Investigating Risk and Behavioral Explanations

So far we have documented that value, momentum, carry and defensive measures can predict corporate bond excess returns. In other markets where these anomalies have been studied, both behavioral and risk-based explanations have been suggested. We run additional tests on credit characteristics portfolios aiming to distinguish between risk and behavioural explanations for their respective premiums.

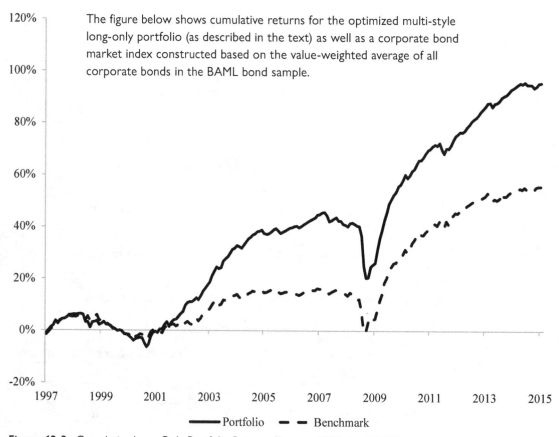

The figure below shows cumulative returns for the optimized multi-style long-only portfolio (as described in the text) as well as a corporate bond market index constructed based on the value-weighted average of all corporate bonds in the BAML bond sample.

**Figure 12.3:** Cumulative Long-Only Portfolio Returns (January 1997–April 2015)

## 4.4.1 Risk Based Explanations

In the first test, we ask whether exposures to traditional macroeconomic variables can explain the premiums that we uncover. We add three macroeconomic variables to the time-series regressions that we had previously run in Table 12.6, specifically we run:

$$CONST\_VOL\_CHAR_t = \alpha + \beta_1 X_t^{Market} + \beta_2 X_t^{Equity} + \beta_7 \Delta LOGVIX_t$$
$$+ \beta_8 \Delta LOGINDPRO_t + \beta_9 \Delta LOGCPI_t + \varepsilon_{i,t}, \tag{3}$$

Where $\Delta LOGVIX$, $\Delta LOGINDPRO$ and $\Delta LOGCPI$ are respectively the one-month change in the log of the VIX, seasonally-adjusted industrial production index and seasonally adjusted consumer price index (CPI). While the intercept cannot be interpreted as a portfolio alpha because the macro variables are not tradable portfolios, we can still examine the regression slope coefficients which are what we report in panel A of Table 12.8. The combination portfolio tends to have higher returns when volatility and inflation rise and when growth falls. If anything, the combo portfolio behaves as a macroeconomic hedge and should have negative expected returns if that hedge is valuable, making its high and positive expected returns even more puzzling.

The single-characteristic portfolios behave much in the same way as the combo—coefficients suggest a macro hedge rather than macro risk profile. Carry is the exception. Its coefficient signs are consistent with the risk story, but only statistically significant for $\Delta LOGVIX$. This suggests that macroeconomic risk may play a role in the carry anomaly but not for the remainder. The conclusions from the time-series regressions, however, have to be caveated by the relatively small sample (about 20 years) for this type of exercise.

In recent years, another class of rational models emerged that focus on financial intermediaries rather than on a single aggregate consumer (e.g. He and Krishnamurthy (2013)). In these models, the conditions of financial intermediaries (wealth, risk aversion, etc.) determine asset prices. Adrian et al. (2014) apply this idea to equity markets and find that exposures to increases in broker-dealers leverage can explain traditional stock factors: size, book-to-market and momentum. We test whether shocks to broker-dealer leverage can explain characteristic factor returns in credit by running time-series regressions of those quarterly returns on quarterly log changes in broker-dealers leverage, controlling for market and equity factor returns. Panel B of Table 12.8 shows that value has a statistically significant loading on broker-dealers leverage shocks of ☐0.18 (t-statistic of 2.2). This suggests that some of the value premium may be due to it being exposed to deterioration in dealer-brokers balance sheet. All other characteristics either have positive loadings (momentum) or loadings that are indistinguishable from zero. In particular, the combo portfolio is a hedge to broker-dealer leverage shocks, though that exposure is not statistically significant. As a consequence, while dealer's balance sheet may play a role in explaining the value characteristic, it cannot be a unified explanation for them all.

**Table 12.8** Long-and-Short Portfolio Betas with Respect to Macroeconomic Variables (January 1997–April 2015)

The table reports monthly excess return regressions of the carry, defensive, momentum, value, and combined characteristic long-top-quintile-short-bottom-quintile, constant-volatility factors onto (i) market excess returns for treasuries, credit and equity; (ii) equity anomaly factors SMB, HML and UMD from Ken French's website and QMJ from Asness et al. (2014); (iii) macroeconomic variables: one-month change in log VIX, one-month change in log industrial production and one-month change in log CPI; (iv) broker-dealer log leverage change (deseasonalized as in Adrian et al. (2014)).

**Panel A: Monthly Volatility, growth and inflation**

|  | Carry | Defensive | Momentum | Value | Combined |
|---|---|---|---|---|---|
| Intercept | 0.00 | 0.01 | 0.01 | 0.01 | 0.01 |
|  | [1.1] | [4.4] | [3.2] | [5.6] | [7.9] |
| ΔLOGVIX | □0.01 | 0.03 | 0.02 | 0.02 | 0.02 |
|  | □[2.5] | [3.1] | [2.2] | [2.3] | [2.2] |
| ΔLOGINDPRO | 0.09 | □0.70 | □0.41 | □0.32 | □0.68 |
|  | [1.0] | □[4.0] | □[2.2] | □[2.0] | □[4.2] |
| ΔLOGCPI | □0.02 | 0.91 | 0.23 | 1.08 | 1.12 |
|  | □[0.1] | [2.2] | [0.5] | [2.8] | [2.9] |
| Market Controls | Yes | Yes | Yes | Yes | Yes |
| Equity Factor Controls | Yes | Yes | Yes | Yes | Yes |
| R-squared | 0.70 | 0.24 | 0.14 | 0.14 | 0.17 |

**Panel B: Quarterly Broker-dealer change in log leverage**

|  | Carry | Defensive | Momentum | Value | Combined |
|---|---|---|---|---|---|
| Intercept | 0.00 | 0.03 | 0.02 | 0.03 | 0.04 |
|  | [1.4] | [5.0] | [4.1] | [6.0] | [8.4] |
| ΔLEV | □0.08 | 0.14 | 0.26 | □0.18 | 0.07 |
|  | □[1.5] | [1.5] | [2.8] | □[2.2] | [0.8] |
| Market Controls | Yes | Yes | Yes | Yes | Yes |
| Equity Factor Controls | Yes | Yes | Yes | Yes | Yes |
| R-squared | 0.77 | 0.17 | 0.33 | 0.26 | 0.20 |

## 4.4.2 Mispricing Explanations

In the next set of empirical tests, we focus on deviations from market efficiency as explanations for the characteristic portfolios positive risk-adjusted returns. Investors deviate from rationality either because they make mistakes or because they are subject to portfolio management frictions (e.g. agency problems due to intermediation, regulations limiting their portfolio choices, etc.); and limits-to-arbitrage (Shleifer and Vishny (1997)) impede arbitrageurs from eliminating the ensuing price distortions. If these deviations from market efficiency are empirically descriptive, then we would expect to see bonds in the most extreme portfolios—those that end up in the top and bottom quintiles–to be illiquid, traded by more error-prone investors, issued by more obscure firms and on the short side would be costlier to borrow (for the bottom quintile). We test these hypotheses by measuring each of these attributes for each characteristic long and short portfolios separately.

We measure liquidity using bond issue size. We use this measure as it has the broadest coverage and has a high correlation with average daily trading volume (Hotchkiss and Jostova (2007)). Volume-based measures typically require coverage in TRACE which is limited for the high-yield market because a large fraction of high-yield bonds are issued under 144A regulations and are not disseminated by TRACE before late 2014. We measure the investor population sophistication by the fraction of a bond which is owned by institutional investors, presumably better equipped than retail investors to avoid mistakes. We measure firm transparency by the number of analysts following the issuer equity (Hong et al. (2000)) and, lastly, the cost of shorting is measured by the shorting fee score from MarkitDataExplorers.

Table 12.9 reports the results. If deviations from market efficiency and/or market frictions are empirically descriptive we would expect to see (i) lower analyst coverage, (ii) lower institutional ownership, and (iii) smaller bonds in the extreme portfolios for each characteristic. We would also expect to see greatest short selling costs in the lowest portfolio for each characteristic. Across all four characteristics we do not see any consistent evidence supporting these explanations. Bonds that score high in carry, momentum and value tend to be smaller, issued by more sparsely covered and owned by fewer institutions. Bonds, on the short side, however, display opposite rather than similar behavior. They are bigger, well covered and owned at a higher rate by institutional investors. Finally, the short side of each characteristic portfolio is in fact cheaper to borrow than its long side. Collectively, these patterns suggest that a simple mispricing hypothesis does not fit the data.

A separate implication of the mispricing hypothesis is that the relation between characteristics and future returns will be stronger among bonds in the segment of the corporate bond universe that are harder to arbitrage, less transparent or populated with a less sophisticated investor base. In Table 12.10, we test this hypothesis by comparing long-and-short portfolios formed on different universes of corporate bonds distinguished by the dimensions discussed above. We find that momentum long-and-short portfolios perform better in the less liquid, less transparent and less sophisticated segments of the corporate bond market. For carry, defensive and value the evidence is more mixed,

**Table 12.9** Average Mispricing Susceptibility of Quintile Portfolios

For each characteristic and mispricing susceptibility proxy, the table reports the cap-weighted average value of the proxy for each one of the quintile portfolios formed on carry, momentum, value and defensive. The proxies for susceptibility are firm transparency measured by the number of equity analysts that follows the issuing company; liquidity as measures by bond issue size; investor base sophistication as measured by institutional ownership and easiness of shorting as measured by the shorting fee score (0 is lowest fee and 5 the highest). The table also displays the difference between the top and bottom quintile portfolios as well as its t-statistic computed using Newey-West standard errors and 18 lags.

**Equity Analyst Coverage**

|  | Carry | Defensive | Momentum | Value |
|---|---|---|---|---|
| Low | 19.36 | 14.87 | 15.19 | 16.48 |
| 40 | 15.13 | 13.90 | 15.20 | 15.61 |
| 60 | 12.46 | 14.50 | 15.04 | 14.47 |
| 80 | 9.42 | 14.95 | 14.59 | 12.98 |
| High | 7.64 | 15.41 | 12.88 | 11.37 |
| High-Low | −11.73 | 0.55 | −2.31 | −5.11 |
| High-Low t-statistic | −18.66 | 2.03 | −4.87 | −13.38 |

**Issue Market Value in Billions**

|  | Carry | Defensive | Momentum | Value |
|---|---|---|---|---|
| Low | 1.28 | 1.34 | 1.06 | 1.10 |
| 40 | 1.04 | 0.87 | 0.98 | 1.05 |
| 60 | 0.79 | 0.85 | 0.93 | 0.93 |
| 80 | 0.66 | 0.72 | 0.85 | 0.74 |
| High | 0.54 | 0.66 | 0.80 | 0.71 |
| High-Low | −0.73 | −0.69 | −0.25 | −0.39 |
| High-Low t-statistic | −17.24 | −9.93 | −3.81 | −5.27 |

**Institutional Ownership of Bond**

|  | Carry | Defensive | Momentum | Value |
|---|---|---|---|---|
| Low | 0.50 | 0.48 | 0.49 | 0.51 |
| 40 | 0.54 | 0.52 | 0.50 | 0.49 |
| 60 | 0.50 | 0.50 | 0.50 | 0.48 |
| 80 | 0.46 | 0.47 | 0.49 | 0.49 |
| High | 0.40 | 0.47 | 0.46 | 0.49 |
| High-Low | −0.10 | −0.02 | −0.03 | −0.02 |
| High-Low t-statistic | −5.18 | −2.20 | −3.50 | −2.66 |

## Average Shorting Cost Score of Bond

| | Carry | Defensive | Momentum | Value |
|---|---|---|---|---|
| Low | 0.05 | 0.10 | 0.14 | 0.10 |
| 40 | 0.05 | 0.09 | 0.10 | 0.10 |
| 60 | 0.08 | 0.12 | 0.10 | 0.14 |
| 80 | 0.17 | 0.20 | 0.12 | 0.19 |
| High | 0.52 | 0.18 | 0.21 | 0.17 |
| High-Low | 0.47 | 0.07 | 0.07 | 0.07 |
| High-Low t-statistic | 9.79 | 7.73 | 4.90 | 3.70 |

**Table 12.10** Average Returns of Characteristic Portfolios across Bonds with Varying Levels of Mispricing Susceptibility

. . . . . . . . . . . . . . . . . . . . . . . . . . . . . . . . . . . . . . . . . . . . . . . . . . . . . . . . . . . . . . . . . . . . . . . . . . . . . . . . . . . . .

The table displays the average credit excess returns and t-statistics of long-and-short characteristic portfolios built from subsets of firms with different values for mispricing susceptibility measures. The proxies for susceptibility are firm transparency measured by the number of equity analysts that follows the issuing company; liquidity as measures by bond issue size; investor base sophistication as measured by institutional ownership and easiness of shorting as measured by the shorting fee score (0 is lowest fee and 5 the highest).

### Panel A: Characteristic Returns across Equity Analyst Coverage Terciles

| | Low | Medium | High | High-Minus-Low |
|---|---|---|---|---|
| Carry | 0.35% | 0.25% | 0.15% | ☐0.20% |
| | [1.9] | [1.6] | [1.1] | ☐[1.8] |
| Defensive | 0.14% | 0.08% | 0.17% | 0.02% |
| | [2.0] | [1.2] | [2.6] | [0.4] |
| Momentum | 0.40% | 0.18% | 0.16% | ☐0.23% |
| | [4.4] | [2.6] | [2.1] | ☐[2.8] |
| Value | 0.42% | 0.39% | 0.22% | ☐0.20% |
| | [6.7] | [7.0] | [2.9] | ☐[2.0] |

### Panel B: Characteristic Returns across Institutional Ownership Terciles

| | Low | Medium | High | High-Minus-Low |
|---|---|---|---|---|
| Carry | 0.32% | 0.30% | 0.28% | ☐0.03% |
| | [1.6] | [1.5] | [1.8] | ☐[0.3] |
| Defensive | 0.11% | 0.10% | 0.17% | 0.05% |
| | [1.7] | [2.5] | [4.5] | [0.9] |
| Momentum | 0.26% | 0.15% | 0.06% | ☐0.20% |
| | [3.1] | [2.1] | [1.2] | ☐[2.3] |
| Value | 0.21% | 0.29% | 0.31% | 0.10% |
| | [3.6] | [4.6] | [6.7] | [1.7] |

**Panel C: Characteristic Returns across Bond Market Value Terciles**

|          | Low    | Medium | High   | High-Minus-Low |
|----------|--------|--------|--------|----------------|
| Carry    | 0.28%  | 0.34%  | 0.23%  | ☐0.06%         |
|          | [1.8]  | [2.1]  | [1.4]  | ☐[0.6]         |
| Defensive| 0.14%  | 0.15%  | 0.11%  | ☐0.02%         |
|          | [2.8]  | [4.3]  | [2.7]  | ☐[0.4]         |
| Momentum | 0.37%  | 0.15%  | 0.12%  | ☐0.25%         |
|          | [6.2]  | [3.4]  | [2.0]  | ☐[3.4]         |
| Value    | 0.28%  | 0.29%  | 0.19%  | ☐0.08%         |
|          | [5.8]  | [7.2]  | [4.4]  | ☐[1.4]         |

**Panel D: Characteristic Returns across of Shorting Costs**

|          | Fee = 0 | Fee > 0 | Fee 0 minus Fee > 0 |
|----------|---------|---------|---------------------|
| Carry    | 0.36%   | 0.35%   | ☐0.01%              |
|          | [1.3]   | [1.0]   | [0.0]               |
| Defensive| 0.16%   | 0.52%   | 0.36%               |
|          | [2.2]   | [1.8]   | [1.3]               |
| Momentum | 0.06%   | 0.08%   | 0.02%               |
|          | [0.6]   | [0.2]   | [0.1]               |
| Value    | 0.32%   | 0.53%   | 0.21%               |
|          | [4.4]   | [2.1]   | [0.9]               |

sometimes performing better in the more mispricing prone arbitrage segments of the market, sometimes performing better in the less vulnerable one, but rarely statistically significant.

As a final test of behavioral explanations, we look at errors in expectations of equity analysts' sales forecasts. A systematic pattern between a characteristic and both future returns and revisions is consistent with mispricing (see e.g. Bradshaw et al. (2001)). We focus on sales instead of EPS because we are assessing senior claims. Increases in EPS can be detrimental for credit if the increase came about through re-leveraging. Our hypothesis is that analysts and investors have similar beliefs and, therefore, we can learn about the (unobservable) mistakes of the latter from the (observable) mistakes of the former. In other words, do the firms in the good carry, momentum, value and defensive portfolio experience more positive revisions than those in the bottom quintile of those characteristics?

To study analyst errors we focus on their forecast revisions for the next 12 months of sales. If analysts are fully rational and free from agency concerns, their revisions should not be predictable by any model relying on public information. If, on the other hand, their revisions are found to be predictable, it means they are ignoring certain information. To the extent that investors and analysts share the same beliefs, prices would not reflect that information as well and as a consequence would be predictable.

We build next-twelve-month revisions by averaging revisions over the next fiscal year sales number (FY1) and that of the subsequent fiscal year (FY2). We set the weights dynamically to assure that the weighted average horizon of the forecast is always 12 months.

The results are displayed in Figure 12.4. The dark lines are the cumulative revisions of the long portfolio and the dotted lines are the revisions for the short portfolio. If there are systematic predictable errors in sales forecasts, then we expect greater downward revisions for the short portfolio and greater upward revisions for the long portfolio. The mispricing hypothesis is consistent with what we see for the momentum portfolio and to a lesser extent for the defensive portfolio: after 12 months the

Average cumulative monthly revisions of analysts sales forecasts for the next 12 months since portfolio formation for issuers in the top and bottom quintile of the four characteristics: Carry, Defensive, Momentum and Value as defined in the text. For every firm, analyst forecasts revisions for the next 12 months are built from an average of the revisions (log difference) of forecasts for the next fiscal year (FY1) and the following (FY2), with weights set to make the average horizon be 12 months. For every portfolio, the revision number is an equal weight of the revisions of all the firms that comprise that portfolio.

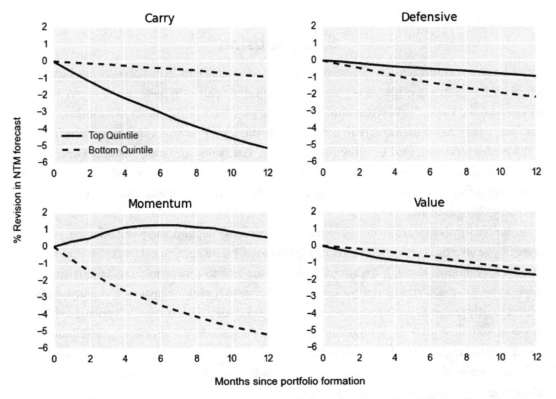

**Figure 12.4:** Analysts Revisions of Top and Bottom Quintile Portfolios Formed on Different Characteristics (January 2001–April 2015)

long portfolio experiences sales revisions that are larger than short by 5.7% (*t*-statistic = 7.28) and 1.2% (*t*-statistic = 1.86) for momentum and defensive, respectively. For value and carry the result goes in the opposite direction of that predicted by the mispricing hypothesis but the difference is only statistically significant for carry (*t*-statistic = 6.17). As a consequence mispricing seems to play less of an obvious role for these two characteristics.

While the revision number for momentum is a sizeable 5.7% sales drop, it is hard to evaluate its impact on the long-and-short portfolio return. To facilitate interpretation we compute the impact on credit spreads of a 5.7% sales drop for the median firm using a simple structural model. The median bond in our sample has an OAS of 302 bps and duration of 5, while its issuer has a leverage of 0.28. We feed those numbers through a structural model (Merton (1974)) to invert the asset volatility that is consistent with this quantity—the credit-implied volatility (Kelly et al. (2016)). We then shock asset value by 5.7% assuming that it drops by the same value as sales and, keeping volatility constant, compute the new credit spread and the credit returns associated with this change. For momentum, a 5.7% sales increase translates into a roughly 112 bps return: about one third of the 290 bps momentum premium displayed in Table 12.4. Errors in expectations offer a partial explanation to the momentum returns in corporate bond markets.

# 5. Conclusion

We undertake a comprehensive analysis of the cross-sectional determinants of corporate bond excess returns. We find strong evidence of positive risk-adjusted returns to measures of carry, defensive, momentum and value. These returns are diversifying with respect to both known sources of market risk (e.g., equity risk premium, credit risk premium and term premium) and characteristic returns that have been documented in equity markets (e.g., size, value and momentum). These conclusions hold whether one examines traditional long-and-short academic portfolios or a long-only, transactions-cost aware portfolio. The latter helps dismiss the hypothesis that the returns are not economically significant.

In our final analysis we examine the source of the value, momentum, carry and defensive premiums in credit. We investigate risk and mispricing explanations. We do not find evidence that the anomalies earn their premiums through traditional risk exposures or to shocks to financial intermediaries' balance sheets—characteristic returns tend to be a hedge to traditional macroeconomic factors and exhibit mostly insignificant loadings on shocks to broker-dealers leverage. Mispricing evidence is strongest for momentum: the momentum strategy has better performance among less liquid bonds issued by less transparent firms and owned by less sophisticated investors; it is also long (short) bonds of firms where analyst forecasts of sales are relatively too pessimistic (optimistic). The evidence for mispricing is mixed for the other characteristics.

# References

Adrian, T., Etula, E., & Muir, T. (2014). Financial Intermediaries and the Cross-Section of Asset Returns. *The Journal of Finance*, 69(6), 2557–2596.

Altman, Edward I. (1968). Financial Ratios, Discriminant Analysis and the Prediction of Corporate Bankruptcy. *Journal of Finance*, 23, 4 189–209

Andersen, T. G., Bollerslev, T., Diebold, F. X., & Ebens, H. (2001). The distribution of realized stock return volatility. *Journal of Financial Economics*, 61(1), 43–76.

Asness, Clifford S., Andrea Frazzini and Lasse Heje Pedersen (2014). Quality minus junk. Working paper.

Asness, C., A. Ilmanen, R. Israel and T. Moskowitz (2015). Investing with Style. *Journal of Investment Management*, 13, 27–63.

Asness, C., T. Moskowitz and L. Pedersen (2013). Value and momentum everywhere. *Journal of Finance*, 68, 929–985.

Asquith, P., A. S. Au, T. Covert and P. A. Pathak (2013). The market for borrowing corporate bonds. *Journal of Financial Economics*, 107, 155–182.

Asvanunt, A., and S. Richardson (2017). The credit risk premium. *Journal of Fixed Income*, Winter 2017.

Ben Dor, A., L. Dynkin, J. Hyman, P. Houweling, E, Van Leeuwen and O. Penniga (2007). DTS (duration times spread). *The Journal of Portfolio Management*, 33, 77–100.

Bessembinder, H., W. Maxwell and K. Venkataraman (2006). Market transparency, liquidity externalities, and institutional trading costs in corporate bonds. *Journal of Financial Economics*, 82, 251–288.

Bharath, Sreedhar T., and Tyler Shumway (2008). Forecasting default with the Merton distance to default model. *Review of Financial Studies*, 21.3, 1339–1369.

Binsbergen, J. H., and R. S. J. Koijen (2015). The Term Structure of Returns: Facts and Theory. Working paper.

Bradshaw, M. T., Richardson, S. A., and Sloan, R. G. (2001). Do analysts and auditors use information in accruals? *Journal of Accounting Research*, 39(1), 45–74

Carvalho, R., P. Dugnolle, L. Xiao and P. Moulin (2014). Low-risk anomalies in global fixed income: Evidence from major broad markets. *The Journal of Fixed Income*, 23, 51–70.

Chen, L., D. A. Lesmond and J. Wei (2007). Corporate yield spreads and bond liquidity. *Journal of Finance*, 62, 119–149.

Chen, N. F., Roll, R. and Ross, S. A. (1986) Economic forces and the stock market. *Journal of Business*, 383–403.

Choi, J., and Y. Kim (2015). Anomalies and market (dis)integration. Working paper, UIUC.

Chordia, T., A. Goyal, Y. Nozawa, A. Subrahmanyam and Q. Tong (2016). Are capital market anomalies common to equity and corporate bond markets? Working paper, Emory University.

Cochrane, J. H. (2009). *Asset Pricing:(Revised Edition)*. Princeton university press.

Correia, M., S. Richardson and I. Tuna (2012). Value investing in credit markets. *Review of Accounting Studies*, 17 (3): 572–609.

DeMiguel, V., Garlappi, L., & Uppal, R. (2009). Optimal versus naive diversification: How inefficient is the 1/N portfolio strategy? *Review of Financial Studies*, 22(5), 1915–1953.

Edwards, A. E., L.E. Harris and M.S. Piwowar (2007). Corporate bond market transaction costs and transparency. *Journal of Finance*, 62, 1421–1451.

Fama, Eugene F., and Kenneth R. French. Common risk factors in the returns on stocks and bonds. *Journal of Financial Economics*, 33.1 (1993): 3–56.

Frazzini, A., R. Israel and T. J. Moskowitz (2012). Trading costs of asset pricing anomalies. Working paper, AQR Capital Management.

Frazzini, A., and L. H. Pedersen (2014). Betting against beta. *Journal of Financial Economics*, 111, 1–25.

Gebhardt, W. R., S. Hvidkjaer and B. Swaminathan (2005a). The cross-section of expected corporate bond returns: betas or characteristics? *Journal of Financial Economics*, 75, 85–114.

Gebhardt, W. R., S. Hvidkjaer, and B. Swaminathan (2005b). Stock and bond market interaction: does momentum spill over? *Journal of Financial Economics*, 75, 651–690.

Grossman, S. J., & Stiglitz, J. E. (1980). On the impossibility of informationally efficient markets. *The American economic review*, 70(3), 393–408.

Haesen, D., P. Houweling and J. van Zundert (2013). Residual equity momentum for corporate bonds. Working paper, Robeco Quantitative Strategies.

Hallerbach, W. G., and P. Houweling. (2013). Ibbotson's default premium: risky data. *The Journal of Investing*, 22, 95–105.

Harris, L. (2015). Transaction costs, trade throughs, and riskless principal trading in corporate bond markets. Working paper, USC.

He, Z., & Krishnamurthy, A. (2013). Intermediary asset pricing. *The American Economic Review*, 103(2), 732–770.

Hong, H., Lim, T. and Stein, J. C. (2000). Bad news travels slowly: Size, analyst coverage and the profitability of the momentum strategies. *The Journal of Finance*, 55(1), 265–295

Hotchkiss, Edith S. and Jostova, Gergana, Determinants of Corporate Bond Trading: A Comprehensive Analysis (July 9, 2007). Working paper.

Houweling, P., and J. van Zundert (2014). Factor investing in the corporate bond market. Working paper, Robeco Quantitative Strategies.

Jostova, G., S. Nikolova, A. Philipov and C.W. Stahel (2013). Momentum in corporate bond returns. *Review of Financial Studies*, 26(7), 1649–1693.

Kelly, B. T., Manzo, G. and Palhares, D., 2016. Credit-Implied Volatility. *Manuscript.*

Koijen, R., T. Moskowitz, L. Pedersen and E. Vrugt (2014). Carry. Working paper, University of Chicago Booth School of Business, New York University, University of Amsterdam.

Kwan, S. H. (1996). Firm-specific information and the correlation between individual stocks and bonds. *Journal of Financial Economics*, 40, 63–80.

Lewellen, J. (2015). The cross-section of expected stock returns. *Critical Finance Review*, 4, 1–44.

Lok, S., and A. Richardson (2011). Credit markets and financial information. *Review of Accounting Studies*, 16, 487–500.

Merton, R. (1974). On the pricing of corporate debt: The risk structure of interest rates. *Journal of Finance*, 29, 449–470.

Moreira, A., & Muir, T. (2016). Volatility managed portfolios (No. w22208). *National Bureau of Economic Research*.

Ng, K. Y., and B. Phelps (2014). Structure of US corporate excess returns: The hunt for a 'low-risk' anomaly. Working paper, Barclays.

Novy-Marx, R. (2013). The other side of value: The gross profitability premium. *Journal of Financial Economics*, 108(1), 1–28.

Palhares, D. (2013). Cash-flow maturity and risk premia in CDS markets. Working paper, AQR Capital Management.

Schaefer, S. M., & Strebulaev, I. A. (2008). Structural models of credit risk are useful: Evidence from hedge ratios on corporate bonds. *Journal of Financial Economics*, 90(1), 1–19.

Shleifer, A. and Vishny, R. W. (1997). The limits to arbitrage. *The Journal of Finance*, 52(1), 35–55.

Shumway, Tyler (2001). Forecasting bankruptcy more accurately: A simple hazard model. *Journal of Business*, 740, 101–124.

# Bonds, Jammed Bonds

## Will Rising Illiquidity in Bond Markets Give ETFS License to Thrill?

By Ed McCarthy

.....................................................................................................................................

T he bond market is experiencing a dichotomy that's challenging investors. Post-Financial Crisis, the volume of outstanding bonds has grown. At the same time, however, consolidation among banks and broker/dealers has cut the number of market makers, and new regulations have reduced the capital these companies can commit to fixed-income inventories. Matthew Tucker, CFA, managing director, head of Fixed-Income iShares Strategy at BlackRock in the San Francisco Bay Area, cites New York Federal Reserve Bank stats that these institutions currently hold 20% of their pre-Crisis bond inventories. These conditions have "caused a shift in liquidity in the bond market where many investors have to reevaluate how they source liquidity [and] where they source liquidity," says Tucker.

The illiquidity is greatest in markets with large numbers of outstanding securities. Tucker notes that there are approximately 250 Treasury notes and bonds with maturities of one year or greater. That relatively small (by number of issues) market has remained liquid. In contrast, BlackRock estimates that less than 20% of investment-grade corporate bonds in the US trade every day. Consequently, corporate bond investors are less likely "to be successful in finding someone to trade with and finding a price at which [they] want to transact," he says.

A third-quarter 2016 report from Stamford, Connecticut–based Greenwich Associates, "Institutional Investors Embrace Bond ETFs," examined the changing bond market. Per the report: "Seventy-one percent of the institutions participating in Greenwich Associates 2016 US Bond ETF Study say the trading and sourcing of securities have become more difficult in the past three years"—up from 34% the previous year. In addition, 60% of study participants reported it was more difficult to complete large-sized bond trades in 2016.

**Key Points:** Illiquidity in bond markets is driving investors to seek alternatives to the dominant over-the-counter (OTC) market structure.

Although assets held in exchange-traded funds (ETFs) account for a tiny share of the bond market, ETF adoption appears to be growing rapidly.

The trend is expected to accelerate, with assets in bond ETFs doubling or tripling over the next two years.

## From OTC to ETF

Andrew McCollum, managing director with Greenwich Associates and the report's author, says the liquidity problem is causing prospective investors to consider how they will sell a position before completing the buy transaction. "We have investors in our research that will say to us, 'Today, I think very carefully not about just getting into a fixed-income security but how I'm going to get out of the fixed-income security,'" says McCollum. "And for some of these bonds that aren't terribly liquid, they consider that when making their decision about what the right vehicle is. I don't think that was a big consideration five years ago."

Tucker says that illiquidity is leading bond investors to seek alternatives to the dominant over-the-counter (OTC) market structure. He estimates that the leading electronic trading platforms now handle about 20% of all corporate bond trades, and that percentage is increasing each year. Fixed-income exchange-traded funds (ETFs) are also attracting more investors. As of late 2016, the average daily trading volume in fixed-income ETFs was roughly $7 billion, and in some instances, fixed-income ETFs can supplement the corporate bond OTC market and provide additional liquidity for investors, Tucker maintains.

## A Small But Growing Role

Assets held in ETFs are still a tiny slice of the overall bond market—less than 1%, says Tucker. But the Greenwich Associates survey points to rapidly growing ETF adoption:

- Sixty-eight percent of survey participants have increased their bond ETF usage over the past three years.

- Institutions are executing larger bond ETF trades. In 2016, 31% reported executing a trade of $50 million or more, up from 19% in 2015.

- Thirty percent of investors surveyed are considering investing with bond ETFs rather than individual bond positions in the next year.

- Eighty-eight percent of institutions using fixed-income derivatives are considering or have considered using bond ETFs as an alternative.

Institutions' ETF usage serves a purpose, and even though bond ETFs are generally passively linked to an index, institutions are using the funds to take active positions, says McCollum. It can be a short-term tactical purpose, such as when an investor is changing managers but wants to maintain exposure to an asset class during the transition, but the uses go beyond those scenarios. "They're taking active positions by thinking, 'There's a real opportunity here in this category or in this asset class, and I want to get in quickly and get out quickly, and I'm going to use an ETF to do that.' Or, 'I'm going to hedge my portfolio for a long period of time, and an ETF could be a good tool to do that,'" says McCollum.

The loss of liquidity has also affected investment managers working with private clients. About five years ago, Mariann Montagne, CFA, a senior investment analyst at Gradient Investments in Arden Hills, Minnesota, began to experience increased difficulty buying bonds for individual investors. Many clients had bond allocations ranging from $50,000 to $200,000 that she would ladder across a range of maturities. Her usual practice was to monitor the OTC markets for investment-grade bonds, with specified parameters to buy for individual clients' accounts. She expected the price markups for small retail positions to be higher than those charged against institutional lots, but between 2011 and 2013, the bid/ask spreads became "onerous, extremely onerous," she says. "You could have a 1% or 2% differential between the bid and the offer in a 2% [rate] environment. I had a devil of a time trying to get good names in the years that I needed and where the client wouldn't automatically get this 1% or 2% haircut."

## Obstacles to Increased Adoption

There are potential roadblocks to the further adoption of ETFs. McCollum says some institutional investors' internal guidelines include restrictions that limit their use of the funds. But those restrictions are becoming less common: Only 24% of the 2016 survey respondents still had such policies, down from about 50% in 2015.

ETF analytics are another challenge. Investors know a specific bond's cash flows and provisions, but an ETF can hold a thousand bonds, making such calculations as yield and duration more difficult. To standardize analytics, Black-Rock, State Street Global Advisors, and Bloomberg, among others, jointly developed the aggregated cash flow methodology and the Fixed Income ETF Metrics Convention. "If you're an investor and you receive information from a broker/dealer about the yield or duration of an ETF, and it's calculated according to the standard, you know how the calculation is done, and you'd be able to replicate it yourself," says Tucker. "And the same thing applies if I go in and look at a provider website and see information about yield or duration or I go onto an analytics platform like Bloomberg and see information about yield and duration."

A third concern has been ETFs' performance during exceptionally volatile or disrupted markets. Specifically, do ETFs experience liquidity and price disruptions during these periods? Fixed-income

ETFs have been in the market since 2002, which means they have gone through the Financial Crisis of 2008, the Taper Tantrum of 2013, and the high-yield market sell-off in December 2015. During these periods, bond ETF prices have reflected their underlying markets, and their trading volumes have increased, says Tucker. The ETF creation and redemption process with authorized market makers helps maintain the value relationship between the fund and the underlying bonds, he adds, and investors have an option to trade ETFs on an exchange versus going to the OTC market, providing them with an incremental source of liquidity.

*I HAD A DEVIL OF A TIME TRYING TO GET GOOD NAMES IN THE YEARS THAT I NEEDED AND WHERE THE CLIENT WOULDN'T AUTOMATICALLY GET THIS 1% OR 2% HAIRCUT.*

A December 2015 BlackRock report, "High Yield ETFs in Stressed Markets," examined the iShares iBoxx $ High Yield Corporate Bond ETF's (symbol HYG) performance for the volatile period of 2 December through 25 December 2015. Secondary market trading in HYG increased significantly during that month to an average of $1.5 billion per day versus $640 million per day for the year's first 11 months. The report states: "Nearly 95% of all HYG investor trading activity during this period occurred on exchange rather than the OTC bond market. High-yield investors were able to execute transactions more efficiently by using HYG, which typically trades at a bid/offer spread of less than 1 basis point, [rather] than by using individual cash bonds, which typically trade at a bid/offer of 50–100 basis points."

## A Bright Outlook

Observers believe bond ETF usage will continue to grow. Greenwich Associates found that one-third of institutions plan to increase their use of bond ETFs in the coming year. Of those, 30% expect to boost ETF usage by more than 10%. Insurance companies' increased use of ETFs is another positive indicator. Among the insurance companies that participated in the 2016 Greenwich Associates study, about half started investing in ETFs within the past two years, and nearly a quarter were using ETFs for 12 months or less. More than half of the surveyed insurers (52%) planned to increase their use of ETFs in the next year.

The development of fixed-term ETFs could also spur usage among institutions looking to match liabilities and among private investors seeking laddered portfolios. The fixed-term ETFs are catching on, says Tucker. The fixed-term corporate and municipal funds from iShares held $1.4 billion at year-end 2015, an amount that grew to $2.6 billion by November 2016. Montagne says her firm uses the Guggenheim dated fixed-term ETFs to create bond ladders in the three- to five-year range for private clients. In a rising rate environment, which the firm expects, the funds allow her to have a predictable series of rolling maturities that can capture higher prevailing rates.

These factors bode well, says Tucker, who believes that it's still the early days for the funds. "I think the ETFs have a long way to go in terms of growth," he says. "I can see assets doubling or tripling easy from here over the next couple of years."

**Ed McCarthy** is a freelance financial writer in Pascoag, Rhode Island.

**Keep Going:** "Fundamental Indexing in Global Bond Markets: The Risk Exposure Explains It All," *Financial Analysts Journal* (posted online 5 December 2016) [www.cfapubs.org]

"Global Inflation-Linked Bonds: A Primer," *Enterprising Investor* (4 November 2016) [blogs.cfainstitute.org/investor]

"Should Bonds Trade More Like Equities?" *CFA Institute Magazine* (September 2016) [www.cfapubs.org]

# Common and Preferred Stock and Stock Valuation

*Go for a business that any idiot can run—because sooner or later, any idiot probably is going to run it.*

**Peter Lynch**

U nlike most bonds and debentures, common and preferred stocks have no maturity date. This means that the company is under no obligation to repurchase issues of common or preferred stock from individual investors.

Common stocks offer residual cash flows in the form of common dividends. These dividends, unlike the interest payments to be received from most bonds, have no fixed rate. They are residual in that they vary in accordance with income earned for a specific period of time. Though they may choose to do so, stock issuers have no obligation to repurchase shares of their stock. In the case of publicly traded shares, investors may resell their shares in the secondary market.

Common stock prices can increase or decrease over time as a result of changes in either or both dividends and risk. First, dividends, which are variable, may be altered over time to affect the rate of return earned on investment in the stock. Second, the stock price itself may be adjusted in the marketplace to reflect required rates of return desired by investors for taking the risk associated with the investment in a particular common stock.

Valuing common stock is more complicated than the process of valuing fixed-income bonds or debentures because they have no maturity or termination date and, more importantly, because the dividends they pay are generally variable. One approach to estimating common stock prices is the use of the Gordon growth or dividend discount model based on estimated future dividends, dividend growth rates, and the return required for perceived risk.

The Gordon growth model, which assumes an investment for a period of infinity, is a stock price estimation method that can also be restructured to allow computation of the required rate of return as based on expected dividends and the current market price. The model provides two components for determination of the required return or yield on an investment in common stock. These are the dividend yield component and the capital gains yield component, both of which are determined based on the price of the stock.

The yield requirements for an investment in common stocks are therefore no different from those for any other investment. Common stock investors, as expected, require compensation for both capital gains and income.

One of the more common ways to assess the required return is the application of the capital asset pricing model. The capital asset pricing model (CAPM) is a market-based model devised to utilize the fact that risk premiums are proportionate to risks undertaken. It therefore utilizes the concept of a risk-free rate of return, which is composed of the real rate of return and an inflation premium to determine the required rate of return for individual investments in consideration of the systematic or undiversifiable risk undertaken in each individual investment. This is accomplished by determining the volatility of investment return with respect to market return and combining this volatility or risk measure of systematic risk to the return required on the market and the return required on a risk-free investment.

The volatility or risk measure of systematic risk is known as the beta factor, which provides an indication of whether or not an asset, be it a security or a portfolio, will react more or less in terms of return change than will the market portfolio. Betas are generally calculated by means of regression in accordance with a least squares regression analysis technique. By regressing the returns of an individual investment against the returns on the market portfolio, we obtain what is referred to as the characteristic line for the investment. The slope of this line provides the beta characteristic of volatility. As a result, we can use the capital asset pricing model to estimate the expected return on an asset with consideration given to the level of systematic or market risk observed in that asset.

In applying the discounted cash flow model for purposes of price estimation, the price a new investor should pay for the common stock should be based on the stream of dividends to be received over the time the investor holds the stock and the price at which the investor expects to be able to sell the stock at some future date. The price will also be based on the required rate of return of that individual investor. Placing a value on common stocks is one of the more difficult financial tasks.

When the term to maturity for any investment, such as a consul bond (a perpetuity) or, in this case, common stock, is equal to infinity, the discounted cash flow models can be reduced to simpler form. In the case of the consul bond, the discounted cash flow model is reduced to the price of the bond being equal to interest payments divided by the required rate of return on the bond. Here, in the case of common stock where $n$ is equal to infinity, the valuation model is equal to the dividend, whether constant or growing, divided by the required rate of return minus the growth rate.

Since the dividends to be received for investments in common stock are residual income benefits, they are based on future earnings, which are uncertain. This implies that it is necessary to utilize a probability distribution in order to come up with an estimate of the expected dividend stream. Similarly, if we are attempting to estimate what the rate of return on an investment will be, given alternative states of nature or the economy, we again are forced to make estimates using a probability distribution approach.

When estimating the price for an issue of common stock, it is necessary to make an assumption about the rate of growth in dividends on that common stock. There are several alternative assumptions that may be made. The first is that dividends remain constant—in other words, the growth rate in dividends will be equal to zero.

The second situation is to assume that dividends will grow or fall at a constant rate of growth $g$. The model for valuation of common stock where dividends are expected to grow or fall at a constant rate $g$ is known as the Gordon growth or dividend discount model. The Gordon model is based on simple time value of money concepts as applied to cash flows in the form of dividend payments to infinity.

One last type of assumption that might be made in the valuation of common stock is that the growth rate of dividends will vary over time. While it is not expected that an accelerated rate of growth can continue indefinitely, variable growth, whether increasing or decreasing, does cause complications in the use of the Gordon growth model. High rates of growth, those beyond the norm for a firm, cause problems because the denominator in the model is stated as the required return less the growth rate. When the rate of growth is greater than the required rate of return, the denominator is a negative value, resulting in the value of the common stock also being defined as a negative value. If, in fact, the rate of growth is defined to be exactly equal to the required rate of return, the price of the common stock is defined as infinity.

In no case can supernormal or abnormal rates of growth continue indefinitely. As a result, it is possible to adjust the Gordon growth model by combining it with the normal discounted cash flow model for situations in which an abnormal period of growth is expected to occur for a specified period of time. When this occurs, the value is determined as the sum of the value over the abnormal growth period (the terminal value) plus the value over the normal growth period to infinity.

Aaron Rotkowski and Evan Clough, in an *Insights* article entitled "How to Estimate the Long-Term Growth Rate in the Discounted Cash Flow Model" (2013), provide one approach to determining the growth of corporate dividend payments for use in the Gordon growth model, as this is an often-disputed factor in the model is the long-term growth rate in dividends.

One of the reasons the growth rate is a topic of concern is that it has a significant effect on the stock price. Even small changes in the estimated percentage of growth in dividends over time can result in relatively large changes in stock price estimation. The importance of the growth rate is common to both the constant growth version of the model and the two-stage version, which requires the determination of a terminal value.

Rotkowski and Clough provide insight as to the factors that affect the rate of dividend growth and why they should be considered carefully. The factors as they describe them include any "qualitative factors such as organic or inorganic growth strategies"; any quantitative factors, including historical financial information, managerial forecasts, or projections; and "expected inflation and/or real growth in the general economy."

An alternative and, due to its simplicity, often-used valuation model for common stocks is the price-earnings (P/E) multiple approach. The P/E model simply requires the development of an estimate of expected earnings and the determination of a P/E multiple of earnings. The product of the two provides an estimate based on earnings rather than dividend cash flows as utilized by the dividend discount model. An obvious issue of concern in the use of the P/E ratio for valuation purposes is that it centers on earnings rather than actual cash flow. One problem encountered here is that simply changing the accounting standards utilized in the determination of a firm's earnings will alter, sometimes significantly, the bottom line and thus the value estimation of the firm's common stock.

P/E multiples for publicly traded firms can be readily obtained from websites and periodicals such as the *Wall Street Journal*, or they can be quantitatively estimated. John Bajkowski, in "Evaluating Valuations Using Price-Earnings Relatives" (2000) in the *AAII Journal*, identifies several different variations in the P/E ratio determination and their use by investors as a means of screening for common stock investments. Bajkowski issues a final warning that when using the multiple, an analyst should "include a number of conditioning criteria that help indicate items such as the future earnings potential of the firm, the financial strength of the firm, as well as the strength of the firm within its industry."

## Selected Readings

Bajkowski, John. "Evaluating Valuations Using Price-Earnings Relatives." *AAII Journal* (October 2000): 2–6.

Rotkowski, Aaron, and Evan Clough. "How to Estimate the Long-Term Growth Rate in the Discounted Cash Flow Method." *Insights* (Spring 2013): 9–20.

# Evaluating Valuations Using Price-Earnings Relatives

By John Bajkowski

......................................................................................................................

> Price-earnings relatives help to establish benchmark comparisons that can help
> identify firms that have deviated from their normal valuation levels, assuming
> nothing has fundamentally changed in the company, industry or market.

The price-earnings ratio, or earnings multiple, is one of the most popular measures of company value. It is computed by dividing the current stock price by earnings per share for the most recent 12 months. It is followed so closely because it relates the market's expectation of future company performance, embedded in the price component of the equation, to the company's actual recent earnings performance. The greater the expectation, the higher a multiple of current earnings investors are willing to pay for the promise of future earnings.

If the market has low earnings growth expectations for a firm, or views earnings as suspect, it will not be willing to pay as much per share as it would for a firm with high and more certain earnings growth expectations.

That does not mean that all stocks with low price-earnings ratios have little or no growth prospects. While most firms deserve their low ratios, value investors seek companies with low price-earnings ratios in the belief that through neglect or overreaction to bad news, the market has not correctly evaluated the earnings potential of the company. Value investors argue that although the market may be efficient in the long term, emotions often dominate in the short run. These emotions can overtake rational analysis, pushing a stock's price above its intrinsic value during periods of euphoria and below its true worth when reacting to bad news.

# Price-Earnings Relative

There are models to help gauge if a company's price-earnings ratio is reasonable. The relative price-earnings ratio approach looks back at the relationship of the price-earnings ratio of a stock either to the price-earnings ratio of the overall market or to the company's industry.

The price-earnings relative is determined by dividing a company's price-earnings ratio by that of the market. Based on relative growth and risk expectations, companies trade at multiples greater or smaller than that of the market multiple. One would expect a company with prospects better than the market, or with lower risk, or both, to have a higher price-earnings ratio than the market. Comparing a firm to its industry is an equally useful technique that has the benefit of isolating interesting candidates within a specific industry.

Changes in the relative levels of the price-earnings ratio may signal that the market, for whatever reason, is changing its expectations about the future earnings potential of a firm, or not paying attention and mispricing the security. It may also signal that a short-term change has already occurred or is expected to occur. The price-earnings relative valuation model, however, assumes that the long-term growth and risk profile of the firm has not fundamentally changed over time. A careful evaluation of each firm's relative price-earnings ratio must be undertaken before investing to determine if it represents a reasonable relationship to the market going forward.

A price-earnings relative average above 1.00 would indicate that a company's price-earnings ratio is typically above the market's price-earnings ratio, while a price-earnings relative average below 1.00 would indicate that a company's price-earnings ratio tends to be lower than the market's. Changes in the price-earnings relatives compared to average levels may indicate a misvaluation.

Publications such as Value Line publish relative price-earnings ratios, but you can also calculate the figure yourself. Table 14.1 provides an example of the price-earnings relative model applied to Pier 1 Imports.

The complete domestic stock market universe within AAII's *Stock Investor Pro* was used to determine median price-earnings ratios for the last five years. The numbers are consistent with the median market figures reported in Value Line's Selection and Opinion publication. Standard and Poor's also reports price-earnings ratios for a number of market indexes. AAII members can view historical ratios and index performance of select S&P indexes on the AAII Web site (www.aaii.com). The S&P Reports link found within the Tools area leads members to data on individual companies and market indexes.

Over the last five years, Pier One Imports has averaged a price-earnings multiple above that of the overall market, leading to an average price-earnings relative of 1.13.

Multiplying the price-earnings relative by the market's current price-earnings ratio provides an adjusted price-earnings ratio. The current median market price-earnings ratio is 14.5, leading to an adjusted price-earnings ratio of 16.39 (14.5 × 1.13). The assumption behind this model is that the market is fairly valued and that the company's relationship to the market has not changed. A stock price valuation can be determined by multiplying this adjusted price-earnings ratio by earnings per share. The example in Table 14.1 uses both trailing earnings per share and expected earnings per share to estimate a fair market value.

**Table 14.1** Calculating the Price-Earnings Relative

............................................................................................................

| | Market Price-Earnings Ratio | | Pier 1 Imports (N: PIR) | | | | | | |
| | | | Stock Price | | | Price-Earnings Ratio | | P/E Relative to Market | |
| | High | Low | High | Low | EPS | High | Low | High | Low |
| | (×) | (×) | ($) | ($) | ($) | (×) | (×) | (×) | (×) |
| 1999 | 21.15 | 11.05 | 12.375 | 5.250 | 0.85 | 14.56 | 6.18 | 0.69 | 0.56 |
| 1998 | 24.85 | 12.59 | 20.750 | 6.063 | 0.77 | 26.95 | 7.87 | 1.08 | 0.63 |
| 1997 | 24.00 | 13.23 | 15.959 | 7.222 | 0.72 | 22.17 | 10.03 | 0.92 | 0.76 |
| 1996 | 21.98 | 13.00 | 7.944 | 4.611 | 0.47 | 16.90 | 9.81 | 0.77 | 0.75 |
| 1995 | 20.42 | 11.92 | 5.500 | 3.444 | 0.11 | 50.00 | 31.31 | 2.45 | 2.63 |
| 5-Year Average | 22.48 | 12.36 | — | — | — | 26.12 | 13.04 | 1.18 | 1.07 |

Average Price-Earnings Relative Ratios:

$\quad$ 1.18 = Five-year high

$\quad$ 1.07 = Five-year low

$\quad$ 1.13 = Five-year average

$\quad$ 14.50 = Current market price-earnings ratio

$\quad$ $0.85 = Trailing 12-month company EPS

$\quad$ $0.94 = Expected next annual company EPS (I/B/E/S)

Price-Earnings Ratio, Based on Relative Ratio and Current Market Ratio:

$\quad$ Adjusted P/E = Current Market P/E × Average Stock P/E Relative

$\qquad\quad$ = 14.50 × 1.13

$\qquad\quad$ = 16.39

---

Stock Valuation (Using Trailing EPS):

$\quad$ Stock Valuation = Adjusted P/E × EPS

$\qquad\quad$ = 16.39 × $0.85

$\qquad\quad$ = $13.93

Stock Valuation (Using Expected EPS):

$\quad$ Stock Valuation = Adjusted P/E × EPS

$\qquad\quad$ = 16.39 × $0.94

$\qquad\quad$ = $15.41

Share Price as a Percent of Valuation

$\quad$ = Current Price ÷ Valuation

$\quad$ = $12.94 ÷ $13.93

$\quad$ = 0.929 or 92.9%

Share Price as a Percent of Valuation

$\quad$ = Current Price ÷ Valuation

$\quad$ = $12.94 ÷ $15.41

$\quad$ = 0.840 or 84.0%

Dividing the current price by the valuation provides a useful screening measure; 1.00, or 100%, indicates that the valuation and current stock price are equal. Figures above 100% may point to stock prices above valuation estimates, while figures below 100% may highlight undervalued companies.

## P/E Relative Screen

Table 14.2 reveals the results of a screen seeking companies with current prices below their valuation estimates computed with trailing earnings per share and five-year average price-earnings relatives. *Stock Investor Pro*, AAII's stock screening program and company database was used to perform the screen.

To ensure reasonable liquidity our first screen looked for stocks traded on Nasdaq, the New York Stock Exchange, and the American Stock Exchange. We also eliminated American depositary receipt firms (ADRs), which are foreign companies that are traded on U.S. exchanges.

The next set of filters required that the firms have five years of data and that the earnings per share be positive for each of the last five years. A price-earnings ratio can only be calculated with positive earnings per share.

Beyond negative earnings, which lead to meaningless price-earnings ratios, unusually low earnings may also throw off standard price-earnings ratio screens. Short-term drops in earnings due to incidents such as special charges, extraordinary events, or in some cases even recessions may lead to unusually high price-earnings ratios. As long as the market interprets the earnings decrease as temporary, the stock price may not fall as dramatically as the earnings, resulting in a high price-earnings ratio. Because the average price-earnings relative model relies on a normal situation, these "outlier" price-earnings ratios should be excluded. In our Pier 1 example, the company had earnings per share of 11 cents in 1995, leading to above-average price-earnings ratios and price-earnings relatives for the year. Pier 1 Imports restated earnings downward in 1995 and 1996 when losses from concealed improper bond investments were discovered and disclosed to shareholders and the SEC. We did not exclude these years in our example in Table 14.1. Calculating the price-earnings relative average over the last three years results in a significantly lower figure of 0.78 compared to our original calculation of 1.13.

When performing a hands-on evaluation, you can manually exclude years with negative earnings or unusually high price-earnings ratios. However, when screening a large universe of stocks, it is best to establish criteria that try to eliminate companies with extreme price-earnings ratios. For our screen, companies with ratios above 100 for any of the last five fiscal years were excluded. If you want to be more conservative, a tighter requirement, such as ratios above 40 or 50, might be specified.

We did not screen for minimum historical or expected growth rates, but Table 14.2 indicates the consensus estimated earnings per share growth for the next three to five years. The expected growth rates range from 3.8% for the utility Consolidated Edison to 41.0% for EOG Resources, an energy stock.

It is important to remember that the growth rate is a raw growth figure that does not necessarily divulge any change in trend or indicate the variability of earnings. The easiest and most direct way to

# Table 14.2 Firms Passing the Price-Earnings Relative Screen

| Company (Exchange: Ticker) | Price 9/15/00 ($) | Price as a % of 52-Wk. High (%) | EPS Last 12 Mo. ($) | Est. EPS Growth Rate (%) | P/E Ratio (X) | Industry P/E Ratio (X) | 5-Yr. P/E Rel. Avg. (X) | P/E Rel. Adj. P/E Ratio (X) | Price as a % of P/E Rel. Val. (%) | Description |
|---|---|---|---|---|---|---|---|---|---|---|
| PolyOne Corp. (N: POL) | 8.94 | 26 | 2.28 | 11.2 | 3.9 | 16.4 | 1.56 | 22.62 | 17.3 | Plastic compounds & servs |
| Toro Company (N: TTC) | 30.69 | 81 | 3.40 | 13.5 | 9.0 | 12.4 | 2.61 | 37.85 | 23.9 | Landscape equip & irrig sys |
| Occidental Petroleum Corp (N: OXY) | 23.81 | 97 | 3.94 | 12.1 | 6.0 | 15.6 | 1.74 | 25.23 | 24.0 | Crude oil, gas & chems |
| EOG Resources, Inc. (N: EOG) | 39.50 | 98 | 4.90 | 41.0 | 8.1 | 15.6 | 1.58 | 22.91 | 35.2 | Crude oil & natural gas |
| BostonFed Bancorp, Inc. (A: BFD) | 18.75 | 98 | 1.91 | na | 9.8 | 11.8 | 1.69 | 24.51 | 40.1 | Bank holding co |
| United Stationers Inc. (M: USTR) | 30.88 | 81 | 2.72 | 15.7 | 11.4 | 11.0 | 1.76 | 25.52 | 44.5 | General line business prods |
| Unocal Corporation (N: UCL) | 37.56 | 91 | 1.88 | 10.9 | 20.0 | 15.6 | 2.97 | 43.07 | 46.4 | Energy resources holding co |
| Texaco, Inc. (N: TX) | 54.25 | 81 | 3.48 | 8.9 | 15.6 | 17.4 | 1.60 | 23.20 | 67.2 | Crude oil & natural gas |
| Chevron Corporation (N: CHV) | 90.19 | 93 | 5.41 | 9.2 | 16.7 | 17.4 | 1.60 | 23.20 | 71.9 | Support for petroleum cos |
| KEMET Corporation (N: KEM) | 32.50 | 73 | 1.69 | 14.3 | 19.2 | 25.2 | 1.82 | 26.39 | 72.9 | Tantalum & ceramic capacitors |
| Florida Progress Corp. (N: FPC) | 52.27 | 98 | 3.64 | 5.3 | 14.4 | 13.9 | 1.33 | 19.29 | 74.5 | Electric holding co |
| Huntington Bancshares (M: HBAN) | 17.75 | 63 | 1.68 | 9.8 | 10.6 | 11.9 | 0.96 | 13.92 | 75.9 | Bank holding co |
| Phillips Petroleum Co. (N: P) | 66.38 | 95 | 4.56 | 10.9 | 14.6 | 17.4 | 1.32 | 19.14 | 76.1 | Crude oil, natural gas & liquids |
| Alcan Aluminium Ltd. (N: AL) | 30.94 | 67 | 3.10 | 9.3 | 10.0 | 18.4 | 0.90 | 13.05 | 76.5 | Aluminum business |
| Heartland Express, Inc. (M: HTLD) | 17.38 | 90 | 1.30 | 13.0 | 13.4 | 10.3 | 1.15 | 16.68 | 80.1 | Nationwide truckload carrier |
| ConAgra, Inc. (N: CAG) | 18.88 | 71 | 0.86 | 10.6 | 21.9 | 14.6 | 1.87 | 27.12 | 80.9 | Food co |
| Centex Corporation (N: CTX) | 30.50 | 92 | 4.09 | 12.0 | 7.5 | 8.7 | 0.62 | 8.99 | 83.0 | Homes, real estate & finan servs |
| M.D.C. Holdings, Inc. (N: MDC) | 23.88 | 93 | 4.49 | 13.4 | 5.3 | 8.7 | 0.44 | 6.38 | 83.3 | Single-family homes |
| ALLETE (N: ALE) | 22.96 | 95 | 2.00 | 7.3 | 11.5 | 13.0 | 0.91 | 13.20 | 87.0 | Electric, water & auto servs |
| Mandalay Resort Group (N: MBG) | 26.19 | 92 | 1.31 | 17.0 | 20.0 | 13.9 | 1.55 | 22.48 | 89.0 | Hotels & casinos |
| Pier1 Imports, Inc. (N: PIR) | 12.94 | 99 | 0.85 | 15.3 | 15.2 | 12.7 | 1.14* | 16.53* | 92.1* | Imported home furnishings |
| UMB Financial Corporation (M: UMBF) | 37.00 | 92 | 3.00 | 14.0 | 12.3 | 11.9 | 0.89 | 12.91 | 95.6 | Bank holding co |
| Casey's General Stores (M: CASY) | 12.25 | 88 | 0.80 | 15.2 | 15.3 | 12.5 | 1.10 | 15.95 | 96.0 | Convenience stores |
| New York Times Co. (N: NYT) | 38.63 | 77 | 2.00 | 12.6 | 19.3 | 19.3 | 1.37 | 19.87 | 97.2 | Media co |
| Consolidated Edison, Inc. (N: ED) | 34.46 | 79 | 3.29 | 3.8 | 10.5 | 13.9 | 0.73 | 10.59 | 99.0 | Energy-related prods & servs |
| Belden, Incorporated (N: BWC) | 24.13 | 79 | 1.92 | 11.3 | 12.6 | 12.5 | 0.87 | 12.62 | 99.6 | Wire, cable & fiber optic prods |

* Numbers do not match Table 14.1 calculations due to rounding.
Source: AAII Stock Investor Pro, Market Guide, I/B/E/S.
Data as of September 15, 2000.

Exchange Key:
N = New York Stock Exchange
A = American Stock Exchange
M = Nasdaq

judge earnings is to examine the earnings directly year-by-year, looking for stability and accelerating growth. As a basic screen, positive earnings per share from continuing operations for the most recent 12 months and each of the last five years are required. Screens that are more stringent would require increases in each of the last five years or even an increase in the year-to-year growth rate for each of the last five years.

It is important to look at factors leading to the growth and determine if the growth is sustainable. When examining a firm's earnings patterns, it is necessary to carefully read both quarterly and annual reports, which can clue you in to possible explanations of the earnings growth pattern. Was a significant portion of the earnings growth achieved through acquisition or internal growth? Did earnings growth from franchises come from increases in same-store sales or the opening of new stores? Did currency translations impact earnings? Are competitive conditions changing within the industry? Are margins increasing or decreasing?

Price momentum is often used as a signal that the market has recognized the stock price is reacting to either proven performance, or an increase in expectations. Investors look for stock price performance superior to that of other stocks with the belief that the rising price will attract other investors, who will drive up the price even more. The current market price as a percentage of the 52-week high price is a popular measure of price strength and momentum. If a firm's stock price continues to be strong, it should be trading near its 52-week high. The figure is provided in the table to help gauge recent price behavior. Pier 1 Imports has been a strong performer recently, with a its current price 99% of its 52-week high. In contrast PolyOne Corp. is well off its 52-week high.

Table 14.2 ranks firms on the price as a percent of price-earnings relative valuation. To arrive at the valuation, the earnings per share for the last 12 months was multiplied by the adjusted price-earnings ratio. We followed the trailing earnings implementation presented in Table 14.1. Our screen looked for companies with current prices below their price-earnings relative valuation.

The current company and industry price-earnings ratio is provided to help gauge the valuation level of each firm's industry. KEMET Corporation's price-earnings ratio of 19.2 is higher than the 12.9 average price-earnings ratio for the firms in Table 14.2, but low compared to the technology industry's price-earnings multiple of 25.2. KEMET produces capacitors that store, filter, and regulate electrical energy and current flow. These are basic elements found in virtually all electronic applications and products and used in every type of electronic equipment, including computers, cell phones, automotive electronics, and consumer electronics. Demand for these components has been extremely strong recently, and the firm has participated in the strong technology price run up in 1999. KEMET has a high historical price-earnings relative of 1.82, but has also traded with price-earnings relative as little as 1.00 five years ago.

In contrast M.D.C. Holdings has a historical average price-earnings relative of 0.44. M.D.C. builds and sells single-family homes in a number of areas including Denver, Virginia, Maryland, California, Arizona, and Nevada. It has a similar expected growth rate to KEMET (13.4 versus 14.3) but trades

## Box 14.1  Definitions of Screens and Terms

**Price as a % of 52-Week High (%):** Most recent stock price divided by the highest stock price over the last 52 weeks. Provides an indication of the recent price strength and momentum of a stock's price. Also highlights the range and movement of share price.

**EPS Last 12 Mo. ($):** Diluted earnings from continuing operations for the most recent 12 months divided by the number of common shares outstanding.

**Est. EPS Growth Rate (%):** The median growth rate in earnings per share from continuing operations over the next three to five years that is being forecasted by analysts as reported by I/B/E/S. An indication of the consensus in earnings growth expectations for the firm.

**P/E Ratio (X):** Price-earnings ratio. Market price per share divided by most recent 12 months' diluted earnings per share from continuing operations. A measure of the market's expectations regarding the firm's earnings growth and risk. Firms with very high price-earnings ratios are being valued by the market on the basis of high expected growth potential.

**Industry P/E Ratio (X):** The median price-earnings ratio for the industry in which a stock is classified by Market Guide. Provides an indication of the valuation levels for the industry in which a company competes.

**5-Year P/E Relative Average (X):** Ratio of historical company price-earnings levels relative to those of the overall market. Calculated over the last five years. Provides an indication as to whether a company normally trades at a premium or discount to the market.

**P/E Relative Adjusted P/E Ratio (X):** Current market price-earnings ratio multiplied by a company's average price-earnings relative. Provides an indication of the company's expected price-earnings ratio if its historical relative price-earnings average holds true.

**P/E Relative Share Valuation ($):** Price-earnings relative adjusted price-earnings ratio multiplied by the company's earnings per share (not shown in table). Gives an estimate of stock price value supported by the historical relationship of the price-earnings ratio to that of the market's considering the current market valuation levels. Can be computed with expected company earnings per share.

**Price as a % of P/E Rel. Valuation (%):** Current price divided by the valuation determined through the price-earnings relative. A figure of 100% indicates the valuation estimate is equal to the current price. A percentage above 100% indicates that the stock price is above the valuation estimates (overvalued), while a figure below 100% indicates the current price is below the valuation estimate (undervalued).

with a current price-earnings ratio of 5.3. While both firms operate in a highly cyclical industry, the market must feel that M.D.C. has a higher risk of an earnings slowdown and therefore it normally trades with a lower multiple.

Investors often look for a catalyst to help attract attention to a company and boost its stock price. The stock prices of many attractively priced stocks often languish until investors find a reason to re-evaluate the prospects of the firm or its industry.

Upward earnings revisions and positive earnings surprises are events that make investors take notice of a company. Revisions to earnings estimates lead to price adjustments. When earnings estimates are revised significantly, stocks tend to show above-average performance. Stock prices of firms with downward revisions tend to show below-average performance after the adjustment.

Changes in estimates reflect changes in expectations of future performance. Perhaps the economic outlook is better than previously expected, or maybe a new product is selling better than anticipated.

For our screen, we required upward revisions to current and next year's earnings over the last month.

While a number of industries are represented in Table 14.2, energy stocks carry some of the most attractive valuations with the price-earnings relative model. The earnings of many energy stocks suffered a few years ago when gas prices were hitting low points. The temporary setback pushed the average price-earnings ratios and corresponding price-earnings relatives up. This distortion shows up in the adjusted price-earnings ratios and valuations. While these stocks may be attractively priced, one must question whether the calculated price-earnings relative represents the long-term norm going into the future.

## Conclusion

Screening for stocks by looking at price-earnings ratios can help highlight firms that have fallen out of favor. Price-earnings relatives help to establish benchmark comparisons that can help identify firms that have deviated from their normal valuation level—with the critical assumption that nothing fundamental to the company, industry, or market has changed significantly. The analysis can highlight companies worthy of further analysis given the expectation that they will move back to their typical levels.

In constructing screening criteria, you may wish to include a number of conditioning criteria that help indicate items such as the future earnings potential of the firm, the financial strength of the firm, as well as the strength of the firm within its industry. Investing in low price-earnings stocks can be rewarding, but caution is required.

Simply looking at historical price-earnings ratios, stock prices, and earnings is informative. The price-earnings approach is far from a secret and will only be successful if the inputs—your expectations—are proven to be well-founded.

# How to Estimate the Long-Term Growth Rate in the Discounted Cash Flow Method

By Aaron Rotkowski and Evan Clough

*In forensic analysis engagements where the value of a company or security is disputed, one topic that the litigants often disagree about is the selection of the expected long-term growth rate used in the discounted cash flow method. The expected long-term growth rate may be contested because (1) small changes in the selected growth rate can lead to large changes in the concluded business or security value and (2) the long-term growth rate is a judgment-based valuation input. Because of these two factors, judges, mediators, and arbitrators may view the analyst's selected long-term growth rate skeptically. This discussion provides qualitative and quantitative factors that analysts may consider to support the selection of an expected long-term growth rate.*

## Introduction

Valuation analysts are often retained to estimate the fair value or fair market value of a company or security for a variety of forensic analysis purposes, including taxation, bankruptcy, lender liability, shareholder disputes, GAAP compliance, intellectual property infringement, contract dispute, condemnation/eminent domain, and other controversies.

In these assignments, the valuation analyst may consider the income approach and, specifically, the discounted cash flow (DCF) method to value the subject company or security.

This discussion focuses on the procedure to estimate one of the important valuation variables in the DCF method: the subject company's expected long-term cash flow growth rate in perpetuity.

The Delaware Chancery Court (the "Chancery Court") "is widely recognized as the nation's preeminent forum for the determination of disputes involving the internal affairs of the thousands

Aaron Rotkowski and Evan Clough, "How to Estimate the Long-Term Growth Rate in the Discounted Cash Flow Method," *Insights*, Spring 2013, pp. 9–20. Copyright © 2013 by Willamette Management Associates. Reprinted with permission.

upon thousands of Delaware corporations and other business entities through which a vast amount of the world's commercial affairs [are] conducted."[1]

The Chancery Court has noted that the DCF method is a generally accepted method to value a business or security. In particular, the Chancery Court notes that "the DCF [method] has featured prominently in this Chancery Court because it 'is the approach that merits the greatest confidence within the financial community'"[2] and "if a [DCF method] reveals a valuation similar to a comparable companies or comparable transactions analysis, [the Chancery Court has] more confidence that both analyses are accurately valuing a company."[3]

The DCF method involves a projection of the company's results of operation for a discrete, multi-year period. The discrete cash flow projection is then converted to a single present value. The DCF method typically involves a terminal value analysis at the end of the discrete projection period.

The terminal value is "the present value of the stabilized benefit stream capitalized into the future,"[4] where the future represents all periods after the discrete projection period.

In the DCF method, it is not uncommon for the terminal value to account for 75 percent or more of the total company or security value. This conclusion is especially true when there are fewer discrete projection periods between the valuation date and terminal period—that is, the terminal value accounts for more of the projected economic benefit of the company and thus a higher proportion of the total value.[5]

The Gordon growth model (GGM) is a method that is often used to calculate the terminal value in a DCF method analysis. This terminal value estimation model can be sensitive to the expected long-term growth (LTG) rate.[6] Because a small change to the LTG rate can have a large impact on the concluded value, the LTG rate is often one of the disputed variables in valuations prepared for forensic analysis purposes.

Figure 15.1 demonstrates the sensitivity of the concluded terminal value to the selected LTG rate (as calculated by the GGM), assuming the following illustrative valuation variables:

1. A 15 percent weighted average cost of capital (WACC)

2. A terminal period cash flow of $10

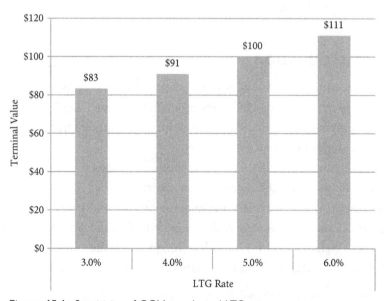

**Figure 15.1:** Sensitivity of GGM to selected LTG rate

As shown in Figure 15.1, an increase in the LTG rate from 3 percent to 4 percent causes an increase in the terminal value of 10 percent. An increase in the LTG rate from 5 to 6 percent causes an increase in the terminal value of 11 percent.[7]

Given the potential controversy regarding the selection of the LTG rate in the DCF method, this discussion considers the following topics:

1. How the LTG rate relates to (a) the subject company or security and (b) the concluded terminal value

2. The factors that affect the LTG rate selection

## The Gordon Growth Model

As previously discussed, one common method used to calculate the DCF method terminal value is the Gordon growth model. The GGM formula[8] is presented as follows:

$$PV = (NCF_0 \times (1 + g)) \div (k - g)$$

where:

PV = Present value

$NCF_0$ = Net cash flow in the final discrete projection period[9]

g = Selected long-term growth rate

k = Selected cost of capital

The first procedure to calculate the terminal value using the GGM is to estimate the normalized long-term income stream (e.g., terminal period net cash flow, or NCF) at the end of the discrete projection period. This income stream should take into account the stable, normalized economic returns of the business.[10]

The next procedure in the GGM is to capitalize the terminal NCF at a risk and growth adjusted capitalization rate (i.e., the direct capitalization rate). The GGM estimates the terminal value based on the premise that the NCF will increase (or decrease) in perpetuity at a constant annual rate. The appropriate GGM direct capitalization rate equals the company WACC (which incorporates the risk of the company cash flow) minus the selected LTG rate (which incorporates the expected growth of the company cash flow).

Once the direct capitalization rate is calculated, the projected terminal period's NCF is divided by that direct capitalization rate to derive the terminal value.

Because the terminal value is calculated as of the end of the discrete projection period, the last procedure in the application of the GGM is to compute the present value of the terminal value.

The long-term growth rate is not used in this procedure. Instead, the same present value factor applied to the final discrete period's projected NCF is also applied to the terminal value in order to convert it to the present value as of the valuation date.

# LTG Rate Definition

The terminal value incorporates the value of all the company's cash flow following the final discrete projection period, into perpetuity. That period is referred to as the "terminal period" for purposes of this discussion. As such, when an analyst selects a long-term growth rate, the analyst is effectively concluding that the company's cash flow will increase (or decrease) at the constant LTG rate forever.[11]

At first glance, it may seem unrealistic to assume that a company will experience positive (or negative) growth forever—especially if the analyst selects a growth rate that is greater than the projected rate of inflation (and, in doing so, implicitly projects that the company will grow to infinite size over infinite time). However, the majority of the terminal value is generated by the cash flow that occurs within the first few periods beyond the discrete projection periods.

Therefore, when the analyst selects a LTG rate for the GGM, he or she is essentially estimating the annual percentage changes in a company's cash flow over the first 10 to 20 years beyond the terminal period.

The GGM is a formula to calculate the net present value (i.e., the "terminal value") for all future periods into perpetuity. In essence, it is a collapsed version of the formula that represents a summation of the present value of each individual period in the terminal period discounted to the beginning of the terminal period at the direct capitalization rate.

Because the direct capitalization rate equals the selected WACC minus the selected LTG, the proportion of the terminal value that is generated in each successive period depends on the spread between these two figures.

In other words, given the same WACC, a lower LTG rate causes a higher proportion of terminal value to be generated in the near term, while a higher LTG rate causes the opposite result.

This is because a higher LTG rate causes cash flow to increase more rapidly into the future, which consequently causes future periods to have relatively higher present values.

Figures 15.2 through 15.4 graphically present the annual and cumulative percentage of the terminal value in the first 20 years of the terminal period, based on the following valuation variables:

1. A WACC of 15 percent
2. Normalized cash flow in the first terminal period of $100
3. LTG rates between 0 percent and 5 percent[12]

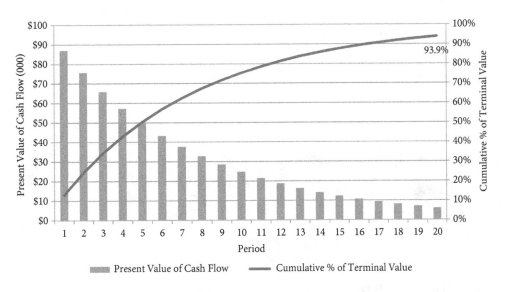

**Figure 15.2:** WACC 15 Percent, LTG 0 Percent

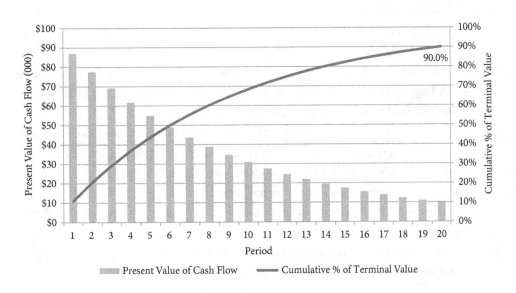

**Figure 15.3:** WACC 15 Percent, LTG 2.5 Percent

The vertical bars in Figures 15.2 through 15.4 present the present value of annual cash flow during the terminal period and the curved horizontal line presents the cumulative percentage of the total terminal value of the presented cash flow for periods 1 through 20.

Figure 15.2 demonstrates that with a selected LTG rate of 0 percent, periods 1 through 20 account for 93.9 percent of the terminal value. Figure 15.3 demonstrates that with a selected LTG rate of 2.5 percent, periods 1 through 20 account for 90.0 percent of the terminal value.

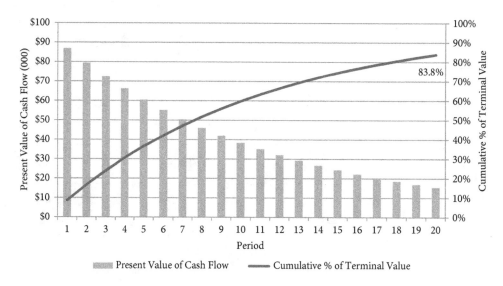

**Figure 15.4:** WACC 15 Percent, LTG 5 Percent

Figure 15.4 demonstrates that with a selected LTG of 5.0 percent, periods 1 through 20 account for 83.8 percent of the terminal value.

The positive correlation between the LTG rate and the proportion of value generated in later periods is paradoxical. Later projection periods and higher selected LTG rates generally drive a greater degree of uncertainty, which means that selecting a higher LTG rate causes uncertainty in later periods to be amplified by their relatively increased proportion of the terminal value.

Nonetheless, this concern is usually mitigated by the fact that the amplitude of this effect is generally somewhat small—that is, sooner periods still generate a much larger proportion of terminal value than later periods, even when the selected LTG rate may be relatively large.

Because of the large proportion of the terminal value that is accounted for in the first 20 or so periods following the discrete projection period, it is possible to make a reasonable directional prediction about the subject company cash flow.

This directional cash flow prediction is captured by the LTG rate. As such, it is necessary that the analyst consider appropriate factors in the selection of the same.

## Selecting The LTG Rate

There are a number of issues that the analyst may consider in selecting an LTG rate. First, the analyst should be careful to match the selected growth rate and the inputs considered with the metric being measured—that is, cash flow.[13]

Second, the analyst should be careful to consider any and all appropriate (and not consider inappropriate) qualitative factors in the selection of the growth rate.

Third, the analyst should consider appropriate (and not consider inappropriate) quantitative factors in the selection of the growth rate.

The next section summarizes the quantitative and qualitative factors that analysts may consider when selecting an LTG rate in the application of the GGM.

## Qualitative Considerations

Some valuation analysts consider the subject company's LTG rate only in terms of historical growth, near-term projected growth, projected or historical inflation, or another similar measurable financial metric. Those factors are all considerations in the selection of the LTG rate.

However, when selecting an LTG rate, the analyst should also have a general understanding from a business perspective of what factors contribute to the subject company's growth. This understanding is important because the period covered by the LTG rate variable within the GGM may start so far into the future that the following may occur:

1. Precisely projecting the LTG rate is difficult.

2. It may not be practical or possible to pinpoint the specific company initiatives that will contribute to the company's growth.

Appropriate qualitative considerations may include an analysis of the historical and projected performance of the company, existing assets of the company, and management's strategy of acquisitions and/or new development.

According to *Investment Valuation, Tools and Techniques for Determining the Value of Any Asset* by Aswath Damodaran, a company's LTG rate should be "determined by a number of subjective factors—the quality of management, the strength of a firm's marketing, its capacity to form partnerships with other firms, and the management's strategic vision, among many others."[14]

Damodaran also includes reinvestment as a factor of a company's expected long-term growth rate. Damodaran writes that "defining reinvestment broadly to include acquisitions, research and development, and investments in marketing and distribution allows you to consider different ways in which firms can grow. For some firms like Cisco, reinvestment and growth come from acquisitions, while for other firms such as GE it may take the form of more traditional investments in plant and equipment."[15]

For any subject company, reinvestment may be viewed as coming from the following three sources:

1. Opportunities to exploit the existing assets

2. New internally developed assets

3. Acquisitions

Let's consider the LTG rate in the context of a hypothetical designer and manufacturer of women's accessories, GrippCo. Let's further assume that (1) the specific segment of the industry that GrippCo competes in was in the growth stage of its life cycle and (2) the industry segment was fragmented.

The next sections explain the three sources of growth described above. And, the next section illustrates each source of growth using the GrippCo example.

### Growth From the Existing Assets

One category of LTG is from the subject company's existing assets, both tangible and intangible. This type of growth is probably what most analysts think of first when they think of the company's long-term growth. Examples of this type of growth include the following:

1. Selling more units of an existing product or service
2. Selling existing products or services at a greater selling price

The factors that the analyst may consider when assessing the expected subject company growth from the existing assets include, but are not limited to, the following:

1. The overall industry growth
2. The company's market share
3. Inflation (e.g., the potential to increase prices)
4. The growth of the existing assets prior to the terminal period

Note that factors one through three should be considered as of the terminal period. For example, if the subject company has projected that it will increase its market position from the tenth largest competitor to the first largest competitor during the discrete projection period, then the company's ability to grow by selling additional units in the terminal period may be limited.

Likewise, if the industry growth is expected to be rapid during the discrete projection period and slow in the subsequent years, then the analyst should focus on the slower, second phase of industry growth.

**Figure 15.5**

Since GrippCo has a small market share, it is possible for the company to grow from both of the following conditions:

1. Increased accessory sales
2. Rising prices

Therefore, the valuation analyst may include GrippCo LTG from existing assets from selling a greater number of products at prices that increase around the same rate of inflation. In this scenario, the analyst could support a selected LTG rate for GrippCo from existing assets that is greater than the projected nominal growth rate for the economy.

### Growth Related to New Internally Developed Assets

Whether it is one year or 100 years, almost every product has a limited life. The stylish and branded GrippCo accessory that is manufactured and sold as of the valuation date will not be around in a decade; but GrippCo likely will be.

If the company does indeed survive 100 years, it will do so by redesigning its existing product offerings or expanding into related lines of business to stay competitive. That is, GrippCo will achieve long-term cash flow growth from new internally developed assets that it did not own as of the valuation date.

For some companies, like the hypothetical GrippCo, developing new assets is a critical component of the company's business plan. For companies like this, if the analyst only considers growth from existing assets in the LTG rate, he or she may understate the company's LTG rate.

Growth from new internally developed assets is more difficult to identify and support than growth from existing assets. This is because, by definition, the valuation analyst is projecting that cash flow will be generated from a product or an idea that hasn't been developed. The analyst is also assuming that this undeveloped idea will be commercially viable.

In spite of the difficulties in explicitly projecting this type of growth, growth from newly developed assets should still be considered. In fact, companies such as GrippCo only survive (1) by regularly reinventing themselves or (2) by "cannibalizing" their existing products with newly developed products.

In order to assess the likelihood and amount of LTG from new internally developed assets, the analyst may consider the following factors:

- The frequency of the subject company product launches. For example, if the subject company launches new products several times a year, then it may be reasonable to assume that it will frequently launch new products during the terminal period.

- The success of the subject company product launches. For example, if demand generally exceeds supply for the first production run of the subject company new products, then it may be reasonable to assume that the company will successfully launch new products during the terminal period.

- The level of innovation in the subject company industry. For example, growth from new internally developed products is more likely if the subject company competes in an innovative industry (e.g., the electronic computers industry) than if the subject company competes in a mature industry (e.g., the petroleum refining industry).

## Growth by Acquisitions

Another category of growth is growth by acquisitions. Growth by acquisitions can (1) create new company assets and (2) create and augment the company's existing assets, including goodwill

Goodwill is the company's business enterprise value in excess of the company individual tangible and intangible assets owned as of the valuation date.

The analyst may consider the following:

1. How likely the subject company is to make acquisitions during the terminal period

2. How much LTG is projected to come from acquisitions

The following discussion presents some specific factors that the analyst may consider to answer the two questions posed above:

- Whether or not the company was a historically acquisitive company. For example, if the subject company was created via an acquisition and reported a material number of acquisitions in the years preceding the valuation date, then it may be reasonable to assume that the company will make a similar number of acquisitions in the future as it did in the past.

- The acquisition policy of company management. For example, if the board of directors' minutes indicate that the subject company management was directed to make acquisitions, then it may be reasonable to assume that the company will grow by making acquisitions.

- The level of acquisition activity in the subject company industry. The analyst can review several of the merger and acquisition databases to analyze the number of transactions that occurred in the subject company industry in the years preceding the valuation date.

    The level of acquisition activity in the industry may provide an indication of the company's likelihood to complete acquisitions in the terminal period.

- The subject company's projected ability, from a financial perspective, to make acquisitions. The analyst can review the historical financial statements as well as the financial statements projected for the discrete projection period.

    Since the relevant period for analysis is the terminal period, the analyst should be most concerned with the company's ability to make acquisitions at the start of the terminal period.

    For example, if the company has planned a major capital expenditure financed with debt capital during the discrete projection period, it may be difficult for the company to complete acquisitions during the first part of the terminal period.

## Excluded Factors

In general, inappropriate considerations may include speculation, hypothetical situations, or opportunities which may have existed as of the analysis date but were as-of-yet unexploited. For valuations prepared for forensic purposes, the valuation analyst should understand how the relevant court (e.g., Tax Court, Delaware Chancery Court, Bankruptcy Court, etc.) has viewed the LTG rate selection in the DCF method.

It may be prudent for the analyst to consult with counsel in order to understand what specific considerations can and cannot be included in the LTG rate variable.

## Quantitative Considerations

Usually, it is also appropriate to consider and support the selected LTG rate with empirical data. Among other things, these data may include both of the following:

1. Company-specific information

2. Projected economic growth, both real and nominal

These data should be corroborative of the selected LTG rate. If qualitative data and quantitative data suggest different LTG rates, the analyst should understand and reconcile the differences.

An important source of information that an analyst can use when selecting an LTG rate is financial information from the company. This can include (1) historical financial information and (2) management-prepared projections

If the business was operating under similar business conditions, historical financial information is useful because it provides snapshots of the economic results of the business.

Management-prepared projections are useful because company management generally has a deep understanding of the economic drivers of the business and is able to isolate and predict the expected results of the business for a number of years into the future.

### Historical Financial Information

When a company is valued as a going concern, as is common in forensic circumstances, it is assumed that it will retain the functioning mechanisms that drove past economic returns.[16] As such, it is likely that the economic factors driving a company in the near past will continue to affect the company in the near future.

In other words, recent trends of increase or decrease in historical cash flow—if not caused by obvious changes in company operation—are often likely to carry on into the future.[17]

This can provide the analyst with a useful idea of what may constitute a reasonable LTG rate for the company cash flow. This is especially true when the company has a long operating history and/or the analyst is able to identify specific factors that have driven these trends.

The age of the company is relevant to the consideration of historical financial trends for the following two reasons:

1. An older company is more likely to exhibit a stabilized economic condition.

2. More time periods provide more data to consider.

When a company has reported stable economic returns over a number of periods with operating conditions similar to those at the valuation date and there are not expected to be any subsequent material changes, trends in historical financial information can carry a significant amount of weight.

The U.S. District Court in Wisconsin observed that "[w]hen a business has a long track record, revenues can be forecasted with greater certainty, and the need to perform a finely calibrated analysis of the various factors affecting revenues may not be as acute." On the other hand, financial trends in the historical financial information of young businesses may carry less weight, and making projections from such information is "notoriously difficult." To do so, "the expert must look to other indicators, such as the track records of other firms that are comparable to the [business]."[18]

This implies that long-term historical trends are useful indicators of future trends, while short-term trends of a business may require a deeper understanding of their economic drivers to predict that they will continue into the future.

As an example, let's consider three different businesses and the impact of their circumstances on the usefulness of their historical financial data in the selection of the LTG rate.

The first business, Company A, was founded three years ago. It is already showing profits and is expected to continue doing so, but it has volatile cash flow and a high dependence on two customers that are not secured by long-term contracts.

The second business, Company B, also has a three-year history, but has exhibited steadily growing cash flow (which is projected to continue increasing at a predictable rate) and no key customer dependence.

Company C has a 30-year operating history with steady cash flow that is increasing at a rate consistent with the industry, and it predicts no material business changes in the foreseeable future.

In the case of Company A, the business does not exhibit stabilized economic drivers, past cash flow is volatile, and customer relationships are uncertain. Therefore, the historical data may be less important when compared to management projections, industry projections and expectations, and/or other factors.

On the other hand, Company B's historical financial information may be more useful than that of Company A. This is because it appears that the Company B economic drivers are more predictable. The historical financial information of Company C would be more useful than that of Companies A or B. This is because it represents many data periods and demonstrates stable economic drivers that are expected to continue in the future.

When management prepared projections are available along with historical financial information, the two can and should be considered side-by-side. The specific factors of the company at hand will determine what information will carry the most weight and what quantitative methods the analyst may use to provide an indication of a supportable LTG rate.

## Management-Prepared Projections

Management-prepared financial projections are similarly useful to historical results of a business, especially if they provide further insight into the economic forces acting on the business. As noted in *Valuing a Business*, "[s]ince the value of a business interest ultimately depends on what the business will accomplish in the future, reasonable estimates of future expectations should help in arriving at a value."[19]

Management-prepared projections also often form the basis for the discrete period projections used in the DCF method.

Reviewing management-prepared projections may be advantageous for a young business that has not exhibited stabilized economic returns. In these situations, the usefulness of historical financial information can be limited, given instability of the historical trends or the limited number of historical data points.

In this case, management's projections over the discrete projection period may be more relevant than the subject company's historical financial statements.

Another example of when management-prepared projections may be particularly helpful to estimate the LTG rate is when the subject company has recently undergone or is projected to undergo a material change in the business. This change could be the rollout of a new product line, closing a facility, or completing an acquisition that was in the diligence stage as of the valuation date.

In each of these examples, the subject company could operate differently as of the start of the terminal period compared to the valuation date, which could render the historical financial information less relevant.[20]

Sometimes, company management includes sufficient detail in the projected financial statements for the analyst to identify the economic drivers that company management believes will affect the projected financial results of the business.

For example, the management-prepared projections may link projected gross domestic product growth with sales volume, and inflation with sales prices. In instances such as these, it is prudent for the analysts to examine the projected economic drivers of the company, as well as the projections themselves.

An examination of projections, coupled with an examination of historical information and the factors that affect similar businesses, can provide insight into the factors that management expects will affect the operation of the business. In this way, projections may provide a view of the LTG potential of a business in the terminal period.

When using management-prepared projections, an analyst may also consider the conditions and care under which the projections were prepared. If the projections were prepared for a purpose that could call their objectivity into question (e.g., they were prepared for litigation purposes where the litigants may hope to achieve a particular value range), an analyst may wish to take care when using these projections.

On the other hand, if the projections are more likely than not to be objective and realistic (e.g., the projections were relied on by a bank that provided financing and were prepared in the ordinary course of business), an analyst may consider carefully any adjustments he or she may wish to make to the management-prepared projections, or risk such adjustments being discarded during litigation.[21]

Consider again Companies A, B, and C, described above. Company A projections would likely be particularly important because, as mentioned, the historical financial information does not reflect stable economic drivers, cash flow, or customer relationships.

Management projections may help to isolate the factors that management expects to influence the company in the near future, driving its economic results. The projections of Company B would likely be nearly as important as those of Company A. This is because this company, though more stable than Company A, is likely to still be in its growth stage. Projections may show that the company is or is not expected to stabilize in the near future.

The projections of Company C would likely carry the least weight compared to the historical financial information. While still important, the business is not expecting any material business changes from the operating conditions reflected in the historical information. Therefore, the projections are likely to be an extrapolation of current financial results.

In any case, an analyst may balance reliance on historical financial information and management-prepared projections carefully, considering the facts and circumstances of the situation at hand.

If, for example, the historical results of a long-operating business and the management-prepared projections of the same show a sharp change in trends, the analyst may carefully consider management's justification of this change and decide whether such change is realistic and appropriate.[22]

Projections can be useful to estimate the LTG rate, but they should be used carefully. As with historical financial information, the characteristics of the projections at hand will influence quantitative methods the analyst may wish to use to provide an indication of a supportable LTG rate.

### Inflation

Another important concern when selecting the LTG rate is the expected rate of inflation. In order to select a reasonable LTG rate, an analyst should understand the relationship between expected inflation and the growth of a business. And, the analyst should be able to explain that relationship.

Inflation is the "rise in the prices of goods and services ... when spending increases relative to the supply of goods on the market"[23] and is a commonly forecast by economists.

By necessity, when all else is equal, this buoyancy on prices pressures all financial metrics of a company to increase at the same rate—that is, a company that is neither gaining nor losing ground will nonetheless see its cash flows increase over time at a rate equal to that of inflation.[24]

This is referred to as nominal growth; in an inflationary environment, a company that is not changing its economic position will still exhibit growth at the rate of inflation. Real growth, on the other hand, is growth that signifies the improvement in economic position of a business. If a company is exhibiting an improvement in economic position, it will exhibit real growth above and beyond the rate of inflation.[25]

In other words, if an analyst wants to select an LTG rate that reflects an improvement in the economic condition of a business, he or she should forecast real growth.

When selecting the LTG rate, it is important to not only consider whether the selected numerical rate appears to be high or low on absolute terms. The valuation analyst may ask what constitutes a reasonable expectation regarding the change in economic position of a company. Is the economic position of the company expected to improve or deteriorate over time?

If the company is expected to show improvement, the selected LTG rate should then be above the expected rate of inflation—and vice versa. The factors to consider in the expectation of change in the economic position of a company may include industry trends, expected real growth of the national economy (i.e., gross domestic product, or GDP), historical financial results and trends, or projected financial results and trends.

The relationship between growth rates and inflation is not linear. Figure 15.6 shows the real (i.e., inflation-adjusted) proportionate change in cash flows after 20 periods with 2.5 percent inflation and nominal growth rates of (1) 7.5 percent, (2) 2.5 percent, and (3) negative 2.5 percent.[26]

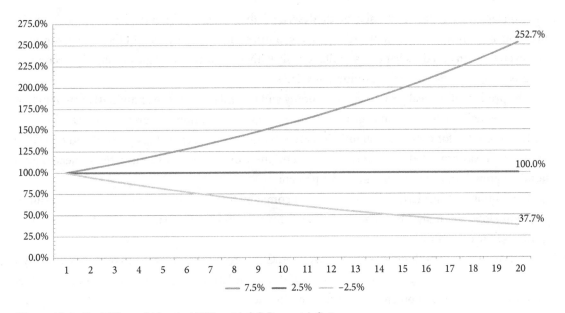

**Figure 15.6:** Real Effect of Nominal LTGs with 2.5 Percent Inflation

As demonstrated, the nominal 7.5 percent growth rate caused cash flow to increase, on a real basis, more than two and a half times over. The nominal growth rate of negative 2.5 percent, on the other hand, caused cash flows to decrease, on a real basis, by nearly two thirds. This relationship is exponential, meaning that for positive real growth rates, the effect increases dramatically after many periods.

Once an analyst has an idea of the direction of a company's real economic position, an effective way to choose an LTG rate may be to consider the following:

1.  Determine the expected rate of real change in economic position of the company
2.  Incorporate this rate to the long-term expected rate of inflation

Such a procedure may allow an analyst to account for expected inflation in a reasonable and supportable manner. However, not every inflation estimate is always appropriate.

If a risk-free rate is being used in the estimation of a discount rate, it may be prudent to use an inflation forecast that matches the maturity period of the instrument that is being used as a proxy for the risk-free rate.

This is because instruments such as non-inflation-adjusted U.S. government bonds, which are often used as proxies for the risk-free rate, include an implicit expectation of a certain rate of inflation during the term of the bond. Thereby, internal consistency is improved if the term of the risk-free proxy instrument and the term of the rate of expected inflation are matched.[27]

### Relation of Inflation and Economic Growth

The concepts of real and nominal growth, described above, also apply to the economy as a whole. Inflation, as mentioned, is the upward buoyancy of prices due to an increase in the money supply—however, this can and does happen simultaneously with a real increase in the output of an economy (in this case, the gross domestic product, or GDP).

The product of the real growth in an economy and the inflationary (i.e., nominal) growth in that economy equals the total nominal growth of the economy, or the nominal growth of GDP.[28]

Let's consider, for example, real inflation growth that was projected at 2.4 percent and real GDP growth that was projected at 2.6 percent. Based on these expected growth rates, the projected total nominal growth rate of the economy is 5.1 percent.

In addition to considering the buoyancy on company financial metrics that come as a result of inflation alone, an analyst may consider the LTG prospects of a company relative to the nominal growth of the economy.

In other words, if both inflationary growth and GDP growth are expected to occur, a company's financial prospects may be more positive than if only inflationary growth were expected—thus supporting the case for a potentially higher growth rate.

# Conclusion

The selection of the LTG rate is an important component in the DCF method of valuing a business or security. It is incorporated into the calculation of the terminal value of the DCF method—which often accounts for a large proportion of the value of the business or security. The GGM, which is often used to conclude the terminal value in the DCF method, is sensitive to changes in the LTG rate.

In spite of how frequently it is estimated, the LTG rate is often selected based on either a consideration or inappropriate factors or a failure to properly consider the appropriate factors. For these reasons it is important that an analyst understand the factors that affect the LTG rate in order to select a supportable rate.

Sources of information that may be considered in the selection of an LTG rate include the following:

1. Qualitative factors such as organic or inorganic growth strategies

2. Quantitative factors, including the following:

    a. Historical financial information

    b. Management-prepared projections

    c. Expected inflation and/or real growth in the general economy

None of these factors may be considered by itself. All of these factors may be considered concurrently. And, the interrelation of these factors may be evaluated to arrive at the appropriate reliance on information from each source.

The specific situation at hand, including the purpose of the valuation, the operating conditions of the business, and the dependability of the information, influence the extent to which an analyst should rely on each source of data.

# Notes

1. http://courts.state.de.us/chancery/

2. Cede & Co. v. JRC Acquisition Corp., 2004 WL 286963, at *2 (Del.Ch. Feb.10, 2004) (quoting Ryan v. Tad's Enters., Inc., 709 A.2d 682, 702 (Del.Ch. 1996)).

3. In re Hanover Direct, Inc. Shareholders Litigation, 2010 WL 3959399, at *2 (Del.Ch. Sept. 24, 2010).

4. Gary Trugman, *Understanding Business Valuation*, 4th ed. (New York: American Institute of Certified Public Accountants, Inc., 2012), 428.

5. Shannon P. Pratt and Roger J. Grabowski, *Cost of Capital: Applications and Examples*, 4th ed. (Hoboken, NJ: John Wiley & Sons, Inc., 2010), 34.

6. Shannon P. Pratt, *Valuing a Business: The Analysis and Appraisal of Closely Held Companies*, 5th ed. (New York: McGraw-Hill, 2008), 243.

7. The proportional effect of the selected LTG rate increases as the LTG rate approaches the WACC. See Aswath Damodaran, *Damodaran on Valuation*, 2nd ed. (Hoboken, NJ: John Wiley & Sons, Inc., 2006), 145.

8. Pratt, *Valuing a Business*, 30.

9. NCF in the terminal projection period is often calculated as NCF in the final discrete projection period × (1 + selected LTG rate), as represented in the GGM formula presented. It should be noted that there may be other valid ways to project terminal NCF.

10. Ibid, 247.

11. Damodaran, *Damodaran on Valuation*, 145.

12. The end-of-period convention is used in the present value calculations.

13. It is entirely possible for a company to realistically forecast increasing cash flows while simultaneously forecasting decreasing revenue, net income, or other figures. For example, a manufacturing company might work to increase productivity and eliminate problematic customers—thus increasing its cash flow while decreasing its revenue—or a company that owns a television show may be subject to declining ratings on its programs but increasing cash flows on the same due to changing industry conditions.

14. Aswath Damodaran, *Investment Valuation, Tools and Techniques for Determining the Value of Any Asset*, 2nd ed. (New York: John Wiley & Sons, Inc., 2002), 300.

15. Ibid.

16. Jay E. Fishman, Shannon P. Pratt, and William J. Morrison, *Standards of Value: Theory and Applications* (Hoboken, NJ: John Wiley & Sons, Inc., 2007), 29.

17. Pratt, *Valuing a Business*, 79.

18. Manpower, Inc. v. Insurance Co. of Pennsylvania, 2010 WL 3730968, at *3 (E.D. Wisc. Sept. 20, 2010).

19. Pratt, *Valuing a Business*, 88.

20. Ibid, 79.

21. See, for example, WaveDivision Holdings, Inc. v. Millennium Digital Media Systems, LLC, 2010 WL 3706624 (Del.Ch. Sept. 17, 2010) stating that the target's expert's valuation "relies on unreliable, self-interested, and thinly justified reductions" to the target's base case projections, which had been prepared for lenders pre-litigation and were "relied upon by a party—the bank—with a strong interest in getting repaid."

22. See Manpower, Inc. v. Insurance Co. of Pennsylvania, 2010 WL 3730968, (E.D. Wisc. Sept. 20, 2010).

23. John Downes and Jordan Elliot Goodman, *Dictionary of Finance and Investment Terms*, 6th ed. (New York: Barron's Educational Series, Inc., 2003), 332.

24. See, for example, Lane v. Cancer Treatment Ctrs. of Am., Inc., 2004 WL 1752847, at *31 (Del.Ch. July 30, 2004), "it must be assumed that [the company] would continue to grow at least at the rate of inflation;" and Global GT LP v. Golden Telecom, Inc., 993 A.2d 497, 511 (Del.Ch. 2010), "the rate of inflation is the floor for a terminal value estimate for a solidly profitable company that does not have an identifiable risk of insolvency."

25. Pratt and Grabowski, *Cost of Capital*, 664.

26. These equate to real growth rates of 5.0 percent, 0 percent, and negative 5.0 percent, respectively.

27. See *Cost of Capital*, 89; *Valuing a Business*, 247.

28. This formula is (1 + expected real GDP growth) (1 + expected inflation rate) − 1 = expected nominal GDP growth.

*Aaron Rotkowski is a manager in the Portland, Oregon, practice office. Aaron's practice includes valuations for litigation support purposes such as shareholder disputes and other commercial litigation matters; and for taxation planning and compliance purposes such as gift tax, estate tax, and ad valorem property tax. Aaron can be reached at 503-243-7522 or at amrotkowski@willamette.com.*

*Evan Clough is an associate in the Portland, Oregon, practice office. Evan performs business valuations and economic analyses for a variety of purposes. He can be reached at 503-243-7529 or at eclough@willamette.com*

# MODULE 10

# Cost of Capital

*We as business owners need to look at our businesses the way those who provide capital look at them. We get frustrated when we are not able to raise the money we need for growth. Too often, however, we keep doing the same things and hope something will change. Instead, owners have to come to a better understanding of what their financial drivers are and figure out ways to produce the needed returns.*

**Josh Patrick**

M anagers should strive to maximize the value of their firms. This objective implies the management of a firm will purchase those assets contributing the most to the value of the firm and will eliminate nonessential or other assets reducing that value. In determining the value of assets being considered for purchase or removal, the discounted cash flow (DCF) method is perhaps most often recommended as the primary technique of valuation.

While employing the DCF method, it is necessary to define a minimally required discount rate of return. The discount rate, when it is used in making long-term or capital asset investment decisions, is the risk-appropriate minimum rate of return or hurdle return required to make an investment acceptable to the firm. Investments providing less than this level of return will decrease the value of the firm, while investments earning a higher return will increase the firm's value.

It is necessary, when determining whether an investment is worthwhile, to define whether the investment provides value to the corporation. One method of determining if projects provide more value to the overall business enterprise is to discount the flows of those projects to a single present value. When the present value is greater than zero, the project adds wealth, or value, to the firm.

In order to discount the flows of such projects, it is necessary to calculate the overall cost of capital for the firm. This cost of capital or discount rate is nothing more than the weighted average of all of the individual component capital or long-term financing costs borne by the firm. Each of the individual after-tax component costs must be weighted by the amount or proportion of that type or component of capital that is actually utilized in the firm. Once the individual long-term capital components have been identified, their costs determined, and the weights applied, the weighted costs are combined and defined as the firm's after-tax weighted average cost of capital, or WACC, at the relevant weight.

A firm's cost of capital is related to its capital structure, and several theories regarding the effect of the capital structure on the cost of capital have been considered over time. Under the traditional cost of capital, adding debt to the firm's capital structure initially decreases the cost until, as gearing, the amount of fixed-cost financing, increases it begins to increase. The firm's optimal cost of capital is obtained at some point where it is the minimum.

In 1958, Modigliani and Miller published a paper that suggested the capital structure would have no effect on a firm's cost of capital in the absence of taxes on the firm. This point of view is known as the *net operating income* or *M&M theory* of capital structure.

Modigliani and Miller (1963), in an *American Economic Review* paper, altered their 1958 perspective, indicating that when corporate tax laws provide pretax deductions of interest expenses, this tax savings or shield does in fact affect the cost of capital by lowering the cost of debt. Under this hypothesis, known as *M&M with Tax*, the optimal capital structure is found with a one hundred percent debt capital structure.

The *pecking order theory* of capital structure proposed in 1984 by Stewart Myers proffers the idea that firms do actually pursue an optimal structure of long-term capital but, because firms tend to maintain relatively stable dividend payout policies and because they prefer to obtain long-term funding from internal operations rather than external offerings, there is a "pecking order" of financing. The "pecking order," according to Myers, is internal retention of earnings; then, when external financing is necessary, the order of preference is safe debt, increasing offerings of risky debt, convertible securities, preferred stock, and finally, common stock financing.

The actual effect of capital structure on cost of capital and, ultimately, therefore, the value of the firm, remains an area of research interest. Additional factors affecting the use of debt in the capital structure, to include agency costs, and the costs of financial distress, to include bankruptcy, complicate the issue.

Minimizing the cost of capital implies all discounted cash flows using that optimal cost will have higher present values and thus have the potential for increasing the value of the firm, as opposed to cash flows discounted at higher rates. Minimizing the cost of capital is thus in line with the theoretically appropriate objective of maximizing the firm's value.

As noted previously, to calculate a weighted average cost of capital, or WACC, it is necessary to determine how the component costs will be weighted. Three options available are the use of book value or historical weights, market or marginal weights, and target weights. Historical weights are really book value weights. In other words, the weights are based on the firm's existing capital structure and thus on historical values.

Market weights are weights determined based on the market value of each of the component sources of capital in the existing capital market. Market or marginal value weights are, of course, preferable to book value weights, since they represent current rather than historical costs.

Target weights are weights determined by the firm based on their desired level of component costing in the firm. Marginal weights are weights based on the amount of financing of each component source the firm actually expects to be able to obtain in the marketplace at a given time. Target weights however, are weights based on the managerial estimate of an optimal structure, which will minimize the firm's weighted average cost of capital.

Once a firm has selected a weighting scheme for use in determining the overall weighted average cost of capital, it is necessary to calculate individual financing component costs. Each of the different types of financing, both external and internal and both debt and equity, has a unique cost attributed to it alone.

In determining the cost of debt, it is necessary to calculate what is commonly referred to as the yield to maturity. This yield is then placed on an after-tax basis. In calculating the cost of preferred stock, we typically use a dividend yield value as our required cost of capital.

In determining the cost of common equity capital, it is necessary to define whether we are talking about internal common equity or common external equity. Internal equity is cheaper than external equity because it is money that has been obtained through internal sources from the operations of the firm. As a result, we do not need to go out into the marketplace and pay excess flotation costs for preparing prospectuses, sales commissions to brokers, or legal fees. As a result, the difference between the costs for internal equity, as opposed to external equity, is the flotation costs associated with external equity financing.

The models most commonly used in equity computation are the Gordon growth model, the capital asset pricing model, and the price/earnings model. These models are applied to both internal and external equity financing sources.

A third model—the abnormal, supernormal growth, or two-stage valuation model—is a hybrid of the Gordon growth model. This model is utilized when we anticipate higher or lower rates of growth than the historical norm.

Another commonly used method for determining the cost of equity capital is the risk-premium approach, also known as a bond plus approach. In this model, the after-tax long-term bond rate is utilized by adding an additional risk premium for the additional risk in equity investment.

In the series of articles authored by Ian Cornelius, the topic of weighted average cost of capital is discussed in detail to include insight into the problems and uses of the cost of capital. The first article, entitled "WACC Attack" (2002), introduces the weighted cost of capital concept and the assumptions on which WACC is based. An engaging discussion of the development of WACC, beginning with traditional and then Modigliani and Miller theories, provides a good basic understanding of the concept and its origins.

The second article in the three-article series, "If the CAPM Fits ..." (2002), addresses the problems of WACC, to include the changing risk characteristics of a firm over time, the difficulties of estimating the cost of equity capital, and an approach to determine a leveraged or geared beta characteristic for use in a capital asset model approach to determining a cost of equity.

Cornelius's third article in the series, "Extremely Well Adjusted" (2002), provides insight as to the issue of changing risk resulting from changing capital structures that result from obtaining additional capital and projects over time. The paper addresses the circular argument of capital structure as well as the process of adjusting the cost of capital in practical terms.

## Recommended Readings

Modigliani, Franco, and Merton H. Miller. "The Cost of Capital, Corporation Finance, and the Theory of Investment." *The American Economic Review* XLVIII, no. 3 (June 1958): 262–97.

Modigliani, Franco, and Merton H. Miller. "Corporate Income Taxes and the Cost of Capital: A Correction." *The American Economic Review* LIII, no. 3 (June 1963): 433–43.

Myers, Stewart C. "The Capital Structure Puzzle." *Journal of Finance* XXXIX, no. 3 (July 1984): 575–92.

Cook, D., and T. Tang. "The Effect of Liquidity and Solvency Risk on the Inclusion of Bond Covenants." *Journal of Corporate Finance* 16 (2010): 73–87.

## Selected Readings

Cornelius, Ian. "WACC Attack." *CIMA Insider* (March 2002): 22–23.

Cornelius, Ian. "If the CAPM Fits." *CIMA Insider* (April 2002): 24–25.

Cornelius, Ian. "Extremely Well Adjusted." *CIMA Insider* (May 2002): 24–25.

# WACC Attack

By Ian Cornelius

········································································································································································

The cost of capital is a huge subject, incorporating many of the most famous and controversial theories in financial management. Given its breadth, it is tempting to treat it as a series of discrete topics with no common thread. This would be a mistake. The key to unlocking the mysteries of the cost of capital is to understand how all of these strands come together. It is particularly important for final-level students to gain a global overview of the subject and to understand how it links with other areas of the syllabus.

In a series of three articles I will cover all of the major topics under the "cost of capital" heading—namely:

- how to make basic weighted-average cost of capital (WACC) calculations;
- how different gearing levels affect the WACC (capital structure theory);
- how to use the capital asset pricing model (CAPM) to calculate the cost of equity;
- how to use the adjusted present value (APV) approach.

All three articles should be of use to final level Financial Strategy (FLFS) students, but those at intermediate level will also find parts in this first article relevant to the syllabus they are studying.

The cost of capital can be thought of as the minimum return required by providers of finance for investing in an asset, whether that is a project, a business unit or an entire company. It needs to reflect the capital structure used to finance the investment. As such, it is likely to include the cost of equity and debt.

Expressed as an annual percentage return, it represents the "hurdle rate" that a company's projects must exceed if they are to increase the investors' wealth. So the cost of capital is used as the discount rate in net present value (NPV) project appraisal techniques. Projects that earn positive NPV at the

Ian Cornelius, "WACC Attack," *CIMA Insider*, March 2002, pp. 22–23. Copyright © 2002 by Chartered Institute of Management Accountants (CIMA). Reprinted with permission.

cost of capital are accepted because they earn more than the investors' required rate of return and will add to their wealth. Negative NPV projects are rejected because they reduce the investor's wealth by earning less than their target rate of return.

The cost of capital therefore has a pivotal role to play in corporate finance, forming the link between the investment decision (what the company should be spending money on) and the finance decision (how it should be funding that spend).

The weighted-average cost of capital (WACC) represents the overall cost of capital for a company, incorporating the costs of equity, debt and preference share capital, weighted according to the proportion of each source of finance within the business.

The models used to calculate the cost of each source all start from the premise that the required rate of return is a function of the investors' expectations of future cash-flow returns, expressed as a percentage of the current value of their investment. The cost of equity share capital is calculated using the dividend valuation model. The usual assumption made is that future dividends are expected to grow at a reasonably even rate.

Preference share capital usually pays a constant dividend each year, so no growth function is required. For debt, the future cash-flow stream is the interest payments. As with preference shares, these cash flows are constant, but, given that a company can deduct interest payments in determining taxable profits, it will experience a tax saving on the interest it pays. This tax shield reduces the cost of debt finance from the company's perspective.

In practice, the firm's WACC is often used as the discount rate to appraise new projects. But it is crucial to realise that this approach makes three key assumptions:

- that the project has the same business risk as existing activities;
- that the project does not change the financial structure of the business;
- that the project is financed from a "pool of funds".

The third assumption is not usually a problem. Most finance is not project-specific. Projects draw on the company's general pool of finance, which incorporates funds from all of the company's finance providers. The cost of using this pool of finance is, of course, the WACC.

The first two assumptions cause the main problems here. The company's WACC reflects the riskiness of its current activities. It also reflects the current financial structure and gearing risk. If a new project changes either of these risk profiles, the WACC becomes an inappropriate discount rate.

When considering the effect of different capital structures on the WACC, it is important to focus on the action of two competing forces as the company gears up. The first force recognises that debt finance is cheaper than equity finance. As a firm increases its gearing, the proportion of this cheap finance within the capital structure increases. All other things being equal, this will reduce the WACC.

The second force focuses on the cost of equity. As a company gears up, shareholders' returns become increasingly volatile, owing to the fixed interest bill that must be repaid before they are given their cut. This extra risk increases their required rate of return. All other things being equal, this increasing cost of equity will increase the WACC.

The overall effect on the WACC depends on the relative size and strength of these two opposing forces. There are two schools of thought here. The traditional view of capital structure theory, based on observation and intuition, suggests that an optimum capital structure exists. This minimises a firm's WACC and therefore maximises its value. So the finance decision is as relevant to a firm's value as the investment decision.

In 1958 two economists, Merton Miller and Franco Modigliani (M&M), presented a radically different view of capital structure theory. They suggested that value was about "what you do" (the investment decision). How you financed it, they argued, was irrelevant. In their "arbitrage proof", they demonstrated that two firms with identical investments would have the same value, regardless of their gearing.

This theory is rock-solid, given the assumptions it makes. In a market with no imperfections, getting obsessed about where the money comes from is indeed misguided—businesses should focus on the quality of their investment decisions. The problem is that the world is not perfect. In particular, the presence of taxation gives debt finance an additional advantage.

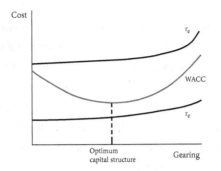

**The traditional view**
- Increasing use of cheap debt finance dominates at low gearing, pushing the WACC down.
- Rapidly increasing cost of equity dominates at high gearing, pushing the WACC up.
- The optimum capital structure exists, minimising the WACC and maximising the firm's value.

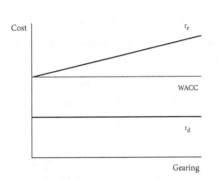

**M&M I – 1958**
- Value is a function of the investment decision, rather than the finance decision.
- Two identical businesses with different gearing should have identical values and WACCs.
- On gearing up, no force dominates. The increased use of debt finance is balanced exactly by an increasing cost of equity, leaving the WACC unchanged.
- In a perfect market there is no optimum gearing level. Companies should focus on the investment decision only.

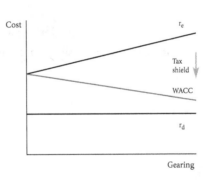

**M&M II – 1963**
- Once tax is introduced, debt finance becomes even cheaper, owing to the tax deductibility of the interest payments.
- Debt becomes the dominant force. Increasing gearing leads to reduced WACC and increased company value.
- The increase in value is the tax shield. To optimise this benefit, firms should gear up to the highest level possible.

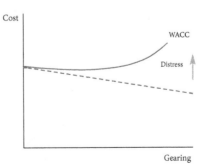

**The compromise view**
- At extreme gearing levels, the costs of financial distress become significant, pushing the WACC back up.
- The position is now consistent with the traditional view.
- In an imperfect world, the tax shield effect and costs of financial distress probably mean there is an optimum capital structure.

**Figure 16.1:** WACC theory in development

Because interest is tax-deductible, the use of debt finance gives rise to a tax saving. So in 1963 M&M republished their model to propose that the value of a geared firm was the value of the equivalent ungeared firm plus the present value of any tax shield generated by the use of debt finance. This suggested that the optimum gearing level was 100 per cent.

In the real world, companies do not raise their debt-to-equity ratios to such extreme levels. This is because at high levels of gearing the costs of financial distress that may lead to liquidation are much more likely. This means that the cost of equity and debt increase significantly at high levels of gearing, causing the WACC to increase.

The traditional view of capital structure theory, leading through M&M's 1958 and 1963 positions, together with the final compromise position taking into account financial distress, is summarised in the panel. It suggests that, given market imperfections, the WACC is affected by changes in the gearing level within the company.

It is clear that the WACC lies at the heart of finance, linking together the key areas of the investment and finance decisions to measure whether the business has created or destroyed value. What is not yet clear is how the WACC is affected for changes in business risk—that is, the fundamental inherent risk of the sector in which the company operates. To grasp this, you need to understand what is arguably the most famous financial theory to appear in the past 40 years: the capital asset pricing model (CAPM). This will be the subject of the next article in this series.

Ian Cornelius is director of ATC's value creation department and specialises in final level Financial Strategy. He has co-written two books on shareholder value. He can be contacted at ian.cornelius@atc.co.uk

# If the CAPM Fits …

By Ian Cornelius

T he first article in this series of three ("WACC attack", March 2002) explored the fundamental importance of the cost of capital. It acts as the link between the investment decision and the finance decision, representing the "hurdle rate" return that a business's investors require. If projects discounted at the firm's cost of capital earn positive net present value, then they will add to the investors' wealth and should be accepted.

A major problem with this theory is that new projects inevitably change the risk profile of the company. A firm's existing weighted-average cost of capital (WACC), calculated using traditional theories such as the dividend valuation model, will not necessarily reflect these new risk profiles.

We have seen how the theories of Franco Modigliani and Merton Miller (M&M) allow us to adjust the WACC for different levels of finance risk. This article focuses on how the WACC can be modified to reflect differing business risk levels.

A key problem in using the dividend valuation model to calculate the cost of equity is that there is no obvious way to modify this cost to reflect different business risk profiles. Costs of capital calculated using this model reflect the company "as it is". This discount rate will be inappropriate for assessing projects with different business risk profiles from the existing activities.

The capital asset pricing model (CAPM) provides a solution to this problem by allowing the calculation of risk-adjusted discount rates for use in project appraisals. It works on the simple premise that investors will require at least the risk-free rate of return when investing in a project. They will also require a premium to compensate them for the particular risk of the investment.

Where CAPM is special is in the nature of the risk considered. There are two types of risk to take into account. The first is termed unsystematic, and is a result of company- or industry-specific factors. By definition, shareholders will be able to diversify away much of this risk by spreading their funds across a wide range of securities from different industries.

The second element, known as systematic risk, is caused by general economic factors. These affect all companies in the same way and therefore cannot be removed by diversification. In an efficient market, shareholders are assumed to have well-diversified portfolios and will therefore require return for systematic risk only. As such, only systematic risk is built into the CAPM risk premium.

A common mistake made by students is to assume that, because systematic risk is caused by general economic factors, all companies have the same systematic risk. This is not so. All companies are affected by general economic factors in the same way, but, depending on their characteristics, they are affected to a greater or lesser extent than the market on average. The measure of the sensitivity of a company's returns to economic factors is the beta factor.

Betas for all quoted companies are published quarterly by London Business School's risk measurement service. These factors, together with an estimate of the risk-free rate of return and the market-risk premium (the difference between the market portfolio return and the risk-free rate of return), allow an estimate of the cost of equity to be made for all quoted companies. Figure 17.1 summarises the basic procedure.

As M&M's work has shown, the cost of equity is affected by increased financial risk within the business. Because shareholders are paid after debt providers, their return becomes more variable as the company gears up. This financial risk is therefore part of the systematic risk that affects them, so beta factors need to reflect this.

---

Investors' required rate of return = risk-free return + premium for risk of investment

$$r_e = r_f + \beta(r_m - r_f)$$

Beta ($\beta$) is a measure of responsiveness of the returns for a particular investment when compared with the average market return:

$\beta > 1$ indicates more systematic risk than the market
$\beta < 1$ indicates less systematic risk than the market
$\beta = 1$ indicates the same systematic risk as the market

$r_f$      = risk-free rate of return
$r_m$     = market portfolio return
$(r_m - r_f)$ = market-risk premium

Sample betas from London Business School (March 2001)

Whitbread: 1.33    $r_e = 5 + 1.33(10 - 5) = 11.65\%$

Lloyds TSB: 1.47    $r_e = 5 + 1.47(10 - 5) = 12.35\%$

Sainsbury's: 0.48    $r_e = 5 + 0.48(10 - 5) = 7.40\%$

Woolwich: 1.00    $r_e = 5 + 1.00(10 - 5) = 10.00\%$

Assuming a return on risk-free investment of 5 per cent and a market-risk premium of 5 per cent.

**Figure 17.1:** CAPM summary

---

XYZ plc, a food retailing company, has an equity beta of 0.5 and a gearing level, measured as the market value of debt to equity, of 1:5.

It is trying to decide whether or not to invest in a construction project. It has identified a quoted company that undertakes similar operations to the project in question. The construction company has an equity beta of 1.2 and a gearing level of 1:3. Corporation tax is 35 per cent.

The equity beta of the quoted construction company is appropriate for establishing a risk-adjusted discount rate for project appraisal, but must first be modified to reflect XYZ plc's gearing level.

- **Stage one**. Degear the comparator beta.
  $1.2 = \beta_u + (\beta_u - 0.20)(1 - 0.35)1 \div 3$
  $\beta_u = 1.02$

- **Stage two**. Regear asset beta to XYZ plc gearing level.
  $\beta_g = 1.02 + (1.02 - 0.20)(1 - 0.35)1 \div 5$
  $\beta_g = 1.13$

- **Stage three**. Calculate cost of equity using CAPM.
  $k_e = 5 + 1.13(10 - 5) = 10.65\%$

This cost of equity can now be combined with the existing cost of debt (which should not be particularly affected by the different nature of the project) to obtain a new weighted-average cost of capital that's appropriate for discounting the project.

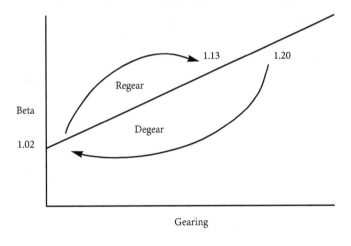

**Figure 17.2:** Geared beta illustration

M&M developed the following with-tax and without-tax equations to adjust any published beta for a different level of gearing:

- without tax: $\beta_g = \beta_u + (\beta_u - \beta_d)D \div E$
- with tax: $\beta_g = \beta_u + (\beta_u - \beta_d)(1 - T)D \div E$

where

$\beta_g$ = equity beta of a geared firm;

$\beta_u$ = equity beta of an ungeared firm;

$\beta_d$ = beta of debt;

E = market value of equity in geared firm;

D = market value of debt in geared firm;

T = corporation tax rate.

Armed with these equations and data from London Business School's risk measurement service, financial managers have a powerful tool enabling them to construct costs of equity allowing for differing levels of business risk and financial risk:

It would seem that CAPM and the work of M&M now give financial managers the theoretical ability to modify the basic WACC formula to deal with differing business and finance risks, and to create risk-adjusted costs of capital suitable for any situation. The third and final article of this series will combine these theories to give a complete methodology for deriving the value of projects that change both the business and financial risk of a company.

Ian Cornelius is director of ATC's value creation department and specialises in final level Financial Strategy. He has co-written two books on shareholder value. He can be contacted at ian.cornelius@ atc.co.uk

# Extremely Well Adjusted

By Ian Cornelius

........................................................................................................

T he first two articles in this series established the importance of the cost-of-capital concept and then discussed the theories of Modigliani and Miller (M&M) and the capital asset pricing model (CAPM) as ways of modifying the basic cost of capital for different levels of financial and business risk respectively.

It would seem that these models give us the theoretical ability to alter the basic formula of the weighted-average cost of capital (WACC) to handle differing risk profiles and to create suitable risk-adjusted costs of capital for any occasion. But one big problem remains. In order to apply these theories we need to know what the new capital structure will be after the new project is accepted. This leads us into a circular argument: if we want to value the project we need a new cost of capital, but to obtain the new cost of capital we need to know the value of the project (*see figure 18.1*, [...]).

The only sensible solution is a "divide and conquer" methodology based on M&M's capital structure work in 1963. Adjusted present value (APV) is the project-specific version of Vg = Vug + PVts. The value of a project is calculated as if it were all equity-financed. The value of any financial side-effects is then added to this, usually limited to the tax shield on debt financing and any issue costs associated with new finance.

The reason why this works is that it does not rely on the calculation of one overarching cost of capital adjusted for business and financial risk. Each element contributing to value is discounted using a rate appropriate to its particular risk profile (*see figure 18.2*, [...], *and figure 18.3*, [...]).

Cost of capital is possibly the most technical area of FLFS. Its precise calculation is, as we have seen, a highly technical process. In practice, though, firms rarely go into the depth of analysis covered in this article—there are simply too many unknowns in the real world.

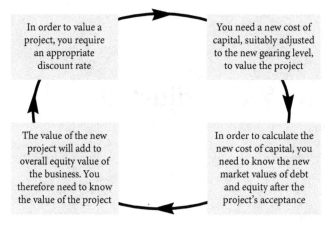

**Figure 18.1:** The circular argument of capital structure

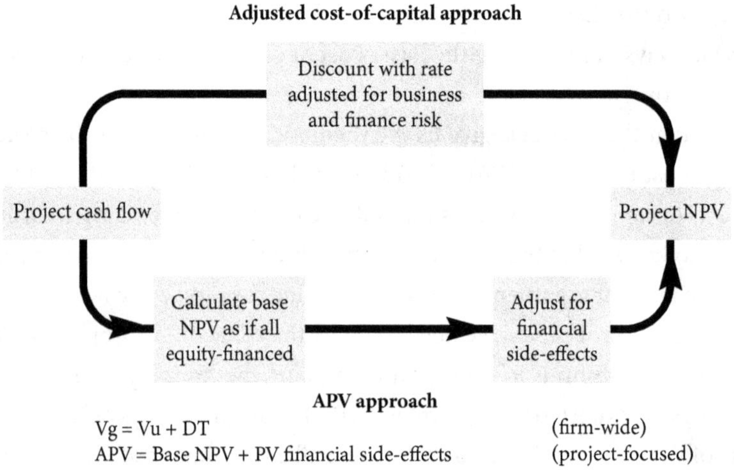

**Adjusted cost-of-capital approach**

Discount with rate
adjusted for business
and finance risk

Project cash flow

Project NPV

Calculate base
NPV as if all
equity-financed

Adjust for
financial
side-effects

**APV approach**

$V_g = V_u + DT$
APV = Base NPV + PV financial side-effects

(firm-wide)
(project-focused)

**Figure 18.2:** Adjusted present value

Cost of capital is not the property of the finance department. Everybody in the organisation responsible for creating value needs to understand its implications. Explaining the concept to non-finance staff in a language they will understand is far more important than calculating it to three decimal places. This is the real challenge for the financial manager.

Ian Cornelius (ian.cornelius@atc.co.uk) is director of ATC's value creation department. He specialises in final level Financial Strategy

PQR plc is considering investing in a new project that would cost £20 million. The project is expected to generate cash inflows to perpetuity of £4 million a year. Half of the necessary finance would be provided from retained earnings. The other half would come from a non-traded irredeemable debenture with a coupon rate of 7 per cent.

Companies within the new projects industry have an average gearing level of 60 per cent equity to 40 per cent debt by market values and an average equity beta of 1.4. The return on the risk-free investment is 5 per cent, the market premium is 5 per cent, the beta of debt is zero and the marginal corporation tax rate is 35 per cent. In order to calculate the adjusted present value of the proposed project, the base case NPV must be calculated as if the business were fully equity-financed.

$$\beta_g = \beta_u + (\beta_u - \beta_d)(1 - T)D/E$$
$$1.4 = \beta_u + (\beta_u - 0)(1 - 0.35)40/60$$
$$\beta_u = 0.98$$

$$r_{eu} = r_f + \beta_u(r_m - r_f)$$
$$r_{eu} = 5 + 0.98(10 - 5)$$
$$r_{eu} = 9.9 \text{ per cent}$$

Base case NPV $= -20 + 4/0.099$
$$= £20.4 \text{ million}$$

The present value of the financing side-effect must now be calculated, being the tax shield on perpetual debt. The annual tax saving is first calculated and then discounted as a perpetuity using the cost of debt as the discount rate.

Annual tax saving on interest
$$= D \times i \times T$$
$$= 10 \times 0.07 \times 0.35$$
$$= £0.245 \text{ million}$$

Present value of savings to perpetuity
$$= 0.245/0.07$$
$$= £3.5 \text{ million}$$

Adjusted present value
$$= £20.4 \text{ million} + £3.5 \text{ million}$$
$$= £23.9 \text{ million}$$

Figure 18.3: APV illustration

Since the capital asset pricing model (CAPM) was expounded by William Sharpe *et al* in the 1960s, it has dominated the academic and practical worlds of investment appraisal. Perhaps because the ideas behind it are so simple, its assumptions are the most tested in the history of finance.

Two key areas of CAPM theory are particularly worthy of note:

- **The value of the risk premium**. The market risk premium—ie, the excess return of the market portfolio over the risk-free rate of return—is usually estimated by looking at long-term historic average returns in the marketplace. A survey by Barclays Capital in 2000 calculated the 100-year average to be 4.7 per cent. The usual practice is to take a long-term average to reduce the effects of year-on-year "lumpiness". The problem, of course, is the further back you look in time the more removed from current market conditions you become. Depending on the study and the timescale used, the premium has been calculated to be as high as 8 per cent. In the late 1990s certain academics and practitioners suggested that a more appropriate current risk premium could be as low as 2 per cent. They pointed to the conquest of inflation, increased diversification and the long bull run to suggest that equities were barely more risky than gilts. Given the current market volatility, the true value of the risk premium is anyone's guess.
- **The concept of a single-factor model**. Many studies have been conducted to identify how well correlated betas seem to be with market returns. The results are spectacularly inconclusive. Certain studies show a good correlation, others find no correlation at all. The pragmatic answer seems to be that the beta is an important factor driving returns, but not the only one. This conclusion has led academics to propose multi-factor models to explain security return. The most famous of these is arbitrage pricing theory (APT). Developed by Stephen Ross in 1976, APT suggests that a number of systematic risk factors are required to explain a securities return. Rather unhelpfully, APT does not specify how many factors there are—or indeed what they are. Research continues in this area.

The inherent uncertainties in CAPM do not seem to have stopped its widespread use in calculating corporate cost of equity. Probably because of CAPM's simplicity and the wide availability of its data inputs, a recent survey suggested that 70 per cent of firms calculating their cost of capital for investment appraisal purposes use CAPM for the cost of equity element. The view from practice seems to be an understanding that CAPM, while not perfect, is good enough.

M&M gave us the mathematics for understanding how WACC changes with different gearing levels. If new projects affect a firm's gearing, its current WACC will not be appropriate for discounting the new project. A more practical solution to this problem is to realise that firms tend to set a target long-term gearing level that's suited to their own circumstances. Individual project finance may affect gearing in the short term, but a long-term target can be used in WACC calculations.

Companies seem less certain about how to deal with the financing issue. The Barclays Capital survey found that, for companies that calculate the WACC to appraise investment projects, only 30 per cent use a long-term target gearing ratio while 44 per cent use the current market value gearing ratio. A further 26 per cent use current book value gearing.

**Figure 18.4:** Weighted-average cost of capital in practice

Anyone who tells you they can calculate a firm's cost of capital to two decimal places is lying. More important than a precise answer is a deep understanding of the assumptions and limitations underlying the models, and some sensible sensitivity analysis based on this.

One last observation is that firms tend to be highly pragmatic about the depth of analysis they perform in calculating the cost of capital. For instance, there's no point making a 0.1 adjustment in your beta to account for a differing gearing level if you can't decide whether the market risk premium is 2 per cent or 7 per cent.

**Figure 18.4:** Weighted-average cost of capital in practice (Continued)

[...]

# Capital Budgeting—Essentials and Cash Flows

*Adhering to budgeting rules shouldn't trump good decision-making.*

**Emily Oster**

The value of the firm is essentially nothing more than the present value of all the firm's assets. Therefore, we can consider the firm to be a portfolio of those individual assets. Academic wisdom suggests a firm should strive to maximize its value and therefore should select only those assets increasing that value. Only the selection of relevant assets with the largest positive value added, or present value, will maximize the firm's value.

The process of selecting capital or long-term projects is defined as capital budgeting. Capital budgeting problems are extremely important due to the length of time for which a firm must commit itself to a project once that capital budgeting project has been selected and purchased. Capital budget projects are also generally expensive, and when asset selection mistakes occur, they are usually very difficult to correct.

The capital budgeting process involves analyzing, ranking, selecting, and monitoring capital or long-term assets. Not all assets found to be acceptable for investment may be selected due to the possible financial constraint of limited financing. Capital rationing is the process of apportioning available financing to acceptable capital investments in accordance with firm-defined minimum requirements.

Business organizations undertake capital asset investments for a variety of reasons, and such assets are therefore often classified by either size or purpose. Capital assets may also be segmented as either independent or mutually exclusive. Mutually exclusive projects are projects that have a direct or indirect impact on other projects. For this reason, for example, if one of two mutually related projects is accepted, the other cannot also be accepted. Independent projects, however, may each be accepted if they meet the firm's capital budgeting selection criteria.

When considering capital asset investment alternatives, one of the important issues considered is cash flow. Each capital investment is evaluated on its own merit, and, as a result, it is necessary to identify the specific incremental cash flows associated with each project under investment consideration. Incremental cash flows are flows that are specifically connected with a project.

Project cash flows can be categorized as either conventional or nonconventional. Conventional cash flows are flows with only one change in sign from positive to negative or negative to positive. Nonconventional cash flows include more than one change in sign. Flows must also be considered in terms of not only the size of the flows but also when they occur.

Business firms utilize a variety of capital budgeting techniques. These include the net present value (NPV), internal rate of return (IRR), profitability index (PI) or benefit-cost ratio, modified internal rate of return, payback period, and discounted payback period methods of analysis.

Perhaps the easiest and quickest of the methods of analysis is the payback method. The payback method, or payback period approach, takes the actual cost of an investment and determines how many years or periods it takes for the cash flows derived from investment in the project to pay back the cost of the project.

The decision criterion for implementing the payback period can either be based on acceptance of the project with the shortest payback period of the feasible project group, or it may be based on some standard payback that the firm sets for all projects of a certain type.

The project meeting this standard and with the shortest payback would be the project selected.

The advantages of the payback period are that it is quite easy to implement, the calculations are simple and easy to understand, and the analysis also allows for the inclusion of risk characteristics via the term to payback. The problems with the payback period method include the fact that it does not consider the time value of money and does not consider additional cash flows derived from a project after the payback period is completed.

To adjust the payback method for the lack of time value is a simple matter. Discounting the cash flows at an appropriate risk-adjusted return and utilizing those discounted present values to determine a payback solves the time-value criticism of the payback approach. Using the appropriate discount rate also adds another risk consideration into the method. This approach to capital budgeting analysis is the discounted payback method.

As with all discounted cash flow methods used in capital budgeting analysis, for projects with approximately the same level of risk as the firm on average, the cost of capital for the firm may serve as the discount rate. For projects exhibiting more or less risk than the firm on average, the discount rate is adjusted to higher or lower required return levels.

The approach commonly considered the most academically acceptable is the net present value, or NPV approach—another discounted cash flow method. To apply the net present value approach, the present value of both the benefits to be received from investment and the present value of all of the cash outflows associated with the project are determined. The difference between these cash flow present values is called the net present value. Deriving these present values requires the determination of an acceptable risk-commensurate required rate of return or discount rate.

When the net present value of the project exceeds zero, the project is deemed acceptable because the project has positive value that will increase the value of the firm. When the net present value is less than zero, the project is considered unacceptable because a negative present value decreases the value of the firm.

Since the net present value method actually determines the value contributed by a project to the firm, it is the academically preferred method of analysis based on the overall objective of maximizing the value of the firm. When ranking projects in accordance with alternative discounted cash flow methods, they may each determine those projects to be acceptable or unacceptable, but they may in fact rank the projects differently due to their uniquely different approaches to the analysis of those projects.

The net present value approach is advantageous in that it provides recognition of the time value of money, utilizes cash flow rather than accounting profit, and allows consideration of risk characteristics for each individual project under consideration.

Another method of analyzing capital budgeting projects, the Internal Rate of Return (IRR) method, again requires discounting cash flows to a present value. In the internal rate of return method, however, the analyst is concerned with identifying not the present value of the project but rather the rate of return earned on the project. That rate of return is defined as the one that equates the present value of the cost of the project with the present value of the cash flows to be derived. Once that rate has been derived, it is referred to as the internal rate of return and is nothing more than the rate that makes the net present value equal to zero.

To apply the internal rate of return method in terms of making a decision, it is necessary to compare the derived internal rate of return to the firm's cost of capital or to a risk-adjusted rate. When the internal rate of return is greater than the risk-adjusted required rate of return, the project will add value to the firm. Thus, the project is acceptable. When the internal rate of return for a project is less than the firm's risk-adjusted rate of return, the project will decrease the value of the firm and therefore is not acceptable.

Roger P. Bey, in a 1998 *Journal of Financial Education* paper, provides an in-depth discussion of the internal rate of return approach, specifically addressing the issue of multiple internal rate of returns. Bey notes that while the basic explanation for multiple IRRs is based on the number of cash flow sign changes, that condition is necessary but not sufficient. Using a variety of examples, he shows, for example, that a negative change in sign in the last period of flows is "rejected" as a sufficient condition for multiple IRRs to exist. Bey provides a graphical approach to reviewing the cash flows for a project with a few simple rules for an understanding of addressing the issue of multiple IRRs.

The net present value and the internal rate of return methods are similar in terms of their rationale for decision-making. The two methods do, however, tend to rank certain projects differently due to the size and timing of the project cash flows. As is the case with the net present value approach, the internal rate of return method has the advantage of considering both time value of money and cash flows. It also allows the explicit consideration of risk. Criticisms of the IRR, however, include the basic time value assumption of reinvestment at the discount rate and that nonconventional cash flows can provide more than one IRR as a solution.

Another discounted cash flow approach, the profitability index (PI) or benefit cost ratio method, is similar to the net present value approach with one significant difference. Rather than subtracting the present values of costs from those of the benefits, the PI approach divides the benefit present value by the cost present value. As a result, a relative index or benefit-cost ratio is derived.

Whenever the present value of the benefits exceeds the present value of the costs, an index greater than one is determined. As the index increases, the project becomes more attractive with regard to its cost. When the present value of the benefits is exactly equal to the present value of the cost, the benefit cost ratio or profitability index is equal to one. An index of less than one indicates a project that provides less present value benefits than costs.

The PI method is advantageous in that it considers time value, cash flows, and consideration of risk, and it is theoretically in line with the NPV and IRR methods. For small projects or small firms, the method allows ranking of projects based on dollars of benefits obtained per dollar of cost incurred on a present value basis.

One final method utilized is the modified internal rate of return (MIRR) method. The MIRR is both lauded and derided in academic circles. While correcting for the time value assumption of reinvestment by requiring reinvestment at the required discount rate, the method is criticized for how intermediate cash flows are treated as well as for the selection of appropriate reinvestment rates over time.

In "MIRR: The Means to an End? Reinforcing Optimal Investment Decisions Using the NPV Rule," R. Brian Balyeat and Julie Cagel (2015) provide an argument that, despite some criticisms, it is useful to teach the MIRR method, since it provides a mechanism for reinforcing students' understanding of the NPV method of capital budgeting analysis. The authors note that considerable attention is paid to the NPV model but that it does not necessarily equate to student understanding.

Balyeat and Cagel further note that research surveys of business financial managers suggest "the IRR is more often used as the primary criteria when decision rules conflict." To this point, two other papers provide interesting evidence with regard to the use of capital budgeting methods. Patricia A. Ryan and Glenn P. Ryan (2002), in "Capital Budgeting Practices of the Fortune 1000: How Have Things Changed," discuss the results of a survey on capital budgeting of Fortune 1000 firm financial officers. Contrary to some earlier studies, the survey found the NPV method was the "most frequently cited capital budgeting tool of choice, followed closely by IRR."

An interesting finding of the Ryan study was that the least popular method was the MIRR model, although, as the authors noted, "some argue MIRR is superior to IRR because it allows the manager to adjust the discount rate of intermediate term cash flows to better match a realistic return for the cash flows."

The selection process or capital budgeting methodology used in small firms can often be very different from the process in a large firm. Morris G. Danielson and Jonathan A. Scott, in their paper "The Capital Budgeting Decisions of Small Business" (2006), surveyed more than seven hundred small business firms to "analyze the capital budgeting practices of small firms," defined as firms with fewer than 250 employees.

Danielson and Scott found that capital asset analysis by those firms was "less sophisticated" than is "recommended by capital budgeting theory." Specifically, relative to large firms, they found that "these businesses use discounted cash flow analysis less frequently than gut feel, payback period, and accounting rate of return"; the last, accounting rate of return, is a model that uses accounting income rather than cash flows.

Conclusions by the authors suggested reasons for the use of less sophisticated models, including the limited formal education of many small business owners, incomplete or small management teams, and small staffs. An additional reason suggested was that in many cases, the capital budget decisions are not discretionary but rather are necessary to avoid going out of business. They make the investment and continue, or they do not, and the business fails. In these firms, then, maximizing the firm value is not the objective. Living for another day is!

It is important to recognize what are considered three of the most common pitfalls in cash flow determination. These are the irrelevant consideration of sunk costs associated with past investments, the omission of the opportunity cost of currently owned assets utilized in conjunction with new projects, and the appropriate allocation of new overhead costs to new projects.

The incremental cash flows attributed to a project are simply the cash flows that pertain to that project itself. Thus, in evaluating the cash flows of a project, only the revenue related to that project should be considered. In addition, any efficiencies providing operating expense reductions must be considered along with cost increases necessary to run or to maintain the project. Combining these cash flows together with tax effects will provide the net cash flows attributable to the project on an incremental basis. It is important to remember, in considering these cash flows, that we do not analyze cash flows attributable to the financing of the projects under consideration. Financing cash flows are separate from investment flows and have nothing to do with the acceptance or rejection of a specific project.

There are a number of sources of error common to capital budgeting analysis. The most important of these error sources are those with regard to sunk costs, opportunity costs, overhead costs, and investment in working capital.

Sunk costs are the costs attributed to past investments and that cannot be recovered regardless of whether or not the new investment is undertaken. As a result, these sunk costs should not be considered in determining whether or not to accept or reject a new project.

Opportunity costs are another source of common error when cash flows are being derived for new projects. When new assets draw beneficial flows from existing projects, this presents an opportunity cost. The loss of these flows or returns on an existing project are costs that must be covered by the new project.

Another common source of error in calculating the incremental cash flows attributable to a specific project arises in the area of overhead costs. Overhead costs are simply those costs not directly related to projects or products but still incurred by the firm in order to operate. These include items such as utility bills and water costs. When an incremental cash flow is derived for a new project, the overhead cost attributable to the project only should be considered. It is clearly incorrect to attribute to a single project cash flows for overhead cost payment that are not directly attributable to that project. Doing so will simply provide a possibility of losing acceptable good projects because of erroneous calculation of cash outflows.

Perhaps one of the most common errors in calculating incremental cash flows for projects lies in the area of net working capital. Net working capital, as we have seen previously, is simply the difference between current asset values and current liability values. When we have projects that require additional investments in working capital—for example, additional cash flow requirements, additional inventory requirements, or an increase in accounts receivable due to additional new sales—those assets must, of course, be financed either by short or long-term financing. When the difference between current assets and current liabilities is positive, this implies that certain short-term assets are being financed with long-term funding.

In consideration of the increase in current asset requirements for a new project, it is entirely possible that the spontaneous financing or current liability financing associated with that increase in current assets will not be adequate to finance all those current assets. When this happens, the resulting change in net working capital from including a new project or from purchase of a new project will be positive.

In short, that there will be an increase in net working capital suggests that the current assets required for the new project are not being spontaneously financed by current liabilities. As a result, this increase in net working capital must be financed by long-term sources. As a result, we must have a return earned on that additional increase in net working capital. Thus, the net working capital increase is the cost that must be included in the incremental cash flow analysis for a new project.

Depreciation is often described as a source of cash flow to the extent that it shelters income from taxation. As a result, any increase or decrease in depreciation is an incremental increase or decrease associated with a new project. This incremental change in depreciation should be considered in terms of the cash flow provided by sheltering income from taxation. It is important to remember to include the depreciation effect when calculating the incremental cash flows for any new project under consideration by a firm.

Once a firm has utilized a project to the extent it deems appropriate, it will necessarily have to salvage or scrap that project. Similarly, when a project requires additional net working capital in order to be utilized over its life, then the firm will no longer need that additional net working capital at the termination of the project.

Both the salvage value or scrap value obtained from the sale of an asset at the termination of its life and the recovery of increases in net working capital at the termination of a project's life should be treated as positive cash flows or benefits being recovered at the end of the project's useful life. It is important to remember to include these values to ensure appropriate positive cash flow benefits are being compared to the cash outflows.

Capital budgeting and other types of financial problems involving annuities sometimes require the comparison of alternatives available. When the various alternatives have the same life expectancy, the analysis is a relatively simple problem. The comparison of alternatives becomes more complicated when the alternatives available have differing life expectancies.

The two commonly utilized approaches to solving the unequal lives problem are the "equivalent annual annuity" and "replacement chain" methods. The equivalent annual annuity model requires the creation of annuity or constant cash flows from the actual cash flows of the projects. The equivalent flows for the alternatives are then compared.

To actually create the flows requires the determination of the net present values of the alternatives based on their unique life expectancies, identifying their equivalent annuity flows based on these net present values, and then comparing the annuities. The project with the highest annuity flow would be the preferred project based on the method.

In their 1997 *Journal of Financial Education* paper, Beadles and Joy provide an example and argument against the use of the equivalent annual annuity (EAA) approach. By providing a problem of mutually exclusive projects with unequal lives, the authors show that the implementation of the EAA method can lead to inappropriate investment decisions, drawing the conclusion that

> since solutions to mutually exclusive choice problems with unequal lives, reinvestment plans and unequal required rates of return are not qualitatively consistent, the EAA method is not a trustworthy technique in this important subclass of capital budgeting problems.

The basic rationale for the problem with the EAA methodology is that it occurs when the risk characteristics of the mutually exclusive projects under review are not similar. Projects with higher risk potential will require a higher required rate of return for determination of their net present values, while projects with less risk will require lower required returns. In these cases, where the risk and thus required return minimums exist, the EAA methodology can lead to erroneous decisions. As the authors point out,

> a present value function is simply a mathematical decay function. The higher the required rate of return, the faster the economic decay. Projects with *both* higher EAAs and required rates of return can be mis-ranked because their decay properties will reduce their present values relatively faster.

The second method, the replacement chain approach, is a bit more complicated. Using this method requires the determination of an equal common-lives time frame. For example, if one of the alternatives has an expected life of seven years and another has an expected life of 14 years, an additional seven-year project must be purchased to make the seven-year project equivalent to the 14-year project, or the 14-year project must include an expected project sale at the end of the seven years in the comparison evaluation. The evaluation can then be undertaken in a normal fashion based on the total equivalent lives of the alternatives.

In "Equivalent Annual Annuity vs. Replacement Chain Approach for Mutually Exclusive Investment Projects," David Fehr (2017) applies both methods to demonstrate that both the equivalent annual annuity and replacement chain models provide acceptable results when considered using the same discount rates for mutually exclusive projects. More importantly, the paper stresses that this is not also true for projects with different risk characteristics and thus different discount rate requirements. In those situations, Fehr suggests that the replacement chain method yields superior results.

# Recommended Readings

Graham, John R., and Campbell Harvey. "The Theory and Practice of Corporate Finance: Evidence from the Field." *Journal of Financial Economics* 60 (2001): 187–243.

Fehr, David. "Equivalent Annual Annuity vs. Replacement Chain Approach for Mutually Exclusive Investment Projects." *Journal of Finance and Accountancy* 22 (October 2017): 1–5.

# Selected Readings

Balyeat, R. Brian, and Julie Cagel. "MIRR: The Means to an End? Reinforcing Optimal Investment Decisions Using the NPV Rule." *Journal of Financial Education* (Spring 2015): 90–102.

Beedles, William L., and O. Maurice Joy. "Mutually Exclusive Projects With Unequal Lives, Reinvestment Plans and Unequal Required Rates of Return." *Journal of Financial Education* (Fall 1997): 81–83.

Bey, Roger P. "Multiple Internal Rates of Return: A Graphical Analysis." *Journal of Financial Education* (Spring 1998): 84–89.

Danielson, Morris G., and Jonathan A. Scott. "The Capital Budgeting Decisions of Small Businesses." *Journal of Applied Finance* 16, no. 2 (Fall/Winter 2006).

Ryan, Patricia, and Glenn P. Ryan. "Capital Budgeting Practices of the Fortune 1000: How Have Things Changed?" *Journal of Business and Management* 8, no. 4 (Winter 2002): 355–364.

# MIRR

## The Means to an End? Reinforcing Optimal Investment Decisions Using the NPV Rule

By Brian Balyeat and Julie Cagle, Xavier University

*Unlike other investment decision techniques, Modified Internal Rate of Return (MIRR) has yielded mixed academic opinions. MIRR is sometimes heralded as a superior decision rule, sometimes seen as having little value, and sometimes ignored altogether. We offer an alternative view; that the value of MIRR lays in improving students' understanding of net present value (NPV) as the primary decision criteria for investment decisions. Results of a classroom experiment support MIRR's pedagogical value for reinforcing the NPV rule.*

## Introduction

The MIRR investment decision criterion yields mixed reviews from academia. Although the MIRR rule dates back to Duvillard in 1787 (Biondi, 2006), MIRR is often ignored in surveys of capital budgeting practices (Graham and Harvey, 2001; and Pike, 1996). Ross, Westerfield, and Jordan (2011) remark the acronym should stand for "meaningless internal rate of return." In contrast, Kierluff (2008) argues MIRR is a more accurate measure of attractiveness of an investment alternative than NPV or IRR, and it is included in many introductory finance texts (Berk, DeMarzo, and Harford, 2012).

We offer a third view of MIRR; as a means to bridge a gap between the practice of capital budgeting and the theory of capital budgeting. Finance texts give considerable space to discussing the cases when NPV and IRR conflict and why NPV should be the primary decision rule. E.g., Ross, Westerfield, and Jaffe (2013) spend approximately three pages discussing NPV, a like number of pages discussing internal rate of return (IRR), but close to nine pages on the problems with IRR. Given this emphasis on problems with IRR, one would assume the flaws are memorable, but Bums and Walkers' (1997) survey results for Fortune 500 CFOs suggest this is not the case. They provide evidence that 41% percent of respondents indicated that IRR took priority in the case of a conflict in decision rules versus 29% that indicated NPV took priority. Since financial theory indicates NPV should take priority, this reflects a gap between the theory of capital budgeting and its practice. Because the calculation of MIRR requires explicit treatment of intermediate cash flows, their reinvestment and discounting, we believe teaching the MIRR technique will reinforce the superiority of NPV over IRR as a decision rule, and work toward reducing this gap.

Most projects involve intermediate cash flows, i.e., cash flows between the initial investment and the termination of the project. Both NPV and IRR make assumptions regarding these cash flows. NPV assumes cash flows are reinvested at the cost of capital, while IRR assumes cash flows are reinvested at the IRR. These reinvestment assumptions are implicit in that students are rarely asked to take the intermediate cash flows and compound them to the termination of the project when calculating NPV or IRR.[1] However, with MIRR they must do exactly that. Students must find the present value of the project's investment cash flows (negative cash flows) and the future value of the positive project cash flows. The MIRR is then the rate that equates the present value of the project's investment cash flows with the future value of the project's positive cash flows. We illustrate this explicit treatment of cash flows below.

## Explicit Treatment of Cash Flows, Discounting and Reinvestment Rates in MIRR Calculations

Finance texts such as Brigham and Daves (2013) usually describe a three step procedure for calculating MIRR. Periodic cash flows must be estimated for the project life, then negative project cash flows are discounted to time zero, while positive project cash flows are compounded until the project terminates (providing a terminal value). The MIRR is simply the rate that equates the required investment base at time zero to the terminal value. While it is generally agreed that the appropriate discount rate is the cost of capital, the choice of the appropriate compounding rate is more controversial. Based on Shull (1992), McDaniel, McCarty, and Jessell (1988), and others, we advocate the cost of capital as the appropriate discounting and compounding rate.

A second issue is how to treat investment funds that occur after the initial investment, e.g., year three of a project requires additional capital investment for a maintenance overhaul, while positive operating cash flows have occurred prior to this outflow. Based on Shull (1992, p. 9), we recommend using positive operating cash flows from the project to fund any subsequent cash outflows during the life of the project. Thus, the firm would be using funds previously generated by the project to fund subsequent cash outflows required by the project. This seems more consistent with the practice of capital budgeting than the alternative of assuming that the company would unnecessarily raise additional capital to fund the project. A more detailed discussion of this MIRR calculation is provided by Balyeat, Cagle, and Glasgo (2013).[2]

Consider this example which requires an initial investment of $80, an additional capital investment for a maintenance overhaul of $35 at year 3, and generates $25 per year in operating cash flows:

```
0     1     2     3     4     5
|-----|-----|-----|-----|-----|   Cost of capital=10%
-80   25    25    25    25    25
                  -35
```

The maintenance overhaul of $35 in year three is not fully funded by the $25 in operating cash flow for the year. We would *modify* the cash flows by using the prior years' operating cash flows to fund the remaining cost of the maintenance overhaul. Thus, $25(1.1)^2 + 25(1.1) + 25 = 30.25 + 27.5 + 25 = 82.75$, which can be used to fund the 35 maintenance overhaul to net $82.75 - 35 = 47.75$. The modified cash flows would be written as:

```
0     1     2     3     4     5
|-----|-----|-----|-----|-----|   Cost of capital=10%
-80   0     0    47.75  25    25
```

In this case, the present value of cash outflows is ☐80 as the maintenance overhaul was fully funded by prior years' operating cash flows, the terminal value is $47.75(1.1)^2 + 25(1.1) + 25 = 110.28$, and the MIRR = 6.63%. The rate of return of 6.63% makes the present value of the outflows grow to the terminal value over the five year life of the project, i.e, $80(1 + MIRR)^5 = 110.28$.

Alternatively, consider the case where previous operating cash flows are insufficient to fund the maintenance overhaul. Operating cash flows are $10 per year for the first three years, and $45 per year for years four and five, while the $80 initial investment and $35 maintenance overhaul in year 3 remain as in the prior example.

```
0     1     2     3     4     5
|-----|-----|-----|-----|-----|   Cost of capital=10%
-80   10    10    10    45    45
                  -35
```

In this case, $10(1.1)^2 + 10(1.1) + 10 = 12.10 + 11 + 10 = 33.10$, accumulated by year 3 is insufficient to fund the maintenance overall. *Modified* cash flows would be:

```
0     1    2 3    4     5
|-----|-----|-----|-----|-----|   Cost of capital=10%
-80   0    0  -1.9 45    45
```

The present value of the outflows is ☐80 + $-1.9/(1.1)^3 = -81.43$, while the terminal value is $45(1.1) + 45 = 94.50$, and the MIRR = 3.02% as $81.43(1.0302)^5 = 94.50$.

The above MIRR calculations require students to make explicit decisions about the treatment of the intermediate cash flows in order to obtain the *modified* cash flows. Students must also use the appropriate discounting and compounding rate. We believe this "explicitness" is the pedagogical value of teaching the MIRR technique. Students are forced to pay attention to these decisions, and thus be more mindful of decisions made not only in the MIRR technique, but other decision criteria as well, such as NPV and IRR. It then becomes more obvious to students that to achieve the IRR a project must reinvest its cash flows at the IRR while achieving the NPV requires reinvestment at the cost of capital.

Given that most corporate finance texts cover NPV and IRR, and discuss issues associated with IRR, teaching the MIRR technique takes a small amount of additional time beyond what is traditionally taught in capital budgeting. The calculation of the MIRR technique is covered, and then it is compared to the NPV and IRR technique in terms of reinvestment rate assumptions and whether investment decisions across the three rules would be consistent or inconsistent. This takes approximately 20 additional minutes of class time. However, we believe that time is well spent and helps reinforce the primacy of the NPV technique. Below we describe a classroom experiment to test this idea.

## Methodology

We developed a classroom experiment using a senior, intermediate level corporate finance class at a private, liberal arts institution taught in a traditional face to face manner. There were two sections of the course both taught by the same instructor. This class is required of finance majors. Introductory finance is the prerequisite to the course, but most students have had two other required finance courses in addition to the introductory class. Capital budgeting is a significant component of the course. Students were taught a variety of decision rules for capital budgeting projects, including NPV, IRR, payback, discounted payback, and profitability index. Students were then administered a five question survey regarding investment decisions. The survey appears in the appendix. After the initial survey, students were then taught the MIRR technique and re-administered the same five question survey. Comparison of the two sets of survey results allows us to assess the impact of teaching MIRR on students' understanding of investment decision rules. A code was assigned to each student and was used to match gender, GPA, and hours worked data and to ensure that survey results were only included in the dataset if the student filled out both the pre- and post-lecture survey. Forty-eight students completed both surveys.

Students were given a score of one for answering the question correctly and a score of zero for answering the question incorrectly. Question 1 of the survey gets most directly at whether teaching MIRR helps reinforce the primacy of the NPV technique by asking students to identify the best primary decision criterion to use for capital budgeting purposes. While question 1 on the survey most directly corresponds to the goal of reinforcing the primacy of the NPV rule, we thought there were other important components to understanding investment performance. Question 2 gets at the issue of mutually exclusive projects with the same scale and whether students understand that NPV, MIRR, and profitability index would give identical decisions as to the ranking of the projects.[3] If a student selected all three of these techniques, they received a score of one, and zero otherwise. The third question ascertains whether students understand which techniques assume reinvestment of intermediate cash flows. Techniques that use time value of money equations that assume compound interest would assume reinvestment of intermediate cash flows, thus the correct answer is IRR, MIRR,

NPV, and Profitability index which is scored as a one, and a zero is scored otherwise. Questions four and five gets at whether students understand WACC as the correct reinvestment rate and discount rate, respectively. Students receive a score of one for answering WACC and a zero otherwise.

$CumScore_i$ is the sum of scores across all five survey questions for student i. The following regression model was used:

$$CumScore_i = a + \beta_1 PostMIRR_i + \beta_2 Gender_i + \beta_3 GPA_i \qquad (1)$$
$$+ \beta_4 \#prior\ FINC\ courses_i + \beta_5 work_i + \varepsilon_i$$

Post MIRR is an indicator variable that is 1 if the survey is taken after the MIRR discussion in class, and zero for the survey taken prior to the MIRR discussion. We hypothesize that the coefficient for Post MIRR is positive and significantly different from zero because teaching MIRR reinforces the primacy of the NPV technique. Gender is an indicator variable that is 1 if the student is female and zero otherwise. While Didia and Hasnat (1998) did not find gender played a role in finance course performance, Trine and Schellenger (1999) did find gender had a role in explaining performance in an upper level finance course. GPA is the student's GPA at the start of the course. Prior research indicates past academic performance is a significant factor in predicting academic performance in an upper level finance course (Trine and Schellenge, 1999), in acquiring time value of money skills (Bianco, Nelson, and Poole, 2010), and in a hybrid finance course (McNally and Smith, 2010).

The variable # of prior FINC courses can be 1, if the student has only had the prerequisite course, or as high as a value of 5. The value would be 5 if all required finance courses have been taken other than the intermediate corporate finance course. We hypothesize the number of prior courses would mean greater exposure to how to measure investment performance and have a positive coefficient. A positive sign for the coefficient for # of prior FINC courses would be consistent with Ely and Hittle (1990).

Work is the self-reported number of hours a student works at a job per week. The sign of this coefficient could be positive or negative. A positive coefficient may indicate good work ethic that favorably affects academic performance. Alternatively, it is also possible that studying becomes a secondary priority to the job and hours worked per week reduce time spent studying which inhibits academic performance (Trine and Schellenger, 1999).

# Results

Survey data was collected from 48 students. The results of the pre- and post-lecture survey appear in Table 19.1. For this analysis, the question was graded under a "full credit" model. Under the "full credit" model, the question is marked correct only if the student marks all of the correct options (a through e) for the question and does not choose any of the incorrect options.

**Table 19.1** Survey Results Number of Correct Responses—Full Credit Model

|  | Q1 Best Decision Criteria | Q2 Mutually Exclusive Projects | Q3 Reinvestment of Intermediate Cash Flows | Q4 Appropriate Discount Rate | Q5 Appropriate Compounding Rate | Total |
|---|---|---|---|---|---|---|
| Pre-lecture | 45 | 0 | 2 | 35 | 28 | 110 |
| Post-lecture | 48 | 5 | 7 | 36 | 36 | 132 |

For each question, the post-lecture results exceeded the pre-lecture results. As indicated in the Total column, the MIRR lecture increased the number of correct responses in the survey by 20%. With 48 responses, the average pre-lecture score was 2.29 and the average post-lecture score was 2.75 for an improvement of 0.46 correct questions. After the MIRR lecture, students better understood not only that NPV is superior to IRR, but why it is superior. Thus, students are potentially less likely to prefer IRR to NPV when the techniques conflict, as documented by Bums and Walkers (1997) for practitioners.

To determine the extent to which the improvements in the student's scores are due to the MIRR lecture, the CumScore regression was run. The results for the CumScore regression model appear in Table 19.2. The model is significant at less than the 1% level, and explains over 20% of the variation in the dependent variable CumScore.

The indicator variable Post MIRR has a coefficient that is positive and is significant at less than the 1% level and has the expected magnitude of 0.460. Thus, the improvement in the survey scores is not only economically significant; it is statistically significant as well. The coefficient for *GPA* has the expected positive sign and is significantly different from zero with a p-value of less than 0.001. Neither *Gender* nor the *# of prior finance courses* was significant in explaining *CumScore*. However, *work* was close to the 5% significance level and the negative coefficient implies that hours worked per week might have a detrimental impact on performance.

To analyze the results question by question, the data was recoded under a "partial credit" model. Questions were graded choice by choice rather than as an entire question as in the previous analysis. For example, if the correct responses for a question are options a, b, c and e (as in question 3) and the student marks b and c, the student would only get 3 points (out of a possible 5) as they correctly

**Table 19.2** Regression Results for Primacy of the NPV Method Dependent Variable is CumScore n = 96 Model F = 5.831, Significance F = 0.000, Adjusted $R^2$ = 0.203

|  | Intercept | Post MIRR | Gender | GPA | # prior INC courses | Work |
|---|---|---|---|---|---|---|
| Coefficient | –0.126 | 0.460 | –0.208 | 0.745 | 0.090 | –0.015 |
| *p-value* | 0.829 | 0.007 | 0.378 | 0.000 | 0.359 | 0.055 |

**Table 19.3** Survey Results Number of Correct Responses—Partial Credit Model

| | Q1 Best Decision Criteria | Q2 Mutually Exclusive Projects | Q3 Reinvestment of Intermediate Cash Flows | Q4 Appropriate Discount Rate | Q5 Appropriate Compounding Rate | Total |
|---|---|---|---|---|---|---|
| Pre-lecture | 235 | 137 | 108 | 218 | 199 | 897 |
| Post-lecture | 240 | 159 | 129 | 216 | 215 | 959 |

marked options b and c and correctly did not mark option d. With 48 survey participants, each question now has 48*5 = 240 possible correct responses.

Table 19.3 details the results of the pre and post-lecture survey under the partial credit model. For all five questions, there were 897 correct responses on the pre-lecture survey and 959 correct responses on the post-lecture survey. In total, the post-lecture results showed a 6.9% increase in the number of correct responses versus the pre-lecture results. The post-lecture results are better than the pre lecture results for 4 of the 5 questions. Even though more students answered question 4 correctly under the "full credit" paradigm after the MIRR lecture, it appears that the students who answered the question incorrectly chose more wrong answers after the MIRR lecture than before. However, the differences in question 4 under both scoring metrics are very slight.

To test the significance of the post-lecture results, regressions were run for each question using the same control variables used in the *CumScore* regressions. The model used under the "partial credit" paradigm for the first question is

$$Q1Score_i = a + \beta_1 PostMIRR_i + \beta_i Gender_i + \beta_3 GPA_i \qquad (2)$$
$$+ \beta_4 \#prior\ FINC\ courses_i + \beta_5 work_i + \varepsilon_i$$

The models for the other 4 questions simply substitute their results for the left-hand side variable. The results for the five regressions can be seen in Table 19.4. Coefficients that are statistically significant at the 10% level are bolded.

For each question (except Question 4), the *Post MIRR* variable is statistically significant. Additionally, for these 4 regressions, while each of the other control variables is significant for at least one of the questions, the *GPA* variable is positive and significant for each question. As expected, the results for question 4 are not significant for the *Post MIRR* variable as the pre and post-lecture score for Question 4 are almost identical. The sum of the *Post MIRR* regression coefficients for all five questions is 1.294. This implies that the MIRR lecture increased the number of correct options chosen in the five question survey by approximately 1.3 choices per student.

The results for the individual questions are consistent with the results for the overall survey. In both specifications, the *GPA* and *Post MIRR* variables are significant and have the expected sign.

**Table 19.4** Regression Results for Primacy of the NPV Method by Question, n = 96

| | Intercept | Post MIRR | Gender | GPA | # prior FINC courses | Work |
|---|---|---|---|---|---|---|
| Q1 Coefficient | **4.727** | **0.103** | −0.287 | **0.116** | −0.049 | −0.001 |
| p-value | 0.000 | 0.080 | 0.001 | 0.077 | 0.156 | 0.814 |
| Q2 Coefficient | **1.911** | **0.455** | −0.224 | **0.406** | −0.142 | **0.011** |
| p-value | 0.000 | 0.002 | 0.263 | 0.011 | 0.089 | 0.091 |
| Q3 Coefficient | −0.653 | **0.438** | −0.284 | **0.879** | 0.047 | 0.005 |
| p-value | 0.427 | 0.067 | 0.394 | 0.001 | 0.737 | 0.670 |
| Q4 Coefficient | **3.649** | −0.038 | −0.003 | 0.219 | **0.187** | **−0.033** |
| p-value | 0.000 | 0.813 | 0.990 | 0.218 | 0.047 | 0.000 |
| Q5 Coefficient | 0.927 | **0.336** | −0.214 | **0.940** | 0.136 | −0.009 |
| p-value | 0.145 | 0.068 | 0.404 | 0.000 | 0.204 | 0.268 |

This implies that the MIRR lecture increases students understanding of investment criteria and more specifically the primacy of NPV.

There are a number of limitations to our study. First, the participants were students as opposed to practitioners and it is unclear how well the results generalize. The results also reflect a limited sample, with only 48 students participating. Of the 48 students, there were only five female students making it difficult to discern gender differences in responses across participants. Also, the surveys were administered in close proximity in time to the lectures on investment performance evaluation techniques, which may have positively affected the students' recall ability. Thus, the extent to which this timely information positively affects recall ability could be overestimating the recall ability of future investment decisions. Finally, the variable *Work* contains noise. The students self-reported their number of hours of work per week, and the number reported may not be accurate and may be highly variable in that the number of hours fluctuate significantly week to week. The label "work" may miss other significant time commitments that affect student studies. A student athlete may spend more hours in practice and competitions per week than a student that works. Also, not all work may be the same. If students are working in a finance related position versus in a food service capacity, the impact of hours worked per week may be different.

## Assurance of Learning

The mission for our college is "We educate students of business, enabling them to improve organizations and society, consistent with the Jesuit tradition." To help achieve our mission, our college has six undergraduate learning goals. One of the learning goals is "Understanding and application of knowledge across business disciplines" and a second is critical thinking. Under the learning goal of knowledge across business disciplines, the objective is that "Students will demonstrate college-level mastery of the body of knowledge and skills relative to their major." To that end, our department has identified 11 program level student learning outcomes (PLSLOs) specific to the finance major. These include applying time value of money principles and describing and applying the capital budgeting process, both of which correspond to understanding and application of finance knowledge and critical thinking. Time value of money and capital budgeting are first introduced in the introductory level course required of all business majors, but are covered with greater depth in the senior level intermediate corporate finance class where the pre and post-MIRR survey was administered.

The calculation of NPV, IRR, and MIRR would all involve applying time value of money principles. In terms of the capital budgeting process, students are also asked to discuss the strengths and weaknesses of NPV and other decision criteria, as well as to identify NPV as the best way to evaluate a project. Given the importance of capital budgeting to businesses and organizations, it is likely that other programs have a similar student learning outcome that must be measured for assessment.

The survey used in this paper can be used to confirm a direct measure of AACSB's Assurance of Learning requirement on the capital budgeting student learning outcome. In our case, the survey shows that students better understand the primacy of the NPV investment criteria and have a better understanding of the strengths and weaknesses of alternative investment criteria. The survey would be used in addition to other course embedded assessment tools such as a case that involves capital budgeting, a comprehensive capital budgeting problem on an exam, or a class project in which students discuss and apply the capital budgeting process.[4]

## Conclusion

Though the finance discipline is fairly *univocal* on the NPV rule being the decision technique most consistent with shareholder wealth maximization, survey evidence on capital budgeting practice indicates the IRR is more often used as the primary criteria when decision rules conflict (Bums and Walkers, 1997). The purpose of the classroom experiment was to examine whether teaching the MIRR technique could reinforce the primacy of the NPV rule. When capital budgeting techniques are taught, students do not generally take intermediate cash flows and reinvest them to calculate the NPV or IRR. Therefore, the assumptions about treatment of these intermediate cash flows and the reinvestment/discount rate are implicit rather than explicit. In contrast, the MIRR calculation forces students to modify the cash flows, and thus makes explicit the treatment of these intermediate cash flows. In so doing, teaching the MIRR technique improves students' awareness of the role of intermediate cash flows, reinvestment rates, and discount rates in not only the MIRR, but also NPV and IRR. The classroom experiment supports that teaching MIRR reinforces the primacy of the NPV decision rule.

# Endnotes

1. While we use the terms student or students throughout [...], the implications may also apply to practitioners.

2. Also see Balyeat et al. (2013) for literature reviews on the practice of capital budgeting, the academic perspective on the MIRR technique, how MIRR is calculated, and alternative reinvestment rate assumptions.

3. Since students may have had multiple finance courses, they may have been exposed to the MIRR rule prior to the intermediate course. E.g., the common text for the introductory finance course includes the MIRR technique.

4. Examples include the Conch Republic Electronics chapter 9 case in the Ross, Westerfield, and Jordan (2011) text, The Power to Cool Off in Florida minicase at the end of chapter 10 in the Emery, Finnerty, and Stowe (2011) text, and both minicases at the back of chapters 12 and 13 in the Brigham and Daves (2013) text.

# References

Balyeat, B., J. Cagle, and P. Glasgo, 2013. Teaching MIRR to Improve Comprehension of Investment Performance Evaluation Techniques, *Journal of Economics and Finance Education* 12, 39–50.

Berk, J., P. DeMarzo, and J. Harford. *Fundamentals of Corporate Finance,* (Prentice Hall, Upper Saddle River, New Jersey). 2th Edition.

Bianco, C., D. Nelson, and B. Poole, 2010. Teaching Time Value of Money, *The Business Review* 16, 25–31.

Biondi, Y., 2006. The Double Emergence of the Modified Internal Rate of Return: The Neglected Financial Work of Duvillard (1755–1832) in a Comparative Perspective, *European Journal of the History of Economic Thought* 13, 311–335.

Brigham, E. and P. Daves, 2013. *Intermediate Financial Management,* (2013), (South-Western Cengage), 11th Edition.

Bums, R. and J. Walker, 1997. Capital Budgeting Techniques Among the Fortune 500: A Rationale Approach, *Managerial Finance* 23, 3–15.

Didia, D. and B. Hasnat, 1998. The Determinants of Performance in the University Introductory Finance Course, *Financial Practice and Education* 8, 102–107.

Ely, D. and L. Hittle, 1990. The Impact of Math Background on Performance in Managerial Economics and Basic Finance Courses, *Journal of Financial Education* 14, 59–61.

Emery, D, J. Finnerty, and J. Stowe. 2011. *Corporate Financial Management,* (Pearson Prentice Hall, Upper Saddle River, New Jersey), 4th Edition.

Graham, J. and C. Harvey, 2001. The Theory and Practice of Corporate Finance: Evidence from the Field, *Journal of Financial Economics* 60, 187–243.

Kierulff, H, 2008. MIRR: A Better Measure, *Business Horizons* 51, 321–329.

McDaniel, W., W. McCarty, and K. Jessell, 1988. Discounted Cash Flow with Explicit Reinvestment Rates: Tutorial and Extension. *The Financial Review* 23, 369–385.

McNally, W. and B. Smith, 2010. Determinants of Performance in a Hybrid Finance Course, *Advances in Financial Education* 8, 22–34.

Pike, R., 1996. A Longitudinal Survey of Capital Budgeting Practices. *Journal of Business Finance and Accounting* 23, 79–92.

Ross, S., R. Westerfield, and J. Jaffe, 2013. *Corporate Finance,* (McGraw-Hill Irwin, New York) 10th Edition.

Ross, S., R. Westerfield, and B. Jordan, 2011. *Essentials of Corporate Finance,* (McGraw-Hill Irwin, New York), 7th Edition.

Shull, D., 1993. Efficient Capital Project Selection Through a Yield-Based Capital Budgeting Technique, *Engineering Economist* 38, 1–18.

Shull, D., 1993. Interpreting Rates of Return: A Modified Rate of Return Approach, *Financial Practice and Education* 5, 67–71.

Shull, D, 1994. Overall Rates of Return: Investment Bases, Reinvestment Rates and Time Horizons, *Engineering Economist* 39, 139–163.

Trine, J. and M. Schellenger, 1999. Determinants of Student Performance in an Upper Level Corporate Finance Course, *Proceedings of the Academy of Educational Leadership,* 4, 91–99.

# Appendix: Survey Instrument

Code: _____

By participating in this survey, you are agreeing to participate in a research study to compare effectiveness of different methods of teaching. Students will be identified by a code not available to the course instructor. No individual will be identified when results are discussed or reported.

Please indicate all previous finance courses completed:

FINC 300_____        FINC 365_____        FINC 492 or 495_____
ACCT 301/FINC 350_____        FINC 485_____

*Directions: Circle the correct answer. You may circle more than one answer if you think more than one answer is correct.*

1. What is the best primary decision criterion to use for capital budgeting purposes?

    a. IRR
    b. MIRR
    c. NPV
    d. Payback
    e. Profitability index

2. If you are considering two mutually exclusive projects with the same size initial investment, which technique would provide the correct ranking of the projects if your goal is to maximize shareholder wealth?

   a. IRR
   b. MIRR
   c. NPV
   d. Payback
   e. Profitability index

3. Which of the following techniques assume intermediate cash flows (cash flows not at the beginning of the project or at the end, but in the middle) will be reinvested?

   a. IRR
   b. MIRR
   c. NPV
   d. Payback
   e. Profitability index

4. When there are positive intermediate cash flows to reinvest, what should be the assumed reinvestment rate for these cash flows?

   a. IRR of the current project
   b. MIRR of the current project
   c. WACC of the current project
   d. Risk-free rate
   e. Market risk premium

5. When there are negative intermediate cash flows to discount, what should be the assumed discount rate for these cash flows?

   a. IRR of the current project
   b. MIRR of the current project
   c. WACC of the current project
   d. Risk-free rate
   e. Market risk premium

# The Capital Budgeting Decisions of Small Businesses

By Morris G. Danielson and Jonathan A. Scott

## The Capital Budgeting Decisions of Small Businesses

### Abstract

[This reading] uses survey data compiled by the National Federation of Independent Business to analyze the capital budgeting practices of small firms. While large firms tend to rely on the discounted cash flow analysis favored by finance texts, many small firms evaluate projects using the payback period or the owner's gut feel. The limited education background of some business owners and small staff sizes partly explain why small firms use these relatively unsophisticated project evaluation tools. However, we also identify specific business reasons—including liquidity concerns and cash flow estimation challenges—to explain why small firms do not exclusively use discounted cash flow analysis when evaluating projects. These results suggest that optimal investment evaluation procedures for large and small firms might differ. [G31]

## The Capital Budgeting Decisions of Small Businesses

[...] The U.S. Small Business Administration estimates that small businesses (which they define as firms with fewer than 500 employees) produce 50 percent of private GDP in the U.S., and employ 60 percent of the private sector labor force. Many small businesses are service oriented, but according to the 1997 Economic Census over 50 percent are in agriculture, manufacturing, construction, transportation, wholesale, and retail—all industries requiring substantial capital investment. Thus, capital investments in the small business sector are important to both the individual firms and the overall economy.

Despite the importance of capital investment to small firms, most capital budgeting surveys over the past 40 years have focused on the investment decisions of large firms (examples include

Morris G. Danielson and Jonathan A. Scott, "The Capital Budgeting Decisions of Small Businesses," *Journal of Applied Finance*, vol. 16, no. 2, pp. 45–56. Copyright © 2006 by Financial Management Association. Reprinted with permission.

Moore and Reichardt, 1983, Scott and Petty, 1984, and Bierman, 1993). An exception is Graham and Harvey (2001), who compare the capital budgeting practices of small and large firms. Even their small firms are quite large, however, with a revenue threshold of $1 billion used to separate firms by size. Indeed, less than 10 percent of their sample report revenues below $25 million. Thus, Graham and Harvey's results do not directly address the investment decisions of very small firms.[1]

There are several reasons small and large firms might use different criteria to evaluate projects. First, small business owners may balance wealth maximization (the goal of a firm in capital budgeting theory) against other objectives—such as maintaining the independence of the business (Ang, 1991, Keasey and Watson, 1993)—when making investment decisions. Second, small firms lack the personnel resources of larger firms, and therefore may not have the time or the expertise to analyze projects in the same depth as larger firms (Ang, 1991). Finally, some small firms face capital constraints, making project liquidity a prime concern (Petersen and Rajan, 1994, and Danielson and Scott, 2004). Because of these small firm characteristics, survey results on the capital budgeting decisions of large firms are not likely to describe the procedures used by small firms.

To document the capital budgeting practices of small businesses, defined here as firms with fewer than 250 employees, we use survey data collected for the National Federation of Independent Business (NFIB) Research Foundation by the Gallup Organization. The results include information about the types of investments the firm makes (e.g., replacement versus expansion), the primary tools used to evaluate projects (e.g., discounted cash flow analysis, payback period), the firm's use of other planning tools (e.g., cash flow projections, capital budgets, and tax planning activities), and the owner's willingness to finance projects with debt. The survey also includes demographic variables that allow us to examine the relations between capital budgeting practice and firm characteristics such as size, sales growth, industry, owner age, owner education level, and business age.

Not surprisingly, we find small and large firms evaluate projects differently. While large firms tend to rely on the discounted cash flow calculations favored by capital budgeting theory (Graham and Harvey, 2001), small firms most often cite "gut feel" and the payback period as their primary project evaluation tool. Less than 15 percent of the firms claim discounted cash flow analysis as their primary criterion, and over 30 percent of the firms do not estimate cash flows at all when they make investment decisions. The very smallest of the surveyed firms (firms with 3 employees or fewer) are significantly less likely to make cash flow projections, perhaps because of time constraints.

Certainly a lack of sophistication contributes to these results, as over 50 percent of the small-business owners surveyed do not have a college degree. Yet, there are also specific business reasons why discounted cash flow analysis may not be the best project evaluation tool for every small firm. For

---

[1] The Federal Reserve Board of Governor's Survey of Small Business Finance serves as the data source in many studies of small business finance. The firms in the Board of Governor's Survey tend to be much smaller than the firms in the Graham and Harvey (2001) sample; in the 1993 Board of Governor's survey, 83 percent of the firms report revenues under $1 million. The firms in the Graham and Harvey sample, therefore, are much larger than firms typically included in studies of small business finance.

example, 45 percent of the sample would delay a promising investment until it could be financed with internally generated funds, suggesting the firms face real (or self-imposed) capital constraints.[2]

We also find that the most important class of investments is "replacement" for almost 50 percent of the firms. Discounted cash flow calculations may not be required to justify replacement investments if the owner is committed to maintaining the firm as a going concern, and if the firm has limited options about how and when to replace equipment.

Finally, investments in new product lines are the most important class of investments for almost one-quarter of the sample firms. Because the ultimate success of this type of investment is often uncertain, it can be difficult to obtain reliable future cash flow estimates, reducing the value of discounted cash flow analysis. Thus, our results suggest that optimal methods of capital budgeting analysis can differ between large and small firms.

## I. Capital Budgeting Theory and Small Firms

Brealey and Myers (2003) present a simple rule managers can use to make capital budgeting decisions: Invest in all positive net present value projects, and reject those with a negative net present value. By following this rule, capital budgeting theory says firms will make the set of investment decisions that will maximize shareholder wealth. And, because net present value is a complete measure of a project's contribution to shareholder wealth, there is no need for the firm to consider alternative capital budgeting tools, such as payback period or accounting rate of return.

Yet, small firms often operate in environments that do not satisfy the assumptions underlying the basic capital budgeting model. And, small firms may not be able to make reliable estimates of future cash flows, as required in discounted cash flow analysis. We discuss these potential problems in detail, and explain why discounted cash flow analysis is not necessarily the one best capital budgeting decision tool for every small firm.

## A. Capital Budgeting Assumptions and the Small Firm

Capital budgeting theory typically assumes that the primary goal of a firm's shareholders is to maximize firm value. In addition, the firm is assumed to have access to perfect financial markets, allowing it to finance all value-enhancing projects. When these assumptions are met, firms can separate investment and financing decisions, and should invest in all positive net present value projects (Brealey and Myers, 2003).

There are at least three reasons to question the applicability of this theory to small firms. First, shareholder wealth maximization may not be the objective of every small firm. As Keasey and Watson

---

[2] Survey participants were asked: "Suppose you had the opportunity to make an investment in your business that would allow earnings to rise 25 percent within the next two years. The project had minimal risk, but you did NOT have the cash right then to make the investment. Would you most likely ...?" The choices included *wait until you accumulate enough cash*, *borrow the money and make the investment*, *seek an outside investor*, and *other*. Forty-five percent of the respondents selected *wait until you accumulate enough cash*.

(1993, p. 228) point out, an entrepreneur may establish a firm as an alternative to unemployment, as a way to avoid employment boredom (i.e., as a life-style choice), or as a vehicle to develop, manufacture, and market inventions. In each case, the primary goal of the entrepreneur may be to maintain the viability of the firm, rather than to maximize its value.[3]

Second, many small firms have limited management resources, and lack expertise in finance and accounting (Ang, 1991). Because of these deficiencies, they may not evaluate projects using discounted cash flows. Providing some support for this conjecture, Graham and Harvey (2001) find that small-firm managers are more likely to use less sophisticated methods of analysis, such as the payback period.[4]

The final impediment is capital market imperfections, which constrain the financing options for small firms. Some cannot obtain bank loans, because of their information-opaqueness and lack of strong banking relationships (e.g., Petersen and Rajan, 1994 and 1995, and Cole, 1998). Ang (1991) notes that access to public capital markets can be expensive for certain small firms, and impossible for others. These capital constraints can make it essential for small firms to maintain sufficient cash balances, in order to respond to potentially profitable investments as they become available (Almeida, Campello, and Weisbach, 2004). Thus, capital constraints provide small privately held firms with a legitimate economic reason to be concerned about how quickly a project will generate cash flows (i.e., the payback period).

## B. Cash Flow Estimation Issues

In his critique of capital budgeting theory, Booth (1996) describes estimation issues managers must confront when implementing discounted cash flow analysis. He concludes that discounted cash flow analysis is less valuable, the more uncertain the level of future cash flows. According to this view, discounted cash flow analysis can be applied most directly to projects with cash flow profiles similar to the firm's current operations (such as projects extending those operations). Discounted cash flow analysis will be less valuable to evaluate ventures that are not directly related to current activities.

Although Booth developed these ideas for large multinational corporations, they can also be applied to small firms. If a small firm is considering investment in a new product line, future cash flows cannot be estimated directly from the past performance of the firm's current operations. In addition, because of the firm's scale, market research studies to quantify future product demand (and cash flows) might not be cost effective. For these reasons, small firms may not rely exclusively on discounted cash flow analysis when evaluating investments in new product lines.

---

[3] In a survey of Swiss firms, Jorg, Loderer, and Roth (2004) find that maintaining the independence of the firm was cited more frequently than shareholder value maximization as a goal of managers. They also find that firms pursuing goals other than shareholder value maximization were less likely to rely on discounted cash flow analysis for investment decisions.

[4] The small firms in the Graham and Harvey (2001) have up to $1 billion in annual revenues. Thus, it is likely that many of these firms have more complete management teams than the small firms envisioned by Ang (1991). In contrast, we evaluate the capital budgeting policies of very small firms—our sample includes only firms with less than 250 employees, and over 80 percent of the firms have less than 10 employees—where the problem of incomplete management teams is likely to be most severe.

There are also reasons why a small firm may not use discounted cash flow analysis to evaluate replacement decisions. In many cases, replacing equipment is not a discretionary investment for a small firm; the firm must replace the equipment to stay in business. In some replacement decisions, a small firm may have limited replacement options, and differences in the future maintenance costs of the various options can be difficult to forecast.[5]

Because small firms do not satisfy the assumptions underlying capital budgeting theory, and because of these cash flow estimation challenges, it would be natural for small firms to evaluate projects using different techniques than large firms. But, evidence about these differences is largely anecdotal. We use survey data to document the capital budgeting practices of small firms, and to provide evidence about whether small-firm project evaluation methods are related to the type of investment under consideration.

## II. Description of Data

The use of survey data to document capital budgeting practices has a long history in the finance literature.[6] Yet, survey results should be interpreted with caution because surveys measure manager beliefs, not necessarily their actions; survey participants may not be representative of the defined population of firms; and survey questions may be misunderstood by some participants (Graham and Harvey, 2001, p. 189). Nonetheless, surveys provide information that cannot be readily gleaned from financial statements. In particular, surveys can shed light on how firms make investment and financing decisions, and why they use these approaches.

The data for this study were collected for the NFIB Research Foundation by the Gallup Organization. The interviews for the survey were conducted in April and May 2003 from a sample of small firms, defined as a business employing at least one individual in addition to the owner, but no more than 249. The sampling frame for the survey was drawn at the NFIB's direction from the files of the Dun & Bradstreet Corporation. Because the distribution of small businesses is highly skewed when ranked by number of employees, interview quotas were used to add more larger firms to the sample. Once the data were compiled, the responses were weighted to reflect population proportions based on U.S. Census data, yielding a sample of 792 observations.

Exhibit 20.1 summarizes the demographic characteristics of the sample—industry, sales growth, business age, employment, owner education, and owner age. For each attribute, we group responses into three to five categories.

---

[5] Booth (1996) also concludes that discounted cash flow analysis might not be used for replacement decisions, but for a different reason. He argues that the payback period combined with judgment can often lead a firm to the correct decision for replacement projects, making discounted cash flow analysis unnecessary.

[6] Scott and Petty (1984) summarize the results of 21 early studies of large firm capital budgeting practices. The selection criteria in these studies include membership in the Fortune 500/1000, a minimum level of capital expenditures, size, or stock appreciation in excess of certain benchmarks. In more recent studies, Moore and Reichardt (1983) surveyed 298 Fortune 500 firms, Bierman (1993) looked at 74 Fortune 100 firms, and Graham and Harvey (2001) investigated the behavior of 392 firms chosen from the membership of the Financial Executives Institute and the Fortune 500.

## Exhibit 20.1　Sample Description

The weighted distributions of the responses to the National Federation of Independent Business' Reinvesting in the Business Survey conducted by the Gallup Organization.

|  | No. of Obs | % of Total |
|---|---|---|
| *Industry* | | |
| Service | 155 | 20 |
| Construction/manufacturing | 194 | 24 |
| Retail/wholesale | 378 | 48 |
| Other | 65 | 8 |
| *Real 2-year sales growth* | | |
| 20 percent or higher | 194 | 24 |
| 10–19 percent | 179 | 23 |
| +/□ 10 percent | 200 | 25 |
| □10 percent or lower | 187 | 24 |
| No answer | 32 | 4 |
| *Business age* | | |
| < 6 years | 183 | 23 |
| 6–10 years | 173 | 22 |
| 11–20 years | 213 | 27 |
| 21+ years | 216 | 27 |
| No answer | 7 | 1 |
| *Employment* | | |
| 1 | 127 | 16 |
| 2–3 | 233 | 29 |
| 4–10 | 287 | 36 |
| 10+ | 145 | 18 |
| *Owner education level* | | |
| Less than college degree | 415 | 52 |
| College degree | 260 | 33 |
| Advanced/prof. degree | 105 | 13 |
| No answer | 12 | 2 |
| *Owner age* | | |
| < 35 years | 81 | 10 |
| 35–44 years | 194 | 24 |
| 45–54 years | 244 | 31 |
| 55+ years | 255 | 32 |
| No answer | 18 | 2 |
| **Total** | **792** | **100** |

Exhibit 20.1 shows 72 percent of the sample firms are in construction, manufacturing, retail, or wholesale, all industries requiring substantial capital investments. Service industries, where capital expenditures may have less importance, account for 20 percent of the sample.

The sample is distributed evenly across four real sales growth categories. The high-growth category is defined as a cumulative (not annualized) increase of 20 percent or more over the past two years, and includes 24 percent of the sample firms. At the other extreme, 24 percent of the firms report two-year sales declines of 10 percent or more. This distribution implies that approximately 75 percent of the sample firms have experienced an average annualized growth rate of 10 percent or less over the last two years. Thus, many of the capital budgeting decisions of small firms may be focused more on maintaining current levels of service and quality, rather than on expansion.

Similarly, the sample is distributed fairly evenly across four business-age categories, ranging from six years in business or less (23 percent of the sample), to 21 years in business or more (27 percent of the sample). The number of years in business could influence both the type of investments a firm will make and the firm's planning process. For example, firms in business longer may have more equipment in need of replacement. A business with a limited operating history may not be able to obtain a bank loan unless it can demonstrate that it has appropriate planning processes in place.

The median (mean) number of total employees is 4 (9). Sixteen percent of the firms have only one employee, and only 18 percent have 10 or more. Thus, it is likely that many sample firms do not have complete management teams, and may not have adequate staff to fully analyze capital budgeting alternatives.

The data in Exhibit 20.1 also suggest that the educational background of owners could influence how the firm makes capital budgeting decisions. Over 50 percent of the business owners do not have a four-year college degree, and only 13 percent have an advanced or professional degree. Therefore, many of the small-business owners may have an incomplete (or incorrect) understanding of how capital budgeting alternatives should be evaluated.

Finally, 63 percent of the business owners are at least 45 years old, and 32 percent are 55 or older. There is some evidence that older managers evaluate capital investments using less sophisticated methods (see Graham and Harvey, 2001).

## III. Survey Results

We use the NFIB survey to address three questions concerning the capital budgeting activities of small firms. We first consider whether the investment and financing activities of small firms conform to the assumptions underlying capital budgeting theory. Then, we look at the overall planning activities of small firms (e.g., use of business plans, consideration of tax implications) and identify firm characteristics that tend to be present when more sophisticated practices are in place. Finally, we provide evidence about the specific project evaluation techniques small firms use (e.g., payback period, discounted cash flow methods). We identify significant differences between the average responses in various subsets of firms and the overall sample averages using a binomial Z-score. We use multinomial logit to evaluate how the choice of investment evaluation tools is related to a set of firm characteristics.

## A. Investment Activity

Exhibit 20.2 describes the investment activities of sample firms. It identifies the firms' most important type of investment over the previous 12 months, and reports the percentage of firms that will delay a potentially profitable investment until the firm has enough internally generated cash to fund the project.

The most important type of investment is replacement for 46 percent of the sample firms. Firms in service industries were more likely than the average sample firm to select this response, and those in construction and manufacturing were less likely. Firms with the highest growth rates and those in business less than six years were less likely than the average sample firm to report replacement activity as the primary investment type. Finally, the importance of replacement activity increases with the age of the business owner; it is significantly less than the overall sample mean when the business owner is younger than 44.[7]

Projects to extend existing product lines are shown as the primary investment activity for 21 percent of the sample firms. Construction and manufacturing firms select this response at a higher rate than the overall sample average. The remaining subsample averages are not significantly different from the overall sample averages (at the 5 percent significance level).

Investments in new product lines are reported as the most frequent investment for 23 percent of the sample firms. Firms in the service industry were less likely than the average sample firm to select this response. Firms with the highest growth rates were more likely (than the overall sample average) to be expanding into new product lines, while those with the lowest growth rate were less likely. The oldest firms were also less likely than the average firm to be considering expansion into new product lines.

Exhibit 20.2 also suggests that many small firms face real (or self-imposed) capital constraints. Forty-five percent of the sample firms report they would delay a promising investment until it could be financed with internally generated funds (*wait for cash*). Firms most likely to *wait for cash* include the youngest firms, the smallest firms, and those whose owner does not have a college degree. As these firms are likely to face capital market constraints, this result supports the prediction in Almeida, Campello, and Weisbach (2004) that capital constraints will make a firm more likely to save cash. Firms with older owners are also slightly more likely to *wait for cash* than firms with younger owners.

---

[7] The significance of the subsample entries depends on the difference between the subsample mean and the overall sample mean in a given column, and on the number of observations in the subsample (most of these numbers appear in Exhibit 20.1). Thus, it is possible for two subsamples to have similar response percentages, one significant and the other not. For example, 54 percent of the service firms identify replacement as the primary investment type, while 55 percent of the firms in the "other" industry category select this investment type. This response percentage is significantly different from the overall sample average for service firms, but not for the "other" firms. As shown in Exhibit 20.1, there are twice as many service industry firms.

## Exhibit 20.2 Investment Activity

Percentage distributions are presented for the question, "Measured in dollars, what was the purpose of the largest share of the investments made in your business in the last 12 months?" The last column presents the percentage of all firms that would delay investments until they could be financed internally with cash. ++ (−−) indicates that the cell percentage is significantly greater than (less than) the column total, at a 5% significance level, and + (−) indicates that the cell percentage is significantly greater than (less than) the column total, at a 10% significance level, using a binomial Z-score.

| | Type of Investment Recently Made | | | | |
| | Replace | Expand Existing Product | New Product Line | Other | Wait for Cash |
|---|---|---|---|---|---|
| *Industry* | | | | | |
| Service | 54++ | 21 | 16− | 3 | 42 |
| Construction/ | 30−− | 31++ | 28+ | 1−− | 42 |
| manufacturing | 49 | 18 | 24 | 5 | 45 |
| Retail/wholesale | 55 | 12− | 22 | 9++ | 56 |
| Other | | | | | |
| *Real 2-year sales growth* | | | | | |
| 20 percent or higher | 37−− | 24 | 31++ | 5 | 45 |
| 10–19 percent | 52 | 21 | 21 | 3 | 50 |
| +/− 10 percent | 50 | 22 | 23 | 3 | 35 |
| ☐10 percent or lower | 47 | 20 | 16−− | 5 | 47 |
| *Business age* | | | | | |
| < 6 years | 38− | 23 | 26 | 4 | 52 |
| 6–10 years | 40 | 27+ | 27 | 2 | 44 |
| 11–20 years | 51 | 16− | 24 | 3 | 38 |
| 21+ years | 51 | 20 | 17−− | 6 | 45 |
| *Employment* | | | | | |
| 1 | 47 | 20 | 20 | 5 | 58 |
| 2–3 | 47 | 20 | 21 | 4 | 43 |
| 4–10 | 42 | 25+ | 26 | 2− | 43 |
| 10+ | 48 | 19 | 23 | 5 | 37 |
| *Owner education level* | | | | | |
| Less than college degree | 44 | 21 | 23 | 4 | 49 |
| College degree | 45 | 20 | 23 | 4 | 38 |
| Advanced/prof. degree | 53 | 22 | 23 | 1 | 44 |
| *Owner age* | | | | | |
| <35 years | 33−− | 23 | 29 | 9++ | 42 |
| 35–44 years | 38−− | 23 | 28 | 4 | 38 |
| 45–54 years | 49 | 21 | 23 | 1−− | 49 |
| 55+ years | 51 | 20 | 19 | 4 | 47 |
| **Total** | **46** | **21** | **23** | **4** | **45** |

These results suggest three reasons small firms might not follow the prescriptions of capital budgeting theory when evaluating projects. First, it is noteworthy that replacement activity is the most important type of investment for almost half of the sample firms. If replacing old equipment is necessary for the firm to remain in business, the owner's capital budgeting decision is essentially a choice between replacing the machine and staying in business, or closing the business and finding employment elsewhere. In this case, maintaining the viability of the firm as a going concern, rather than maximizing its value, might be the owner's primary objective.

Second, the results suggest that many small firms place internal limits on the amount they will borrow. Thus, many small firms cannot (or choose not to) separate investment and financing decisions, contrary to capital budgeting theory.

Finally, the results suggest that the personal financial planning considerations of business owners may affect the investment and financing decisions of small firms. In particular, older owners are more conservative in their strategies than younger owners (older owners focus more on replacement activity and are more likely to report that they will *wait for cash*). These results conflict with an assumption of capital budgeting theory: that the transferability of ownership interests (at low cost) allows managers to separate the planning horizon of a business from the planning horizon of its owners.

## B. Planning Activity

Exhibit 20.3 analyzes three dimensions of each firm's planning environment: how frequently firms estimate cash flows in making capital budgeting decisions; whether they have written business plans; and whether they consider tax implications in making capital budgeting decisions.

Exhibit 20.3 reports that only 31 percent of the sample firms have a written business plan. Over 30 percent of the sample firms do not estimate future cash flows when making investment decisions, and 26 percent of the firms do not consider the tax implications of investment decisions. Thus, many small firms do not have a formal planning system that guides capital budgeting decisions.

Firms with the highest growth rates (over 20 percent growth) are more likely to use each of these planning tools, particularly written business plans and consideration of tax effects. Similarly, firms that extend existing product lines or invest in new lines of business engage in more planning activities than the average sample firm. As firms expand, they use up more of their borrowing capacity, reducing their future financial flexibility (assuming that they face capital constraints). For these firms, it may be essential to plan ahead, so the firm is not forced to pass up promising opportunities in the future.

Newer firms (less than 6 years old) and younger owners (less than 45 years old) are more likely than other firms to use written business plans. This is an expected result, given that banks require evidence of planning before extension of credit to firms with short operating histories.

The smallest firms (three or fewer employees) are less likely to make cash flow projections, while firms with ten or more employees are more likely to make these estimates. This finding supports conjectures made by Ang (1991) and Keasey and Watson (1993) that personnel constraints (incomplete management teams) may hamper small firms in planning.

## Exhibit 20.3  Investment Planning Tools

Responses are presented to three questions about planning tools used in the evaluation of capital investments. "Make CF Projections" presents the percentage of respondents who said they typically make cash flow projections prior to making a major investment in their business. "Written Business Plan" presents the percentage of respondents who said they had a written business plan projecting the major investments planned over the next few years. "Taxes Calculated/Considered" presents the percentage of respondents who reported they typically calculated or considered the tax implications of a major investment in their business. ++ (−−) indicates that the cell percentage is significantly greater than (less than) the column total, at a 5% significance level, and + (−) indicates that the cell percentage is significantly greater than (less than) the column total, at a 10% significance level, using a binomial Z-score.

| | Planning Tools | | |
| --- | --- | --- | --- |
| | Make CF Projections | Written Business Plan | Taxes Calculated/ Considered |
| *Industry* | | | |
| Service | 71 | 34 | 72 |
| Construction/manufacturing | 68 | 32 | 71 |
| Retail/wholesale | 70 | 30 | 75 |
| Other | 67 | 27 | 83+ |
| *Real 2-year sales growth* | | | |
| 20 percent or higher | 74 | 38++ | 79+ |
| 10–19 percent | 66 | 29 | 75 |
| +/− 10 percent | 68 | 28 | 74 |
| −10 percent or lower | 70 | 29 | 68 |
| *Business age* | | | |
| < 6 years | 80++ | 46++ | 79+ |
| 6–10 years | 71 | 28 | 72 |
| 11–20 years | 71 | 28 | 72 |
| 21+ years | 58− | 23−− | 74 |
| *Employment* | | | |
| 1 | 61− | 35 | 75 |
| 2–3 | 64− | 24− | 77 |
| 4–10 | 72 | 33 | 72 |
| 10+ | 81++ | 36 | 74 |

(continued)

**Exhibit 20.3   Investment Planning Tools (Continued)**

| | Planning Tools | | |
| --- | --- | --- | --- |
| | Make CF Projections | Written Business Plan | Taxes Calculated/ Considered |
| *Owner education level* | | | |
| Less than college degree | 65⁻ | 27⁻ | 73 |
| College degree | 73 | 35 | 75 |
| Advanced/prof. degree | 81⁺⁺ | 38 | 83⁺⁺ |
| *Owner age* | | | |
| <35 years | 80 | 40+ | 73 |
| 35–44 years | 73 | 37+ | 78 |
| 45–54 years | 69 | 34 | 73 |
| 55+ years | 66 | 21⁻⁻ | 74 |
| *Wait for cash* | 69 | 32 | 77 |
| *Investment type* | | | |
| Replacement | 67 | 23⁻⁻ | 72 |
| Expand existing product | 71 | 37⁺ | 76 |
| New product line | 74 | 42⁺⁺ | 80⁺ |
| Other | 81 | 49⁺ | 83 |
| **Total** | **69** | **31** | **74** |

The planning activities of small firms are also strongly related to the educational background of the business owner. If the business owner does not have a college degree, the firm is less likely than the average firm to make cash flow projections or to use written business plans. If the business owner has an advanced/professional degree, the firm is more likely to engage in such activities.

## C. Project Evaluation Methods

Exhibit 20.4 summarizes responses about the primary tool firms use to assess a project's financial viability: payback period, accounting rate of return, discounted cash flow analysis, "gut feel," or combination. The most common response is the least sophisticated, gut feel—selected by 26 percent of the sample firms.[8]

---

[8] Vos and Vos (2000) report "intuition" as the most frequently used project evaluation technique in a survey of 238 small New Zealand businesses.

## Exhibit 20.4  Investment Decision Tools

Responses are presented to the question about the investment tools used to assess the financial viability of a major investment in the business. Each of the five responses are reported under Investment Tools. ++ (−−) indicates that the cell percentage is significantly greater than (less than) the column total, at a 5% significance level, and + (−) indicates that the cell percentage is significantly greater than (less than) the column total, at a 10% significance level, using a binomial Z-score.

| | Investment Tools | | | | |
|---|---|---|---|---|---|
| | **Payback** | **ARR** | **DCF** | **Gut Feel** | **Combination** |
| *Industry* | | | | | |
| Service | 18 | 11 | 13 | 33++ | 11 |
| Construction/manufacturing | 19 | 14 | 11 | 22 | 15+ |
| Retail/wholesale | 19 | 16 | 13 | 25 | 8− |
| Other | 23 | 6− | 9 | 29 | 14 |
| *Real 2-year sales growth* | | | | | |
| 20 percent or higher | 15 | 17 | 14 | 26 | 9 |
| 10–19 percent | 26++ | 14 | 11 | 27 | 9 |
| +/□ 10 percent | 21 | 12 | 11 | 24 | 12 |
| □10 percent or lower | 18 | 11 | 14 | 31 | 9 |
| *Business age* | | | | | |
| < 6 years | 21 | 14 | 18++ | 24 | 8 |
| 6–10 years | 19 | 10 | 12 | 29 | 9 |
| 11–20 years | 17 | 19++ | 13 | 23 | 11 |
| 21+ years | 20 | 11 | 7−− | 28 | 14 |
| *Employment* | | | | | |
| 1 | 22 | 14 | 13 | 25 | 11 |
| 2–3 | 20 | 15 | 11 | 25 | 12 |
| 4–10 | 16 | 12 | 13 | 28 | 10 |
| 10+ | 21 | 16 | 12 | 25 | 9 |
| *Owner education level* | | | | | |
| Less than college degree | 18 | 12 | 12 | 29 | 10 |
| College degree | 20 | 18+ | 10 | 23 | 12 |
| Advanced/prof. degree | 24 | 11 | 17++ | 17− | 13 |

*(continued)*

## Exhibit 20.4 Investment Decision Tools (*Continued*)

| | Investment Tools | | | | |
|---|---|---|---|---|---|
| | **Payback** | **ARR** | **DCF** | **Gut Feel** | **Combination** |
| *Owner age* | | | | | |
| <35 years | 26 | 10 | 14 | 19 | 14 |
| 35–44 years | 14⁻ | 19⁺⁺ | 18⁺⁺ | 21 | 11 |
| 45–54 years | 24⁺⁺ | 15 | 7⁻ | 31⁺ | 10 |
| 55+ years | 16 | 11 | 13 | 27 | 11 |
| *Wait for cash* | 21 | 12 | 15 | 24 | 8 |
| *Investment type* | | | | | |
| Replacement | 20 | 11 | 12 | 31⁺⁺ | 13 |
| Expand existing product | 20 | 14 | 17⁺ | 20⁻ | 8 |
| New product line | 19 | 20⁺⁺ | 9 | 23 | 13 |
| Other | 21 | 17 | 14 | 14 | 3 |
| *Planning tools* | | | | | |
| Cash flow projection made | 23⁺⁺ | 15 | 14 | 22⁻ | 13 |
| Written business plan | 19 | 18⁺ | 16⁺ | 20⁻⁻ | 13 |
| Taxes calculated/considered | 20 | 16 | 14⁺ | 24 | 12 |
| **Total** | **19** | **14** | **12** | **26** | **11** |

The use of gut feel is strongly related to the business owner's educational background. Owners without a college degree resort to it most frequently, and owners with advanced degrees least. The use of gut feel is also inversely related to a firm's use of planning tools. Firms with written business plans and firms that make cash flow projections are significantly less likely to rely on gut feel.

While the use of gut feel is concentrated in the least sophisticated of small firms, it is also widely used by firms that make primarily replacement investments. A firm may have limited options when it replaces equipment, and estimating future cash flows (i.e., incremental maintenance costs or efficiency gains) for each option might be difficult. For example, if a firm must replace a delivery truck, it may be difficult for the firm to estimate differences in the future annual operating costs of two replacement vehicles under consideration. Moreover, if an investment is necessary for the firm's survival (and the owner is committed to maintaining the business as a going concern), the maximization of firm value may not be the business owner's primary objective. Instead, the owner may simply look for the alternative promising the required level of performance at the most reasonable cost. Thus, it is not surprising to find that small business owners use relatively unsophisticated methods of analysis to evaluate replacement options.

Gut feel is also used extensively by firms in the service industry. Although some service firms make substantial capital expenditures, the investments of many service firms might be limited to business vehicles or office equipment. Because a firm's primary considerations when evaluating this type of purchase decision may be cost, reliability, and product features, structuring a discounted cash flow analysis of these investments can be difficult.

Payback period is the second most common response, selected by 19 percent of the sample. The payback period is used slightly more often by firms that will *wait for cash*, as expected. Firms using the payback period are significantly more likely than other firms to estimate future cash flows (because cash flow estimates are required for this calculation). Finally, use of the payback period appears to increase with the formal education of the business owner.

These results suggest that the payback period conveys important economic information in at least some circumstances. For example, the payback period can be a rational project evaluation tool for small firms facing capital constraints (i.e., firms that do not operate in the perfect financial markets envisioned by capital budgeting theory). In this case, projects that return cash quickly could benefit a firm by easing future cash flow constraints.

The accounting rate of return is the next most frequent choice, identified by 14 percent of the firms as their primary evaluation method. The use of accounting rate of return increases with firms' growth rates; it is significantly higher than the sample mean for firms entering new lines of business. Each of these characteristics can indicate high borrowing needs. The accounting rate of return is thus especially important if a firm must provide banks with periodic financial statements, or is required to comply with loan covenants based on financial statement ratios.

The most theoretically correct method—discounted cash flow analysis—is the primary investment evaluation method of only 12 percent of the firms. Not surprisingly, owners with advanced/professional degrees are most likely to use this method; 17 percent of these firms identify it as their primary evaluation tool. Firms with written business plans and those that consider the tax implications of investments are also significantly more likely to use discounted cash flow techniques. Thus, firms using this project evaluation method are among the most sophisticated of the small firms.

Firms extending existing product lines are also significantly more likely to use discounted cash flow analysis. This result is evidence that discounted cash flow analysis is most useful when evaluating projects with cash flow profiles similar to current operations (such as projects extending existing product lines), because it is easier to obtain reliable cash flow estimates in this case.

Another noteworthy finding is that 18 percent of the firms in business less than six years use this method, the most of any age group. Although younger firms are less likely to have complete management teams in place, it is also possible that banks may encourage newer firms to demonstrate adequate planning (and project evaluation) procedures before qualifying for credit.

Of the specific evaluation techniques firms could choose from, combination of methods was selected least often, by 11 percent of firms. Use of this approach does not appear to be strongly related to any of the firm characteristics listed in Exhibit 20.4.

The results in Exhibit 20.4 are very different from results in Graham and Harvey (2001). Approximately 75 percent of their firms evaluate projects using estimates of project net present value or internal rate of return. The vast majority of their firms also appear to consider multiple measures of project value in making investment decisions. However, even the smaller firms in the Graham and Harvey study are much larger than the firms in our sample, and are thus more likely to have complete management teams. It is therefore not surprising that their firms use more sophisticated methods of project analysis.

## D. Multivariate Analysis

To provide a multivariate perspective on how small firms make investment decisions, we use multinomial logit to jointly identify factors influencing the choice of a project evaluation tool. This technique is appropriate when an unordered response, such as a set of project evaluation tools, has more than two outcomes.

Exhibit 20.5 reports the results of this exercise; gut feel is the omitted category. Thus, the coefficients listed in Exhibit 20.5 should be interpreted as the increase (a positive coefficient) or the reduction (a negative coefficient) in the log odds between the evaluation tool specified and gut feel.

The results show that firms using any of the formal investment evaluation tools are more likely to make cash flow projections than firms using gut feel. Firms using the accounting rate of return, discounted cash flow, or a combination of methods are more likely to consider tax implications when they evaluate projects. These results corroborate the results in Exhibit 20.4—firms using gut feel to evaluate projects have much less structured planning environments than other firms.

Exhibit 20.5 also identifies factors that differentiate between firms attaching primary importance to the various investment evaluation tools. The results suggest that capital constraints and the type of investment (e.g., replacement, expand product line, new product line) can influence how firms evaluate projects.

The *wait for cash* coefficient is positive and significant for both payback period and discounted cash flow analysis. These results suggest that firms committed to funding projects internally are not necessarily irrational or unsophisticated. Instead, the decision to wait for cash might be an acknowledgment that the firm does not operate in a perfect financial market, and faces capital constraints. Because the firm knows it may not be able to fund all valuable projects, it will evaluate projects using the payback period (to help it allocate investment funds over a multiyear horizon) or discounted cash flow analysis (to help it identify the best projects).

The accounting rate of return is frequently the choice of firms pursuing either growth strategy: expand product line or new product line. The coefficients for both of these variables are positive and significant for accounting rate of return. As a firm grows, it may need to raise new capital, either by

## Exhibit 20.5 Multinomial Logit Results

Mulitnomial logit estimates are presented of the factors that affect the decision tool most frequently used to assess the financial viability of a project. All of the dependent variables are 1/0 variables that take a value of 1 if the method of investment evaluation in each column is reported for large investments. The omitted choice is Gut Feel; thus the significance of the coefficients should be interpreted as the effect on the log odds of the evaluation tool choice relative to Gut Feel. In each case where there is a set of 1/0 variables for the independent variable, the omitted variable is identified and significance should be interpreted relative to this omitted variable. *** indicates significance at the 0.01 level, ** significance at the 0.05 level and * significance at the 0.10 level. The observations included in these estimates are limited to those respondents reporting one of the five investment analysis techniques, which limits the sample size to 583 observations.

| | Payback | | Rate of Return | | DCF | | Combination | |
|---|---|---|---|---|---|---|---|---|
| | Coeff | Std Err | Coeff | Std Err | Coeff | Std Err | Coeff | Std Err |
| *Industry* | | | | | | | | |
| Manufacturing/construction | 0.221 | 0.332 | 0.512 | 0.383 | 0.040 | 0.399 | 0.512 | 0.379 |
| Retail/wholesale | −0.063 | 0.287 | 0.621 | 0.333* | 0.259 | 0.334 | −0.505 | 0.362 |
| Service/other (omitted) | | | | | | | | |
| *Real 2-year sales growth* | | | | | | | | |
| 10 percent or higher (omitted) | | | | | | | | |
| No change (+/☐ 10 percent) | 0.374 | 0.296 | −0.142 | 0.336 | 0.347 | 0.360 | 0.250 | 0.356 |
| 10 percent or lower | −0.330 | 0.305 | −0.420 | 0.338 | 0.226 | 0.342 | −0.252 | 0.366 |
| *Business age* | | | | | | | | |
| Under 6 years (omitted) | | | | | | | | |
| 6–10 years | 0.151 | 0.362 | −0.216 | 0.411 | −0.179 | 0.400 | 0.349 | 0.489 |
| 11–20 years | 0.451 | 0.381 | 0.924 | 0.391** | 0.314 | 0.403 | 1.404 | 0.485*** |
| 20+ years | 0.604 | 0.384 | 0.442 | 0.422 | −0.482 | 0.461 | 1.671 | 0.499*** |
| *Employment* | | | | | | | | |
| Under 4 (omitted) | | | | | | | | |
| 10-Apr | −0.666 | 0.278** | −0.570 | 0.310* | −0.346 | 0.321 | −0.838 | 0.336** |
| Over 10 | −0.503 | 0.331 | −0.336 | 0.358 | −0.243 | 0.397 | −1.067 | 0.418** |
| *Owner education level* | | | | | | | | |
| College (BA or AA) | 0.251 | 0.268 | 0.299 | 0.287 | −0.206 | 0.322 | 0.085 | 0.327 |
| Graduate school | 0.915 | 0.388** | 0.059 | 0.461 | 0.683 | 0.439 | 1.104 | 0.472** |
| No college (omitted) | | | | | | | | |
| *Owner age* | | | | | | | | |
| Under 35 | 1.367 | 0.486*** | 0.249 | 0.578 | 0.448 | 0.551 | 1.712 | 0.603*** |
| 35–44 | 0.448 | 0.371 | 0.881 | 0.374** | 0.565 | 0.378 | 0.803 | 0.441* |
| 45–54 | 0.432 | 0.296 | 0.164 | 0.336 | −0.845 | 0.384** | 0.089 | 0.370 |
| 55 up (omitted) | | | | | | | | |

(*continued*)

## Exhibit 20.5  Investment Decision Tools (*Continued*)

| | | | | | | | | |
|---|---|---|---|---|---|---|---|---|
| Wait for cash | 0.426 | 0.241* | −0.084 | 0.269 | 0.593 | 0.280** | −0.452 | 0.305 |
| *Investment type* | | | | | | | | |
| Replacement (omitted) | | | | | | | | |
| Expand product line | 0.381 | 0.313 | 0.640 | 0.339* | 0.880 | 0.343** | −0.018 | 0.395 |
| New product line | 0.255 | 0.305 | 0.637 | 0.322** | 0.031 | 0.377 | 0.334 | 0.361 |
| *Planning tools* | | | | | | | | |
| Cash flow projection made | 1.297 | 0.286*** | 0.635 | 0.296** | 0.731 | 0.323** | 1.157 | 0.357*** |
| Written business plan | −0.041 | 0.275 | 0.363 | 0.297 | 0.422 | 0.308 | 0.397 | 0.322 |
| Taxes calculated/considered | −0.047 | 0.274 | 0.744 | 0.344** | 1.020 | 0.394*** | 0.762 | 0.388** |
| Constant | −3.836 | 1.512** | −1.849 | 1.646 | −0.461 | 1.738 | −3.402 | 1.898* |

obtaining a bank loan or by attracting new equity investors. In either case, the firm's historical and projected financial statements will be used to communicate information about the firm to investors. The accounting rate of return can be valuable to firms pursuing growth strategies because it provides information about how a project will affect a firm's financial statements (and its ability to meet accounting-based loan covenants).

The importance of discounted cash flow analysis depends on the type of growth the firm is pursuing. The coefficient for expanding an existing product line is positive and significant for discounted cash flows, but the coefficient for new product line is not. Firms will use discounted cash flows to evaluate projects that extend existing product lines because future cash flow estimates can be based on past performance in this case. But, if it is contemplating a new product line, where obtaining future cash flow estimates can be difficult, the firm is less likely to use a discounted cash flow method of analysis.

## IV. Summary

Firms with fewer than 250 employees analyze potential investments using much less sophisticated methods than those recommended by capital budgeting theory. In particular, survey results show these businesses use discounted cash flow analysis less frequently than gut feel, payback period, and accounting rate of return.

Many small-business owners have limited formal education, and their firms may have incomplete management teams. Therefore, a lack of financial sophistication is an important reason why the capital budgeting practices of small firms differ so dramatically from the recommendations of theory. Small staff sizes also constrain the amount of capital budgeting analyses the firms can perform. Beyond this, there are also substantive reasons a small firm might choose to use methods other than discounted cash flow analysis to evaluate projects.

The primary reason is that many small businesses do not operate in the perfect capital markets that capital budgeting theory assumes. Most of the firms in our sample are very small (with fewer than 10 employees); they have short operating histories (almost half have been in business under 10 years), and their owners are not college educated. These characteristics may limit their bank credit, posing credit constraints. If so, these firms may be required to finance some future investments using internally generated funds, and it would not be surprising for the owners to consider measures of project liquidity (such as the payback period) when making investment decisions.

Second, many of the investments that small firms make cannot easily be evaluated using the discounted cash flow techniques recommended by capital budgeting theory. Many investments by small firms are not discretionary (a firm either makes a specific investment or it goes out of business), and future cash flows can be difficult to quantify. For example, if a firm is introducing a new product line, estimates of future cash flows can be imprecise (and market research studies required to obtain better cash flow estimates may not be cost effective). When future cash flows cannot be easily estimated, discounted cash flow analysis may not provide a reliable estimate of a project's contribution to firm value, and it is not surprising that a firm might resort to gut feel to analyze the investment.

For these reasons, small firms face capital budgeting challenges that differ from those faced by larger firms. Thus, it is possible that optimal capital budgeting methods for large and small firms may differ. However, a fully integrated capital budgeting theory—identifying the conditions under which discounted cash flow analysis is appropriate—has yet to be developed. The question of how to better tailor the prescriptions of capital budgeting theory for small firms remains unanswered.

# References

Almeida, H., M. Campello, and M. Weisbach, 2004, "The Cash Flow Sensitivity of Cash," *Journal of Finance* 59 (No. 4, August), 1777–1804.

Ang, J., 1991, "Small Business Uniqueness and the Theory of Financial Management," *The Journal of Small Business Finance* 1 (No. 1), 1–13.

Bierman, H., 1993, "Capital Budgeting in 1992: A Survey," *Financial Management* 22 (No. 3, Autumn), 24.

Booth, L., 1996, "Making Capital Budgeting Decisions in Multinational Corporations," *Managerial Finance* 22 (No. 1), 3–18.

Brealey R. and S. Myers, 2003, *Principles of Corporate Finance*, New York, McGraw-Hill/Irwin.

Cole, R., 1998. "The Importance of Relationships to the Availability of Credit," *Journal of Banking and Finance* 22 (Nos. 6–8, August), 959–977.

Danielson, M. and J. Scott, 2004. "Bank Loan Availability and Trade Credit Demand," *Financial Review* 39 (No. 4, November), 579–600.

Graham J. and C. Harvey, 2001. "The Theory and Practice of Corporate Finance: Evidence from the Field," *Journal of Financial Economics* 60 (Nos. 2–3, May), 187–243.

Jorg, P., Loderer, C., Roth, L., 2004, "Shareholder Value Maximization: What Managers Say and What They Do," *DBW Die Betriebswirtschaft* 64 (No. 3), 357–378.

Keasey K. and R. Watson, 1993, *Small Firm Management: Ownership, Finance and Performance,* Oxford, Blackwell.

Moore J. and A. Reichert, 1983. "An Analysis of the Financial Management Techniques Currently Employed by Large U.S. Corporations," *Journal of Business Finance and Accounting* 10 (No. 4, Winter), 623–645.

Petersen, M. and R. Rajan, 1994. "The Benefits of Firm-Creditor Relationships: Evidence from Small Business Data," *Journal of Finance* 49 (No. 1, March), 3–37.

Petersen, M. and R. Rajan, 1995. "The Effect of Credit Market Competition on Lending Relationships," *Quarterly Journal of Economics* 60 (No. 2, May), 407–444.

Scott, D. Jr., and W. Petty II, 1984. "Capital Budgeting Practices in Large American Firms: A Retrospective Analysis and Synthesis," *Financial Review* 19 (No. 1, March), 111–123.

Vos, A. and E. Vos, 2000. "Investment Decision Criteria in Small New Zealand Businesses," *Small Enterprise Research* 8 (No. 1), 44–55.

# Mutually Exclusive Projects with Unequal Lives, Reinvestment Plans and Unequal Required Rates of Return

By William L. Beedles and O. Maurice Joy

The equivalent annual annuity (EAA) approach is widely used when ranking mutually exclusive investment proposals with unequal lives that require reinvestments. EAA solutions are particularly prominent in some of the most popular introductory finance textbooks. We present a simple example showing that when proposals also have unequal risks, and therefore unequal required rates of return, the EAA does not always provide correct investment decisions.

## Introduction

Mutually exclusive choice decisions arise when economically attractive investment proposals compete for funding. We investigate here a well-known subclass of investment decisions where mutually exclusive proposals have (1) unequal lives and (2) reinvestment plans later in the lives of the proposals. The second point refers to the common condition that one or more future reinvestment cycles are expected if the proposal is undertaken. The capital budgeting literature invariably uses examples where the required rates of return of the alternatives are equal, implying that project risks are equal. Our contribution is to introduce into that environment the complicating, but realistic feature of (3) unequal proposal risks, and hence, unequal required rates of return. We present an example where this complication destroys the general usefulness of the commonly employed equivalent annual annuity (EAA) capital budgeting technique.

The EAA is one of the more popular current textbook presentations for solving the capital budgeting problem of concern here. See for examples Brealey, Myers, and Marcus [1995], Emery and Finnerty [1997], Pinches [1996], and Ross, Westerfield, and Jaffe [1993]. These authors and others point out common difficulties that lurk in the uncritical use of EAA: inflation problems and changing technology effects on replacement cash flows [Pinches] and situations where no replacement is needed [Ross, Westerfield and Jaffe].

The research literature tackles more difficult problems, an especially noteworthy example being Howe and McCabe's [1983] analysis of model specification. However, we have never seen a text or research article that considers the possibility of unequal risks among proposals and the consequent effect on EAA usage. Because of the popularity of EAA, and because many real world comparisons likely involve proposals with unequal risks, the shortcoming we point out is noteworthy.

## The Most Common Unequal Lives Problem

If proposals have unequal lives, but no future reinvestment plans are anticipated, a straightforward comparison of net present values is sufficient to identify the best course of action. If, however, proposals anticipate future reinvestments *and* have unequal lives, more complex analytical procedures must be employed to assure that the resulting solution is consistent with the principle of maximizing present value.

One important issue is identification of an appropriate evaluation interval. Emery [1982] has presented an exhaustive taxonomy that compares proposal lives and the life of the economic project to which the proposals relate. He considers it likely, and we concur, that the most frequently encountered case is where the mutually exclusive proposals' lives are less than the economic project's life. As an example, two rivet gun alternatives are used in the manufacturing of planes, one more durable than the other. Emery notes the correct evaluation interval for this type of problem is the lesser of the project life and the least common multiple years of the alternative proposals. We will focus on this type of case below.

## An Example

Consider two mutually exclusive proposals. Alternative A is shorter lived and presumed to be safer than B; estimated required rates of return are 10% and 12%, respectively, reflecting the risk difference. Cash flows are shown below. Expectations are that, whichever proposal is accepted, future reinvestments will be made. Also, estimates of cash flows after tax (CFAT) for the future reinvestment cycles for the two proposals are identical to the original estimates shown. Finally, the economic project associated with proposals A and B has a life longer than the least common multiple (LCM) of 12 years. This example is the kind described earlier as the most common unequal lives scenario.

| Year | Alternative A<br>CFAT | Alternative B<br>CFAT |
|---|---|---|
| 0 | –1,000 | –1,000 |
| 1 | +482 | +415 |
| 2 | +482 | +415 |
| 3 | +482 | +415 |
| 4 | | +415 |
| | NPV = +199 | NPV = +260 |

We next contrast two solution techniques with the end purpose of demonstrating the deficiency in the EAA method.

## Analysis #1: Compute NPV for the Least-Common-Multiple Period

NPV of 1 cycle of A = +199
NPV of 4 cycles of A = +544
NPV of 1 cycle of B = +260
NPV of 3 cycles of B = +531
Therefore: *Choose A*

This is a straightforward application of present value to a properly framed problem. Absent use of a computer, the solution is tedious and would be more so if the least common multiple configuration involves more cycles. But, the solution is unambiguously correct. A is indeed the choice that maximizes net present value and shareholder wealth.

## Analysis #2: Compute Equivalent Annual Annuities (EAA)

The EAA approach reduces the original investment cash flows to a net present value, then computes an annual annuity cash flow equivalent in time value to that net present value. This is a popular technique for handling mutually exclusive investments with unequal lives. Most texts that discuss the unequal lives problem present this technique. (PVA(R,H) represents an annuity present value factor for R% and H periods.)

EAA for A = 199/PVA(10,3) = $80 per year
EAA for B = 260/PVA(12,4) = $86 per year
Therefore: *Choose B*

The most attractive feature of the EAA method is its ease of solution. There is no need to project cash flows out to multiple investment cycles as was done in Analysis #1. But, as this example shows, using EAA here leads to the wrong decision.

# Discussion

In the usual unequal lives capital budgeting problem, the two analytical methods shown above give consistent answers: they correctly and identically rank competing proposals. This is obviously not the case in the example above. The reason for the inconsistent ranking is the presence of unequal required rates of return for the alternatives. Not all EAA applications lead to incorrect decisions, just as not all internal rate of return applications are erroneous. But the possibility of error being present when the EAA method is applied defeats its generality.

EAA solutions are not completely consistent with NPV solutions in our subclass of unequal lives problems. The presence of unequal required rates of return destroys the ability to compare annual cash flow results directly. If required rates of return are equal for investment alternatives, then there is a consistent mapping of EAAs into NPVs. EAA solutions will always give correct answers to the ranking problem. When alternatives have unequal required rates of return, reflecting unequal project risks, the EAA method is no longer perfectly aligned with present value. This lack of consistency in solutions is not recognized in the capital budgeting literature, but should be.

On a more technical level, the mathematical conditions under which the methods give conflicting decisions has no general solution. The problem has more unknowns (NPVs, discount rates, and horizons) than equations (LGM-NPVs and EAAs).

However, the economic logic is straightforward. Recall that a present value function is simply a mathematical decay function. The higher the required rate of return, the faster the economic decay. Projects with *both* higher EAAs and required rates of return can be mis-ranked because their decay properties will reduce their present value relatively faster. Project B in our example above had both a higher required rate of return and EAA than Project A. But B's economic value (NPV) decayed more rapidly than in A's case.

The general conclusion from our analysis is that since solutions to mutually exclusive choice problems with unequal lives, reinvestment plans and unequal required rates of return are not qualitatively consistent, the EAA method is not a trustworthy technique in this important subclass of capital budgeting problems.

# References

Brealey, Richard A., Myers, Stewart C. and Marcus, Alan J., *Fundamentals of Corporate Finance,* Mc-Graw-Hill, 1995, pp. 181–83, Emery, Douglas R., and Finnerty, John D., *Corporate Financial Management,* Prentice Hall, 1997, pp. 375–79. Emery, Gary W., "Some Guidelines for Evaluating Capital Investment Alternatives with Unequal Lives", *Financial Management,* Spring 1982, pp. 14–19, Howe, Keith M. and McCabe, George M., "On Optimal Asset Abandonment and Replacement," *Journal of Financial and Quantitative Analysis,* September 1983, pp. 295–305. Pinches, George E., *Essentials of Financial Management,* 5th ed., Harper Collins, 1996, pp. 197–200. Ross, Stephen A., Westerfield, Randolph W., and Jaffe, Jeffrey F., *Corporate Finance,* 3rd ed., Richard D. Irwin, Inc., 1993, pp. 204–10.

# Multiple Internal Rates of Return

## A Graphical Analysis

By Roger P. Bey

The concept of multiple internal rates of return (IRRs) has existed for 60 years. However, contemporary financial management textbooks provide incomplete discussions of multiple IRRs, which can lead to incorrect conclusions concerning identification of multiple IRRs. [...] it is shown that complex mathematics are not necessary for identifying IRRs, but by understanding the HPV map, counting changes in signs on cash flows, and the application of a spreadsheet, the multiple IRR problem can be addressed in a very simple manner. However, caution must be exercised in applying the spreadsheets, since the spreadsheet IRR function is sensitive to the initial IRR guess and may yield a solution that isn't the closest root to the initial guess.

## Introduction

Many authors of contemporary financial management textbooks [Brealey and Myers, 1988; Brigham and Gapenski, 1993; Bussey, 1978; Copeland and Weston, 1988; Emery and Finnerty, 1991; Herbst, 1982; Lee, 1985; Levy and Sarnat, 1994; Peterson, 1994; Pinches, 1994; Ross, Westerfield, and Jordan, 1993; Shapiro, 1990; Van Horne, 1995; Weston and Brigham, 1993; Weston and Copeland, 1992; and Wilkes, 1977] state that one limitation of the internal rate of return (IRR) is the fact that multiple solutions may exist. It is then common for the authors to illustrate the multiple IRR problem with an example, often Lorie and Savage's [1955] pump problem, which has two IRRs. Many authors then go on to indicate that projects with cash outflows in the final period of the project's life, such as reclamation of a strip mine, may have multiple IRRs. Although most of the textbook presentations are technically correct, they are incomplete, sometimes make implicit statements which may lead the reader to incorrect conclusions, and do not provide the reader with an understanding about the nature of multiple IRRs, the conditions required for multiple IRRs to occur, or the frequency of the multiple IRRs. Therefore, given the lack of clarity in finance textbooks and

Roger P. Bey, "Multiple Internal Rates of Return: A Graphical Analysis," *Journal of Financial Education,* vol. 24, pp. 84–89. Copyright © 1998 by Roger P. Bey. Reprinted with permission.

the continued popularity of the IRR, the objectives [...]: (1) to provide a non-mathematical analysis of the cash flow patterns required for multiple IRRs; (2) to provide guidelines and a procedure for the identification of multiple IRRs; and (3) to illustrate the potential problems associated with the application of spreadsheet functions (Lotus and Excel) in solving for IRRs.

## Historical Perspective

The concept of the IRR as a measure of economic return has existed at least since Fisher [1907] implicitly introduced it. Boulding [1935] adapted the concept of rates of return for financial assets to real assets and explicitly developed the mathematical relationships associated with the IRR. Although Lorie and Savage [1955] often are cited for identifying the multiple root problem of the IRR, Samuelson [1937] identified this problem 18 years earlier. Lorie and Savage's article stimulated a large number of authors [Bernhard, 1979a, 1979b, 1980; de Faro, 1974; de Faro and Soares, 1978; Hajdasinski, 1983; Herbst, 1978; Norstrom, 1972; Teichroew, Robichek and Montalbano, 1965; Ward, 1985; and Wohl, 1985] to suggest solutions to the multiple IRR problem and to identification of when a unique IRR exists. A good summary of these issues is provided by Cannaday, Colwell, and Paley [1986], Jean [1968, 1969] and Hirshleifer [1969] discussed the mathematics associated with identifying the number of IRRs possible. Jean's work is very helpful in understanding the nature of multiple IRRs, but unfortunately has not been incorporated into textbooks.

## Graphical Analysis

The question of whether a series of cash flows may have multiple IRRs can be addressed through relatively simple graphical analysis. However, first it is necessary to classify a project's cash flows into two broad categories:

1.  Investment projects: projects in which the first cash flow at time zero is negative, but the following cash flows may be either negative or positive.

2.  Borrowing projects: projects in which the first cash flow at time zero is positive, but the following cash flows may be either positive or negative.

Second, a further breakdown is whether the sum of the undiscounted cash flows is positive or negative. In other words, there are four classes of projects to consider.

### Investment Project—Sum of Undiscounted Cash Flows is Positive

A simple investment project would have an initial investment ($CF_0$) followed by a series of positive cash inflows such as −$1,000, $500, $500, $300. The undiscounted sum of the cash flows, r = 0, is $300. If the discount rate becomes very large or approaches infinity, the net present value of the cash flows approaches the initial cash flow, □$1,000, since the present value of all cash flows after time 0 approaches 0 as r becomes large. This project's NPV map is given in Figure 22.1.

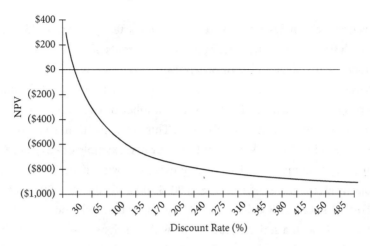

**Figure 22.1:** Investment project sum of undiscounted cash flows in positive

The important feature of the NPV map is that it always starts (assuming r = 0) at the sum of the undiscounted cash flows and approaches $CF_0$ as r becomes large. The relevancy of understanding the beginning and ending points of the NPV map is that this information can be used to determine if the number of IRRs is an even or odd number. That is, if the sum of the undiscounted cash flows is positive and the NPV map crosses the X-axis a second time, the NPV must cross the X-axis a third time so that the NPV may approach $CF_0$ as r becomes large. Likewise, if the NPV map crosses the X-axis a fourth time, it must cross it a fifth time so that the NPV may approach $CF_0$ as r becomes large. Hence, if an investment project's undiscounted sum of cash flows is positive, the maximum possible number of IRRs is an odd number (1, 3, 5, ...) which does not exceed the number of sign changes. This point is illustrated in Figure 22.2 for a project with cash flows of –$160, $920, –$1,700, $1,000 and IRRs of 25,100, and 150 percent.[1]

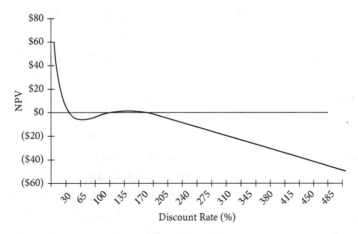

**Figure 22.2:** Investment project sum of undiscounted cash flows is positive

The foregoing graphical analysis is consistent with Descartes' rule of signs [Skrapek, Korkie, and Daniel, 1976], which states that the number of positive real roots of a polynomial equation with real coefficients is either equal to the number of variations in sign or is less than this number by a positive even integer. Therefore, by using Descartes' rule of signs and determining if the undiscounted sum of cash flows is positive or negative, the maximum number of IRRs and whether the number of IRRs is an odd or even number can be established. This determination is helpful in knowing if all possible IRRs have been identified. For example, in our first example of –$1,000, $500, $500, $300, there is one sign change, so multiple IRRs cannot exist. Likewise, if an investment in a strip mine consists of the following cash flows: –$10,000, $5,000, $5,000, $5,000, –$1,000, where the last –$1,000 is reclamation cost, only one IRR exists. If the foregoing is true, why do so many textbooks have examples with two IRRs with a series of cash flows with the signs of – + + + –? The answer is that in the textbook examples, although not explicitly stated, the sum of the undiscounted cash flows is negative.

If the sum of the undiscounted cash flows is positive, there must be at least one negative cash flow in the middle of the cash flow series such as – + + – + +, – + + – + – +, or + + – + – +, to allow multiple IRRs to occur. The number or signs in the same direction (+ + + or – – – –) doesn't change the number of possible IRRs. The necessary, although not sufficient, condition for multiple IRRs to exist is the number of sign changes. Therefore, the common textbook implication that a negative cash flow in the last period is a sufficient condition for multiple IRRs to exist can be rejected for all investment projects which have a positive sum of undiscounted cash flows. Likewise, other than projects with a scheduled major upgrade or mid-life maintenance, few projects have negative cash flows forecasted during the life of the project except at the beginning and the end. Hence, the frequency of multiple IRRs occurring may be much less than textbooks often imply.

### Investment Project—Sum of (Undiscounted Cash Flows is Negative

Analysis of investment projects when the sum of the undiscounted cash flows is negative is very easy since the same conditions prevail for multiple IRR's to exist as when the sum of the undiscounted cash flows is positive. The major difference is that the NPV map starts below the X-axis rather than above. Lorie and Savage's general pump example with explicit cash flows provided by Solomon [1956] of –$1,600, $10,000, □$10,000 with IRRs of 25 and 400 percent meets the multiple IRR criteria. Graphically, this example is illustrated in Figure 22.3.

Following the previous statements that the NPV equals the sum of the undiscounted cash flows for r = 0 and approaches $CF_0$ as r becomes large, an even number of IRRs (0, 2, 4, …) must occur if the sum of the undiscounted cash flows is negative. It is possible that no positive rate of return causes the NPV to equal zero, but if one IRR does exist, a second IRR also exists since the NPV map must be below the X-axis and approach $CF_0$, as r becomes large. A similar condition exists if a third IRR exists; that is, a fourth IRR also exists since the NPV must cross the X-axis so that it can approach $CF_0$, as r

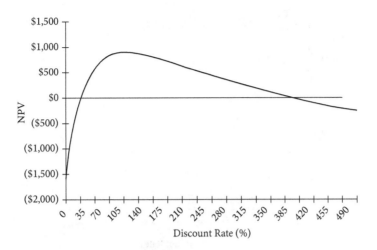

**Figure 22.3:** Investment project sum of undiscounted cash flows is negative

becomes large. Therefore, if the sum of the undiscounted cash flows is negative, the maximum possible number of IRRs is an even number (0, 2, 4, ...) which is not greater than the number of sign changes.

## Borrowing Project—Sum of Undiscounted Cash Flows is Positive

For borrowing projects, $CF_0 > 0$, the results are reversed from the investment project conditions. That is, if the sum of the undiscounted cash flows is positive, the maximum number of IRR's is an even number (0, 2, 4, ...) which does not exceed the number of sign changes. The same logic holds for borrowing projects. The major difference from the investment project is that the NPV starts and ends above the X-axis as r ranges from 0 to ∞. Graphically, a borrowing project with cash flows of $384, –$4,000, $14,000, –$20,000, $10,000 and IRRs of 25, 67, 150, and 400 percent is illustrated in Figure 22.4.

## Borrowing Project—Sum of Undiscounted Cash Flows is Negative

The same logic applies again. If $CF_0 > 0$ and the sum of the undiscounted cash flows is negative, the NPV map starts below the X-axis and must be above the X-axis and approach $CF_0$ as r becomes large. Therefore, since the NPV map starts and ends on opposite sides of the X-axis, the maximum possible number of IRRs is an odd number (1, 3, 5, ...) and is not greater than the number of sign changes. Graphically, this borrowing situation for a project with cash flows of $800, –$1,720, □$9,660, $34,800, □$35,000, $10,000 and IRRs of 25, 100, and 150 percent is illustrated in Figure 22.5.

## Summary of IRR Rules

The foregoing IRR rules are summarized in the decision chart shown in Figure 22.6.

The results of the two questions in the decision chart lead to a very simple decision rule for students or practitioners to follow in the analysis of IRRs. If the answers to the two questions are identical

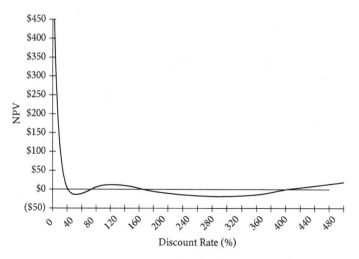

**Figure 22.4:** Borrowing project sum of undiscounted cash flows is positive

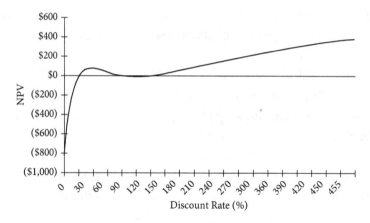

**Figure 22.5:** Borrowing project sum of undiscounted cash flows is negative

(both Yes or both No), an even number of IRRs exists. If the answers to the two questions are mixed (one Yes and one No), an odd number of IRRs exists. Conclusion: the number of IRRs for a set of cash flows is less than or equal to the number of sign changes in the cash flows; is an odd number if only one response to the two questions is Yes; and is an even number if both responses to the two questions are identical (either Yes or No).

## Implementation

The preceding section focused on determining the maximum possible number of IRRs but did not address the issue of the actual number of IRRs. Identification of the actual IRRs can be accomplished

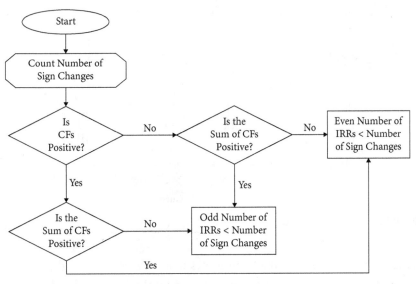

**Figure 22.6:** Decision chart for multiple IRRs

through mathematical procedures such as numerical analysis (e.g., Newton-Raphson), However, most managers and financial analysts would prefer a less mathematical and more intuitive solution. Spreadsheets (Excel, Lotus, etc.) have functions to solve for IRRs, but care must be exercised in using the IRR functions because, if multiple IRRs exist, the IRR obtained is dependent upon the initial guess (the spreadsheet functions require an initial IRR guess by the user or, in the case of Excel, a default rate of 10 percent). For example, a project with cash flows of $384, ☐$4,000, $14,000, ☐$20,000, $10,000 has IRRs of 25, 67, 150, and 400 percent. If the initial guess is 0, the Excel and Lotus IRR solutions are 25 percent, the nearest root. However, the spreadsheet search procedures do not necessarily converge to the root that is closest to the initial guess, but sometimes will skip the closest root and return a more distant root as the solution. For example, if the initial guess in this example is 40 percent, the Excel IRR function skips the 67 percent root and yields a solution of 150 percent, whereas Lotus yields a solution of 25 percent. However, if the initial guess is 45 percent, Excel returns an IRR solution of 67 percent and Lotus a 150 percent solution. Also, if the initial guesses are 99, 100, and 101 percent, the Excel IRR solutions are 150 percent, an error, and 25 percent, but Lotus yields solutions of 67 percent, 67 percent, and an error. The Excel and Lotus IRR functions are very sensitive to the initial guess (sec Figure 22.7) and it is not possible to predict which solution the Excel and Lotus IRR functions will yield. In Figure 22.7, the zero IRR solutions correspond to errors in the Excel solution (i.e., # NUM). The Excel error occurs whenever an IRR solution cannot be found in 20 iterations. If the spreadsheet IRR solutions always yield the root closest to the initial guess, the plot of the initial IRR guess versus the IRR solution would be a simple step function.

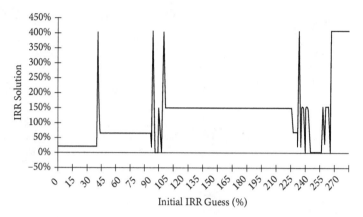

**Figure 22.7:** IRR Guess vs. IRR solution

A comparison of Figures 22.4 and 22.7 indicates that the errors and high volatility in the IRR solutions occur at points where the NPV function is a local minima or local maxima. The Excel solution procedure is not known. However, if Excel utilizes something such as a derivative search, the zero slope of the NPV function at the local minima or maxima could cause the search routine to behave in a very erratic fashion. For example, with an initial IRR guess of 40 percent, the zero slope may imply that r should be increased by such a large amount that the 67 percent root is skipped and the 150 percent becomes the solution.

Since application of the IRR function may lead the user to misinterpret the results, the following spreadsheet solution is suggested for determining and calculating multiple IRRs.

1. On the basis of the rules concerning the number of sign changes described in the previous section, determine the maximum possible number of IRRs and if this number is even or odd.

2. If only one IRR is possible, use a spreadsheet IRR function to solve.

3. If more than one IRR is possible, plot the NPV map for a wide range of r values; for example, $0 \leq r \leq 500\%$, in increments of 5%. The data table function makes this a very easy task.

4. Count the number of times the NPV map crosses the X-axis. If the number of X-axis crossings equals the maximum possible number of IRRs determined in step 1, all IRRs have been identified.

5. If the NPV map crosses the X-axis fewer times than the maximum possible number of IRRs, first check to determine if the NPV is on the correct side of the X-axis as r becomes large. If this isn't true, increase the maximum r in the NPV map until the NPV crosses the X-axis and approaches $CF_0$. If the NPV map approaches $CF_0$ as r becomes large, the actual number of IRRs simply may be less than the maximum possible by some even number. This may be true for two reasons: (1) the actual number of IRRs is less than the maximum possible, or (2) some of the IRRs have not been identified due to the large incremental r used in the NPV plot. To determine if some IRRs have been missed, check the NPV map to see if the NPV map approaches the X-axis but does not cross it for some range of r-values. If this is true, decrease the incremental r value and

create a new NPV map for this range of r values. If the difference between the identified and maximum number of IRRs is an odd number and the NPV approaches $CF_0$ as r becomes large, the NPV must be tangent to the X-axis and two IRRs have the same value.

6. To calculate a more precise IRR than can be read from the NPV map, simply use each IRR value from the NPV profile as the initial guess in the IRR function.

The foregoing procedure easily can be programmed into a spreadsheet so that the user essentially only has to enter the cash flows.

## Conclusions

The question of whether a project has multiple IRRs has plagued financial analysts and managers for a long period of time. Unfortunately, the only solutions to resolving this problem have been mathematical in nature and have not been adopted by textbook authors. [...] it is shown that complex mathematics are not necessary for identifying IRRs, but by understanding the characteristics of an NPV map, a few simple rules, and the application of a spreadsheet, the multiple IRR problem can be addressed in a very easy manner which easily can be included in undergraduate textbooks.

The increased understanding of the IRR provided [...] is not meant to suggest that the superior NPV decision rule should be replaced by the IRR. Also, there is no intent to imply that the modified internal rate of return should not be used to avoid the multiple root IRR problem. The objective simply is to clarify the limitations associated with the IRR and to allow a more complete analysis for individuals who apply the IRR.

## Endnote

1. The IRRs in this example were intentionally selected to cover a wide range so that the graphical illustration in the figure would be more definitive. The same reasoning holds for the following example. There is no intent to imply that actual multiple IRRs must cover a wide range. In fact, theoretically, there is no limit as to how close together multiple IRRs may be.

## References

Bernhard, Richard H. "A More General Sufficient Condition for a Unique Nonnegative Internal Rate of Return." *Journal of Financial and Quantitative Analysis,* 14 (June, 1979), 337–342.

_____. "A Simpler Internal Rate of Return Uniqueness Condition Which Dominates That of de Faro and Soares," *The Engineering Economist,* 24 (Winter, 1979), 71–74.

_____. "A Simplification and an Extension of the Bernhard-de Faro Sufficient Condition for a Unique Non-Negative Internal Rate of Return," *Journal of Financial and Quantitative Analysis,* 15 (March, 1980), 337–342.

Boulding, K.E. "The Theory of Single Interest," *Quarterly Journal of Economics,* 49 (May, 1935), 475–494.

Brealey, Richard A. and Stewart C. Myers. *Principles of Corporate Finance,* 3rd Ed. (New York, 1988) McGraw-Hill Book Company.

Brigham, Eugene F. and Louis C. Gapenski. *Intermediate Financial Management,* 4th Ed. (New York, 1993) The Dryden Press.

Bussey, Lynn E, *The Economic Analysis of Industrial Projects,* (Englewood Cliffs, 1978), Prentice-Hall, Inc.

Cannaday, Roger E., Peter F. Colwell, and Hiram Paley. "Relevant and Irrelevant Internal Rates of Return," *The Engineering Economist,* 1 (Fall, 1986), 17–38.

Copeland, Thomas E. and J. Fred Weston, *Financial Theory and Corporate Policy,* 3rd Ed., (New York, 1988) Addison-Wesley Publishing Company.

de Faro, Clovis. "On the Internal Rate of Return Criterion," *The Engineering Economist,* 19 (Spring, 1974), 165–194.

de Faro, Clovis and Luiz Soares. "A Flexible Sufficient Condition for a Unique Nonnegative Internal Rate of Return," *The Engineering Economist,* 23 (Winter, 1978), 117–127.

Emery, Douglas R. and John D. Finnerty. *Principles of Finance with Corporate Applications,* (New York, 1993), West Publishing Company.

Fisher, Irving. *The Rate of Interest,* (New York, 1907), The Macmillan Company.

Hajdasinski, Miroslaw M. "A Complete Method for Separation of Internal Rates of Return," *The Engineering Economist,* 28 (Spring, 1983), 207–250.

Herbst, Anthony. "The Unique, Real Internal Rate of Return: Caveat Emptor!" *Journal of Financial and Quantitative Analysis,* 14 (June, 1978), 363–370.

_____. *Capital Budgeting Theory, Quantitative Methods, and Applications,* (New York, 1982), Harper & Row, Publishers.

Hirshleifer, Jack. "On Multiple Rates of Return: Comment," *The Journal of Finance,* 24 (March, 1969), 98.

Jean, William H. "On Multiple Rates of Return," *Journal of Finance,* 23 (March, 1968), 35–38.

_____. "On Multiple Rates of Return: Reply," *The Journal of finance,* 24 (March, 1989), 99–100.

Lee, Cheng F. *Financial Analysis and Planning; Theory and Application,* (Reading, 1985) Addison-Wesley Publishing Company.

Levy, Haim and Marshall Sarnat. *Capital Investment and Financial Decisions,* 5th Ed., (New York, 1994), Prentice Hall.

Lorie, James and Leonard Savage. "Three Problems in Rationing Capital," *The Journal of Business,* 28 (October, 1955), 229–239.

Norstrom, Carl J. "A Sufficient Condition for a Unique Nonnegative Internal Rate of Return," *Journal of Financial and Quantitative Analysis,* 7 (June, 1972), 1835–1841.

Peterson, Pamela P. *Financial Management and Analysis,* (New York, 1994), Mc-Graw, Inc.

Pinches, George E. *Financial Management,* (New York, 1994), Harper Collins College Publishers.

Ross, Stephen A., Randolph W. Westerfield, and Bradford D. Jordan. *Fundamentals of Corporate Finance,* 2nd Ed., (Homewood, 1993), Irwin.

Samuelson, Paul A. "Some Aspects of the Pure Theory of Capital," *The Quarterly Journal of Economics,* 51 (May, 1937), 469–496.

Shapiro, Alan C. *Modem Corporate finance,* (New York, 1996), Macmillan Publishing Company.

Skrapek, Wayne A., Bob M. Korkie, and Terrence E. Daniel, *Mathematical Dictionary for Economics and Business Administration,* (Boston, 1976), Allen and Bacon, Inc.

Solomon, Ezra. "The Arithmetic of Capital-Budgeting Decisions," *The Journal of Business,* 29 (April, 1966), 124–129.

Teichroew, Daniel, Alexander A. Robichek, and Michael Montalbano. "An Analysis of Criteria for Investment and Financing Decisions Under Certainty," *Management Science,* 12 (November, 1965), 151–179.

Van Horne, James C. *financial Management and Policy,* 10th Ed., (Englewood Cliffs, 1995), Prentice Hall.

Ward, Thomas L. "Internal Rates of Return: A Linear Systems Theoretic View," *The Engineering Economist,* 30 (Winter, 1985), 135–156.

Weston, J. Fred and Eugene F. Brigham. *Essentials of Managerial Finance,* 10th Ed., (New York, 1995), The Dryden Press.

Weston, J. Fred and Thomas E. Copeland. *Managerial Finance,* 9th Ed., (New York, 1992), The Dryden Press.

Wilkes, F. M. *Capital Budgeting Techniques,* (New York, 1977), John Wiley & Sons.

Wohl, Marlin. "A New Ordering Procedure and Set of Decision Rules for the Internal Rate of Return Method," *The Engineering Economist,* 30 (Summer, 1985), 363–387.

# Capital Budgeting Practices of the Fortune 1000

## How Have Things Changed?

By Patricia A. Ryan and Glenn P. Ryan

.......................................................................................................

Corporate capital budgeting and cost of capital estimation are among the most important decisions made by the financial manager. In this process, it is crucial that management use accurate methods that will result in the maximization of shareholder wealth. Over time, managers have used various commonly taught capital budgeting models and cost of capital estimations procedures; however, the use of models has not always aligned with what is taught in collegiate finance. This study re-examines the capital budgeting decision methods used by the Fortune 1000 companies. We show management views net present value (NPV) as the most preferred capital budgeting tool. Both NPV and internal rate of return (IRR) are superior to other capital budgeting tools, a result that represents alignment between corporate America and academia.

[...] Section I provides a review of prior capital budgeting studies. Section II discusses the sample selection and survey methodology. Section III presents the results and Section IV concludes.

## I. Review of Prior Capital Budgeting Studies

Over the past four decades, financial research has recorded how business use capital management methods and how large corporations determine the cost of capital used in capital budgeting decisions. Financial managers and academics have not been in full agreement as to the choice of the best capital budgeting method. In Exhibit 23.1, Miller (1960), Schall, Sundam, and Geijsbeek (1978), and Pike (1996) report payback technique as the most preferred method, while Istvan (1961) reports a preference for accounting rate of return. Early studies generally report discounted cash flow models to be the least popular capital budgeting methods. This might be attributed to the lack of financial sophistication and limited use of computer technology in that era. Mao (1970) and Schall,

## Exhibit 23.1   Comparative Results of Prior Studies

The first 11 results were compiled from Scott and Petty (1984). DCF was used when specific discounted cash flow techniques were not enumerated. The following abbreviations are used: Payback: PB, Internal Rate of Return: IRR, Net Present Value: NPV, Profitability Index: PI, and Accounting Rate of Return: AROR.

| Authors | Journal | Year Published | Population | Most Popular Capital Budgeting Tool | Least Popular Capital Budgeting Tool |
|---|---|---|---|---|---|
| Miller | NAA Bulletin (now Management Accounting) | 1960 | Fortune 500 and "Manual of Excellently Managed Companies" | PB | DCF |
| Istvan | Bureau of Business Research | 1961 | Selected large companies | AROR | DCF |
| Mao | Journal of Finance | 1970 | Selected large and medium companies | IRR | NPV and PI |
| Williams | Managerial Planning | 1970 | Fortune 500 and selected small companies | IRR | PI |
| Klammer | Journal of Business | 1972 | Compustat | DCF | PB |
| Fremgen | Management Accounting | 1973 | Dun and Bradstreet's Reference Book | IRR | PI |
| Brigham | Financial Management | 1975 | Selected financial managers | IRR | PI |
| Petry | Business Horizons | 1975 | Fortune 500 and Fortune 50 retailing, transportation and utilities | IRR | NPV |
| Petty, Scott, Bird | Engineering Economist | 1975 | Fortune 500 | IRR | PI |
| Gitman and Forrester | Financial Management | 1977 | Sample from Forbes | IRR | PI |
| Schall, Sundam, and Geijsbeek | Journal of Finance | 1978 | Compustat | PB | NPV |
| Oblak and Helm | Financial Management | 1980 | Fortune 500 MNC's in at least 12 countries | IRR | PI |
| Hendricks | Managerial Planning | 1983 | Some of Fortune 500 | IRR | PI |
| Ross | Financial Management | 1986 | 12 large manufacturers | IRR | PB |
| Jog and Srivastava | Financial Planning and Education | 1995 | 582 Canadian companies | IRR | AROR |
| Pike | Journal of Business Finance and Accounting | 1996 | Large UK companies | PB | AROR |

Sundam, and Geijsbeek (1978) specifically point to NPV as the least popular capital budgeting tool; a result in contrast to modern financial theory. Klammer (1972) reports a preference for general discounted cash flow models, and subsequently, the overwhelming majority of published research indicate management prefer the use of internal rate of return (IRR) over all other capital budgeting methods.[1] Eight studies dating from 1970 to 1983 show profitability index, a ratio of present value and initial cost, to be the least most popular capital budgeting tool. Recently, Jog and Srivastava (1995) and Pike (1996) indicate a decreased acceptance of accounting rate of return in Canada and the United Kingdom, respectively.[2] Interestingly, throughout the literature, NPV has always trailed IRR in management preference. Managers have argued the perception of a percentage return is more easily understood and comparable than an absolute dollar value increase in shareholder wealth. Therefore, in the past, managers have chosen IRR over NPV. Evans and Forbes (1993) argue management view IRR as a more cognitively efficient measure of comparison. In a comparison of past studies, it is seen that managers are moving toward NPV as a method of choice, but never to the level of IRR.

Academics have long argued for the superiority of NPV over IRR for several reasons. First, NPV presents the expected change in shareholder wealth given a set of projected cash flows and a discount rate. For mutually exclusive projects, there is some dispute over the appropriate method. Second, when cash flows come in over a longer time period, NPV assumes the intermediate term cash flows are reinvested at the cost of capital. Internal rate of return, on the other hand, assumes the intermediate term cash flows are reinvested at the IRR, which for any positive NPV project is higher than the cost of capital.[3] Finally, NPV is not sensitive to multiple sign changes in cash flows. It is a method that presents the expected dollar amount that shareholder wealth would increase or decrease upon the acceptance of a project.

## II. Sample Selection Process

The interpretation of survey data presents some limitations as discussed in Aggarwal (1980). While the survey was mailed to the CFO, the responses were the opinion of one individual and thus may not fully reflect the firm's position. It is possible this person may not be the best to assess the capital budgeting process if he/she is far removed from capital management. There is also potential concern about a non-response bias. In an attempt to limit this limitation, two personalized mailings were sent six weeks apart. While the survey technique is not without flaws, it has been generally accepted as a reasonable proxy given the time and personal constraints in large corporations.

---

[1] See Williams, 1970; Fremgen, 1973; Brigham, 1975; Petry, 1975; Petty, Scott, and Bird, 1975; Gitman and Forrester, 1977; Oblak and Helm, Jr., 1980; Hendricks, 1983; Ross, 1986.

[2] In a recent multinational study of the Asia-Pacific, Kester (et.al) found internal rate of return and net present value the most popular capital budgeting tools for large companies in that region.

[3] Brealey and Myers (1995) dispute this point and argue the reinvestment rate assumptions are not essential to evaluating a given project since reinvestment rates represent the return on another, separate project.

A two-page questionnaire was mailed to the Chief Financial Officers (CFO's) of each of the Fortune 1000 companies. In an attempt to increase the response rate, each letter was personalized and signed. Furthermore, we mailed a copy of the results to interested respondents. Each survey was coded to avoid duplication in a second mailing.

Ten surveys were returned as undeliverable and thirty-two firms indicated they did not respond to mail surveys. Two hundred and five usable responses were received, for a response rate of 20.5%, which is comparable to similar surveys.[4] One hundred twenty responses were received from the first mailing and eighty-five from the second mailing.

## III. Results

Although all the firms are large, the size of the annual capital budget did vary among the respondents. The size of the capital budget is subdivided as follows:

| Size of Capital Budget | Number | Percentage |
| --- | --- | --- |
| Less than $50 million | 35 | 17.1% |
| $50—$99.9 million | 42 | 20.5% |
| $100—$499.9 million | 78 | 38.0% |
| $500—$1 billion | 22 | 10.7% |
| Greater than $1 billion | 28 | 13.7% |
| | 205 | 100.0% |

Next, the CFO's were asked at what level a formal capital budgeting analysis was required. As can be seen, 99.5% of the companies require a formal analysis; however, the minimum capital expenditure for the analysis varied substantially.

| Amount of Capital Expenditure Required for Formal Capital Budgeting Analysis | Number | Percentage |
| --- | --- | --- |
| Less than $10,000 | 42 | 21.2% |
| $10,000—$99,999 | 54 | 27.3% |
| $100,000—$500,000 | 63 | 31.8% |
| Greater than $500,000 | 38 | 19.2% |
| Never | 1 | 0.5% |
| | 198 | 100.0% |

[4] For example, Jog and Srivastava (1995) have a response rate of 22.9%; Trahan and Gitman (1995), 12%; Gitman and Maxwell (1985), 23.6%; and Poterba and Summers (1995), 26.3%.

## A. Use of Basic Capital Budgeting Methods

Respondents were asked how frequently they used seven capital budgeting methods: net present value, profitability index, internal rate of return, modified internal rate of return, payback, discounted payback, and accounting rate of return. The responses were on a five point Likert scale with the following percentages attached to each alternative in an attempt to quantify the responses: "always" (100%), "often" (approximately 75%), "sometimes" (approximately 50%), "rarely" (approximately 25%), and "never" (0%).

In Exhibit 23.2, it is seen that NPV was always utilized by 49.8% of the respondents and frequently (always and often combined) used by 85.1% of the respondents. Finally, when including the "sometimes" category, the cumulative use of NPV climbs to 96% of the firms. Net present value gains the highest positive response in comparison to other basic capital budgeting techniques. Internal rate of return was always used by 44.6% of the firms, and frequently (always and sometimes combined) used by 76.7% of the respondents. Finally, when including the "sometimes" category, the usage rates increase to 92.1% of all respondents. The results show that NPV and IRR are preferred over all other capital budgeting methods. This is a notable alignment of theory and practice.

The size of the capital budget is a significant factor in the choice of capital budgeting methodology. Within NPV, the Pearson Chi-squared test of independence is significant at the 1% level; within IRR, it is significant at the 5% level.[5] This indicates a positive relationship between the size of the capital budget and the use of NPV and IRR. Similar analyses were performed based on the size of the capital expenditure. The results are qualitatively similar.

The third model was the payback, a favorite of business in the 1960's and used at least half of the time by 74.5% of the respondents. Fourth in popularity was the discounted payback model, used at least half of the time by 56.7% of the companies. Finally, at least half time usage was reported for the last three models as follows: profitability index ranks fifth at 43.9%, followed by accounting rate of return at 33.3% and finally, modified internal rate of return (MIRR) at 21.9%. Examination of within model proportions for profitability index, accounting rate of return, and modified internal rate of return reflect chi-squared significance at the 1% level, while the proportion distributions for payback are chi-squared significant at the 5% level. The only model that is not chi-squared significant when subdivided by the size of the capital budget is discounted payback. Payback and profitability index are more frequently used by firms with smaller capital budgets, while modified internal rate of return appears to be used more frequently by firms with capital budgets in the range of $100-$500 million.

Modified internal rate of return is the least popular of all discounted and non-discounted models. Some argue MIRR is superior to IRR because it allows the manager to adjust the discount rate of intermediate term cash flows to better match a realistic return for the cash flows. Samuel C. Weaver,

---

[5] The Pearson Chi-squared test of independence is frequently used to test for differences in proportions between two or more groups. The Chi-squared test is used to see of grouped data fit into declared groups. Rejection indicates the data do not fit into the group. The statistical tests were performed in Excel.

## Exhibit 23.2 Comparison of Basic Capital Budgeting Tools

Response to the question: "Please classify how frequently your firm utilizes each of the following budgeting tools. "Often" would generally mean that you use this tool about 75% of the time, "sometimes" would refer to about 50%, and "rarely" would mean about 25% of the time." The absolute percentages are in columns 3–7 and the cumulative percentages are in columns 8–10. Results are based on 205 responses by size of capital budget. All tools can be completed with basic Excel or other spreadsheet functions.

| Capital Budgeting Tool (level of technical difficulty, L=Low, M=Medium, H=High)* | Size of Capital Budget (in millions) | Always (100%) | Often (75%) | Sometimes (50%) | Rarely (25%) | Never (0%) | Always or Often (>=75%) | Always, Often, or Sometimes (>=50%) | Rarely or Never (<=25%) |
|---|---|---|---|---|---|---|---|---|---|
| Net Present Value (NPV) *** (L) | Less than $100 | 32.9% | 52.6% | 13.2% | 1.3% | 0.0% | 85.5% | 98.7% | 1.3% |
| | $100–$499.9 | 56.0% | 25.3% | 10.7% | 5.3% | 2.7% | 81.3% | 92.0% | 8.0% |
| | Greater than $500 | 67.3% | 22.5% | 8.2% | 2.0% | 0.0% | 89.8% | 98.0% | 2.0% |
| | **Full Sample** | **49.8%** | **35.3%** | **10.9%** | **3.0%** | **1.0%** | **85.1%** | **96.0%** | **4.0%** |
| Internal Rate of Return (IRR) **(L) | Less than $100 | 30.3% | 43.4% | 21.1% | 3.9% | 1.3% | 73.7% | 94.8% | 5.2% |
| | $100–$499.9 | 49.3% | 25.3% | 12.0% | 12.0% | 1.4% | 74.6% | 86.6% | 13.4% |
| | Greater than $500 | 60.0% | 24.0% | 12.0% | 2.0% | 2.0% | 84.0% | 96.0% | 4.0% |
| | **Full Sample** | **44.6%** | **32.2%** | **15.3%** | **6.4%** | **1.5%** | **76.7%** | **92.1%** | **7.9%** |
| Payback ** (L) | Less than $100 | 26.0% | 37.7% | 20.8% | 13.0% | 2.5% | 63.7% | 84.5% | 15.5% |
| | $100–$499.9 | 14.1% | 33.8% | 22.5% | 12.7% | 16.9% | 47.9% | 70.4% | 29.6% |
| | Greater than $500 | 17.0% | 25.5% | 23.4% | 27.7% | 6.4% | 42.5% | 65.9% | 34.1% |
| | **Full Sample** | **19.4%** | **33.2%** | **21.9%** | **16.8%** | **8.7%** | **52.6%** | **74.5%** | **25.5%** |

Exhibit 23.2  Comparison of Basic Capital Budgeting Tools (Continued)

| | | | | | | | | | |
|---|---|---|---|---|---|---|---|---|---|
| **Discounted Payback (L)** | Less than $100 | 17.6% | 28.3% | 20.3% | 20.3% | 13.5% | 45.9% | 66.2% | 33.8% |
| | $100–$499.9 | 11.3% | 18.3% | 23.9% | 22.6% | 23.9% | 29.6% | 53.5% | 46.5% |
| | Greater than $500 | 18.8% | 18.8% | 10.4% | 20.8% | 31.2% | 37.6% | 48.0% | 52.0% |
| | **Full Sample** | **15.5%** | **22.2%** | **19.1%** | **21.1%** | **22.2%** | **37.6%** | **56.7%** | **43.3%** |
| **Profitability Index* (L)** | Less than $100 | 2.8% | 22.2% | 25.0% | 20.8% | 29.2% | 25.0% | 50.0% | 50.0% |
| | $100–$499.9 | 11.4% | 14.3% | 17.1% | 18.6% | 38.6% | 25.7% | 42.8% | 57.2% |
| | Greater than $500 | 2.3% | 6.8% | 27.3% | 29.5% | 34.1% | 9.1% | 36.4% | 63.6% |
| | **Full Sample** | **5.9%** | **15.5%** | **22.5%** | **21.9%** | **34.2%** | **21.4%** | **43.9%** | **56.1%** |
| **Accounting Rate of Return * (L)** | Less than $100 | 8.2% | 5.5% | 24.6% | 9.6% | 52.1% | 13.7% | 38.3% | 61.7% |
| | $100–$499.9 | 1.4% | 12.7% | 11.3% | 23.9% | 50.7% | 14.1% | 25.4% | 74.6% |
| | Greater than $500 | 6.8% | 11.4% | 20.4% | 15.9% | 45.5% | 18.2% | 38.6% | 61.4% |
| | **Full Sample** | **5.3%** | **9.5%** | **18.5%** | **16.4%** | **50.3%** | **14.7%** | **33.3%** | **66.7%** |
| **Modified IRR * (M)** | Less than $100 | 0.0% | 4.2% | 14.1% | 25.4% | 56.3% | 4.2% | 18.3% | 81.7% |
| | $100–$499.9 | 1.5% | 13.2% | 13.2% | 28.0% | 44.1% | 14.7% | 27.9% | 72.1% |
| | Greater than $500 | 7.0% | 2.3% | 9.3% | 32.6% | 48.8% | 9.3% | 18.6% | 81.4% |
| | **Full Sample** | **2.2%** | **7.1%** | **12.6%** | **27.9%** | **50.3%** | **9.3%** | **21.9%** | **78.1%** |

where *** is $\chi^2$ significant within the specific capital budgeting method at the .01 level,
** is $\chi^2$ significant within the specific capital budgeting method at the .05 level, and
* is $\chi^2$ significant within the specific capital budgeting method at the .10 level.

Director of Financial Planning and Analysis of Hershey Foods, commented at the 1988 FMA meeting (Financial Management Panel Discussion; 1989),

> ... modified internal rate of return ... is a subject that is thinly written about. (In his discussion, he referred to modified IRR as terminal IRR) terminal internal rate of return will always give an answer that is consistent with net present value, as long as the reinvestment rate is identical to the discount rate that would have been used for net present value. ... (MIRR) gives the right answer and in such a way that management can understand it as a rate of return.

Given strong theoretical support and the inclusion of MIRR in popular financial spreadsheet packages, it may appear surprising that MIRR has garnered so little acceptance from the CFO's in this study. It is possible MIRR will gain acceptance in the delayed manner that NPV gained acceptance over a period of several decades. If this is to be the case, we may see a surge in MIRR applications over the next decade as more financial managers work with this technique especially if the reinvestment rate argument is valid.[6]

## B. Use of Advanced Capital Budgeting Methods

The same format was used to ask about the use of more specialized methods. In Exhibit 23.3, it is shown that sensitivity analysis was the most popular tool, followed by scenario analysis. Inflation adjusted cash flows were used by 46.6% of the responding firms on a regular basis.

Stern Stewart's Economic Value Added (EVA®) and Market Value Added (MVA®) models receive strong acceptance and use despite the relative youth of the methods. Stern Stewart argues that EVA is the financial performance measure that comes closer than any other to capturing the economic profit of an enterprise. They define EVA as the difference between a firm's net operating after tax income and the cost of capital while MVA is a cumulative measure of wealth creation. EVA was used by over half of the respondents while MVA was used by approximately one third.

Incremental IRRs were used by 47.3% of the respondents, while simulation models were used by 37.2%. PERT/CPM charting and decision trees were each used by about 31% of the firms. From this point, the more complex mathematical models, such as linear programming and option models, receive less corporate acceptance.

## C. Management Determination of Appropriate Cost of Capital

Several studies examine the cost of capital for large firms [Gitman and Mercurio (1982), Jog and Srivastava (1995), and Oblak and Helm, Jr. (1980)] and other studies examine the approximate cost of capital

---

[6] If, as posited by Brealey and Myers (1995), the assumption of reinvestment rates is not required, modified internal rate of return may not gain additional support.

## Exhibit 23.3 Relative Usage of Various Supplementary Capital Budgeting Tools

Response to the question: "Please classify how frequently your firm utilizes each of the following budgeting tools. "Often" would generally mean that you use this tool about 75% of the time, "sometimes" would refer to about 50%, and "rarely" would mean about 25% of the time." The absolute percentages are in columns 2–6 and the cumulative percentages are in columns 7–9. Results are based on 205 responses.

| Supplemental Capital Budgeting Tools* (level of technical difficulty, L=Low, M=Medium, H=High) | Always (100%) | Often (75%) | Sometimes (50%) | Rarely (25%) | Never (0%) | Always or Often (>=75%) | Always, Often, or Sometimes (>=50%) | Rarely or Never (<=25%) |
|---|---|---|---|---|---|---|---|---|
| Sensitivity Analysis (M) | 20.5% | 44.6% | 20.0% | 4.1% | 10.8% | 65.1% | 85.1% | 14.9% |
| Scenario Analysis (M) | 10.5% | 31.1% | 25.3% | 12.1% | 21.1% | 41.6% | 66.8% | 33.2% |
| Inflation Adjusted Cash Flows (M) | 12.0% | 19.4% | 15.2% | 25.1% | 28.3% | 31.4% | 46.6% | 53.4% |
| Economic Value Added (EVA) (M) | 12.0% | 18.8% | 23.0% | 19.9% | 26.2% | 30.9% | 53.9% | 46.1% |
| Incremental IRR (M) | 8.5% | 19.1% | 19.7% | 16.5% | 50.3% | 27.7% | 47.3% | 52.7% |
| Simulation (H) | 3.1% | 16.2% | 17.8% | 27.2% | 35.6% | 19.4% | 37.2% | 62.8% |
| Market Value Added (MVA) (M) | 3.7% | 11.2% | 18.1% | 26.6% | 40.4% | 14.9% | 33.0% | 67.0% |
| PERT/CPM (M) | 1.1% | 7.1% | 22.8% | 26.1% | 42.9% | 8.2% | 31.0% | 69.0% |
| Decision Tree (M) | 1.1% | 6.8% | 23.2% | 33.7% | 35.3% | 7.9% | 31.1% | 68.9% |
| Complex mathematical models (H) | 1.1% | 6.5% | 13.5% | 22.2% | 56.8% | 7.6% | 21.1% | 78.9% |
| Linear Programming (H) | 0.0% | 5.4% | 11.4% | 23.2% | 60.0% | 5.4% | 16.8% | 83.2% |
| Option Pricing Model (H) | 0.0% | 5.3% | 15.5% | 26.7% | 52.4% | 5.3% | 20.9% | 79.1% |
| Real Options (H) | 0.5% | 1.1% | 9.7% | 23.2% | 65.4% | 1.6% | 11.4% | 88.6% |

*All models can be constructed in Excel or similar spreadsheets with embedded macros for the more advanced models.

facing large companies [Schall, Sundem, and Geijsbeek, Jr. (1978), and Gitman and Forrester (1977)]. Oblak and Helm, Jr. (1980) examine the cost of capital practices of multinationals and found weighted average cost of capital (WACC) was used by 54% of the respondents. Other measures cited in their study include the cost of debt, past experience, expected growth rate, and CAPM. Jog and Srivastava (1995) found WACC to be used by 47% of Canadian firms, but significant numbers of firms also use the other measures found in Oblak and Helm, Jr. (1980). In academia, it is argued that WACC is the superior base level for cost of capital determinations. The following closed ended question was posed; "In general, which of the following does your company consider to be the best discount rate?" The vast majority, 83.2% chose WACC, while 7.4% chose the cost of debt, 1.5% chose the cost of retained earnings, and 1.0% chose the cost of new equity. A minority (5.4%) chose cost of equity for a project financed with equity and cost of debt for a project financed with debt and 1.5% indicated they had another measure for calculating the base discount rate. The results indicate that WACC was the strong preference among the respondents, in alignment with academia.

## IV. Conclusion and Implications

It appears the views of academics and senior financial managers of Fortune 1000 companies on basic capital budgeting techniques are in stronger agreement than ever before. Discounted capital budgeting methods are generally preferred over non-discounted techniques. While it is possible the survey results reflect the increased financial sophistication and availability of inexpensive computer technology, it was shown that net present value is the most frequently cited capital budgeting tool of choice, followed closely by IRR. Additionally, firms with larger capital budgets tend to favor NPV and IRR. The vast majority of respondents agree that WACC is the best starting point to determine the appropriate discount rate. Popular supplemental methods include sensitivity analysis, scenario analysis, inflation adjusted cash flows, economic value added, and incremental IRR. It will be interesting to track the progression of MIRR over the next decade to see if this technique gains more acceptance, especially for those firms with large capital budgets.

Brief description of supplementary capital budgeting tools:

- Sensitivity analysis allows for the change in one input variable at a time, such as sales or cost of capital, to see the change in NPV.

- Scenario analysis allows for the change in more than one variable at a time, including probabilities of such changes, to see the change in NPV.

- Inflation Adjusted Cash Flows adjusts expected future cash flows by an estimated inflation factor.

- Economic Value Added (EVA) measures managerial effectiveness in a given year or period (net operating profit after taxes–after tax cost of capital required to support operations)

- Incremental IRR is the IRR of the difference in cash flows of two comparison projects; commonly used in replacement decisions

- Simulation is a method for calculating the probability distribution of possible outcomes.

- Market Value Added (MVA) is the market value of equity—equity capital supplied by shareholders.

- PERT/CPM is the analysis and mapping of the most efficient financial decision.

- Decision trees are graphical illustrations used to model a series of sequential outcomes, along with their associated probabilities.

- Complex mathematical models a general term inclusive of various option pricing model techniques, complex real options, and firm specific proprietary models and methods.

- Linear programming identifies a set of projects that maximizes NPV subject to constraints (such as maximum available resources)

- Option pricing model include either binomial option pricing model or the Black-Scholes option pricing model, the latter used by firms such as Merck with high R&D expenditures and relatively few, albeit large positive NPV investments.

- Real options include the opportunity for expansion, contraction, or abandonment of a capital project before the end of its life.

# References

Aggarwal, Raj, 1980, "Corporate Uses of Sophisticated Capital Budgeting Techniques: A Strategic Perspective and a Critique of Survey Results," Interfaces 10 (No. 2, April) 31–34.

Brealey, Richard A. and Stewart A. Myers., 1997, Principles of Corporate Finance, 5th edition, McGraw-Hill Companies, New York.

Brigham, Eugene F., 1975, "Hurdle Rates for Screening Capital Expenditure Proposals," Financial Management 4 (No. 3, Autumn), 17–26.

Evans, Dorla A. and Shawn M. Forbes, 1993, "Decision Making and Display Methods: The Case of Prescription and Practice in Capital Budgeting," The Engineering Economist 39 (No. 1, Fall), 87–92.

Financial Management Panel Discussion on Corporate Investment, (1989), Samuel C. Weaver, moderator, Financial Management 18 (No. 1, Spring), 10–17.

Fremgen, James M., 1973, "Capital Budgeting Practices: A Survey," Management Accounting 54 (No. 11, May), 19–25.

Gitman, Lawrence J. and John R. Forrester, Jr., 1977, "A Survey of Capital Budgeting Techniques Used by Major U.S. Firms," Financial Management 6 (No. 3, Fall), 66–71.

Gitman, Lawrence J. and Charles E. Maxwell, 1985, "Financial Activities of Major U.S. Firms: Survey and Analysis of Fortune's 1000," Financial Management 14 (No. 4, Winter) 57–65.

Gitman, Lawrence J. and Vincent A. Mercurio, 1982, "Cost of Capital Techniques Used by Major U.S. Firms: Survey and Analysis of Fortune's 1000," Financial Management 14 (No. 4, Winter), 21–29.

Hendricks, James A., 1983, "Capital Budgeting Practices Including Inflation Adjustments: A Survey," *Managerial Planning* (January-February), 22–28.

Istvan, Donald F., 1961, "Capital-Expenditure Decisions: How They Are Made in Large Corporations," Bureau of Business Research, Indiana University.

Jog, Vijay M. and Ashwani K. Srivastava, 1995, "Capital Budgeting Practices in Corporate Canada," *Financial Practice and Education* 5 (No. 2, Fall-Winter), 37–43.

Kester, George W., Rosita P. Chang, Erlinda S. Echanis, Shalahuddin Haikal, Mansor Md. Isa, Michael T. Skully, Kai-Chong Tsui, and Chi-Jeng Wang, 1999, "Capital Budgeting Practices in the Asia-Pacific Region: Australia, Hong, Kong, Indonesia, Malasia, Philippines, and Singapore," Financial Practice and Education, (Spring/Summer) 25–33.

Klammer, Thomas, 1972, "Empirical Evidence of the Adoption of Sophisticated Capital Budgeting Techniques," *The Journal of Business* 45 (No. 3, July), 387–397.

Mao, James C.T., 1970, "Survey of Capital Budgeting: Theory and Practice," Journal of Finance 25 (No. 2, May), 349–360.

Miller, James H., 1960, "A Glimpse at Practice in Calculating and Using Return on Investment," *N.A.A. Bulletin (now Management Accounting)*, June, 65–76.

Oblak, David and Roy J. Helm, Jr., 1980, "Survey and Analysis of Capital Budgeting Methods Used by Multinationals," *Financial Management* 9 (No. 4, Winter), 37–41.

Petry, Glenn H., 1975, "Effective Use of Capital Budgeting Tools," *Business Horizons* 5 (October), 57–65.

Petty, J. William, David F. Scott, Jr., and Monroe M. Bird, 1975, "The Capital Expenditure Decision-Making Process of Large Corporations," *The Engineering Economist* 20 (No. 3, Spring), 159–172.

Pike, Richard, 1996, "A Longitudinal Survey on Capital Budgeting Practices," *Journal of Business Finance and Accounting* 23 (No. 1, January), 79–92.

Poterba, James M. and Lawrence H. Summers, 1995, "A CEO Survey of U.S. Companies' Time Horizons and Hurdle Rates" *Sloan Management Review* 37 (No. 1, Fall), 43–53.

Ross, Marc, 1986, "Capital Budgeting Practices of Twelve Large Manufacturers," *Financial Management* 15 (No. 4, Winter), 15–22.

Schall, Lawrence D., Gary L. Sundem, and William R. Geijsbeek, Jr., 1978, "Survey and Analysis of Capital Budgeting Methods," *Journal of Finance* 33 (No. 1, March), 281–288.

Scott, Jr. David and J. William Petty, II, 1984, "Capital Budgeting Practices in Large American Firms: A Retrospective Analysis and Synthesis," *Financial Review* 19 (No. 1, March), 111–123.

Shapiro, Alan, 1978, "Capital Budgeting for the Multinational Corporation," *Financial Management* 7 (No. 1, Spring), 7–16.

Trahan, Emery A. and Lawrence J. Gitman, 1995, "Bridging the Theory-Practice Gap in Corporate Finance: A Survey of Chief Financial Officers," *Quarterly Review of Economics and Finance* 35 (No. 1, Spring), 73–87.

Williams, Jr., Ronald B., 1970, "Industry Practice in Allocating Capital Resources," *Managerial Planning* (May-June), 15–22.

# Capital Structure and Firm Value

*The researches of many commentators have already thrown much darkness on this subject, and it is probable that, if they continue, we shall soon know nothing about it.*

**Mark Twain**

A firm's market-weighted cost of capital, based on the market's perception of the organization and its risk characteristics, is an opportunity cost for asset investment. This market or marginal cost is therefore the minimum required return for an investment project exhibiting the average level of investment risk for the firm.

Because it is the firm's investments that create value for the firm, a firm's cost of capital is directly related to the value of the firm. Investments earning exactly the risk-adjusted marginal cost of capital maintain the firm's value. Investments providing returns in excess of that cost increase the value of the firm, while investments returning less reduce the value of the firm.

The question addressed here is whether the cost of capital, which directly affects the value of the firm, will change if the long-term financing or capital structure of the organization changes. If, in fact, the cost of capital is affected by the firm's capital structure, an additional question of whether or not there is an optimal capital structure that minimizes the cost of capital and simultaneously maximizes the firm's value must be addressed.

Recognized as the seminal work on the theory regarding capital structure and its effect on the cost of capital and the value of the firm, a 1958 paper by Franco Modigliani and Merton Miller—commonly referred to as MM—assumed a world of perfect markets and rational market participants. In their perfect markets world, the assumptions were extremely strict, including a world in which all participants have the ability to borrow and lend at the same interest rate, relevant information is costless and available to all investors, there are no transactions costs, and there is a large, sufficient number of buyers and sellers, thus eliminating the possibility of one investor having a significant influence on trading prices. Further, the 1958 paper also assumed a world of no taxes, threat of bankruptcy, or financial distress.

Applying these perfect market conditions, MM developed two propositions: "Proposition One," which states that the firm's value is unaffected by the financial structure of the firm, and "Proposition Two," which suggests that a firm's value is, in fact, dependent on three separate factors. These factors include the cost of the firm's debt financing, the amount of debt financing relative to equity financing, and the returns earned by the firm on its asset investments.

The MM argument has its foundation in an underlying assumption of market arbitrage in which the securities of levered and unlevered firms with similar levels of business risk trade so rapidly that their market values will be equal. Their conclusion, therefore, is that under these assumptions, the value of a firm is not related to or is independent of its capital structure.

In a 1963 follow-up paper, MM relaxed the strict no-tax assumption for corporations. This relaxed assumption creates a situation of financing cost and benefit trade-offs. The 1963 paper concluded that because corporate tax laws allow pretax deductibility for debt interest expenses, while equity dividend payouts are strictly post-tax, capital structure does affect the value of the firm. Under this relaxed corporate tax scenario, an optimal debt-equity mix can exist, and that optimal mix would be in the form of a one hundred percent debt financing capital structure. Under the corporate tax assessment assumptions of MM, the value of the firm is actually composed of the sum total of the value of the firm without taxes plus the value of the tax shield provided by interest expenses.

Merton Miller (yes, he of MM fame) clarifies in his 1977 "Debt and Taxes" paper some of the issues dealing with the importance of interest as a tax shield in the capital structure decision and how that structure affects investors. Miller provides insight via the inclusion of not only corporate income taxes but personal taxation as well. In doing so, he presents an aggregate supply-and-demand argument for corporate debt, suggesting that an equilibrium position will occur as a result of the personal taxes paid by investors, simply serving as an offset to the savings provided to corporations by the tax shelter of interest expenses.

Miller notes that debt interest is generally taxed at a normal or ordinary tax rate, while the capital gains on equity investments is taxed at a capital gains rate that is set at a lower level to encourage investors to fund equity rather than debt investments. Further, he notes that the taxes on capital gains are not actually assessed and paid until an actual transaction occurs with the equity investment. Miller concludes that the lower rate of taxation applied to stock investment provides for a lower equity return requirement, which offsets the tax benefits to corporations via debt instrument financing. The combination of the two tax results in a sort of net trade-off, although the actual effect is not clearly defined.

Accepting the idea that the theoretically best financial objective for a firm is to maximize value or shareholder wealth, one approach to accomplishing this task is to minimize the cost of capital utilized to finance the firm. When a firm minimizes its cost of capital, more potential projects will be acceptable, and all projects will provide more value to the firm. Under the corporate tax assumption with the possibility of both financial distress and agency costs, the conclusion is that an optimal capital structure exists at a point with less than one hundred percent debt financing.

The specific question, then, is whether the capital structure, or how the firm structures its long-term financing, actually has an impact on the value of the firm. If, in fact, financing does have an effect on the value of the firm, it is necessary to identify the debt-equity mix that is optimal and will therefore provide the lowest possible cost of capital and thus maximize the value for the firm. If, on the other hand, the financing mix has no effect on the value of the firm, it is inconsequential as to how the firm's assets are financed, since the financing or capital structure is separate from and has no effect on the value of the firm.

It is important to remember at this point that when we talk of the value of the firm, we are not talking simply of the value of the equity portion of the firm but rather the value of the entire firm—the value of its assets. The value of assets, it must be remembered, is determined as the summation of the value of both the equity financing and the value of the debt financing in the marketplace. Thus, the value of the firm is equal to the value of its equity or stock financing plus the value of its debt financing. Since the use of debt provides an increase in the value of the firm in the form of a value from sheltering income from taxes, it follows then that the value of debt increases as leverage increases. Conversely, as the value of debt increases due to an increase in leverage, the value of equity decreases. This is not meant to imply, however, that the stock's price decreases.

In providing the proof that the value of the firm has increased by the use of tax-advantaged debt, it is important to note that the analysis uses a trade-off of debt for equity financing. This means that to increase the amount of tax-beneficial financing in the firm, the firm issues more debt and repurchases outstanding stock. The value of this stock increases with the increase in leverage, and the old shareholders whose stock is purchased to make room for the new debt financing are paid a price greater than the original value of their shares prior to the disclosure of intent to increase leverage. Thus, these initial stockholders or old stockholders receive an increase in market value.

Since a firm's value increases with the use of tax-advantaged debt, what prevents firms from using a maximum amount of debt financing? Since firms do not use one hundred percent debt financing—the maximum amount possible, or at least a percentage close to one hundred percent—there must be considerations other than tax benefits.

Two considerations that, from a practical standpoint, are not accounted for in the tax analysis are the effects of financial distress costs and agency costs. Financial distress exists when a firm has difficulty in meeting its contractual obligations to creditors. Agency costs exist when there is a dissimilarity between the needs or goals of two or more groups.

The potential for financial distress increases as the level of fixed cost debt financing increases. When the level of debt reaches a level considered excessive, the cost of additional debt and, ultimately, of equity financing as well, will rise. The potential for financial distress also brings with it other costs, to include the loss of managerial flexibility, higher administrative costs, and possible legal costs.

In general, since stockholders desire to have the value of the firm increased, their goals are somewhat different from the goals of creditors, who would be primarily interested in making sure cash flow is adequate to provide payment of both interest and principal. As a result, creditors are more interested in short-term benefits as opposed to long-term benefits.

The existence of agency costs to the firm will exist due to the disparate objectives of the debt and equity investors. The objectives for the two groups of investors pertain to their investment objectives with regard to both payment streams and safety. Creditors prefer that the firm take lower levels of risk to ensure a higher probability of payment, while the equity investors, as residual investors, accept the additional risk of equity investment with the expectation that the firm will earn higher investment and operating returns.

The specific type of agency costs related to an organization's capital structure are essentially trade-offs between the creditors and equity investors in the firm. The agency costs of debt increase with increases in leverage, while the agency costs associated with equity financing decrease with increases in leverage. As the amount of leverage increases, additional creditors will require more protective covenants and will pay a smaller price for the debt they purchase. This price reduction is an agency cost borne by the stockholders. In addition, the equity investors also pay agency costs. As the amount of leverage increases, new or external equity investors reduce the price they are willing to pay for shares and thus provide an agency cost to internal or continuing shareholders. This again is an agency cost borne by the shareholders. As a result, the true value of the firm is diminished by the cost of financial distress as well as associated agency costs.

In a 2013 *Journal of Finance* paper entitled "How Stable Are Corporate Capital Structures?" the authors, Harry DeAngelo and Richard Roll, via a study of industrial firms, found some interesting items with regard to the stability of corporation capital structures. First, the amount of financial leverage—measured as debt/total assets—in industrial firms was infrequently stable, and when it was stable, it was usually at a level of low financial leverage. Second, a number of firms had both high and low levels of leverage, but measures above .5 were, with the exception of a few firms, rare.

In his *Journal of Finance* paper "The Capital Structure Puzzle," Stewart Meyers, by discussing the positive and negative aspects of various theories and models that attempt to explain capital structure decisions and whether or not an optimal structure exists, addresses the difficulty of such endeavors. Meyers discusses some of the well-known theories and provides some insights into their underlying rationale and assumptions. The frustration of attempting to study capital structure theory is illustrated by his comment in the opening paragraph of the paper, which reads, "I will start by asking, 'How do firms choose their capital structures?' Again, the answer is, 'We don't know.'" The first theory addressed by Myers is the static trade-off, or simply the trade-off theory, which suggests that firms will seek an optimal leverage value as measured by the firm's debt-equity ratio in the determination of their ideal capital structure. The optimal ratio will provide an optimal cost of capital and is determined by trading the costs of debt against the benefits of that debt in the capital structure.

The second theory presented by Myers is the pecking order theory, which suggests that firms will consider obtaining funds internally via retaining earnings, issuing debt, or issuing new equity, in that order. The "pecking order," according to Myers, is then first to obtain the funds internally, then to secure debt financing, and finally, as a last resort, equity funding will be utilized. Equity funding is considered the source bearing the most risk and, according to the theory, there is no optimal debt-equity ratio.

Myers finds fault with both theories and presents a modified pecking order theory that might be referred to as a "timing of the market" theory. According to Myers, neither the static nor the pecking order theories seem to reflect the true nature of management practice when it comes to capital structure decision-making in the real world. Under this modification, management observation of the debt and equity markets provides insight as to the preferred financing source optimal at any given time.

Murray Frank and Vidhan Goyal (2009), in their *Financial Management* paper "Capital Structure Decisions: Which Factors Are Really Important?" conduct a survey of firms looking at the actual capital structures in publicly traded US firms in an attempt to explain the most important factors related to capital structure decisions. They conclude that the most important decision factors include the median industry leverage, the market-to-book assets ratio, tangibility, profits, the log of assets, and expected inflation.

Frank and Goyal assert that while the three basic theories of capital structure—trade-off, pecking order, and market timing—all have advocates, none seems to provide a clear understanding of managerial decision-making in creating a firm's capital structure. They further note that an additional complication in this search for a model that accurately describes the real-world capital structure decision is the issue of "agency concerns," or simply the basic principal-agent problem.

In identifying the list of concerns or factors they find as being the most important in the capital structure decision of publicly traded firms, they note first that "it is likely that patterns of corporate financing decisions have changed over the decades ..." and secondly, that "it has been argued that different theories apply to firms under different circumstances." Frank and Goyal conclude that "the pecking order theory provides an intuitively pleasing explanation for the fact that more profitable firms tend to have lower leverage ..." They further note, however, that in their survey, it is not company ratios but rather industry leverage ratios that are considered the "single most important empirical factor."

The authors also conclude that the trade-off theory seems to match well with a number of the important factors, to include "industry leverage, firm size, tangibility, and market-to-book," but, as suggested in other studies, "the main empirical weakness of the trade-off theory is commonly thought to be the fact that more profitable firms generally have lower leverage."

While there are numerous studies about capital structure, cost of capital, and the value of firms, none, as pointed out in the readings, provide a solid understanding of the decision process found in real corporations. In their conclusions, Frank and Goyal note their hope that while none of the suggested models are perfect, the identification of the factors considered important in determining the capital structure can provide some insight as to a process for making that decision. They also, however, provide a 1979 quote from George E. P. Box that seems to summarize the issue fairly well: "All models are wrong, but some are useful."

## Recommended Readings

Modigliani, Franco, and Merton H. Miller. "The Cost of Capital, Corporation Finance, and the Theory of Investment," *The American Economic Review* XLVIII, no. 3 (June 1958): 262–97.

Modigliani, Franco, and Merton H. Miller. "Corporate Income Taxes and the Cost of Capital: A Correction." *The American Economic Review* LIII, no. 3 (June 1963): 433–43.

Miller, Merton H. "Debt and Taxes." *Journal of Finance* 32, no. 2 (May 1977): 261–75.

Myers, Stewart C. "The Capital Structure Puzzle." *Journal of Finance* XXXIX, no. 3 (July 1984): 575–92.

DeAngelo, Harry, and Richard Roll. "How Stable Are Corporate Capital Structures?" *Journal of Finance* 70, no. 1 (August 2013): 373–418.

Frank, Murray Z., and Vidhan K. Goyal. "Capital Structure Decisions: Which Factors Are Reliably Important?" *Financial Management* 38, no. 1 (2009): 1–37.

Ross, Stephen. "Capital Structure and the Cost of Capital." *Journal of Applied Finance* 15, no. 1 (Spring/Summer 2005): 5–23.

Fu, X., and T. Tang. "Corporate Debt Maturity and Acquisition Decisions." *Financial Management* 45, no. 3 (2016): 737–768.

# MODULE 13

# International Financial Management

*When once we have recognized how close is the connection between finance and trade, we have gone a long way towards seeing the greatness of the service that finance renders to mankind, whether it works at home or abroad.*

**Hartley Withers**

D omestic corporations invest capital to set up operations in foreign countries for a number of different reasons. These include increasing return due to cheaper labor or materials costs and attempting to decrease risk characteristics through international diversification investment. A third possibility involves an expansion of products into international markets under what is referred to as the product cycle hypothesis. An additional explanation for domestic firms making investments in foreign countries deals with the imperfections of foreign currency exchange or securities markets.

The two major factors that are generally considered to influence the rate of exchange in currencies are inflation and interest rates. How to finance international trade is one of the most important considerations and problems of the multinational corporation financial manager. When dealing on an international basis, there are three basic risk factors that must be considered. These are political risk, exchange risk, and credit risk.

Problems encountered in international financial management have become extremely critical areas of concern to most major corporations. The basis upon which foreign investment by US corporations is undertaken is, quite simply, the risk-and-return trade-off decision. With regard to return, the firm may find it beneficial to invest in foreign countries due to the low cost of either raw materials or labor (or both). The high return available from these low-cost investments alone is not enough to entice US corporations to invest in foreign countries. Another significant factor is the fact that international diversification by a firm reduces the risk of a company's overall operations.

It is necessary to point out that the diversification benefit by itself is not a sufficient reason for a firm to invest in a foreign country. This is based on the rationale that investors can obtain such international diversification by independent investment rather than by having the firm do it for them. The prime consideration for a firm's decision to invest in foreign corporations should be based on the overall characteristics of risk and return and cost and benefit. Several hypotheses provide an explanation for why firms invest in foreign countries.

Under the product cycle hypothesis, the product cycle begins when a new product is developed. As competing firms emerge, new markets must be obtained for continuation of the sale of the product. This leads to exporting of the product to foreign countries. Following the exporting decision, it is often a decision to actually invest in a foreign country and to produce the product there. This provides an ability for the company to avail itself of lower costs in either the materials or labor areas (or both) as well as to allow it to exploit such items as patent rights, to avoid barriers in the form of tariffs, and to compete on a more advantageous basis with local producers. Additionally, it is possible to explain the large amount of foreign investment in terms of securities markets. Because the securities markets of many foreign countries are not as organized or efficient as the market to which we are accustomed in the United States, some international diversification benefit can be provided for investors as a result of these market imperfections.

The foreign exchange market is the market where the currencies of one country are exchanged for those of another. Such exchanges provide for currency delivery, either immediately or at some point in the future. The interbank market, which is a composite organization composed of the large financial institutions around the world, is the location of most foreign exchange trading.

Exchange rates are identified or defined as the rates at which currencies of different countries can be traded for one another, and these trades can be identified as spot or forward market trades. Stated differently, the exchange rate is quite simply the price that must be paid for one medium of exchange in terms of another.

As noted by Harry G. Johnson in his 1969 paper published by the Federal Reserve of St. Louis, it is important to distinguish between flexible rates and those determined under the adjustable peg approach, which was in place until 1971, when the floating exchange rate system was adopted. As Johnson notes, flexible exchange rates can be defined as "rates of foreign exchange that are determined daily in the markets for foreign exchange by the forces of demand and supply, without restrictions imposed by governmental policy on the extent to which rates can move." Professor Johnson pays homage to Milton Friedman and his 1950 essay "The Case for Flexible Exchange Rates," as published in his 1953 tome entitled *Essays in Positive Economics*, as a solid foundation for all who write on the topic of flexible exchange rates.

Thus, as Johnson points out, flexible rates are substantially different than the adjustable peg rate approach, which he defines as a system

> under which countries commit themselves to maintain the foreign values of their currencies within a narrow margin of a fixed par value by acting as residual buyers or sellers of currency in the foreign exchange market, subject to the possibility of effecting a change in the par value itself in case of "fundamental disequilibrium."

As he points out in the Federal Reserve paper, the basic argument in favor of flexible rates is that individual governments are able to consider the needs of their citizens when using the basic tools of

> monetary, fiscal, and other policy instruments, consistent with the maintenance of whatever degree of freedom in international transactions they chose to allow their citizens, by automatically ensuring the preservation of external equilibrium.

Professor Johnson makes a strong and interesting argument for flexible rates, providing discussions on issues such as international immobility, regional imbalances, a lack of centralized control of currencies, and the effects of fixed-rate disequilibrium.

Several hypotheses have been proffered in an attempt to explain the relationships of foreign exchange rates over time. The purchasing power parity hypothesis says that the relationship between expected inflation rates for two countries must remain equal to the ratio of the expected spot rate at the end of one period to the current spot rate. Stated another way, this simply means that any change in the exchange rate between the two currencies over time eliminates any difference in the relative price levels between the two countries involved.

An alternative hypothesis is known as the "interest rate parity" hypothesis. According to this hypothesis, the ratio between interest rates must equal the ratio between the forward and spot rates for the countries being examined. Adjustments in the exchange rates will occur in accordance with the interest rate parity hypothesis due to the supply-and-demand factor in the marketplace.

When one country provides interest rates that are above those of another country, investor funds will be funneled into the country providing the greatest amount of return on investment. As a result, the demand for the currency in the country providing the high interest rates will increase, while the demand for currency in other countries providing lower interest rates will decrease. As a result, the change in demand for currency will provide a change in exchange rates that exactly offset the difference in interest rates.

When investing in foreign countries, it is important for a corporation to consider the principal sources of risk involved in international investment. In addition to the normal risks faced in domestic operations, additional risks include political risk, exchange rate risk, and credit risk. Political risk is the risk related to changes in the political arena of the country under consideration for foreign investment. The more stable a foreign government is, the lower the risk, from a political standpoint, of foreign investment.

The risk of changes in exchange rates is an important characteristic that needs to be examined. Since most business operations involve both payments and receipts on a time basis, the change in exchange rates between the time of a sale or a purchase and the time of a receipt or a payment can have substantial effects on the financial profitability of a corporation involved in international business. It is important, therefore, that the corporation seriously consider the effects of international foreign exchange.

The third unique factor of importance to international business decisions is credit risk. Credit risk can be defined as risk related to potential default in terms of payment. Credit risk, or default risk, can be a function of not only the corporations or business institutions with which a domestic entity deals but also of the default or credit risk associated with the country in which that organization is located. In those countries where protection by regulation is greatest, the risk of default from doing business with a foreign corporation is reduced. For those countries in which regulation is minimal, the risk of default by a foreign corporation is increased.

To reduce the risks involved in foreign country investment, many domestic corporations engage in what is defined as hedging. To hedge against a decrease in the value of accounts receivable in foreign countries, a corporation may sell the currency of that foreign country for dollars based on a future delivery date. Alternatively, when a corporation engaged in foreign trade has accounts payable in foreign currency, it may buy the foreign exchange of the country based on a future delivery date. Either of these fixes the amount of cash to be received or delivered at a specific amount.

When business between two corporations in foreign countries is undertaken, it is often necessary to try to protect against a situation in which one of the corporations or entities does not meet its contractual obligations. There are several methods of protecting against this nonperformance problem of foreign corporations. These include letters of credit, drafts, banker's acceptances, and bills of lading.

Several alternatives are also available to corporations wishing to raise funds for foreign investment. The funds to be utilized may be raised in the domestic markets and then transferred or utilized in the foreign country. Alternatively, a subsidiary can be set up in the foreign country and the funds raised at that location.

Rob Hayward (2015), in a recent article in the *Journal of International Financial Studies*, considered the issue of foreign exchange rates and changes in those rates relative to speculative sentiment. Of importance in international operations is the speed of change or liquidity existing in foreign markets and the time necessary for a new level of equilibrium to be attained.

Hayward cites a 1936 paper by John Maynard Keynes, noting Keynes's view that "speculation is a myopic, sentiment-driven activity, dominated by the desire to 'beat the gun' or 'outwit the crowd.'" According to Hayward, "speculation is a problem that will cause booms, reversals and will discourage fundamental, long-term investment. It is noise that emerges from the interaction of collective sentiment to create trends in asset prices."

Considering speculation from the perspective of Milton Friedman (1953), he notes that "speculation is a stabilizing force, providing liquidity and helping to ensure that markets swiftly find equilibrium." Specifically, the argument proffered by Friedman was that "the speculative process would reward those able to access or utilize information relative to the uninformed and through a Darwinian process, informed speculation would dominate." This belief suggests that speculation "facilitates the process of price discovery" as well as financial market liquidity.

Hayward's study concludes that it "appears that speculation drives prices towards equilibrium and that speculation is informed." This finding is important in that uninformed speculators, known as "noise-traders or liquidity traders" provide market orders in a random fashion. As Hayward notes, "if foreign speculation is uninformed noise, extreme speculation, whether measured by sentiment or weight of activity, will coincide with deviations from fundamental value; if speculation is informed, speculation is part of the process of price discovery and extremes will provide no information about future prices."

# Recommended Readings

Friedman, M. "The Case for Flexible Exchange Rates." In *Essays in Positive Economics*, 157–203. Chicago: University of Chicago Press, 1953.

Hayward, Rob. "Speculation in the Foreign Exchange: Noise or Information?" (July 16, 2015). https://ssrn.com/abstract=2631584 or http://dx.doi.org/10.2139/ssrn.2631584.

Keynes, John Maynard. *The General Theory of Employment, Interest and Money*. Macmillan Cambridge University
   Press, for Royal Economic Society, 1936.

## Selected Reading

Johnson, Harry G. *The Case for Flexible Exchange Rates, 1969*. Federal Reserve Bank of St. Louis (June 1969):
   12–24.

# The Case For Flexible Exchange Rates, 1969*

By Harry G. Johnson

......................................................................................................................................................

B y "flexible exchange rates" is meant rates of foreign exchange that are determined daily in the markets for foreign exchange by the forces of demand and supply, without restrictions imposed by governmental policy on the extent to which rates can move. Flexible exchange rates are thus to be distinguished from the present system (the International Monetary Fund system) of international monetary organization, under which countries commit themselves to maintain the foreign values of their currencies within a narrow margin of a fixed par value by acting as residual buyers or sellers of currency in the foreign exchange market, subject to the possibility of effecting a change in the par value itself in case of "fundamental disequilibrium." This system is frequently described as the "adjustable peg" system. Flexible exchange rates should also be distinguished from a spectral system frequently conjured up by opponents of rate flexibility— wildly fluctuating or "unstable" exchange rates. The freedom of rates to move in response to market forces does not imply that they will in fact move significantly or erratically; they will do so only if the underlying forces governing demand and supply are themselves erratic—and in that case any international monetary system would be in serious difficulty. Finally, flexible exchange rates do not necessarily imply that the national monetary authorities must refrain from any intervention in the exchange markets; whether they should intervene or not depends on whether the authorities are likely to be more or less intelligent and efficient speculators than the private speculators in foreign exchange—a matter on which empirical judgment is frequently inseparable from fundamental political attitudes.

The fundamental argument for flexible exchange rates is that they would allow countries autonomy with respect to their use of monetary, fiscal, and other policy instruments, consistent with the

---

* The title acknowledges the indebtedness of all serious writers on this subject to Milton Friedman's modem classic essay, "The Case for Flexible Exchange Rates," written in 1950, and published in 1953 (M. Friedman, *Essays in Positive Economics* (Chicago: University of Chicago Press, 1953), pp. 157–203, abridged in R. E. Caves and H. G. Johnson (eds.), *Readings in International Economics* (Homewood, Illinois: Richard D. Irwin, for the American Economic Association, 1968), chapter 25, pp. 413–37.

Harry G. Johnson, "The Case for Flexible Exchange Rates, 1969," *Federal Reserve Bank of St. Louis Review*, pp. 12–24, Federal Reserve Bank of St. Louis, 1969.

maintenance of whatever degree of freedom in international transactions they chose to allow their citizens, by automatically ensuring the preservation of external equilibrium. Since in the absence of balance-of-payments reasons for interfering in international trade and payments, and given autonomy of domestic policy, there is an overwhelmingly strong case for the maximum possible freedom of international transactions to permit exploitation of the economies of international specialization and division of labour, the argument for flexible exchange rates can be put more strongly still: flexible exchange rates are essential to the preservation of national autonomy and independence consistent with efficient organization and development of the world economy.

The case for flexible exchange rates on these grounds has been understood and propounded by economists since the work of Keynes and others on the monetary disturbances that followed the First World War. Yet that case is consistently ridiculed, if not dismissed out of hand, by "practical" men concerned with international monetary affairs, and there is a strong revealed preference for the fixed exchange rate system. For this one might suggest two reasons: First, successful men of affairs are successful because they understand and can work with the intricacies of the prevalent fixed rate system, but being "practical" find it almost impossible to conceive how a hypothetical alternative system would, or even could, work in practice; Second, the fixed exchange rate system gives considerable prestige and, more important, political power over national governments to the central bankers entrusted with managing the system, power which they naturally credit themselves with exercising more "responsibly" than the politicians would do, and which they naturally resist surrendering. Consequently, public interest in and discussion of flexible exchange rates generally appears only when the fixed rate system is obviously under serious strain and the capacity of the central bankers and other responsible officials to avoid a crisis is losing credibility.

## Pressures Towards a More Flexible Exchange Rate System

The present period has this character, from two points of view. On the one hand, from the point of view of the international economy, the long-sustained sterling crisis that culminated in the devaluation of November 1967, the speculative doubts about the dollar that culminated in the gold crisis of March 1968, and the franc-mark crisis that was left unresolved by the Bonn meeting of November 1968 and still hangs over the system, have all emphasized a serious defect of the present international monetary system.[1]

This is the lack of an adequate adjustment mechanism—a mechanism for adjusting international imbalances of payments towards equilibrium sufficiently rapidly as not to put intolerable strains on the willingness of the central banks to supplement existing international reserves with additional credits, while not requiring countries to deflate or inflate their economies beyond politically tolerable limits. The obviously available mechanism is greater automatic flexibility of exchange rates (as distinct from

---

[1] The exchange speculation in favor of the Deutsche Mark in early May 1969 is only the latest example of instability in the present fixed exchange rate system.

adjustments of the "pegs"). Consequently, there has been a rapidly growing interest in techniques for achieving greater automatic flexibility while retaining the form and assumed advantages of a fixed rate system. The chief contenders in this connection are the "band" proposal, under which the permitted range of exchange rate variation around parity would be widened from the present one per cent or less to, say, five per cent each way, and the so-called "crawling peg" proposal, under which the parity for any day would be determined by an average of past rates established in the market. The actual rate each day could diverge from the parity within the present or a widened band, and the parity would thus crawl in the direction in which a fully flexible rate would move more rapidly.

Either of these proposals, if adopted, would constitute a move towards a flexible rate system for the world economy as a whole. On the other hand, from the point of view of the British economy alone, there has been growing interest in the possibility of a floating rate for the pound. This interest has been prompted by the shock of devaluation, doubts about whether the devaluation was sufficient or may need to be repeated, resentment of the increasing subordination of domestic policy to international requirements since 1964, and general discontent with the policies into which the commitment to maintain a fixed exchange rate has driven successive Governments—"stop-go policies," higher average unemployment policies, incomes policies, and a host of other domestic and international interventions.

From both the international and the purely domestic point of view, therefore, it is apposite to reexamine the case for flexible exchange rates. [...] For reasons of space, the argument will be conducted at a general level of principle, with minimum attention to technical details and complexities. It is convenient to begin with the case for fixed exchange rates; this case has to be constructed, since little reasoned defense of it has been produced beyond the fact that it exists and functions after a fashion, and the contention that any change would be for the worse. Consideration of the case for fixed rates leads into the contrary case for flexible rates. Certain common objections to flexible rates are then discussed. Finally, some comments are offered on the specific questions mentioned above, of providing for greater rate flexibility in the framework of the IMF system and of floating the pound by itself.

## The Case for Fixed Exchange Rates

A reasoned case for fixed international rates of exchange must run from analogy with the case for a common national currency, since the effect of fixing the rate at which one currency can be converted into another is, subject to qualifications to be discussed later, to establish the equivalent of a single currency for those countries of the world economy adhering to fixed exchange rates. The advantages of a single currency within a nation's frontiers are, broadly, that it simplifies the profit-maximizing computations of producers and traders, facilitates competition among producers located in different parts of the country, and promotes the integration of the economy into a connected series of markets, these markets including both the markets for products and the markets for the factors of production (capital and labour). The argument for fixed exchange rates, by analogy, is that they will similarly encourage the integration of the national markets that compose the world economy into an international network of connected markets, with similarly beneficial effects on economic efficiency and growth. In other words, the case for fixed rates is part of a more general argument for national economic policies conducive to international economic integration.

## International Immobility

The argument by analogy with the domestic economy, however, is seriously defective for several reasons. In the first place, in the domestic economy the factors of production as well as goods and services are free to move throughout the market area. In the international economy the movement of labour is certainly subject to serious barriers created by national immigration policies (and in some cases restraints on emigration as well), and the freedom of movement of capital is also restricted by barriers created by national laws. The freedom of movement of goods is also restricted by tariffs and other barriers to trade. It is true that there are certain kinds of artificial barriers to the movement of goods and factors internally to a national economy (apart from natural barriers created by distance and cultural differences) created sometimes by national policy (e.g., regional development policies) and sometimes by the existence of state or provincial governments with protective policies of their own. But these are probably negligible by comparison with the barriers to the international mobility of goods and factors of production. The existence of these barriers means that the fixed exchange rate system does not really establish the equivalent of a single international money, in the sense of a currency whose purchasing power and whose usefulness tends to equality throughout the market area. A more important point, to be discussed later, is that if the fixity of exchange rates is maintained, not by appropriate adjustments of the relative purchasing power of the various national currencies, but by variations in the national barriers to trade and payments, it is in contradiction with the basic argument for fixed rates as a means of attaining the advantages internationally that are provided domestically by a single currency.

## Concern Over Regional Imbalance

In the second place, as is well known from the prevalence of regional development policies in the various countries, acceptance of a single currency and its implications is not necessarily beneficial to particular regions within a nation. The pressures of competition in the product and factor markets facilitated by the common currency instead frequently result in prolonged regional distress, in spite of the apparent full freedom of labour and capital to migrate to more remunerative locations. On the national scale, the solution usually applied, rightly or wrongly, is to relieve regional distress by transfers from the rest of the country, effected through the central government. On the international scale, the probability of regional (national in this context) distress is substantially greater because of the barriers to both factors and goods mobility mentioned previously; yet there is no international government, nor any effective substitute through international co-operation, to compensate and assist nations or regions of nations suffering through the effects of economic change occurring in the environment of a single currency. (It should be noted that existing arrangements for financing balance-of-payments deficits by credit from the surplus countries in no sense fulfill this function, since deficits and surpluses do not necessarily reflect respectively distress in the relevant sense, and its absence.)

## Lack of Central Control of Currencies

Thirdly, the beneficent effects of a single national currency on economic integration and growth depend on the maintenance of reasonable stability of its real value; the adjective "reasonable" is meant to allow for mild inflationary or deflationary trends of prices over time. Stability in turn is provided under contemporary institutional arrangements through centralization of control of the money supply and monetary conditions in the hands of the central bank, which is responsible for using its powers of control for this purpose. (Formerly, it was provided by the use of precious metals, the quantity of which normally changed very slowly.) The system of fixed rates of international exchange, in contrast to a single national money, provides no centralized control of the overall quantity of international money and international monetary conditions. Under the ideal old-fashioned gold standard, in theory at least, overall international monetary control was exercised automatically by the available quantity of monetary gold and its rate of growth, neither of which could be readily influenced by national governments, operating on national money supplies through the obligation incumbent on each country to maintain a gold reserve adequate to guarantee the convertibility of its currency under all circumstances at the fixed exchange rate. That system has come to be regarded as barbarous, because it required domestic employment objectives to be subordinated to the requirements of international balance; and nations have come to insist on their right to use interventions in international trade and payments, and in the last resort to devalue their currencies, rather than proceed farther than they find politically tolerable with deflationary adjustment policies.

The result is that the automatic mechanisms of overall monetary control in the international system implicit in the gold standard have been abandoned, without those mechanisms being replaced by a discretionary mechanism of international control comparable to the national central bank in the domestic economic system, to the dictates of which the national central banks, as providers of the currency of the "regions" of the international economy, are obliged to conform. Instead, what control remains is the outcome on the one hand of the jostling among surplus and deficit countries, each of which has appreciable discretion with respect to how far it will accept or evade pressures on its domestic policies mediated through pressures on its balance of payments, and on the other hand of the ability of the system as a system to free itself from the remnants of the constraint formerly exercised by gold as the ultimate international reserve, by using national currencies and various kinds of international credit arrangements as substitutes for gold in international reserves.

In consequence, the present international monetary system of fixed exchange rates fails to conform to the analogy with a single national currency in two important respects. Regions of the system are able to resist the integrative pressures of the single currency by varying the barriers to international transactions and hence the usefulness of the local variant of that currency, and in the last resort by changing the terms of conversion of the local variant into other variants; moreover, they have reason to do so in the absence of an international mechanism for compensating excessively distressed regions and a mechanism for providing centralized and responsible control of overall monetary conditions. Second, in contrast to a national monetary system, there is no responsible centralized institutional arrangement for monetary control of the system.

This latter point can be rephrased in terms of the commonly held belief that the fixed rate system exercises "discipline" over the nations involved in it, and prevents them from pursuing "irresponsible" domestic policies. This belief might have been tenable with respect to the historical gold standard, under which nations were permanently committed to maintaining their exchange rates and had not yet developed the battery of interventions in trade and payments that are now commonly employed. But it is a myth when nations have the option of evading discipline by using interventions or devaluation. It becomes an even more pernicious myth when it is recognized that abiding by the discipline may entail hardships for the nation that the nation will not tolerate being applied to particular regions within itself, but will attempt to relieve by interregional transfer payments; and that the discipline is not discipline to conform to rational and internationally accepted principles of good behavior, but discipline to conform to the average of what other nations are seeking to get away with. Specifically, there might be something to be said for an international monetary system that disciplined individual nations into conducting their policies so as to achieve price stability and permit liberal international economic policies. But there is little to be said for a system that on the one hand obliges nations to accept whatever rate of world price inflation or deflation emerges from the policies of the other nations in the world economy, and on the other hand obliges or permits them to employ whatever policies of intervention in international trade and payments are considered by themselves and their neighbours not to infringe the letter of the rules of international liberalism.

## "Harmonization" and "Surveillance"

The defenders of the present fixed rate system, if pressed, will generally accept these points but argue the need for a solution along two complementary lines: "harmonization" of national economic policies in accordance with the requirements of a single world currency system, and progressive evolution towards international control of the growth of international liquidity combined with "surveillance" of national economic policies. The problem with both is that they demand a surrender of national sovereignty in domestic economic policy which countries have shown themselves extremely reluctant to accept. The reasons for this have already been mentioned; the most important are that there is no international mechanism for compensating those who suffer from adhering to the rules of the single currency game, and that the nations differ sharply in their views on priorities among policy objectives, most notably on the relative undesirability of unemployment on the one hand and price inflation on the other. The main argument for flexible exchange rates at the present time is that they would make this surrender of sovereignty unnecessary, while at the same time making unnecessary the progressive extension of interventions in international trade and payments that failure to resolve this issue necessarily entails.

The case for fixed exchange rates, while seriously defective as a defense of the present system of international monetary organization, does have one important implication for the case for flexible exchange rates. One is accustomed to thinking of national moneys in terms of the currencies of the major countries, which currencies derive their usefulness from the great diversity of goods, services and assets available in the national economy, into which they can be directly converted. But in the contemporary world there are many small and relatively narrowly specialized countries, whose national currencies lack usefulness in this sense, but instead derive their usefulness from their rigid convertibility at a fixed price into the currency of some major country with which the small country trades extensively or on which it depends for capital for investment. For such countries, the advantages of rigid convertibility in giving the currency usefulness and facilitating international trade and investment outweigh the relatively small advantages that might be derived from exchange rate flexibility. (In a banana republic, for example, the currency will be more useful if it is stable in terms of command over foreign goods than if it is stable in terms of command over bananas; and exchange rate flexibility would give little scope for autonomous domestic policy.) These countries, which probably constitute a substantial numerical majority of existing countries, would therefore probably choose, if given a free choice, to keep the value of their currency pegged to that of some major country or currency bloc. In other words, the case for flexible exchange rates is a case for flexibility of rates among the currencies of countries that are large enough to have a currency whose usefulness derives primarily from its domestic purchasing power, and for which significant autonomy of domestic policy is both possible and desired.

## The Case For Flexible Exchange Rates

The case for flexible exchange rates derives fundamentally from the laws of demand and supply—in particular, from the principle that, left to itself, the competitive market will establish the price that equates quantity demanded with quantity supplied and hence clears the market. If the price rises temporarily above the competitive level, an excess of quantity supplied over quantity demanded will drive it back downwards to the equilibrium level; conversely, if the price falls temporarily below the competitive level, an excess of quantity demanded over quantity supplied will force the price upwards towards the equilibrium level. Application of this principle to governmental efforts to control or to support particular prices indicates that, unless the price happens to be fixed at the equilibrium level—in which case governmental intervention is superfluous—such efforts will predictably generate economic problems. If the price is fixed above the equilibrium level, the government will be faced with the necessity of absorbing a surplus of production over consumption. To solve this problem, it will eventually have to; either reduce its support price, or devise ways either of limiting production (through quotas, taxes, etc.) or of increasing consumption (through propaganda, or distribution of surpluses on concessionary terms). If the price is fixed below the equilibrium level, the government will be faced with the necessity of meeting the excess of consumption over production out of its own stocks. Since these must be limited in extent, it must eventually either raise its control price, or devise ways either to limit consumption by rationing, or reduce the costs of production (e.g., by producer subsidies, or by investments in increasing productivity).

## Effects of Fixed-Rate Disequilibrium

Exactly the same problems arise when the government chooses to fix the price of foreign exchange in terms of the national currency, and for one reason or another that price ceases to correspond to the equilibrium price. If that price is too high, i.e., if the domestic currency is undervalued, a balance-of-payments surplus develops and the country is obliged to accumulate foreign exchange. If this accumulation is unwelcome, the government's alternatives are to restrict exports and encourage imports either by allowing or promoting domestic inflation (which in a sense subsidizes imports and taxes exports) or by imposing increased taxes or controls on exports and reducing taxes or controls on imports; or to appreciate its currency to the equilibrium level. If the price of foreign exchange is too low, the domestic currency being overvalued, a balance-of-payments deficit develops and the country is obliged to run down its stocks of foreign exchange and borrow from other countries. Since its ability to do this is necessarily limited, it ultimately has to choose among the following alternatives: imposing restrictions on imports and/or promoting exports (including imports and exports of assets, i.e., control of international capital movements); deflating the economy to reduce the demand for imports and increase the supply of exports; deflating the economy to restrain wages and prices and/ or attempting to control wages and prices directly, in order to make exports more and imports less profitable; and devaluing the currency.

In either event, a deliberate choice is necessary among alternatives which are unpleasant for various reasons. Hence the choice is likely to be deferred until the disequilibrium has reached crisis proportions; and decisions taken under crisis conditions are both unlikely to be carefully thought out, and likely to have seriously disruptive economic effects.

All of this would be unnecessary if, instead of taking a view on what the value of the currency in terms of foreign exchange should be, and being therefore obliged to defend this view by its policies or in the last resort surrender it, the government were to allow the price of foreign exchange to be determined by the interplay of demand and supply in the foreign exchange market. A freely flexible exchange rate would tend to remain constant so long as underlying economic conditions (including governmental policies) remained constant; random deviations from the equilibrium level would be limited by the activities of private speculators, who would step in to buy foreign exchange when its price fell (the currency appreciated in terms of currencies) and to sell it when its price rose (the currency depreciated in terms of foreign currencies).

On the other hand, if economic changes or policy changes occurred that under a fixed exchange rate would produce a balance-of-payments surplus or deficit, and ultimately a need for policy changes, the flexible exchange rate would gradually either appreciate or depreciate as required to preserve equilibrium. The movement of the rate would be facilitated and smoothed by the actions of private speculators, on the basis of their reading of current and prospective economic and policy developments. If the government regarded the trend of the exchange rate as undesirable, it could take counter-active measures in the form of inflationary or deflationary policies. It would never be forced to take such measures by a balance-of-payments crisis and the pressure of foreign opinion, contrary to its own policy objectives. The balance-of-payments rationale for interventions in international trade and capital movements, and for such substitutes for exchange rate change as changes in border tax adjustments or the imposition of futile "incomes policies," would disappear.

If the government had reason to believe that private speculators were not performing efficiently their function of stabilizing the exchange market and smoothing the movement of the rate over time, or that their speculations were based on faulty information or prediction, it could establish its own agency for speculation, in the form of an exchange stabilization fund. This possibility, however, raises the questions of whether an official agency risking the public's money is likely to be a smarter speculator than private individuals risking their own money, whether if the assumed superiority of official speculation rests on access to inside information it would not be preferable to publish the information for the benefit of the public rather than use it to make profits for the agency at the expense of unnecessarily ill-informed private citizens, and whether such an agency would in fact confine itself to stabilizing speculation or would try to enforce an official view of what the exchange rate should be—that is, whether the agency would not retrogress into *de facto* restoration of the adjustable peg system.

## Freeing Domestic Economic Management

The adoption of flexible exchange rates would have the great advantage of freeing governments to use their instruments of domestic policy for the pursuit of domestic objectives, while at the same time removing the pressures to intervene in international trade and payments for balance-of-payments reasons. Both of these advantages are important in contemporary circumstances. On the one hand, there exists a great rift between nations like the United Kingdom and the United States, which are anxious to maintain high levels of employment and are prepared to pay a price for it in terms of domestic inflation, and other nations, notably Western Germany, which are strongly adverse to inflation. Under the present fixed exchange rate system, these nations are pitched against each other in a battle over the rate of inflation which is to prevail in the world economy, since the fixed rate system diffuses that rate of inflation to all the countries involved in it. Flexible rates would allow each country to pursue the mixture of unemployment and price trend objectives it prefers, consistent with international equilibrium, equilibrium being secured by appreciation of the currencies of "price stability" countries relative to the currencies of "full employment" countries.

On the other hand, the maximum possible freedom of trade is not only desirable for the prosperity and growth of the major developed countries, but essential for the integration of the developing countries into the world economy and the promotion of efficient economic development of those countries. While the postwar period has been characterized by the progressive reduction of the conventional barriers to international trade and payments—tariffs and quotas, inconvertibility and exchange controls—the recurrent balance-of-payments and international monetary crises under the fixed rates system have fostered the erection of barriers to international economic integration in new forms—aid-tying, preferential governmental procurement policies, controls on direct and portfolio international investment—which are in many ways more subtly damaging to efficiency and growth than the conventional barriers.

The removal of the balance-of-payments motive for restrictions on international trade and payments is an important positive contribution that the adoption of flexible exchange rates could make to the achievement of the liberal objective of an integrated international economy, which must be set against any additional barriers to international commerce and finance, in the form of increased uncertainty, that might follow from the adoption of flexible exchange rates. That such additional uncertainty would be so great as to seriously reduce the flows of international trade and investment is one of the objections to flexible rates to be discussed in the next section.

## The Mechanics of Flexible Exchange Rates

At this point, it is sufficient to make the following observations. First, as pointed out in the preceding section, under a flexible rate system most countries would probably peg their currencies to one or another major currency, so that much international trade and investment would in fact be conducted under fixed rate conditions, and uncertainty would attach only to changes in the exchange rates among a few major currencies or currency blocs (most probably, a U.S. dollar bloc, a European bloc, and sterling, though possibly sterling might be included in one of the other blocs). For the same reason—because few blocs would imply that their economic domains would be large and diversified—the exchange rates between the flexible currencies would be likely to change rather slowly and steadily. This would mean that traders and investors would be able normally to predict the domestic value of their foreign currency proceeds without much difficulty.

But, secondly, traders would be able to hedge foreign receipts or payments through the forward exchange markets, if they wished to avoid uncertainty; if there were a demand for more extensive forward market and hedging facilities than now exist, the competitive profit motive would bring them into existence.

Third, for longer-range transactions, the economics of the situation would provide a substantial amount of automatic hedging, through the fact that long-run trends towards appreciation or depreciation of a currency are likely to be dominated by divergence of the trend of prices inside the currency area from the trend of prices elsewhere. For direct foreign investments, for example, any loss of value of foreign currency earnings in terms of domestic currency due to depreciation of the foreign currency is likely to be roughly balanced by an increase in the amount of such earnings consequent on the relative inflation associated with the depreciation. Similarly, if a particular country is undergoing steady inflation and its currency is depreciating steadily in consequence, money interest rates there are likely to rise sufficiently to compensate domestic investors for the inflation, and hence sufficiently to compensate foreign portfolio investors for their losses from the depreciation.

Finally, it should be noted that the same sort of political and economic developments that would impose unexpected losses on traders and investors through depreciation under a flexible exchange rate system, would equally impose losses in the form of devaluation, or the imposition of restrictions on trade and capital movements, under the present fixed rate system.

## The Case Against Flexible Exchange Rates

The case against flexible exchange rates, like the case for fixed exchange rates, is rarely if ever stated in a reasoned fashion. Instead, it typically consists of a series of unfounded assertions and allegations, which derive their plausibility from two fundamentally irrelevant facts. The first is that, in the modern European economic history with which most people are familiar, flexible exchange rates are associated either with the acute monetary disorders that followed the First World War, or with the collapse of the international monetary system in the 1930's; instead of being credited with their capacity to function when the fixed exchange rate system could not, they are debited with the disorders of national economic policies that made the fixed exchange rate system unworkable or led to its collapse. The second, and more important at this historical distance from the disastrous experiences just mentioned, is that most people are accustomed to the fixed exchange rate system, and are prone to assume without thinking that a flexible rate system would simply display in an exaggerated fashion the worst features of the present fixed rate system, rather than remedy them.

The historical record is too large a topic to be discussed adequately in a brief essay. Suffice it to say that the interwar European experience was clouded by the strong belief, based on pre-First World War conditions, that fixed exchange rates at historical parity values constituted a natural order of things to which governments would seek eventually to return, and that scholarly interpretation of that experience leaned excessively and unjustifiably towards endorsement of the official view that any private speculation on the exchanges based on distrust of the ability of the authorities to hold an established parity under changing circumstances was necessarily "destabilizing" and anti-social. It should further be remarked that European interwar experience does not constitute the whole of the historical record, and that both previously (as in the case of the United States dollar from 1862 to 1879) and subsequently (as in the case of the Canadian dollar from 1950 to 1962) there have been cases of a major trading country maintaining a flexible exchange rate without any of the disastrous consequences commonly forecast by the opponents of flexible rates.

The *penchant* for attributing to the flexible rate system the problems of the fixed rate system can be illustrated by a closer examination of some of the arguments commonly advanced against floating exchange rates, most of which allege either that flexible rates will seriously increase uncertainty in international transactions, or that they will foster inflation.

## Flexible Rates and Uncertainity

*Instability of the Exchange Rate*—One of the common arguments under the heading of uncertainty is that flexible rates would be extremely unstable rates, jumping wildly about from day to day. This allegation ignores the crucial point that a rate that is free to move under the influence of changes in demand and supply is not forced to move erratically, but will instead move only in response to such changes in demand and supply—including changes induced by changes in governmental policies—and normally will move only slowly and fairly predictably. Abnormally rapid and erratic movements will occur only in response to sharp and unexpected changes in circumstances; and such changes in a fixed exchange rate system would produce equally or more uncertainty-creating policy changes in the form of devaluation,

**Canadian Foreign Exchange Rate**

Note: Canada was on a floating exchange rate from late 1950 to mid-1962. The sharp movements at both ends of the period represent the transition from fixed rates to flexible rates. Once the free market equilibrium rate was established, it moved in a relatively narrow quarter-to-quarter range.

Source: Bank of Canada

deflation, or the imposition of new controls on trade and payments. The fallacy of this argument lies in its assumption that exchange rate changes occur exogenously and without apparent economic reason; that assumption reflects the mentality of the fixed rate system, in which the exchange rate is held fixed by official intervention in the face of demand and supply pressures for change, and occasionally changed arbitrarily and at one stroke by governmental decisions whose timing and magnitude is a matter of severe uncertainty.

*Reduction of Foreign Trade*—A related argument is that uncertainty about the domestic currency equivalent of foreign receipts or payments would seriously inhibit international transactions of all kinds. As argued in the preceding section, trends in exchange rates should normally be fairly slow and predictable, and their causes such as to provide more or less automatic compensation to traders and investors. Moreover, traders averse to uncertainty would be able to hedge their transactions through forward exchange markets, which would, if necessary, develop in response to demand. It is commonly argued at present, by foreign exchange dealers and others engaged in the foreign exchange market, that hedging facilities would be completely inadequate or that the cost of forward cover would be prohibitive. Both arguments seek to deny the economic principle that a competitive system will tend to provide any good or service demanded, at a price that yields no more than a fair profit. They derive, moreover, from the experience of recent crises under the fixed rate system. When exchange rates are rigidly fixed by official intervention, businessmen normally do not consider the cost of forward cover worth there while; but when everyone expects the currency to be devalued, everyone seeks to hedge his risks by selling it forward, the normal balancing of forward demands and supplies ceases to prevail, the forward rate drops to a heavy discount, and the cost of forward cover becomes "prohibitive." Under a flexible exchange rate system, where the spot rate is also free to move, arbitrage between the spot and forward markets, as well as speculation, would ensure that the expectation of depreciation was reflected in depreciation of the spot as well as the forward rate, and hence tend to keep the cost of forward cover within reasonable bounds.

*Incentive to "Destabilizing Speculation"*—A further argument under the heading of uncertainty is that it will encourage "destabilizing speculation." The historical record provides no convincing supporting evidence for this claim, unless "destabilizing speculation" is erroneously defined to include any speculation against an officially pegged exchange rate, regardless of how unrealistic that rate was under the prevailing circumstances. A counter-consideration is that speculators who engage in genuinely destablilizing speculation—that is, whose speculations move the exchange rate away from rather than towards its equilibrium level—will consistently lose money, because they will consistently be buying when the rate is "high" and selling when it is "low" by comparison with its equilibrium value; this consideration does not however exclude the possibility that clever professional speculators may be able to profit by leading amateur speculators into destabilizing speculation, buying near the trough and selling near the peak, the amateurs' losses being borne out of their (or their shareholders') regular income. A further counterconsideration is that under flexible rates, speculation will itself move the spot rate, thus generating uncertainty in the minds of the speculators about the magnitude of prospective profits, which will depend on the relation between the spot rate and the expected future rate of exchange, neither of which will be fixed and independent of the magnitude of the speculators' transactions. By contrast, the adjustable peg system gives the speculator a "one-way option": in circumstances giving rise to speculation on a change in the rate, the rate can only move one way if it moves at all, and if it moves it is certain to be changed by a significant amount—and possibly by more, the stronger is the speculation on a change. The fixed exchange rate system courts "destabilizing speculation," in the economically incorrect sense of speculation against the permanence of the official parity, by providing this one-way option; in so doing it places the monetary authorities in the position of speculating on their own ability to maintain the parity. It is obviously fallacious to assume that private speculators would speculate in the same way and on the same scale under the flexible rate system, which offers them no such easy mark to speculate against.

## Flexible Rates and Inflation

The argument that the flexible exchange rate system would promote inflation comes in two major versions. The first is that under the flexible rate system governments would no longer be subject to the "discipline" against inflationary policies exerted by the fixity of the exchange rate. This argument in large part reflects circular reasoning on the part of the fixed rate exponents: discipline against inflationary policies, if necessary for international reasons, is necessary only because rates are fixed, and domestic inflation both leads to balance-of-payments problems and imposes inflation on other countries. Neither consequence would follow under the flexible exchange rate system. Apart from its external repercussions, inflation may be regarded as undesirable for domestic reasons; but the fixed rate system imposes, not the need to maintain domestic price stability, but the obligation to conform to the average world trend of prices, which may be either inflationary or deflationary rather than stable.[2] Moreover, under the adjustable peg system actually existing, countries can evade the discipline against excessively rapid inflation by drawing down reserves and borrowing, by imposing restrictions on international trade and payments, and in the last resort by devaluing their currencies. The record since the Second World War speaks poorly for the anti-inflationary discipline of fixed exchange rates. The reason is that the signal to governments of the need for anti-inflationary discipline comes through a loss of exchange reserves, the implications of which are understood by only a few and can be disregarded or temporized with until a crisis descends—and the crisis justifies all sorts of policy expedients other than the domestic deflation which the logic of adjustment under the fixed

---

[2] A good example is Germany, which is suffering from balance-of-payments surpluses, because its price increases have been less than the average world trend.

rate system demands. Under a flexible rate system, the consequences of inflationary governmental policies would be much more readily apparent to the general population, in the form of a declining foreign value of the currency and an upward trend in domestic prices; and proper policies to correct the situation, if it were desired to correct it, could be argued about in freedom from an atmosphere of crisis.

The second argument to the effect that a flexible exchange rate would be "inflationary" asserts that any random depreciation would, by raising the cost of living, provoke wage and price increases that would make the initially temporarily lower foreign value of the currency the new equilibrium exchange rate. This argument clearly derives from confusion of a flexible with a fixed exchange rate. It is under a fixed exchange rate that wages and prices are determined in the expectation of constancy of the domestic currency cost of foreign exchange, and that abrupt devaluations occur that are substantial enough in their effects on the prices of imports and of exportable goods to require compensatory revision of wage bargains and price-determination calculations. Under a flexible rate system, exchange rate adjustments would occur gradually, and would be less likely to require drastic revisions of wage- and price-setting decisions, especially as any general trend of the exchange rate and prices would tend to be taken into account in the accompanying calculations of unions and employers. Apart from this, it is erroneous to assume that increases in the cost of living inevitably produce fully compensatory wage increases; while such increases in the cost of living will be advanced as part of the workers' case for higher wages, whether they will in fact result in compensatory or in less than compensatory actual wage increases will depend on the economic climate set by the government's fiscal and monetary policies. It is conceivable that a government pledged to maintain full employment would maintain an economic climate in which any money wage increase workers chose to press for would be sanctioned by sufficient inflation of monetary demand and the money supply to prevent it from resulting in an increase in unemployment. But in that case there would be no restraint on wage increases and hence on wage and price inflation, unless the government somehow had arrived at an understanding with the unions and employers that only wage increases compensatory of previous cost of living increases (or justified by increases in productivity) would be sanctioned by easier fiscal and monetary policy. That is an improbable situation, given the difficulties that governments have encountered with establishing and implementing an "incomes policy" under the fixed rate system; and it is under the fixed rate system, not the flexible rate system, that governments have a strong incentive to insist on relating increases in money incomes to increases in productivity and hence are led on equity grounds to make exceptions for increases in the cost of living. It should be noted in conclusion that one version of the argument under discussion, which reasons from the allegation of a persistent tendency to cost-push inflation to the prediction of a persistent tendency towards depreciation of the currency, must be fallacious: it is logically impossible for all currencies to be persistently depreciating against each other.

# Contemporary Proposals for Greater Exchange Rate Flexibility

## Increased Flexibility in the IMF System

The extreme difficulties that have been encountered in recent years in achieving appropriate adjustments of the parity values of certain major currencies within the present "adjustable peg" system of fixed exchange rates, as exemplified particularly in the prolonged agony of sterling from 1964 to 1967 and the failure of the "Bonn crisis" of November 1968 to induce the German and French governments to accept the revaluations of the franc and the mark agreed on as necessary by the officials and experts concerned with the international monetary system, have generated serious interest, especially in the United States Administration, in proposals for reforming the present IMF system so as to provide for more flexibility of exchange rates, it has been realized that under the present system, a devaluation has become a symbol of political defeat by, and a revaluation (appreciation) a symbol of political surrender to, other countries, both of which the government in power will resist to the last ditch; and that this political symbolism prevents adjustments of exchange rates that otherwise would or should be accepted as necessary to the proper functioning of the international monetary system. The aim therefore is to reduce or remove the political element in exchange rate adjustment under the present system, by changing the system so as to allow the anonymous competitive foreign exchange market to make automatic adjustments of exchange rates within a limited range.

The two major proposals to this end are the "wider band" proposal and the "crawling peg" proposal. Under the "wider band" proposal, the present freedom of countries to allow the market value of their currencies to fluctuate within one per cent (in practice usually less) of their par values would be extended to permit variation within a much wider range (usually put at five per cent for argument's sake). Under the "crawling peg" proposal, daily fluctuations about the par value would be confined within the present or somewhat wider limits, but the parity itself would be determined by a moving average of the rates actually set in the market over some fixed period of the immediate past, and so would gradually adjust itself upwards or downwards over time to the market pressures of excess supply of or excess demand for the currency (pressures for depreciation or appreciation, rise or fall in the par value, respectively).

Both of these proposals, while welcomed by advocates of the flexible exchange rate system to the extent that they recognize the case for flexible rates and the virtues of market determination as contrasted with political determination of exchange rates, are subject to the criticism that they accept the principle of market determination of exchange rates only within politically predetermined limits, and hence abjure use of the prime virtue of the competitive market, its capacity to absorb and deal with unexpected economic developments.[3] The criticism is that *either* economic developments will not be such as to make the equilibrium exchange rate fall outside the permitted range of variation, in which case the restriction on the permitted range of variation will prove unnecessary, *or* economic

---

[3] It is quite likely that a crawling peg would not have provided an equilibrium exchange rate in France after the events of May 1968.

change will require more change in the exchange rate than the remaining restriction on exchange rate variation will permit, in which case the problems of the present system will recur (though obviously less frequently). Specifically, sooner or later the exchange rate of a major country will reach the limit of permitted variation, and the speculation-generating possibility will arise that the par value of that currency will have to be changed by a finite and substantial percentage, as a result of lack of sufficient international reserves for the monetary authorities of the country' concerned to defend the par value of the currency.

In this respect, there is a crucial difference between the wider band proposal and the crawling peg proposal. The wider band system would provide only' a once-for-all increase in the degree of freedom of exchange rates to adjust to changing circumstances. A country that followed a more inflationary policy than other nations would find its exchange rate drifting towards the ceiling on its par value, and a country that followed a less inflationary policy than its neighbours would find its exchange rate sinking towards the floor under its par value. Once one or the other fixed limit was reached, the country would to all intents and purposes be back on a rigidly fixed exchange rate. The crawling peg proposal, on the other hand, would permit a country's policy, with respect to the relative rate of inflation it preferred, to diverge permanently from that of its neighbours, but only within the limits set by the permitted range of daily variation about the daily par value and the period of averaging of past actual exchange rates specified for the determination of the par value itself. For those persuaded of the case for flexible exchange rates, the crawling peg is thus definitely to be preferred. The only question is the empirical one of whether the permitted degree of exchange rate flexibility would be adequate to eliminate the likelihood in practice of a situation in which an exchange rate was so far out of equilibrium as to make it impossible for the monetary authorities to finance the period of adjustment of the rate to equilibrium by use of their international reserves and international borrowing power. This is an extremely difficult empirical question, because it involves not only the likely magnitude of disequilibrating disturbances in relation to the permitted degree of exchange rate adjustment, but also the effects of the knowledge by government of the availability of increased possibilities of exchange rate flexibility on the speed of governmental policy response to disequilibrating developments, and the effects of the knowledge by private speculators that the effects on the exchange rate of current speculation will determine the range within which the exchange rate will be in the future, on the assumption that the crawling peg formula continues to hold.

Evaluation of how both the wider band and the crawling peg proposals should work in practice requires a great deal of empirical study, which has not yet been carried out on any adequate scale. In the meantime, those persuaded of the case for flexible exchange rates would probably be better advised to advocate experimentation with limited rate flexibility, in the hope that the results will dispel the fears of the supporters of the fixed rate system, than to emphasize the dangers inherent in the residual fixity of exchange rates under either of the contemporary popular proposals for increasing the flexibility of rates under the existing fixed rate systems.

# A Floating Pound?

The argument of the preceding sections strongly suggests the advisability of a change in British exchange rate policy from a fixed exchange rate to a market-determined flexible exchange rate. The main arguments for this change are that a flexible exchange rate would free British economic policy from the apparent necessity to pursue otherwise irrational and difficult policy objectives for the sake of improving the balance of payments, and that it would release the country from the vicious circle of "stop-go" policies of control of aggregate demand.

A flexible exchange rate is not of course a panacea; it simply provides an extra degree of freedom, by removing the balance-of-payments constraints on policy formation. In so doing, it does not and cannot remove the constraint on policy imposed by the limitation of total available national resources and the consequent necessity of choice among available alternatives; it simply brings this choice, rather than the external consequences of choices made, to the forefront of the policy debate.

The British economy is at present riddled with inefficiencies consequential on, and politically justified by, decisions based on the aim of improving the balance of payments. In this connection, one can cite as only some among many examples the heavy protection of domestic agriculture, the protection of domestic fuel resources by the taxation of imported oil, the subsidization of manufacturing as against the service trades through the Selective Employment Tax, and various other subsidies to manufacturing effected through tax credits. One can also cite the politically arduous effort to implement an incomes policy, which amounts to an effort to avoid by political pressure on individual wage- and price-setting decisions the need for an adjustment that would be effected automatically by a flexible exchange rate. A flexible exchange rate would make an incomes policy unnecessary. It would also permit policy towards industry', agriculture, and the service trades to concentrate on the achievement of greater economic efficiency, without the biases imparted by the basically economically irrelevant objectives of increasing exports or substituting for imports.

The adoption of flexible exchange rates would also make unnecessary, or at least less harmful, the disruptive cycle of "stop-go" aggregate demand policies which has characterized British economic policy for many years. British Governments are under a persistently strong incentive to try to break out of the limitations of available resources and relatively slow economic growth by policies of demand expansion. This incentive is reinforced, before elections, by the temptation to expand demand in order to win votes, in the knowledge that international reserves and international borrowing power can be drawn down to finance the purchase of votes without the electorate knowing that it is being bribed with its own money—until after the election the successful party is obliged to clean up the mess so created by introducing deflationary policies, with political safety if it is a returned government, and with political embarrassment if it is an opposition party newly come to power. If the country were on a flexible exchange rate, the generation of the "political cycle" would be inhibited by the fact that the effort to buy votes by pre-election inflationary policies would soon be reflected in a depreciation of the exchange rate and a rise in the cost of living. Even if this were avoided by use of the Government's control of the country's international reserves and borrowing powers to stabilize the exchange rate, a newly elected Government of either complexion would not be faced with the absolute necessity of introducing deflationary economic policies to restore its international reserves. It could instead allow the exchange rate to depreciate while it made up its mind what to do. Apart from the question of winning elections, Governments that believed in demand expansion as a means of promoting growth could pursue this policy *a outrance,* without being forced to reverse it by a balance-of-payments crisis, so long as they and the public were prepared to accept the consequential depreciation of the currency; Governments that believed instead in other kinds of policies would have to argue for and defend them on their merits, without being able to pass them off as imposed on the country by the need to secure equilibrium in the balance of payments.

## The Feasibility of Floating

While these and other elements of the case for a floating pound have frequently been recognized and advocated, it has been much more common to argue that a flexible exchange rate for sterling is "impossible," either because the position of sterling as an international reserve currency precludes it, or because the International Monetary Fund would not permit it. But most of the arguments for the presumed international importance of a fixed international value of sterling have been rendered irrelevant by the deterioration of sterling's international position subsequent to the 1967 devaluation, and in particular by the Basle Facility and the sterling area agreements concluded in the autumn of 1968, which by giving a gold guarantee on most of the overseas sterling area holdings of sterling have freed the British authorities to change the foreign exchange value of sterling without fear of recrimination from its official holders. Moreover, the relative decline in the international role of sterling, and in the relative importance of Britain in world trade, finance and investments that have characterized the post-war period, has made it both possible and necessary to think of Britain as a relatively small component of the international monetary system, more a country whose difficulties require special treatment than a lynch-pin of the system, the fixed value of whose currency must be supported by other countries in the interests of survival of the system as a whole.

Under the present circumstances, adoption of a floating exchange rate for the pound would constitute, not a definitive reversal of the essential nature of the IMF system of predominantly fixed exchange rates, but recognition of and accommodation to a situation in which the chronic weakness of the pound is a major source of tension within the established system. The International Monetary Fund is commonly depicted in Britain as an ignorantly dogmatic but politically powerful opponent of sensible changes that have the drawback of conflicting with the ideology written into its Charter. But there is no reason to believe that the Fund, as the dispassionate administrator of an international monetary system established nearly a quarter of a century ago to serve the needs of the international economy, is insensitive to the tensions of the contemporary situation and blindly hostile to reforms that would permit the system as a whole to survive and function more effectively.

CPSIA information can be obtained
at www.ICGtesting.com
Printed in the USA
LVHW112000131221
706089LV00003B/16

9 781516 528158